P9-CNG-333

BISON
BOOKS

By Hank Davis

With a new afterword by the author

Small-Town Heroes

Images of Minor League Baseball

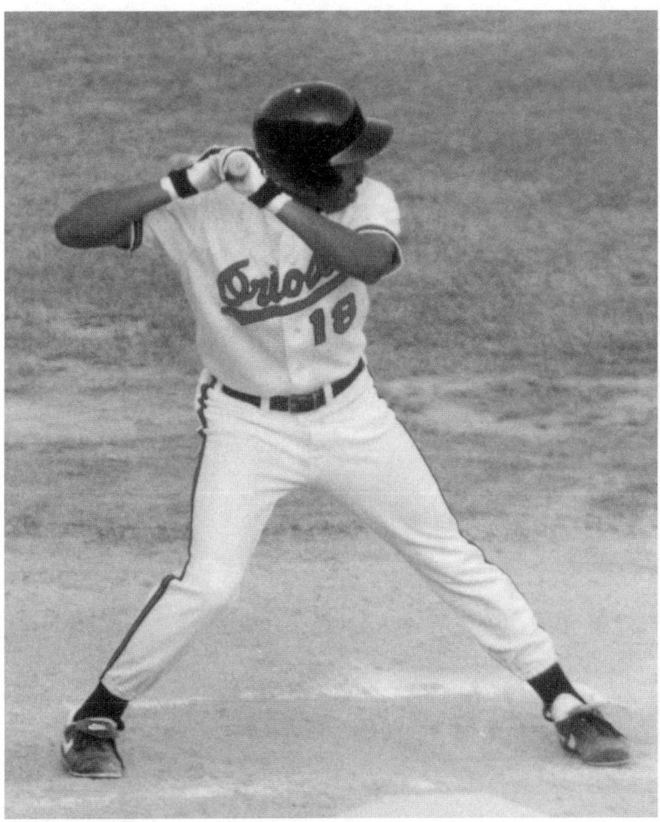

University of Nebraska Press
Lincoln and London

Manufactured in the United States of America

∞

First Nebraska paperback printing: 2003

Library of Congress Cataloging-in-Publication Data
Davis, Hank, 1914–
Small-town heroes: images of minor league baseball / by Hank Davis.
p. cm.
Includes index.
ISBN 0-8032-6639-1 (pbk.: alk. paper)
1. Minor league baseball—United States. 2. Minor league baseball—Canada. I. Title.
GV875.A1D38 2003
796.357′64′0973—dc21 2003051351

To Doug, who casually told me there was a minor league team just an hour and a half down the road and went to those first games with me; to Geoff, who shared my early Journey, sitting in the freezing rain with me in nearly empty stadiums; to Sue, who unselfishly encouraged me to "go for it" as my Journey took me farther and farther from home; to the many GMs, players, and coaches who gave willingly of their time and expertise; to my mother, Sarah, who took an unprecedented interest in my Journey and listened to my experiences in late-night collect phone calls from small towns; and to my dad, Al, my first baseball partner. He never knew about any of this Journey, but he would have loved every minute of it.

Contents

Preface

Steve Scarsone was the first professional baseball player I saw in his jockstrap. Way before I thought of writing this book, I walked into what I thought was the ticket office at Labatt Park in London, Ontario. It wasn't. It was the visitors' clubhouse. Scarsone, the second baseman for the AA Reading Phillies, was the first guy I encountered. Standing there in his jockstrap, he was in no position to sell me tickets.

"How ya doin'?" he said.

"Good," I replied. "You?"

"I need to bring my average up a bit," he said.

It turns out that was an understatement. Scarsone was having a terrible year. Although he was their second selection in the January 1986 draft, the Phillies were on the brink of giving up on Scarsone. He finished the season at Reading hitting .179 and struck out several times the afternoon I saw him. The next year, Scarsone was sent down to Clearwater, a demotion to Class A that had "last chance" written all over it. He hit .275, improvement enough to earn a midseason return to Reading.

I saw him that next summer. He looked better, still not exactly Robbie Alomar out there, but no longer overmatched by AA pitching. I remember the day vividly, because Reading lost both ends of a double header to London. It was a long, hot, frustrating afternoon. At the end of it, Scarsone sat alone in the dugout, his head in his hands, looking thoroughly dejected. I was transfixed and stood there unnoticed for several minutes. It was as naked a scene as when I first met him.

When Scarsone became aware of me, he rallied what little energy was left and asked if there was something I wanted him to sign. "No, I don't want anything from you," I told him. "I just wanted to tell you something. I saw you play here last year and I saw you today. I wanted you to know it was like seeing two different guys. You've really improved."

Scarsone got up and came over to the corner of the dugout closest to where

Steve Scarsone. Photo courtesy Donruss Trading Card Company.

I was standing. He reached up his hand and said, "I can't tell you how much it means to me to hear that. Especially today."

We shook hands warmly and made eye contact. "Good luck," I said. My knees felt a little rubbery as I walked to my car. It was an unplanned moment and more intense than I had anticipated. Obviously, I haven't forgotten the encounter, and part of me wonders if it's still in Scarsone's memory as well. More likely, it's part of an experience he'd like to erase.

In any case, Steve Scarsone finished the season hitting .265 for Reading, enough of an improvement to wake up the front office. When he began the '91 season at Reading by hitting .306, he was promptly promoted to Scranton–Wilkes Barre. He played well enough in AAA to make the International League All Star Team, where he was named Most Valuable Player. In 1992, Scarsone continued to blossom in AAA and got a callup to play some infield for the injury-plagued Phillies. His major league experience didn't amount to much, and in August he was traded to Baltimore for Juan Bell, whom the Phillies viewed as their shortstop of the future. They were wrong, of course, and Bell was released in shame early in the '93 season with the Phillies on their way to a Pennant. More to the point, Scarsone was gone. In thirty major league at bats in 1992, he hit a combined .167 for the Phillies and Orioles.

That might have closed the book on Steve Scarsone, only it didn't. During the off-season, Scarsone was traded by the Orioles to the Giants, who sent him to AAA Phoenix to get a few at bats while he worked through some nagging injuries. When Giant third baseman Matt Williams was hurt in late June '93, Scarsone was called up to replace him.

This is not necessarily a rags-to-riches story, and there is every chance that Scarsone will be at best a journeyman infield reserve. So far, he has hung on for three major league seasons with the Giants. He's never embarrassed himself, and there are plenty of teams that wouldn't mind having him on the bench. Perhaps his sweetest moment came on July 9, 1993, against the Philadelphia Phillies. Scarsone had his first four-hit game, including his first major league home run.

This saga holds the essential message of the book you're about to read. The minor leagues are full of stories, and almost anything can happen. The one about Steve Scarsone is still being written. It is probably more meaningful to me than to many fans, because I've watched it unfold from the very first minor league game I ever attended.

Small-Town Heroes

The Pregame Show

A Teenager in New York

I grew up in New York City in the fifties. When I was fourteen years old and obsessed with baseball, I had three major league teams to choose from. I naturally assumed everybody had it so good.

It seemed there was always a game being played near me. The Yankees were just a subway ride away. Better yet, my uncle had season tickets. He saved the best games for himself and his clients, but come September, when the Yanks had their usual twenty-one-game lead on the second-place Indians, he sent me and my friends to see every second division team that came to town. To this day, I can tell you who played first base for the Philadelphia Athletics, St. Louis Browns, and Washington Senators.

The New York Giants were more to my liking. They, too, were a train ride from me, although the Polo Grounds were a little trickier to find. You had to get off the main line and take a shuttle to Coogan's Bluff. I remember the New York Giants as a "real" team, meaning they lost on a semiregular basis and their roster included some black guys. For most of my youth, nobody could say either of those things about the Yankees.

The Dodgers were another story. Although Brooklyn doesn't look very far away on a map of New York, it might as well have been on a different planet. My parents would *never* have let me go to Brooklyn with my friends. Certainly not when I was fourteen. It was enemy territory. There were tough guys on every street corner in Brooklyn, and their New York accents were even more guttural than in the Bronx. If I wanted to see National League teams, I could go to the Polo Grounds.

I did end up in Brooklyn a couple of times before the Dodgers broke the faith and moved three thousand miles west. Ebbets Field was a strange place, full of the sound of Gladys Gooding's skating rink organ. Before the game, there was Roy Campanella on the field being interviewed by Happy Felton for his *Knothole Gang* TV show, which preceded Dodger telecasts. Who was Happy Felton, that large, bespectacled man crammed so awkwardly into a Dodger uniform? Where is he today?

Living in New York meant that major league baseball was everywhere. It was played live within a subway ride of my house. It appeared on the front page of the sports section every day, was on the radio continuously, and was a daily occurrence on TV. The Dodgers were on channel 9. The Yankees or the Giants were on channel 11. Red Barber, Vin Scully, Russ Hodges, Mel Allen: their voices seem permanently etched in my memory.

Taking the Majors for Granted

I took major league baseball for granted. Even after the Giants and Dodgers fled for the West Coast, we had the Mets. I just assumed that everyone was surrounded by major league baseball. This sounds like arrogance today, but it reflects the kind of insularity, even an unexpected naïveté, that comes from growing up in New York.

My thinking about the majors didn't change at all when I left to do graduate work in Boston. Major league baseball was again played in my neighborhood. From there, I moved to a suburb of Washington, D.C., near Baltimore. Again, an embarrassment of major league riches. I then took my first job in Los Angeles. My innocence seemed to have no end in sight.

It wasn't until I moved to Toronto in the early seventies that I finally learned you could live without a major league team. I was just getting used to this humility when the Blue Jays moved in. I revised my conclusion. One might live without major league baseball, but the condition is only temporary. It's just a matter of time before a team finds you.

The Minors Come Calling

I finally got my initiation into the minor leagues in 1989. The Blue Jays were still playing within an hour's drive of my house, but I was losing interest. Their games were almost always sold out. Ticket selection wasn't good. Things became intolerable when the SkyDome opened. The eighth wonder of the world, indeed! Overpriced tickets in the nosebleed section, pricey watered-down beer: the thrill was fading fast.

Somewhere in the midst of this creeping angst, my buddy Doug called to tell me there was a minor league team just down the road in London, Ontario. London is the least likely town to have a minor league team. If baseball has a gritty, blue-collar identity, London has the opposite: it's an upscale palace of pretensions that hosts a major university and teaching hospital, along with the corporate headquarters of just about every insurance company in Canada. The place is crawling with white collars, and most of them are highly starched.

But London did have a minor league baseball team in the AA Eastern League. Truthfully, I wasn't quite sure what that meant. I was a creature of the big leagues. What did I really know about the minors? They were a mystery to me. Like most New Yorkers, I always knew that big leaguers played *somewhere* before they appeared in Yankee Stadium. I was just a little fuzzy on the details. I had heard expressions like "triple-A" all my life, but I had no images to pair with them. Like many of us, my vision of minor league baseball had become a little sharper when the movie *Bull Durham* became a runaway hit in 1988. But just how accurate were those pictures? What was really going on in the bush leagues? Was there truly a world full of Crash Davises and Nook LaLooshes out there?

I drove to this tiny little ballpark in London not knowing what to expect. And I went as a fan. I was far from being a baseball journalist at that point. I was an adolescent; a grown man with the baseball psyche of a fourteen year old. An incurable romantic who half expected to find the heroes of his youth out there. Instead I discovered a bunch of twenty-one year olds I had never heard of.

To my surprise, it didn't matter. These unknowns were wearing Phillies and Tigers uniforms! I could smell the hot dogs, and I heard all the old familiar sounds — the crack of the bat, the slap of leather. It all looked and sounded and smelled right. These guys may not have been Robin Roberts, Willie Mays, and Duke Snider, but everything was recognizable. At some very primitive level it all fell into place.

Now Batting: Ivan Pavlov

The most important name in the park that afternoon never appeared on the scorecard. Ivan Pavlov. Not a utility infielder for the London Tigers. Not a left-handed reliever for the visiting Reading Phillies. This was Pavlov, the Nobel Prize–winning physiologist and psychologist who taught us that simple sensations — like the smell of a hot dog or the sight of a Phillies jersey or the slap of a baseball glove — can reduce us to the awestruck adolescent who lives within.

It was better to be in this condition in London, Ontario, than to be trapped at the SkyDome. In London, I could freely wander down to the first row and listen to on-field conversations. When these guys walked off the field and into the dugout they made eye contact with the fans. You could say "Hi!" and they'd greet you back. You go to a major league game and you're as likely to have a two-way conversation with the players as you are with the image of Kevin Costner on the screen in *Bull Durham*. But here, in London, Ontario, there was a *connection*. Everything was so much more intimate. The worst seats in the house were better than anything I'd ever had in Blue Jay country.

And so I sat through my first minor league game. The experience was intense and intimate, and I was flooded with adolescent impulses. I gawked and stared at everything around me. I talked to players. Miraculously, I drew the line at asking for autographs. I knew I had to keep some semblance of the adult on the scene. I still had to drive home, and they'd never let a starry-eyed fourteen year old operate a car on the freeway.

Long before the game was over, I knew I'd be back, and, before long, my enthusiasm carried me back to Labatt Park in London. And then I started to branch out. Initially, I stayed within my own territory. Then I began to explore farther and farther afield. At first I made day trips. Later, they became journeys with planned itineraries through the minor league byways of North America.

Mysteries of the Minors

What would I find out there? What was minor league life like behind the scenes? Would there be differences in the minor leagues as I changed locales? As I moved from single-A teams all the way to triple-A? Would the parks and personnel differ? The towns? What about the system itself? Were the minors about the development of skills or about winning at any cost? It's true that these young men were getting paid to play baseball, but were their lives really carefree? Was this a stress-free world of perpetual summertime? Given the chance, what would these players complain about?

I learned one thing very quickly. There are a lot more average guys out there than superstars in the making. Forget what the baseball cards and *Baseball Weekly* or *Baseball America* might have told you. The minors are full of also-rans. Guys who have had a taste and guys who never will. Some have had their proverbial "cup of coffee" in the majors and are fading fast, hanging on by their fingernails to avoid slipping back into real life. And there are those, the vast majority, who will never make it to "The Show." For every highly touted number one draft pick, there are fifty guys drafted without media attention. Some weren't even drafted; they had to claw their way through tryout camps and beat the odds by making the team. What is it like for the 95 percent who will never make it? At what point do they realize that they're no longer considered "prospects"? That they're just putting in time?

I also learned that players may be the most visible part of minor league baseball, but there is a rich supporting cast just waiting to be discovered. There are coaches, men in their forties and beyond, with checkered careers behind them, making arduous bus trips with kids half their age. There are concession workers and twenty-two-year-old assistant general managers, happy to scrub toilets and paint dugouts just to be close to the game. There are broadcasters and scorekeepers and scoreboard operators. The nine-year-old kids selling Cracker Jacks in Bluefield, West Virginia, the lady operating the "mechanical" bull in Durham Athletic Park: they are all a part of minor league baseball, and they too would become part of my journey.

The Adolescent versus the Journalist

There was a lesson I had to learn in order to write this book. I was going to have to control that adolescent romantic and become an observer. A journalist. There's a vast difference between leaning over the railing that separates players from supplicants, holding out a baseball card, and saying, "Please mister, would you sign this?" and sitting *in* the dugout during batting practice, chatting with the guy who just hit one over the 380 sign in left center, discussing food or women or his career.

If this journey were to succeed, I would have to wear the journalist/observer suit with grace. I knew I would never abandon the adolescent, not in the face of all the memories that led me here in the first place, but I would have to keep that youthful romantic in check.

Once, in an awkward moment, I blew it. I absolutely lost my detachment and got caught immediately. There I was, sitting in the dugout in some small southern town, listening to that night's pitcher go over the opposition with one of his teammates. No problem, so far. As I thumbed casually through the souvenir program, I came upon a full-page picture of the manager. I remembered him vividly from his major league playing days. And there he sat, two players down to my right. I looked at him, I looked at the picture. Before I knew what I was doing, I asked him if he'd sign the photo and extended my pen to him. Without thinking, he started to oblige me, and then he suddenly stopped.

"Hey!" he proclaimed, rearing back from me. "Who *are* you?"

I had been caught: an intruder in their midst! A journalist was welcome, but *fans* do not sit with players. For a moment a hushed silence fell over the dugout. It was the tone of his voice. An unmistakable alert that an outsider had penetrated the force field. Everyone looked at me. Guys who had talked to me minutes ago seemed to recoil. “Hey, I *trusted* you,” their eyes seemed to say. “But you're not one of us. You're just a *fan*. You belong up there with the rest of them.”

It was an awful moment and it only lasted mere seconds. But it taught me an unforgettable lesson. The adolescent may have led me here in the first place, but he had to stay out of sight when I was working. I had to be cool, professional, and, above all, unimpressed. You're either one of us or you're one of *them*. And *they* don't belong on the field.

Another lesson I learned as the romance flickered is that the guy in the dugout or standing by the batting cage is very little different from the guys I played ball with as a kid or hung out with in high school. The romantic in me, the wide-eyed adolescent, still finds that incomprehensible. He still believes that untold wisdom is exchanged during those secret conversations on the mound between managers and beleaguered pitchers. How can a guy who had his face on an Upper Deck Hot Prospect card be sitting around the dugout telling me he misses his parents or his girlfriend or how concerned he is about facing better pitching than he's ever seen in his life?

A Thumbnail Sketch of the Minors

My journey took place over seven years, although most of the traveling occurred during the final three. My destinations included everything from AAA cities, some of which admittedly push the boundaries of “small town,” to rural sites of the lowest Rookie League teams. From the grimy steel mills of Hamilton, Ontario, to the lush mountains of Hickory, North Carolina; from the sweltering heat of the American Midwest to the icy winds of London, Ontario; from the tightly orchestrated professionalism of Columbus, Ohio, to the unfettered zaniness of the Durham Bulls.

Unexpectedly, my journey occurred at a unique time. Minor league baseball stands at a crossroads. It is in danger of losing its innocence. Until now, the success of minor league baseball has usually followed suit with the majors. Both tend to be driven by external factors such as war and economic cycles. Like the major leagues, the minors have not prospered during wartime or periods of economic depression, but they have thrived when times were good.

The National Association of Professional Baseball Leagues set up shop in 1901 and began keeping official minor league records the following season. By 1910 there were fifty-two different leagues in operation. As the effects of World War I gradually took their toll on the economy and available manpower, teams were forced to fold. By 1917, the number of minor leagues in operation had dropped to twenty-one. The following year, only ten leagues began play at the start of the season, and of them, only the International League finished its schedule.

But the minors weren't dead. Postwar prosperity ushered in renewed interest, and the 1920s were known as a golden decade. Attendance, as well as the number of franchises, again soared until the Great Depression sent owners scurrying for cover. The cycle was repeated with economic recovery and yet another world war to decimate the minors.

The success of minor league baseball reached its all-time peak in 1949. More than 40 million fans paid to see over 400 teams. But the party was soon over. The dawn of televised baseball sent shock waves through the minor league marketplace. Recovery has been gradual. Just when things were starting to heat up again, the Vietnam War turned America away from traditional pastimes, apple pie and baseball. The minors were dealt a body blow. During the Vietnam era, franchises could be bought and sold for a dollar, assuming the new owner was willing to shoulder existing debt and face uncertain prospects.

Things have been on the rise ever since. Many of those one-dollar investments turned out to be goldmines. Although the number of teams and leagues is down from historic levels, attendance is again at near-record highs. In 1994 there were 15 leagues and approximately 150 teams, but over 33 million fans came to see them play. The A-level Midwest League, a barometer of the American heartland, drew nearly 2.5 million fans. In their first season, the West Michigan Whitecaps alone played to nearly half a million fans.

A Parting of the Ways?

For maybe the first time, the majors and minors are headed in different economic directions. Major league baseball has weathered a debilitating strike that fans have yet to forgive and forget. Through it all, the minors have prospered. No longer a well-kept secret, the minors are beginning to attract the attention of a mass audience. The players appear on their own baseball cards, including a premier set issued in 1992 by industry trendsetter Upper Deck. Their exploits are documented in movies, TV documentaries, and Sunday supplements. Even the redoubtable *New York Times* has paid its respects with a feature on then-AAA pitcher Turk Wendell. Minor league stats are published in national magazines and weekly newspapers. In 1991, the *National Geographic* published a photo essay about the minors. The road to respectability was fully paved. Minor league baseball has never received more media attention.

The public has responded in kind. Minor league attendance is at record levels. The merchandizing of minor league logos and memorabilia has become as lucrative as ticket sales. A cap with a Hickory Crawdads logo can be worn with assertive pride in posh urban settings: a touch of primitive exotica that only a sophisticate would flaunt. Even virtual reality has come to call. The Internet features a minor league discussion group, and many franchises have their own sites on the World Wide Web.

Most of what follow are "small" stories. It's a cinch they won't make the six o'clock news. The people, by and large, aren't famous and the events aren't earth shattering. Yet these people are as essential a part of the fabric of baseball as the headline-grabbing superstars who dominate the sport. In many cases, they are far more interesting, and their stories have rarely been told.

Sometimes, what started out being a passing glance at a struggling athlete became the first chapter in the story of a major league career. Alternatively, some of the young men portrayed here have dropped out of sight and are back home leading normal, less glamorous lives. Others are still slogging it out in the obscurity of the lower minors. The relatively brief period between my journey and the publication of this book can be a lifetime in the career of a professional athlete. The fortunate few have already made it all the way to "The Show." They are in the national spotlight they so deeply desired. In some cases their promotions were not surprising. In others, like so many things about the minors, they were totally unpredictable.

London, Ontario

"Once we get here we love to play. The problem is getting here."
—Don McCormack, Reading Phillies manager

Labatt Park in London, Ontario, is one of the most beautiful places to play baseball I've ever seen. It's a gorgeous little stadium adjacent to the downtown area, yet nearly surrounded by parkland. The Thames River runs behind it, an inviting target for aspiring Cecil Fielders who play for this AA Detroit affiliate. Behind the row of trees that border the outfield fence is a spectacular view of the London skyline. Architects have made fortunes designing those concrete towers, and the contrast between natural and manmade splendor is truly inspiring.

I live about an hour and a half from this little palace on the Thames. They say it's easy to ignore the treasures in your own backyard, but this is one exception to the rule. I've been going to London Tigers games since they opened the franchise in 1989. In fact, I may never have discovered the delights of minor league baseball if not for the London Tigers.

From my point of view, the London park may be a dream come true. But there is clearly another side to the story. I talk to a lot of players who agree how lovely the park is but are quick to remind me what London, Ontario, does to their travel schedule. Reading manager Don McCormack speaks for many when he says, "You've really got a beautiful place here. Once we get here, we love to play. The problem is getting here. When you've just finished a night game in Albany, New York, the thought of getting on the bus and driving all night is pretty awful. It's hard to be enthusiastic about any place other than home when you have to drive ten hours to get there."

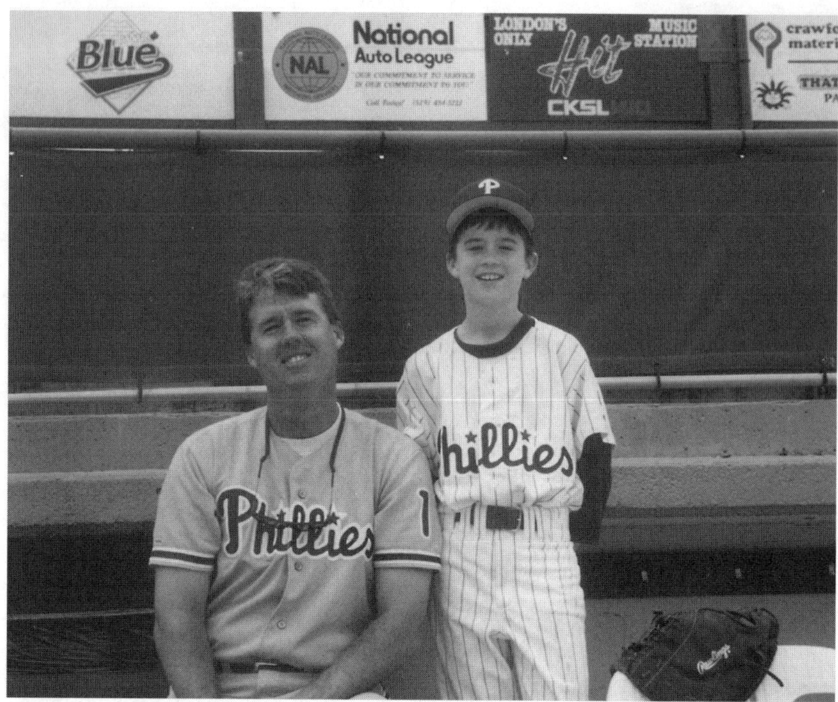

Reading manager Don McCormack and son Taylor.

As if to complicate things further, little wisdom seems to have gone into the Eastern League schedule. While it's true there are no tropical locations in the Eastern League, Canada is colder than most. Spring comes late to London, Ontario. Why not let the Tigers open on the road, far from the frozen North, and gradually work their way back home as the ice melts?

"That never happens," laughs Assistant General Manager John Belford. "We always seem to be playing here far too early. You'd think they'd just give us a couple of weeks to get things warmed up."

Not bloody likely, as the locals say. On April 15, 1992, a date literally frozen in my memory, I ventured forth to see the London Tigers at home. The afternoon sun was pleasant, and the temperature during batting practice squeaked up past 50 degrees. The trouble is, this was a night game. While the sun shone, we stood several feet behind Reading catcher Ed Rosado while he warmed up first round draft choice Tyler Green. It was an incredible experience, watching Green's knuckle-curveball dance in the crisp afternoon air. If anyone still believes that curveballs are optical illusions, this afternoon would have been a revelation.

Later that night, after the sun set and the temperature plummeted, Green pitched four very strong innings. When the knuckler was dancing, he was virtually unhittable. The London hitters looked very bad, swinging off balance, striking out more often than putting the ball in play. But if Green's pitches were unhittable, they were also uncallable. That night's umpire was as baffled by the movement as were the London hitters, and things ultimately unraveled.

At the start of the game, there were approximately one hundred people in the stands. When the gentle freezing rain started, that number was halved. Somewhere around the sixth inning, I saw a foul ball coming for me and was literally too cold to move. I wasn't thinking about souvenirs but survival. My friend reached out his left hand and saved us both. When we left at the end of the game, which went into extra innings, there were fewer than thirty fans left in the park. There were literally more people in the London dugout than in the stands.

Even when the London weather is fine, which it tends to be once you move into June, some strange things happen in Labatt Park. Earlier this year, Tigers pitcher Ben Blomdahl pitched a hell of a game against this same Reading team. The game ended with Blomdahl throwing a one hitter and losing 1–0. He's not the first to experience that frustration. What makes the story notable is the way London lost. They did it on the most difficult kind of mental error to correct. Reading had one of the game's rare base runners on third with less than two out. Jeff Jackson hit a long foul ball into the right field corner. The right-fielder gave chase, thinking it might drop in for an extra base hit. But the ball stayed up just long enough for him to make a really nice running catch in foul territory, which was the worst thing he could have done. Doc Palmer, broadcasting the game, was screaming "Drop it! Drop it!" into the mike. But the right-fielder was nowhere near a radio when he made the running catch. The Reading runner at third tagged up and could have crawled home. How do you suppress the impulse to catch a ball when you're on the run?

P.S. The Detroit front office was sufficiently impressed with Blomdahl, despite his loss, to promote him to Toledo (AAA).

Sid Monge is the London Tigers pitching coach. Monge has impressive major league credentials. He stayed around for a decade, pitching for the Angels, Indians, Phillies, and Tigers. His final stint for Detroit came in September 1984, when he pitched in nineteen games during the Tigers' drive to the playoffs. Monge's best year was 1979. He made the All-Star team and had a 2.40 ERA and nineteen saves for the Indians.

Sid Monge knows his stuff. He learned it in the trenches, and he is here to teach it to a whole new generation of pitchers. He is also opinionated and articulate. Long before I talked to Monge, I watched him work from the sidelines. He had Tigers pitchers lined up and was showing them his pickoff move. Over and over, he drilled it into them. If these guys had come to learn some fancy new kind of curveball, they were disappointed that afternoon. All they got was moves to first.

But they listened. And several hours later it was obvious they had learned. That night it was pathetic. Was it Albany? New Britain? It doesn't even matter anymore. The pickoffs were coming fast and furious, one after another. The incredible thing is, the opposition never adapted. They kept taking leads and they kept getting picked off.

"Oh, I love to teach them that move," Monge told me. "It's so valuable. And it's so underrated. I mean, look, a guy gets to first. He can hurt you. Especially if he can steal second. All it takes is a single, and I'm down a run. I figure in most cases I have a better chance to pick that guy off first than I do to strike out the next batter.

"I remember one game I was pitching back in the American League. We were playing the Yankees. Mickey Rivers gets on, I don't remember how. And up comes Bucky Dent. Now Dent is a little guy. I figure he's not going to go long ball on me, but he sure can hit a single. The last thing I want is Mickey Rivers on second. And you know Rivers is standing there at first with just one thing on his mind. He's going, the first chance he has.

"But I'm not going to give him that chance. It's between Rivers and me. So I throw over there. And he gets back. And I throw over again. And again he gets back. And the fans are booing. They're yelling 'Pitch to him!' But I'm thinking, Dent isn't getting anything to hit until I settle this thing with Rivers. I must have thrown over there fifteen times. On the sixteenth time, I got him. Now Dent can't hurt me."

What Monge taught his young Tigers that afternoon was very simple. The mechanics were only one part of it. Maybe the easy part. The rest was the mental stuff. He taught them not to show their best move.

"Let him think he's seen your best a couple of times. Then he gets cocky and wham! you've got him. He underestimates you and you nail him. They always walk away shaking their heads," Monge tells me, and he's right. Even from the stands, I've seen that mixture of embarrassment and surprise.

The other part of what Monge taught them had to do with attitude. He taught them just to *do* it.

"Very few coaches stress pickoffs," he tells me. "I see it as one of baseball's fundamentals. It's something that every pitcher should know and be ready to use. It's one more way of getting the edge. Taking another out away from them. Taking the bat out of their hands. If I screw up and they get a hit or a walk off me, I'm mad. I want it back. I pick him off, it's like it never happened. He can't come around to score."

I kid Monge that he's teaching his craft right out in broad daylight.

"If I saw you doing it, why didn't they?" I ask him. "Why weren't they prepared for you? Why don't they come into London knowing this is pickoff city?"

Monge laughs. "They just don't. Nobody believes it can happen, even while it's happening. Remember that game with the Blue Jays?"

I do. I can still picture that awful night in August 1983, when Tippy Martinez picked off three consecutive Jays in one inning. They must have known it was coming, at least after the first runner got nailed. But it didn't matter. They kept taking leads, and, like Monge, Martinez kept throwing over there. And he got every last one of them.

Keith Kimberlin had his twenty-seventh birthday the day he played against his former team in London. Keith is built like a shortstop and barely looks his age. You wouldn't be surprised to find him playing in a pickup game on a Sunday afternoon in some small town. He'd be the skinny kid with the good glove. He'd also be the one to keep his teammates laughing. He's verbal and funny. He's a nice guy.

But he didn't fit into the Tigers' plans, especially after he tore up his knee prior to the '92 season and spent the whole campaign rehabbing. In December 1992, he was released by the Tigers and signed by the Phillies. It is unlikely the Phillies saw him as a prospect any more than the Tigers did, but he met a need within the Phillies farm system, so he had a job.

That's a harsh verdict. The usual wisdom is that everybody in A ball sees himself as a prospect. Somewhere around AA that vision gets blurred, and by AAA the label "prospect" is no longer a certainty. Some guys are on their way up, and some are on their way down or, more aptly, out. There are also career AAA players. These guys aren't going to make it to "The Show," but they play adequately at the AAA level to hold teams together so that genuine prospects can develop. They also make a decent living at something they do well. There are examples galore. One of the most familiar is Tommy Barrett, whose brother Marty played for the Red Sox for years. Tommy was most recently with Tucson in the Pacific Coast League; before that he played for Scranton. Barrett leads all minor leaguers in stolen bases, a record that may never be eclipsed simply because it is unlikely that anyone will have so many opportunities to steal bases in the minors. Usually, if you're that fast, you're also that good. And if you're that good, you get called up. Except for a cup of coffee with the Phillies, Barrett has played his career in the minors. It is unlikely he is the

Astros third baseman of the future, even though he is presently hitting .280 and fielding competently for their AAA team. It is also unlikely, indeed it would be somewhat sad, if Tommy Barrett saw himself as a prospect.

Which gets us back to Keith Kimberlin. In AA ball, the distinction between prospect and suspect is often fuzzy, or at least in transition. In Kimberlin's case, he was hired to do a job. He is in danger of doing it so well that the organization may have to rethink his status. When last seen, he had just been elected to the Eastern League All-Star team. He was also hitting .270 and behaving like a Hoover at shortstop, even playing a portion of the year with a broken finger. But despite his youthful appearance, Kimberlin *is* twenty-seven years old. When you look at a AA roster, you want to see a lot of guys twenty-two and twenty-three years old. Not twenty-seven.

True, there are exceptions. Every year, there is a story like Seattle's Rich Amaral. Someone has to win the oldest rookie award. But those cases are anomalies; that's why they attract all the media attention. Still, they happen, and there is precedent on Kimberlin's own team. Two years ago, the aforementioned Steve Scarsone was a journeyman Reading infielder headed nowhere. Likewise, Tom Marsh was a reserve outfielder. He hadn't even evolved to journeyman status. No one, their manager, their teammates, perhaps even Scarsone or Marsh themselves, expected the kind of dramatic improvement seen in the months ahead. Both men were promoted and became stars in AAA, as well as seeing time in the majors.

Where does that leave Keith Kimberlin? For one thing, he, Marsh, and Scarsone were born within seven months of each other. They are essentially the same age. Marsh and Scarsone were late bloomers, but they have already bloomed. The world is still waiting for the flower of Kimberlin's abilities. He undoubtedly turned a few heads playing against London during a four-game series in July 1993, and I told him so in no uncertain terms. He thanked me for noticing but admitted, "That's just what I wanted to do. I always turn it up a notch when I come back into London."

Who can blame him? When you've been jilted, you want to look good in front of your ex-lover. Show her she was wrong to let you go so easily. Whether or not Keith Kimberlin can keep it "turned up a notch" for the rest of the season is an open question. He's got a month and a half to put up more good numbers and wake up a few more folks. And maybe start next season in AAA. But he's got to do it the hard way. There are no more games to play in London.

There is bad news in the air that even the charms of Labatt Park can't hide. London is on the brink of losing its franchise. It's no fun to watch anything die, and that includes a minor league team. This one has been dying slowly but surely over the course of three seasons, ever since they won the Eastern

League championship in 1990. It's hard to say exactly what happened. Maybe fan support, which peaked during the championship year, was fickle.

"These fans want a winner," Assistant GM John Belford tells me. "I'm not sure they're ready to support a team just because it's in their hometown."

Maybe Belford is right. London just may not be a baseball town. It certainly doesn't fit the usual stereotypes. It is a very white-collar place, strongly associated with insurance company head offices. The joke in London is that there are more CEOs in town than garage mechanics. There may be as many doctors and university professors as well.

Do these folks go to Tigers games? In fact, does *anybody* from London come to Labatt Park? During a recent Canada Day holiday sellout, prompted more, I suspect, by the postgame fireworks display than the game itself, I meet more fans who have driven in from Detroit than from London. A lot of people tell me, "Oh, we try to come over a couple of times every summer. This is a lovely place. Much nicer than going to Tiger Stadium."

And they usually add the punchline. "And much safer."

Safety is the last thing you'd worry about in this park. Plus you get to see a bunch of players who will likely be wearing Detroit uniforms within a couple of years. The list of former London Tigers who now play for Detroit is long, given this brief affiliation. Like any good minor league franchise, London will be happy to impress you with that list in their souvenir program for just two dollars. The litany includes Travis Fryman, Milt Cuyler, Scott Livingstone, Scott Aldred, Chris Gomez, John Dougherty, and José Lima. Before it's over, even if it ends this year, the list will be longer.

Like a virus, this lack of support is contagious. Both the fans and the local media have come down with it. It's hard to tell who had it first. On a gorgeous July afternoon, you'll rarely find more than a thousand fans sitting here in the sunshine. So you figure, maybe they're home listening to the game on the radio, right? Wrong. They couldn't if they wanted to. During a recent Sunday game against Reading, the only voice in the radio booth comes from Steve Degler, the Reading announcer, who is broadcasting the game *back* to Pennsylvania. Reading fans care about their baseball, and they get the coverage they deserve.

To be fair, some games are broadcast over London radio. But that owes more to the enthusiasm of one local fan than it does corporate support. John "Doc" Palmer, an economics professor at the University of Western Ontario, broadcast nineteen of the London games over CHRW, the 3000-watt campus FM station. But it is a noncommercial labor of love for which Palmer sees not a penny. And if he stopped tomorrow, it is doubtful anyone would rush to take his place.

In many minor league towns, local baseball games are front-page news. If they don't bump the Middle East off page 1, they are certainly lead items in the sports section. Even that isn't the case in London. I've rarely seen a Tigers result, even when they play at home, displayed more prominently than page 3 of the sports section. And the coverage ranges from minimal to inaccurate. For example, on July 22, 1993, fans in Labatt Park witnessed a triple play. I saw it, broadcaster Doc Palmer saw it, but London *Free Press* reporter Brenda Bouw was apparently looking elsewhere. Her coverage in the next morning's paper, on page 3 of the sports section, managed to work the wrong players and wrong positions into her description. If you don't know, just guess. It's only the AA Tigers.

The triple play that the London reporter got wrong was, in fact, the second one that Reading had pulled that week. That, in itself, is a little strange. But it is no stranger than the rest of the game played that July evening. It was like a conspiracy of low probability events; they had chosen *this* game to surface. Maybe it had something to do with Reading's all night bus trip from Binghamton. No one had slept particularly well. Some of the players were wired, others were tired. A perfect night for a strange game.

You might have thought the Reading batters were comatose, the way London pitcher Felipe Lira mowed them down. He struck out twelve hitters on what looked like a very good split-finger fastball. Pretty strong stuff for the Eastern League. But he also gave up nine hits, eight of them for extra bases. It was feast or famine out there.

The other side of the game was no less exciting. Craig Holman pitched for Reading and managed to hit three London batters. The fans really got on Holman, but there were no warnings issued and no bench-clearing brawls. Holman didn't seem to be throwing at anybody; he was just, well, wild inside. Other than that, Holman pitched a little gem as well: a complete game two-hit shutout. In truth, it might have been a no-hitter. Both hits by the Tigers were solid enough: one went for a double, the other a triple. But on both, outfielder Jeff Jackson *almost* made spectacular catches. He had his glove on both balls but just couldn't hang on. A slower outfielder might not have even gotten to either ball, so there was no question surrounding the scoring. But it makes you realize how fragile no-hitters are.

Then there was the triple play. First there was a hit batter, then a walk. Tigers manager Tom Runnells figured he had Holman on the ropes, so with nobody out he called for the hit and run. Both runners took off like deer, and the batter hit a line drive into right field. The trouble is, it was hit right at David Tokheim, who simply threw back into Ron Lockett at first. Lockett tagged the bag for the second out, then checked the situation at second base. He was surprised to find runner Rudy Pemberton about halfway to third. The final out wasn't even close. I remember thinking, if London had the bases loaded, Reading could have probably gotten the fourth out at third base.

So what you had on a lovely July evening in London was twelve strikeouts in a losing cause, versus a two-hit complete game shutout, that might have been a no-hitter, with three hit batsmen and a triple play. Just your average ballgame.

I'm walking around Labatt Park watching the Tigers go through their pregame rituals when manager Tom Runnells saunters over to me. Runnells is a product of the Expos organization. He managed their AAA franchise in Indianapolis and won the championship with his team in 1989. He was promoted to the third base coaching job with the Expos next season and eventually became their manager. He was thirty-six at the time, marking him as something of a prodigy. He left the Expos amid the usual swirl of acrimony and rumors that accompanies managerial firings. I had never met the man and I had no idea what to expect.

"Can I ask you a favor?" he says.

"Sure," I reply. I can't imagine where this is going. Can I borrow ten bucks? Can you take a couple of throws from the outfield while I hit some flies out there? Would you move your camera bag off the third base line? Nothing will surprise me. Including the espionage Runnells proposes.

"Can you take a couple of pictures for me?" he begins. "You see that guy over by the batting cage? Number 21? That's Rudy Pemberton. Look at his feet. You see that?"

I look over at Pemberton, then down at his feet. What I see is a piece of rope tied between his ankles. A strange sight indeed. Is this a practical joke? Is Rudy about to fall on his ass when he tries to walk?

"Can you take some pictures of that?" Runnells continues. "Don't let him see you. You know, get a close up of his ankles, then get one of him standing there. And try to get one of him in the cage when he's hitting."

I agree and set off on my undercover mission. The first two shots are easy since Pemberton is facing away from me. It becomes a little trickier when he gets in the cage. I have to move around to the first base side and hope he doesn't decide to foul some off down the right field line. I'm not exactly a delegate from *Candid Camera*, standing out there between home and first. I also feel rather vulnerable with a camera attached to my face.

Fortunately, Rudy hits to left. When I finish shooting, I walk back to Runnells.

"Mission accomplished," I report. "Now can you tell me why he does it?"

"Ask Rudy. See what he tells you," Runnells suggests.

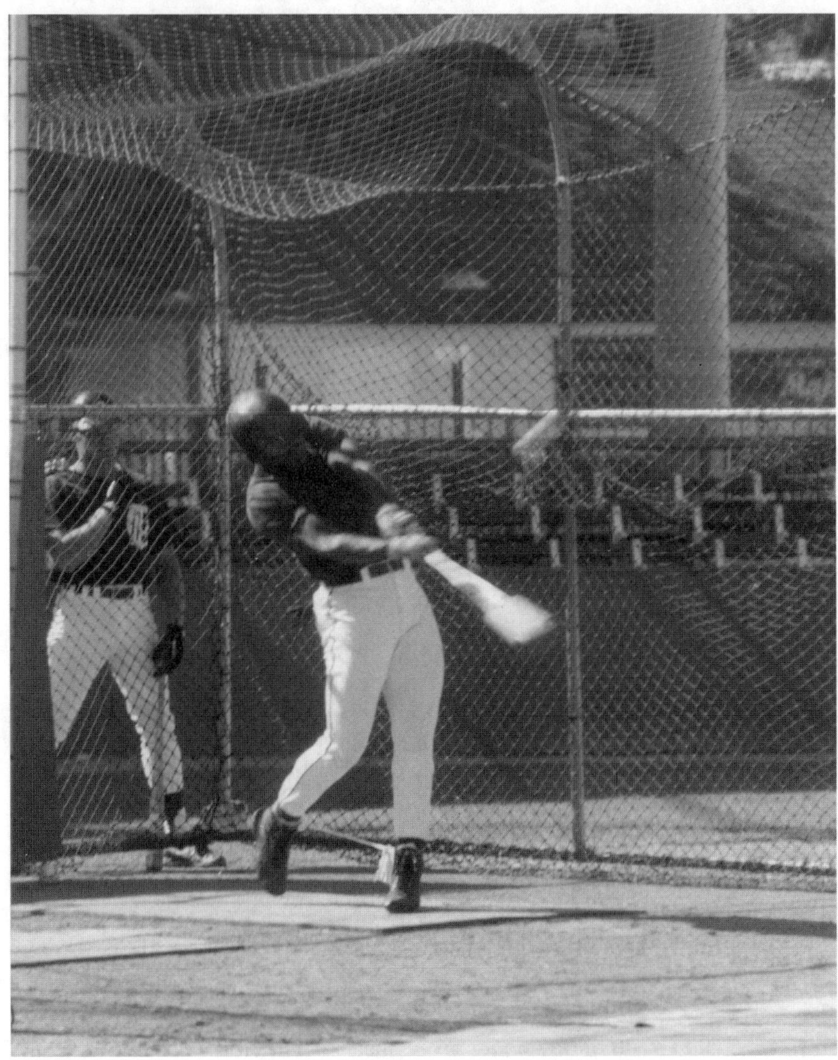

Rudy Pemberton strides into one as best he can with his feet tied together.

So I do. It seems a pretty straightforward question.

"Hey Rudy, how come you're walking around with a piece of rope tied between your ankles?"

Pemberton looks at me for what seems like a long time.

"My coach in winter ball told me I was striding too much when I hit," he explained in somewhat accented English. "He said to use the rope to limit how much I can step into the pitch."

This time I look at him for a while.

"It must really slow you down on the bases," I venture. I thought it was pretty funny, but Pemberton just looks at me. I think about explaining it, but I figure, what the hell. So I thank him and walk back to Runnells.

"He told me it was something he learned in winter ball. It's supposed to help his swing, keep him from striding too much."

Runnells just shakes his head and makes a kind of noise that suggests he doesn't agree with such methods.

"Can you send me the pictures?" he asked.

"Sure. Glad to. What are you going to do with them?" I wonder.

"I'm going to use them as ammunition when we have our talk about his hitting."

Next week, the pictures come back, and I send a second set of prints off to Runnells. Rudy is hitting .265 with twelve home runs at the time. You can bet I'm going to be watching his stats for the rest of the season.

P.S. Later that day, I recount the tale to John Belford, the Tigers' assistant general manager. When I get to the line about the rope slowing Pemberton down on the bases, Belford laughs. That makes me feel better.

"Yeah, I thought that was pretty funny too. I can't believe Pemberton never cracked a smile."

Belford laughs again. "You probably didn't know it," he explains. "Rudy hardly understands a word of English. He's Dominican. You wouldn't know it looking at him, and his name doesn't give it away either. He probably had no idea what you were talking about."

So much for cross-cultural humor.

The Phillies took what turns out to have been a big gamble when they drafted seventeen-year-old high school star Jeff Jackson in the first round back in 1989. He may have seemed like a sure thing at the time, but Jackson has been languishing in the low minors ever since, and the Phillies have been taking heat over their blown choice. The standard rap against them goes, "They could have had Frank Thomas. Instead they took this untested high school kid."

Phillies scouting director Mike Arbuckle sees it differently. From his point of view, Jackson is just where you might expect him to be had he gone to college and been drafted at age twenty-one. Arbuckle believes that Jackson is still an athlete with exceptional tools who can develop into a major league star. Arbuckle has an extra measure of credibility since he was not part of the original scouting machine that selected Jackson. When he claims that critics are being impatient with Jackson, no one can accuse Arbuckle of being defensive.

Like Jackson, first baseman Ron Lockett comes from Chicago. He came to the Phillies with far less fanfare. Lockett was the eighth selection in the 1990 draft. Unlike Jackson, Lockett has put up some good numbers in his brief minor league experience, hitting .310 during his rookie season.

Now their paths have crossed. Jackson and Lockett are teammates on the Reading Phillies. It is Lockett's fourth pro season. He is still developing and isn't plagued by "first round" or "can't miss" labels. Jackson is in his fifth season, which may turn out to be something of a watershed in his career. How much longer are the Phillies prepared to nurture him in the low minors?

I first saw Jackson play for Batavia during his second season. He was fast on the bases but didn't get on enough to be a threat. He struck out eighty times in a short season league and batted .198. Today he looks very different.

"Man, I was a *kid* then. A skinny kid," he laughs. "I've put on thirty-five pounds since then. I'm much stronger now."

It is easy to see. Jeff Jackson is now a strong twenty-one-year-old man. When he makes contact, the ball jumps. The problem, of course, is how often he makes contact.

"JJ is real laid back," one of his teammates tells me. "He's real easygoing. Nonchalant. It's helped him to cope with all the pressure, but it probably hasn't helped his game any. There's no telling what he could do if someone lit a fire under him."

Perhaps that's where Lockett comes in. How much of their being on the same team is an accident? Sure, both players are developing, and they both happen to be at the AA level, but it's hard not to see more to it. For one thing, there is undeniable comfort in having someone from your own hometown, someone with shared cultural experience, as a teammate. But Lockett provides more than comfort. He is good for Jackson. He's the more aggressive of the two. The more assertive as well.

"I push him sometimes," Lockett admits to me, standing in the dugout in Labatt Park. "I get on him to do things. He's very easygoing, you know. He doesn't like to bother people."

Lockett offers a prime example. "This spring, we were in the Phillies camp. Dennis Menke was spending a lot of time working with Jeff on his hitting. He told him, if you have any problems, any questions, you call me. He gave us his number. He didn't have to do that. He meant it. He really cared. Later on, when Jeff went into a slump, I said, 'Call him! You got his number. Call him.' But Jeff didn't want to. He didn't want to bother him. If it was me, I wouldn't have hesitated. You got to look out for yourself. Make the most of these chances."

That's good advice. It's doubly good coming from a teammate rather than from management. But Lockett isn't on Reading just to be a guru or a role model for Jeff Jackson. He has a career of his own to look after. Lockett is also

Jeff Jackson.

a prospect. He was proud to be featured on Upper Deck's inaugural series of minor league cards. Only ten players from each organization were selected, and Lockett was one of them. So was Jackson.

Ironically, the two men have virtually identical stats through two-thirds of the '93 season. At the start of their series with London, their records looked like this.

	AVG	AB	R	H	2B	3B	HR	RBI	SB
Jackson	.233	227	26	53	7	2	5	31	11
Lockett	.236	212	28	50	9	2	6	32	8

Ideally, you'd like to add fifty points to those averages and get those power stats up a bit. But for now, what you see is not just what you get; it's what you get from both guys.

"I don't know if we're bringing each other up, keeping each other down, or what," laughs Lockett. "Whatever it is, we sure do have similar records."

Maybe the numbers are similar, but the personalities are not. Jackson sweats as much as anybody, but he seems to glide through the work with a smile on his face. He gives the impression that it comes very easily. That could work against him at some point. Lockett, on the other hand, does not glide and has no illusions about what it takes.

"This is hard work," he tells me, looking very serious. "Don't ever let anyone tell you it isn't. People think, being out here, taking your swings, it's all fun. Maybe it is when you're playing on a street corner, but out here, it's something else. These pitchers are learning how to get you out. They're working on new pitches. They're doing everything they can to make you look bad. That's their job. You got to learn to adapt. To stay on top of things. Every day, you got to be thinking. Preparing mentally. You got to be tough. The physical stuff is just part of it. If you make it, even this far, you've done some hard work. I wish more people understood that."

It's 4:30 on a gorgeous July afternoon in London. The Reading team bus has just arrived, and players are starting to find their way onto the field. They've just woken up after an all-night bus trip and a few hours' shut-eye at the motel. Out in deepest right field, lying safely away from the bullpen or outfield drills, is a solitary figure. It is sprawled in the sunshine like a reptile, seeking maximum contact between body surface and warmth. The body is in uniform. It doesn't move, but as I walk by, taking care not to step on it, it asks me if I know the time. It seems an odd request from an area of Labatt Park where time seems to be standing still.

I reply, and before long I am stretched out on the same outfield grass. It becomes obvious within minutes, probably less, that this is no ordinary ballplayer I'm talking to. I ask some usual interview-type questions, but things always seem to head off in odd directions. Pretty soon we're lying out in right field laughing like a couple of certifiable loonies.

So who is this guy I'm talking to? I've never seen him before, although his name is vaguely familiar. But from where? He's a pitcher named Chris Marchok. Have I seen him on any of the Phillies minor league rosters? No. Have I seen him pitch here before? No again. Why do I know about him? Gradually, it all comes together.

Chris graduated from Harvard with a degree in applied mathematics. Then he came up through the Expos system.

"Come on, stop laughing," he pleads. "I'm not the first guy from Harvard to play pro ball. In fact, there was even a guy on the Expos about ten years ago. An outfielder."

I accuse him of making the guy up to save face, but I know he's right. Neither of us can retrieve the name at the moment, but later I find out it was Mike Stenhouse. Not that Stenhouse and his career .190 average are a major source of Crimson pride. Neither is pitcher Jeff Musselman, another Harvard product, who faded from view in a career tainted by substance abuse. But the future may be brighter. I tell Chris about Nick Delvecchio, the first baseman from Harvard I saw playing for Greensboro. He seems relieved not to be carrying the Harvard stigma alone.

Chris has been pitching in the Expos minor league system since he was drafted in '87. He spent part of two seasons in AAA Indianapolis and was on the Expos' forty-man roster. They seemed to be taking him quite seriously. Last season he pitched for AA Harrisburg, where he finished with a 6–0 record and an ERA of 3.09. Then he was cut. Chris is not exactly an Expos fan anymore.

"If you think I'm turned off to them, go talk to Tom Runnells," he says, gesturing across the field. I see his point. Even though Runnells has made me his official photographer, I wouldn't discuss the Expos with him in casual conversation.

"So how did you get from being an out-of-work Expos pitcher to the Reading Phillies?" I ask.

Chris laughs and begins this tale.

"I was sitting there in the off-season without a job. I'm twenty-eight years old and I figure I can still pitch. I wasn't real happy with my agent and the phone wasn't exactly ringing off the wall. I knew there were some things about me that might interest some team, so why didn't I try to sell myself? My wife and I sat down and put together this flyer. In one corner we put one of my old baseball cards from when I was in AAA. Then opposite it we wrote, in large type, 'Hire This Man!' Then we added a bunch of career highlights that made me sound indispensable. At the bottom, we warned them, 'Don't let this opportunity pass you by!' It was really great. Even if it didn't work, we had fun doing it. I figured no one else in baseball goes looking for work this way. At least I'll be noticed."

"What did you do with them?" I wondered. "Did you scatter them from a plane?"

"No. That's the old fashioned way. We were very nineties. I faxed them off to every major league club. Except the Expos, of course. In the middle of sending all these faxes, I get a call from my agent. He says, 'I don't know what you're doing, but my phone is starting to ring. Maybe you'd better send me a copy of it too.'"

All this time, Chris and I are lying on our backs in right field, laughing and soaking up rays.

"But it still wasn't that easy," he continues. "So I started pestering the Phillies. I was calling every day. I was relentless. Del Unser's secretary knew my voice by heart. Finally I got through to him. He said, 'I can see we're not going to get rid of you too easily! Why don't you come down to Reading and show us what you have.' So I did, and I had pretty good stuff that day. They signed me and that's how I got the job here."

Chris Marchok: "Hire This Man!"

"So after all that," I wonder, "how are you doing?"

Chris makes a noise to suggest this wasn't unfolding as a Cy Young season. I take out my stat sheet and start to check.

"Oh, let's see what it says," Chris says eagerly, almost grabbing the paper from my hand. "Mmmm. Good thing I had those last scoreless innings. I've got the ERA down to 7.04."

I never thought I'd laugh right in a guy's face about his ERA. But there was something about Chris's relief in getting it *down* to 7.04 that gave me license. That and the fact that he was laughing.

It was somehow OK to giggle at how badly things were going. It wasn't that Chris didn't care. He cared a lot, and he had the ability to do something about it. That was another reason it was OK to laugh. His lifetime ERA over six previous seasons is 2.61. The guy can pitch. It was best to see this season's ERA as an anomaly, maybe have a disbelieving chuckle over it, and then get back to work at getting it down.

Somewhere during our talk, it occurs to me that Chris might have been teammates with Steve Fireovid, who also pitched for Indianapolis. Fireovid's book *The 26th Man* is one of the best chronicles of the frustrations of minor league life I've ever read.

"Don't you remember me from the book?" Chris asks.

At first, I think he's kidding me. But then it starts to dawn. For the first half of the book, Fireovid talks about his young teammate from Harvard. It's a wonderful portrait, presented mostly as a contrast between smart, funny, enthusiastic Chris and the plodding, self-effacing author. The details are, of course, three years out of date, but the essentials are on target. No wonder Chris Marchok seems familiar to me. I've already read all about him. That night, as soon as I get home from the park, I grab *The 26th Man* and reread the entire first half. How could I have forgotten all this? I'm ready for Chris when I see him two days later.

We hang out a bit before Sunday's game and I ask him a rather cosmic question.

"Where do you see yourself in five years?"

"The truth?" he starts, as if there were an alternative. "Probably out of the game. I needed a really great year and I'm not having one. Even if I turn it around from here, I don't know if it's enough. I'm twenty-eight years old. I've been married for a year and a half. We'd like to have a family. It's nice having a degree from Harvard, but I've also got a student loan from Harvard. Much as I love playing ball, I may have to go out and get a real job."

I ask Chris if he thinks it'll be that easy to get baseball out of his system. He pitched in college and now he's pitched professionally for seven years.

"I don't know. I hope so." Then he shrugs. "Maybe not." Then Chris tells me a story to suggest that baseball may not be so easy for him to kick cold turkey.

"Last winter after I was released by the Expos, I thought about what I was going to do. I could have quit right then. It would have been a logical place to stop. I had my shot. I'd been released. But I still knew I could pitch. So I figured I'd give it another chance. That meant I better stay in shape. The trouble is I can't always find somebody to catch me. So I went out to this playground by myself. I took my glove and ball and started throwing against this wall. Just to keep in shape. I'm throwing, and the ball is rolling back to me, and I'd throw again. Then all of a sudden the ball takes a bad bounce off the wall and rolls off to the side. So I reach for it and miss it, and I fall down and I'm lying there on the ground, my knee is skinned, it's freezing cold, mist all around me, and I say, 'Wait a minute! What am I doing! Am I crazy? It's freezing out here, my knee is bleeding . . . Look at me! I've got a degree from Harvard! Do I need this?'"

Chris hasn't forgotten the moment. Or the fact that he went back to throwing the ball. All of which may help him anticipate how easy it's going to be to put the ball down after this season, or whenever he chooses to.

Before I leave, I give Chris my copy of Bill Lee's book *The Wrong Stuff*. In some ways, Chris reminds me of Lee. Both are bright, talented guys who push the ever-present boundaries of corporate baseball. Bill Lee was more of a renegade. He pitched for about ten big league seasons and earned the right to act out a bit. Still, it cost him his career. Ironically, it was the Expos who finally pulled the plug.

Chris may never make it to the majors and may have to fight his guerrilla war from down here, in the netherworld of AA and AAA. It's not that he's consciously rattling the cage or trying to make trouble. It's just that he's a bit different. Guys like him give baseball some dimension. They define new possibilities and breathe new life into the game. But baseball doesn't take kindly to change. You only buy the right to push the limits when you're hitting over .300 or your career ERA is below 3.00. Right now, Chris Marchok is just trying to hang on.

Casey Waller came to the Phillies in the same June 1989 draft that brought Jeff Jackson. Waller was the Phillies' eleventh selection. He didn't have "can't miss!" written all over him, but he was far from being taken for granted.

Waller has played at all three levels of the Phillies minor league system, although AA Reading seems to be his home. Earlier in his career, Waller split the season between A Clearwater and Reading. Now that's he's more advanced, Waller has split his time between Reading and AAA Scranton. After a couple of split seasons, the verdict seems to be that Waller doesn't seem quite up to AAA competition but thrives on AA play.

1993 is the fourth season Casey Waller has played for Reading. There aren't a lot of guys who play four seasons in AA, where an unspoken "up or out" policy is a fact of life. Like his teammate Sean Ryan, with whom Waller has traveled through the Phillies minor league system, Casey began 1993 in AAA. Don McCormack, their manager at Reading, puts the case simply. "This was their year to show what they could do. We already knew they could play at AA. They were sent up and given a chance to show whether they had it."

I saw Scranton play several games in late June. It was good seeing Sean and Casey again, especially in AAA uniforms. Sean was more upbeat than Casey. He had been hitting the ball well and was feeling optimistic. Still, his average was hovering around .230. Casey wasn't playing as often as Sean, and his average was nearly fifty points lower. Things were not looking good.

Three weeks later Reading came to London. One of the first guys I saw on the field was Casey Waller. I was truly surprised to see him.

"Yeah, we're seeing a lot of each other this year," he jokes.

"How does it feel being back in AA?" I venture.

"I'm a little disappointed things didn't go better, but I'm glad to be here. I'm playing every day. At least I'm getting my at bats. I come to the park, I know I'm going to be in the lineup."

There was a double irony in seeing Casey back in London. As long as I've known him, Casey has hit uncommonly well in Labatt Park. I kid him about it every time I see him.

"You ought to just get traded to London," I used to say only half-jokingly. I often gave him the local sports section that featured his heroics, although Casey doesn't seem to be much of a collector. But he could hit! On July 1, 1991,

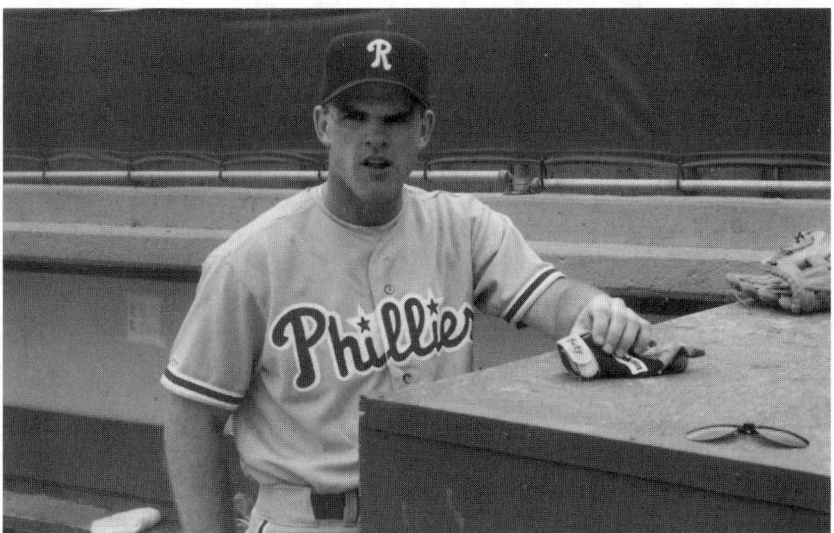

Casey Waller.

Casey launched his seventh and eighth home runs to contribute to a Reading win at Labatt Park. A year later on July 18, Casey hit a dramatic eighth-inning three-run homer into the Thames River for a come-from-behind Reading win over London. It wasn't just my imagination. Casey was building a career in London. I even tried unsuccessfully to export the magic. When I saw Casey playing in AAA, I brought him a small London Tigers schedule to keep in his pocket. It obviously wasn't enough. He was back in London.

I ask McCormack if it isn't unusual having Waller back yet again.

"Yes, it is," he replies. "But we had to make a decision on him and he made it easier for us. He said he didn't mind coming back here. He just wanted to play."

Just before game time, Casey comes over and says, "I know there's lots of ups and downs. But the main thing is I'm still here. I'm still working."

Not so his buddy Sean Ryan.

"Sean was released last week," Don McCormack tells me. "There was just no place for him to play anymore. Gene Schall moved up from here and he's going to play first base in Scranton. He's hit everywhere we've had him and it was time for him to move to AAA. Sean couldn't come back down here. We've got Lockett at first, and he needs the at bats to develop. There was just no place to put Sean. It's a tough decision, but he had his shot."

Sean Ryan isn't the first guy to get cut from AAA, but the timing was pretty poor. Even McCormack admitted that.

"This is a bad time of year to be looking for a job. At the beginning of the season, maybe. But going into the last couple of months, it'll be a real long shot for Sean to find a place to play."

I've known Sean for several years. I've seen him play everything from rookie ball to AAA. But his fate underscored Casey's simple words even further.

"I'm still working."

Saturday night, August 28. Things are pretty festive in the London press box. Tomorrow is officially the final home game of the season, but the partying has started early. Rumors have been flying all season about the Tigers' demise, and there is an unspoken sense that tonight will be the swan song. There is sadness and joy. There is champagne to go with the hot dogs and fries. Keith, the official scorer, figures that tonight is his 199th game. Tomorrow, during the last of the season, he can end his career in round numbers.

PA announcers from the past five years are staging an impromptu reunion. The fans have a treat. Each of these guys takes an inning and reminisces about his favorite memories. During the seventh-inning stretch, the entire press box sings a rousing version of "Take Me Out to the Ballgame." The fans love it. For once, the stands are full. Over three thousand people are on hand to celebrate Fan Appreciation Night with all its giveaways. It is a happy time. At least it starts out that way.

The mood changes abruptly at the very end. Here's what causes the melodrama. The Canton Indians breezed into town on Thursday only to find that their rooms at the Sheraton have been given away. The Ladies PGA tour was in session, and apparently professional golf beats AA baseball in London. Finding someone else in your bed is no way to cap off an eight-and-a-half-hour bus trip. Since hotel space in London is at a premium, the Indians are shunted off to some undergraduate dormitory rooms at the University of Western Ontario. Hardly the Ritz.

On top of the accommodation blues, the Indians have lost three games in a row, two of them by one run. They are not happy campers. The game on Saturday is a strange, loosely played contest. In the second inning, London scores four runs against Canton in one of the sloppiest innings I've ever seen in pro ball. Indians left fielder Patrick Lennon moves in, then freezes in his tracks and watches a line drive sail over his head. The ball is retrieved by the center fielder, who apparently thinks the cutoff man is fifteen feet tall. Infield throws go sailing past the bases. Canton ends up with four errors. They aren't alone. Sloppiness is often contagious, and London kicks in with two errors of their own. After nine innings, the score is tied at five.

In the ninth, Canton reliever Calvin Jones mows the Tigers down. He looks overpowering. Arguably, he should. Jones has already pitched in The Show, baseball's affectionate shorthand for playing in the major leagues. Jones split last season between AAA and Seattle. He's twenty-nine years old and he's been around. These days, he's pitching for AA Canton, trying to put some decent numbers on the board and hoping for a September callup with the Indians. Coming into the game, he has a 5–3 record and a 3.14 ERA. Respectable. He's also got sixty-seven strikeouts in fifty-seven innings and twenty-two saves. More than respectable. Still, every bit counts. He wants to look good when decision time comes.

In the tenth, things start to unravel. Jones gets a strikeout, but then he gives up a walk to Shannon Penn. Not a good beginning. Penn steals second. Definitely not a good omen. Then Jones uncorks a wild pitch, and the winning run is standing on third. Probably unknown to Calvin Jones, Penn has just been named by *Baseball America* as the best base runner in the Eastern League. In any case, soon there are two out and a 3–2 count on London outfielder Dan Bautista. Bautista is a twenty-year-old kid who can fly. He already has twenty-seven stolen bases. The pitch comes in, and Bautista hits a slow grounder deep in the hole. The shortstop gets to it, but it's going to take a miracle to beat Bautista at first. Jones does not get a miracle from his shortstop. What he gets is a terrible throw that pulls the first baseman off the bag. Bautista slides head first and beats the throw. The runner scores from third, London wins, and both Jones and Canton lose. Bautista is credited with a hit. It's a marginal call, but arguably Bautista, who has just been named by the aforementioned *Baseball America* as the fastest runner in the Eastern League, is going to beat the throw anyway. The official scorer makes his judgment, the results are called into the wire services, and we're all getting ready to go. Hands are being shaken, notebooks packed away. Then all of a sudden word comes that a player is coming up to the press box to dispute a call.

It suddenly gets very quiet in the press box.

"Stick around," somebody says to me. "It'll give you something to write about."

They're right. What happens in the next two or three minutes is some of the rawest, most intense anger I've ever seen. It's born of frustration, a sense of helplessness, and the sense that a career, indeed a livelihood, may be on the line. Calvin Jones has come to register his dissent.

Jones isn't a small man. The press guide lists him at 6′3″ and 185 pounds. I'd add fifteen or twenty pounds to that estimate. He's far from the biggest guy on the team, but he's a damn sight bigger and stronger than anybody in the press box. He comes storming in, and his radar directs him right to Keith, the official scorer. Jones seems to be reeling in disbelief.

"You giving him a hit on *that*?" he fumes.

Keith says yes.

Jones can't believe his ears.

"That throw was way off. Didn't you see that?" he shouts. "How could that not be an error?"

Keith tells him that he thinks Bautista is going to beat it out, no matter how good the throw is.

"That's bullshit!" Jones screams. "I can't believe you're giving me an earned run for that shit!"

In truth, Jones's ERA has just gone from 3.14 to 3.20. It seems unlikely his future has been imperiled, but that's not how it feels at the moment.

Keith just sits there and keeps his cool. He's in survival mode. Deep in his brain is a circuit that says, "You stand up, you get killed." He remains seated, deceptively calm. Jones is becoming more frustrated. He keeps vacillating between shock and anger. He does some more screaming and a lot more cursing. Then *his* survival mode kicks in. A little voice says, "You stay here, you hurt somebody." So he leaves. On his way out, he kicks over the huge garbage can that contains three hours' worth of press box food. Half-eaten hot dogs, fries, onion rings, greasy wrappers, and Coke cartons go flying in every direction. It seems a small price to pay.

On the way out to the parking lot, broadcaster Doc Palmer points out that the official scorer gets paid $18 per game.

"That's why I'm not looking for work as an official scorer," he observes.

Mike Lumley is one of those rare guys in pro ball who's pitching for his own hometown.

"I grew up here. I played Little League ball in London. I played in this park when I was a kid," he tells me. "Now I'm pitching here professionally. Sure, it's a bit more pressure with all those people knowing you. But it feels good. This is my home."

Lumley has been quietly putting together a solid career in the Detroit organization since he signed back in 1988. In 1992 he had his best season and was named London's Pitcher of the Year. Lumley appeared in a career high fifty-five games and finished with an 8–3 record and a stellar 2.52 ERA. Opposing batters hit just .227 off him. Lumley followed his season at London with winter ball in Mexico, where he again posted impressive numbers, including the second best ERA in the league. While he was in Mexico, Detroit rewarded him with a promotion to AAA Toledo and a spot on their forty-man roster. Things could not have been going better. Then all of a sudden everything turned sour.

"This has been the worst season of my career," Mike Lumley tells me, shaking his head. "I've really struggled. It's been just . . . unimaginable. I suppose it's good for everything difficult to happen in one year. How can you go through a season like this and not get tougher? I feel like, based on mental toughness, I should already be in the big leagues."

Things started going wrong gradually.

"First, I didn't get a lot of pitching in spring training because something was wrong with my shoulder. We don't know what it is. I really haven't been checked out. It might be tendinitis. It comes and goes.

"Then I got to Toledo and that didn't work out either. They didn't know what to do with me up there. They just put me on the team because I had done well last year. The promotion was really a reward. But nobody there knew how to use me. I sat in the pen a lot waiting to pitch. I started a couple of games and pitched four in relief. I wasn't very effective. I can't blame them for that."

Then things became complicated. The Detroit Tigers were desperate for pitching at the start of the season. They went on a well-publicized hunt for castoffs, signing most of them to minor league contracts. That meant Toledo, which meant they needed space on the minor league roster. Maybe even the forty-man roster.

"I was the guy most likely to get cut. I knew that. It didn't surprise me so much," Lumley admits, although he regrets not having had a better chance to show his stuff in Toledo.

"They really put themselves in a spot by buying so many other pitchers to help them in the big leagues. They had to make sure, if they're going to buy these people, that their money doesn't go to waste. They had Toledo stocked with insurance policies. I wasn't one of them."

But Lumley's return to AA London was clouded by an even more troubling event.

In a well-publicized episode, Mike Lumley hit Boo Moore, a member of the New Britain Red Sox, in the head. The incident seems to have created more problems for Lumley than it did for Moore, the man he hit.

"It's not just because I hit somebody," Lumley explains. "I hit eighteen batters in Lakeland one year and it never affected me. If I'm pitching inside, it's no big deal. My attitude has always been, I hit somebody, I hit somebody. But this time it was different. I felt like I had no control over my pitches. The first pitch, I came up and in. It was pretty close, and I hadn't even been trying to come inside. Then I tried to pitch away just to be safe, and I ended up hitting him. I'm trying to hit the outside corner, and I hit him in the head.

"It's one thing to say, I was pitching inside or trying to brush back a hitter. You miss by a couple of inches, or the guy dives into the pitch and you hit him. You say, it's his fault, or I missed by a couple of inches. That's part of the game.

Mike Lumley.

It's not that big a deal. But I don't want to hit someone in the head. I'm not saying I've never hit somebody intentionally, because I have. But I've never aimed for anybody's head. I would never do that.

"After that it became a thing. I started thinking about it. Something triggered inside me that I couldn't control my arm whatsoever. It felt like I was shooting for one spot, and my arm was shooting for another, like it had its own mind.

"The next time I was pitching back home, against Harrisburg. The batter was Mike Hardge. I started thinking, uh oh, here comes another right-handed hitter. I tried to aim one across the middle of the plate and I ended up throwing it right above his head, all the way to the backstop. I didn't get through that inning too well. I was struggling, walking people.

"The next time I was pitching against Harrisburg, and Hardge came up again. I started feeling it even stronger, and I threw it over his head again. I was struggling just to get through the inning. All I wanted to throw was my slider. I figured even if it was headed inside, it would break back over the plate and not hit somebody. I was throwing probably 98 percent sliders just to keep from hitting anybody again. I couldn't use my other pitches. I'd get a couple of strikes that way, but I ended up walking too many guys."

I ask Mike what kind of reaction he got from his manager or pitching coach.

"I don't think they really understood what was happening. They just kept pitching me. They figured, even if it's in my head, it'll probably stop as quickly as it started. That's how they approached it at first. Just a 'Don't worry about it' attitude rather than 'Let's address the problem and find out what's going on.' It seemed like a bit of a brush-off.

"I remember that night against Harrisburg. After I was done, I went into the clubhouse and I was just sitting there thinking, What am I doing? What am I thinking? What's wrong with me? My manager came in to see how I was doing. He wanted to know what was going through my mind. I think it was after that he realized what was happening."

Finally London did something about it.

"They put me on the DL for ten or eleven days. All they had me doing was throwing in the bullpen. There were times I was struggling even there to throw a strike. It seemed like I was aiming the ball even when there was nobody in the batter's box. It took a while for me to get past that. For a while we put some tires up for me to throw through. I don't care if I hit tires. You're not going to hurt a tire.

"Then when I got to throwing strikes again, my manager stepped in and let me pitch against him. He's a rightie. So I threw to him and it started coming around a bit. They changed my mechanics and it helped. My confidence started coming back. Then they took me off the DL and I pitched again. I faced a couple of lefties first and that made a difference. I was able to find my strike zone. Then I could go on. Then a rightie came up and I did OK.

"Then I went through a really good streak. I had a start against Reading and I only gave up two hits. That was important to me. Reading really helped because they have a lot of left-handed batters."

So is it over?

"Not completely," Mike concedes. "It comes back. It's like it's still up there, a voice in the corner of my head saying, 'Here comes a right-handed batter.' And I'm saying, 'So what.' It's distant, but it's still there. I have to concentrate more when a rightie comes up. I wrote stuff on the brim of my hat. Stuff about my mechanics, and little sayings like 'Even keel' and 'Me and Catcher.' That meant, there's just me and the catcher, no one else. Forget the batter. It's getting easier to brush away the little voice when I hear it."

I mention to Mike that baseball does not have a great track record for being sensitive to psychological problems.

"That's really incredible," he replies. "Everybody tells you this game is at least 75 to 80 percent mental. They all accept that. But if you run into any kind of mental problems, they just want to dismiss it. They don't know what to do with you. I think there should be more counselors, more sports psychologists available. I know there's a few guys who have used them. But they're really exceptions."

Mike and I discuss some of the well-publicized examples we know about. Guys like second baseman Steve Sax, who ran into problems throwing to first. Or Mackey Sasser, the catcher who could barely throw the ball back to the pitcher but could nail base runners at second on a dime. We talk about John Smoltz, who publicly credited a psychologist for contributing to his success pitching for Atlanta. And I think of Joe Cowley, whose career ended, even after throwing a no-hitter, when home plate became a totally elusive target to him.

Mike sums up his feelings simply.

"I believe major league teams should acknowledge these kinds of problems more. After my experience, I think a person who can help in these situations is just as important to have as a trainer. I could have used somebody to talk to, even a hypnotist, to help get my confidence back. My manager and pitching coach did everything they could for me, but they're not trained to deal with those things. The best thing they did really was to put me on the DL."

Why was that so important?

"Just to keep me off the field. So I didn't have to worry about whether I was going to have to come in and pitch. It took the pressure off so I could go off on the sidelines and deal with the problem."

I ask Mike if this year has done any permanent damage to his record.

"It's amazing that after all of this I still don't have a terrible ERA. It's a lot higher than my career level, but compared to the rest of the staff, it's not that bad. When things were at their worst, my ERA got up as high as 8.00 or 9.00. When I went on the DL, it was at 6.66. Talk about omens! Someone who believes in devil worship would have loved that! Since I'm off the DL, I've been able to drop about two more points off my ERA. It's at 4.57 now. Through all of this, my opponents' batting average has stayed low. It's .211, which is the lowest on the team. In fact, it's even lower than I had last year, which was my best season."

Lumley's record is not going to get any better. When I talked to him, he hadn't pitched in over two weeks. He will finish the season on the DL, with an undiagnosed soreness in his shoulder.

"I really wish they'd be a little more aggressive about diagnosing this shoulder thing. If I'm going to need surgery, I want to have it now. I want lots of time to recover and get ready so I can be 100 percent for next season. I want to remove all the question marks. I can't understand why they haven't gone ahead and done something. They don't need to fly me down to the States." Lumley points over the left field fence. "I could walk over to the hospital from here. I'm a Canadian citizen. My medical care is free. I want to get something done about this soon. It's very frustrating.

"I think I've had a pretty decent career in the Tigers organization. But the message they keep giving me is that I have to be more consistent. I'm not even sure what that means at this point. I may not have the best ERA in our organization, but it's pretty close."

Lumley is right. Prior to this season, he has accumulated six pitching lines. His ERAs in five of them have been 2.91, 2.69, 2.38, 2.84, and 2.52. It's hard to imagine a more consistent record.

The next season is Lumley's sixth. He becomes a free agent. He would like to stay with the organization that drafted him back in 1988. But this is baseball and anything can happen. After this season, nothing would surprise Mike Lumley.

P.S. I wondered about Boo Moore, the player Lumley had hit.

"He's OK. I talked to him afterward, and he was all right. He's been doing fine since."

"So he knew you weren't trying to hit him?" I checked.

"Absolutely. Hardge is OK also. Even though I didn't hit him, I talked to him a couple of times. He knew about what I was going through. It had got around that I was having some problems with control. It was no big deal."

On September 2, 1993, it became official. After five years of operation, the London Tigers closed up shop. The franchise was sold to a group of investors who moved the team to Trenton, New Jersey.

There was sadness and frustration among the team's supporters, who were no longer numerous enough to make the franchise economically viable. Whose fault was it? The fans, for not turning out? Or management, for their failure to market the product effectively? Like a group of naughty kids caught by their teacher, the fingers pointed in all directions. Most fans I talked to blamed management.

"Those guys are idiots. Why didn't they give away half-price tickets on slow nights? Or even half-price hot dogs? Or free coffee on those cold nights? Just some kind of gesture! There was never any of that."

Management, in turn, blamed the parent organization. General manager Bob Gilson told the London *Free Press*, "If you don't put a good product on the field, you don't get a lot of fans. You don't have to be a Rhodes scholar to know what kind of minor league system the Detroit Tigers have."

36 *London, Ontario*

Shortly before the team's departure, broadcaster Doc Palmer interviewed Gilson on his pregame show. Putting the question as directly as possible, he asked Gilson, "After five years as general manager of the London Tigers, surely you've learned something from the experience. Is there anything you'd do differently now?"

Completing his rendition of "It Ain't Me, Babe," Gilson replied, "No. Not a thing."

Hamilton, Ontario

"Twenty-four bucks for a case of beer! How does anybody afford to drink up here?"
—Ron Blazier, Batavia pitcher

Even by the humble standards of the New York–Penn League, Bernie Arbour Stadium in Hamilton is a pretty marginal place to see a ball game. You'd think the Hamilton area, drawing on a population base of nearly a million people, could do better than this.

Hamilton seems like it should be a baseball town: a sprawling, working-class city with enough factories and steel mills to pollute the sky for miles around. Surely these folks could rally support for a decent facility and a team in the high minors. Instead what you get is a short-season A-league team and a rinky-dink park located out in the middle of nowhere. Actually, it's "up on the mountain," as they say in Hamilton. Which means that downtown residents will have to make a trip to the suburbs. It also means that the folks who live around Bernie Arbour Stadium who didn't mind when high school kids played there aren't thrilled about a pro team taking it over and drawing traffic and noise to their tidy little neighborhood. Stories about pending legal action against the team are as plentiful as box scores in the morning paper.

Having a team in the New York–Penn League is nothing to be ashamed of. The league has been around since 1939, which makes it the oldest continuously operating A league in professional baseball. When things were just getting started in 1938, you could have bought a franchise for the princely sum of $630. Along with teams in Batavia, New York, and Bradford, Pennsylvania, Hamilton was one of the original franchises. In fact, the earlier name "PONY League" was a lot more apt than its present title. PONY wasn't meant to suggest anything diminutive, as in tiny horse or *minor* league; it was an acronym for Pennsylvania, Ontario, and New York.

There have been a lot of changes and city shuffles in the fifty-odd years of the league's existence. Even London, Ontario, Hamilton's upscale neighbor to the west, had a team as early as 1940. Hamilton rejoined the New York–Penn League back in 1988 when it became one of eight St. Louis Cardinals minor league affiliates. Like all its competitors, the Cardinals' farm system is bottom heavy: six of eight teams are below the AA level.

Hamilton's park may be substandard, but I never saw a bad ballgame there. My very first visit was in August 1989, early in my minor league journey. I was so enthusiastic, I would have sat in a cornfield during a summer storm. Actually, I came close. The vegetation was missing, but the weather was about right. I dragged a friend with me through some of the grayest skies either of us had ever seen. I kept assuring him the storm clouds would blow over. He didn't believe me for a second, but he enjoyed my enthusiasm. Two outs into the top of the first inning, the sky opened up. There is hardly any cover to run for at Bernie Arbour Stadium.

Most of the two hundred stalwart souls were into their cars and gone within five minutes. It was that kind of rain. Several of us hung around a bit longer. I noticed a guy in his forties who looked as disappointed as I did. Standing off to the side, looking as patient as my friend, were his wife and daughter. When we left, I noticed the family was still there.

The next night was relatively pleasant. The skies had cleared by midday and there was no threat of rain. My friend had headed home shaking his head when I told him I was prepared to make a second try for it. He left me his rain check in case I saw an eager-looking kid. I was off for the second time in two days, this time to see a doubleheader.

Doubleheaders in Hamilton start at six P.M. and go seven innings. I got there early and had the park nearly to myself, except for three familiar-looking faces behind home plate. I sat down next to the family and introduced myself. Hadn't they been at the park last night? I asked.

"Oh yeah, we were here. We've been traveling all over watching our son play," the father told me.

"Your son plays for Hamilton?"

"No, Batavia," he explained. "He's on the Clippers."

"So you travel around following the team?" I asked.

This time the wife and daughter replied, nearly in unison. "Yeah. We have their schedule. We've been to Batavia, their home park, then Auburn, Elmira, Geneva . . ."

The father was not much of a conversationalist, but over the course of the evening, I learned that he had two weeks' vacation from his job in Missouri.

The family had decided to spend the time traveling together watching their son play ball. They were staying in motels along the journey, and they were in the stands every night.

"Last night wasn't the first time we got rained out," the mother told me. "But we're there whenever we can. We're probably seeing more of him now than when he lived at home."

The target of all this attention was a utility player on the Batavia Clippers named Steve Bieser. Bieser was having a solid if undistinguished season. He made himself useful, perhaps even indispensable, by playing quite a few positions as well as switch hitting. Guys who can play anywhere in the infield and outfield, and even catch a bit, are bound to stick around the organization a bit longer than most. Two years later, during his 1991 season, Bieser redefined the term "useful" by playing all nine positions for Spartanburg.

In 1993, Steve Bieser was still playing pro ball. He started the season at AA Reading. As usual, he was filling in wherever they needed him most. During the spring, there was even a call up to Scranton (AAA). It was just a cup of coffee, and Bieser was back down in AA by the time I saw him in late July. He was catching for Reading that afternoon. His average was around .270 and, although he doesn't *look* like a catcher, he seemed comfortable behind the plate. One guy tried to steal on him early in the game and was thrown out neatly. That was the last time anyone tried to run on his arm. I didn't see Bieser's family in the stands that day, although he told me they do come to see him when Reading plays in Canton, Ohio.

"That's as close as this league gets to my home," he told me. "And it's still not that close. But they come."

I remember the evening in Hamilton vividly, even though it took place over seven years ago. Images of a dad going to see his son play are sweet enough. Add a mom to the picture, and it's even closer to Norman Rockwell. What really got me, though, was the sister. She was a healthy teenager who no doubt had other pursuits she might have been following back home in Missouri. Instead she seemed content traveling with mom and dad watching her big brother play ball. It was a small moment, but it still gives me goosebumps.

Two seasons after that first rainout, Hamilton's stadium looks about the same. There have been no visible renovations. My friend is finishing a sandwich as we walk in, and the gatekeeper asks him to eat it outside. League rules prohibit bringing food into the park, and this guy is a bit zealous about enforcing them.

I go off to the bullpen to talk to some of this year's crop of draft picks. The Phillies split choices from the June draft between Batavia and Martinsville.

The older, more polished players typically end up here. I meet a couple of pitchers named Ronnie Allen and Ron Blazier. Allen is starting his second pro game tonight. After working out a bit, these guys change into their playing uniforms standing out in right field in the open-air bullpen. There's nobody around, and it hardly seems worth the trek back into the clubhouse. It seems completely natural at the time. Looking back, I try to imagine talking to Steve Carlton in the bullpen, before a start, while he changes into his game duds. For a few moments the place looks like a game of "shirts vs. skins."

Blazier has an uncle in Toronto, and he's heard tales about the cost of living. Some of the guys wander over and are amazed to hear how high prices are in Canada. I look for some purchases we have in common in order to convince them how bad things really are. It becomes obvious that the international standard is a case of beer. When I tell them the Ontario price, around $24 at the time, they nearly fall off their chairs.

"Twenty-four bucks for a case of beer! How does anybody afford to drink up here?" Blazier asks me.

"They find a way," I assure him.

I try to explain the currency differential, but international finance does not go down too well in the Batavia bullpen. All they know is that if you're using things that look like dollars, you should not have to trade twenty-four of them for a case of beer. *Even* if it's better beer than they can buy around Buffalo, and *even* if those dollar bill–looking things are only worth about seventy-five cents in "real money."

If Blazier doesn't have a future in high finance, he also nearly missed the boat with professional baseball. When area scouts first saw him pitch in high school in 1989, they were impressed with his potential but considered him so raw they didn't even send him to the lowest Rookie League team in the organization. He was given the princely sum of $500 as a signing bonus and told to go home and work on his skills. Blazier was given a list of twenty things he needed to practice.

The $500 was his to keep, whether or not he managed to impress the Phillies in spring training the following year. It turns out he did, and, after a season in Princeton (a co-op team in the Appalachian League), Blazier was starting his second year with the Phillies when I met him. In professional baseball, not many kids are given a list of mechanical shortcomings and a year to work them out in the privacy of their own backyards. But Blazier was and did. In 1996, Ron Blazier started the season in AAA and quickly asserted himself as his team's closer. By the end of May, he was pitching for the Phillies in the major leagues.

Of course, I didn't know any of this when I asked Blazier and Ronnie Allen where they were staying that night. I'm ready to offer a free night at my place and a chance to sample some of that Canadian beer after the game. I can have them back to the park in plenty of time for tomorrow night's game.

"We're not staying anywhere tonight," Allen informs me. "We're going back to Batavia."

I can hardly believe it. These guys are going to get on the bus after the game and drive back across the border to Batavia, New York. They're going to go through U.S. Customs hassles, then the bus will drop these dead-tired guys off at the park, where they will make their separate ways to wherever it is they stay in Batavia. And tomorrow morning, they will again assemble at the park, board the bus, and drive back across the border, enduring Canadian Customs this time, and make their way back to Hamilton, Ontario, arriving in time for batting practice. And why go through all this? The answer is simply to avoid having to pay for one night's lodging in Hamilton. What, then, is the point of having two consecutive away games in the same town? Absolutely none. I think about this any time someone talks about the glamour of life in professional baseball.

Ronnie Allen pitches a hell of a game that night, winning his second consecutive start. He has a no-hitter going for the first five innings. Part of the reason Allen wins the game (final score 10–3) is an offensive show by Patrick Cheek, the Clippers' second baseman. Cheek is a tall, skinny kid playing his second year for Batavia. He has not been leaving a trail of numbers behind to impress anybody. In fact, coming into tonight's game he's hitting .087.

His first couple of at bats aren't memorable. The Clippers are being shut out 3–0 when they suddenly come to life in the top of the seventh. Suddenly, they have the bases loaded and up comes Cheek, his average now sitting at .068. The pitcher glances at Cheek's stats on the scoreboard and breathes a sigh of relief. But, like most deities, the gods of baseball have a sense of humor. In comes a fastball, around goes the bat, and wham! out it goes into the Ontario night. Cheek is grinning from ear to ear as he rounds the bases. His teammates are waiting for him when he gets near the dugout. There are high fives all over the place. The local fans are booing and looking away.

Cheek comes up again one more time. This time there are two guys on. I start to yell, "Come on, Pat. Hit another one out . . ." But I never get that far. He cuts me off midsentence with a sweet swing that sends another projectile into the Hamilton skyline.

The line on Patrick Cheek is pretty simple: two swings, two home runs, seven RBIs. After the game, I take a ball I caught during BP and ask Cheek to sign it. I don't want anybody else's signature on it, including first round draft pick Tyler Green, who is on the same team. The night belongs to Cheek. He looks about sixteen years old and he's still smiling. I tell him, you keep hitting like this, this ball is going to be worth a million bucks. We both laugh.

My last view of Cheek, and all his teammates, is seeing them lined up, still in uniform, to buy some postgame hot dogs and Cokes. No fancy buffet in an air-conditioned clubhouse away from the clamoring fans. No sir. Stand in line *in your spikes* and wait your turn with the paying customers.

After the season, I review the final minor league stats to see how all these guys have done. There at the bottom of the organizational report is a brief paragraph saying "The following players have been released." The list is alphabetical, so I don't have far to read. Patrick Cheek. I'm ready to shout "No way!" until I look at Cheek's final stats for the season. Batting average around .170. Home run total: 2. RBIs for the season: 11. The man had virtually his entire offensive season in one night in Hamilton.

At the end of the 1992 season, after a five-year association with the Cardinals, the Hamilton Redbirds ceased to be. The team packed up and moved to Glens Falls, New York. A year later, they relocated to New Jersey. You want Cardinals baseball in the New York–Penn League, you go see the New Jersey Cardinals play in lovely Skylands Park in Augusta, New Jersey.

The story of how Hamilton lost its franchise is a political saga worth a chapter on its own. The simplified version runs like this: although the attendance was OK, the stadium needed upgrading to meet league standards. The city was not willing to pay for it. Neither were the team owners. They were already paying out enough in legal fees to counteract neighborhood opposition to Bernie Arbour Stadium.

What Hamilton *really* wanted was a AA franchise. They were in contention for one of the '94 expansion teams in the Eastern League. That might have worked. There was a decent chance a AA-quality stadium could have been built in time for the '94 season. Lord knows, a million people can support a AA team. But they never got the chance. Hamilton was not selected for Eastern League expansion, and when the dream of a AA team died, support for their A team dried up as well. Professional baseball in Hamilton, Ontario, is now a memory.

Welland, Ontario

"They'll never know what it took for that guy to hit 1.000."
—Jeff Banister, Welland manager

Welland is not a baseball town. Forty-five thousand people live here, most of whom could not tell an RBI from an Arby's. They care about other things like soccer and curling. The ones who do care about baseball would probably be more attentive if the Welland Pirates, a team in the New York–Penn League, were an affiliate of the Toronto Blue Jays. I mean, who the hell are the Pittsburgh Pirates? They're not even in the American League.

Brian Sloan, in his first year as the Pirates' general manager, shakes his head in frustration.

"It got so bad at one point that we called individuals randomly from the phone book. We were giving away tickets. Whoever we got on the line, if they wanted a ticket, they had it. 70 percent of the people we spoke to either didn't even know what we were talking about or weren't interested. There's a limit to what you can do in a market like that."

Still, things could be worse. The Pirates are averaging about a thousand people a game.

"That's just about even with St. Catharines," Sloan points out proudly. "St. Catharines has three times our population and is affiliated with the Blue Jays."

The bottom line is that neither Welland nor St. Catharines is thriving. End-of-franchise rumors are swirling in both cities.

Despite its present-day doldrums, baseball is no stranger to Welland. The Pirates franchise, which arrived in 1989, is the city's first pro team, although organized baseball began in Welland about a hundred years ago. There are records from

1896 detailing a Welland team's journey via horse and buggy to neighboring cities like St. Catharines. Semipro ball came just after the turn of the century, followed by an era of industrial baseball.

Semipro games in the 1940s were played in a place called Burgar Park. Crowds of three thousand were not uncommon. Welland's best pitcher at the time was a guy called Sal Maglie. He went straight from Welland to pitch for the New York Giants. Maglie's legacy in the Niagara peninsula is strong. Until 1993, the Niagara Falls Rapids of the New York–Penn League played their games in Sal Maglie Stadium.

The Pirates play their games in Welland Sports Complex. It is a typical aluminum "instant stadium," pleasant and devoid of character. In January 1989 it was a snow-covered hole in the ground. By mid-June it was a new ballpark, welcoming locals to the delights of A-level baseball. Older fans could see the improvement immediately. They may have remembered Ellis Morningstar, an outfielder with the 1922 Welland team who fell into a four-foot ditch and broke his leg while chasing a fly ball in right field. In contrast, the present facilities are a dream come true. On the other hand, if you sit in the Welland dugout, you can hear the players grousing about the facility. They'll tell you how rough the infield is, or how difficult it is for a left-handed batter to pick up the pitch against the fancy new scoreboard. You can't please everyone.

It's Thursday night and Batavia is in town. The crowd is pretty thin. Six hundred and eighty-eight are announced, and that includes about 150 season ticket holders. What the crowd lacks in number, it makes up in enthusiasm. There are several families dressed in Pirate outfits. Even the babies are wearing team caps. The Welland food vendor wears a colorful court jester suit. He's a cute kid, but he looks a little embarrassed by the costume.

"I don't have an official name," fifteen-year-old Scott MacLeod tells me. "Some people call me Bucko the Clown."

When he isn't selling Cracker Jacks aisle to aisle, Bucko can be found hanging out with the Pirates' mascot. This mascot stands out in a couple of ways. He sports the most cumbersome name in minor league baseball. "Pierre Le Claire, the Pirate Extraordinaire" is a hell of a moniker to hang on anyone.

"Can you believe we had a contest to select that name?" Sloan tells me. "You wouldn't believe some of the losing entries!"

On the other hand, this giant toy Pirate is the only mascot I have seen who patrols his stadium on roller blades. Sometime around the fifth inning, the PA system plays Billy Swan's record "I Can Help." As soon as he hears the eight-bar intro to Swan's record, which features skating rink organ music, Pierre Le Claire takes off on his roller blades. It is an odd moment, to say the least.

I've been around dozens of batting cages, but I've never seen or heard anything like the ruckus that's going on here. The Pirates squad has split into two teams, and they're taking turns batting, keeping track of how many hits they get. There's all kinds of good-natured arguing over whether somebody's fly ball or grounder would have gotten through.

My first thought is, Wait until the manager sees this! He'll put an end to this foolishness. But Jeff Banister, the Pirates skipper, is right in the center of the action. He's contributing as much laughter and good-natured razzing as anyone. This team is loose!

"Yeah, I try to keep things pretty easy-going around here," he tells me in the dugout as swarms of mosquitoes gnaw on us. We're having a postgame chat. The Pirates have just come from behind for a 2–1 win, and Banister is feeling pretty good.

"This is a good bunch of guys. We're not winning as much as we did early in the season, but they've promoted most of my best players. I guess that means I'm doing my job. You work with what they give you and do your best with it."

Banister is anyone's definition of a company man. "I've been with the Pirates all my professional life. They drafted me out of college, I spent seven years in their minor league system, and I got to play with them in The Show. Now I'm managing here for them. I guess you could say my blood flows Pirates black and gold."

Banister has been rewarded for his loyalty. His is one of those rare cases where longevity paid off, an antidote for the thousands who'll tell you baseball is an unfair business. In his sixth minor league season, Banister was toiling away for the Buffalo Bisons, Pittsburgh's AAA affiliate.

"On the night of July 22, 1991, I got a phone call from Terry Collins. He starts out by asking me, 'How long have you waited for this call?' I said, 'I don't know. Who is this?' He says, 'This is Terry Collins. You're going to the big leagues.' I said, 'Yeah, sure. Who is this?' We went back and forth like that for quite a while until he convinced me.

"I went up and the next day, July 23, 1991, Jim Leyland gave me an opportunity to pinch-hit. I batted for Doug Drabek against the Atlanta Braves. Dan Petrie was pitching. I hit a single to left field."

It turns out that was Banister's only hit in the majors. But since it was also his only at bat, he retired with a 1.000 batting average. To this day, that brings him some notoriety and quite a bit of good-natured heckling.

"Yeah, I'm in the record books," Banister tells me with both laughter and pride. "I'm right there between Sal Bando and Ernie Banks. Both those guys have pages of stats. I have one line. One at bat, one hit. It may not be much,

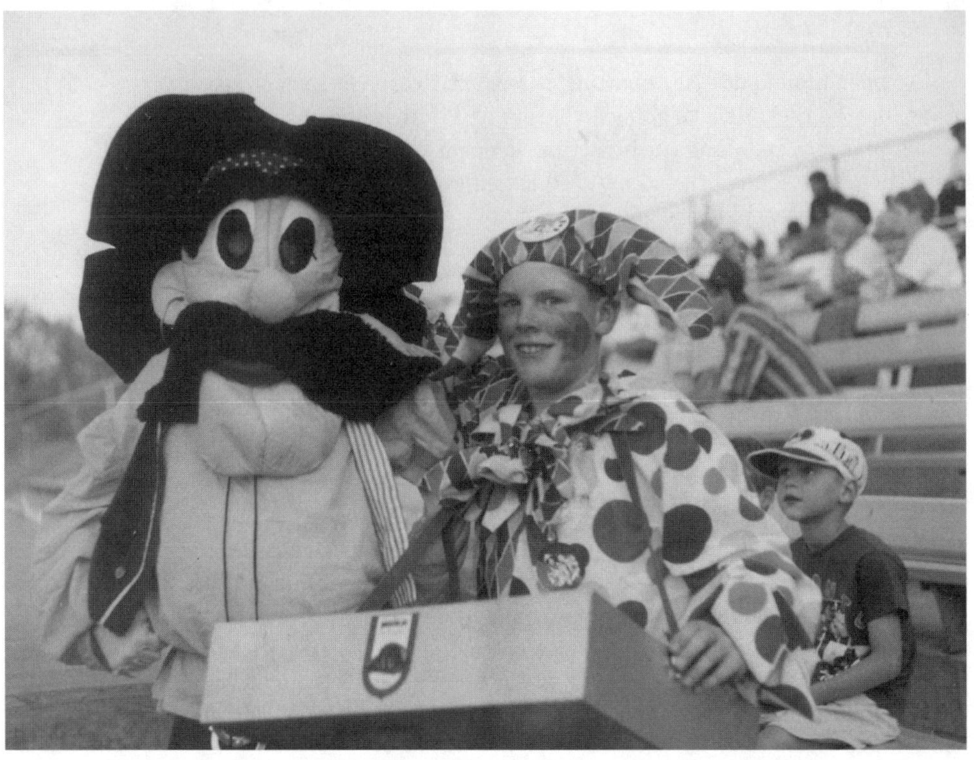

Pierre Le Claire, the Pirate Extraordinaire, meets Bucko the Clown.

---

but it's mine. And no one can take it away. Whenever I'm in a bookstore, I check out *The Baseball Encyclopedia*, just to see it. Just to make sure they haven't erased it."

Banister's pride goes beyond his career average. "It wasn't just playing in the big leagues and getting a hit. It was survival. Just having the opportunity to walk from the dugout to the plate."

Banister is being literal when he talks about survival. Just being alive and healthy were major accomplishments.

"I've been through quite a bit," he acknowledges. "It started when I was a sophomore in high school. I grew up in LaMarque, Texas. I got hurt playing football and had to have knee surgery. That was just the beginning. The next year I found out I had bone cancer. I spent my seventeenth birthday in a hospital getting that news. I stayed there for the next four and a half months having a whole bunch of surgeries. At one point they were talking about amputating my left leg just to save my life. But they were able to cure me with surgery and medication, and they finally released me.

Jeff Banister, happy to be alive.

"I thought it was over, but late that summer I got ill again. I had to go back into the hospital for about three more weeks and some more operations. I had seven in all. The doctors told me to forget about playing football. They said I probably wouldn't be able to run. But I came back and played baseball during my senior year in high school. I don't think I was very good, but I was able to trick some people into giving me a scholarship to the University of Houston.

"Then it started again. In my freshman year in college I was in an accident. On October 23, I was involved in a collision at home plate. I was catching and the batter hit a fly ball to right field. The guy on third tagged up and tried to score. The throw was a little offline, and I went to my knees to block the ball. Just as I did that, the runner hit me. I had my head down and the collision broke my neck.

"The impact crushed three vertebrae in my neck. I had to have two more surgeries just to save my life. I was paralyzed from the neck down for about ten days. My left leg was partially paralyzed for about six weeks just from the trauma to the spinal cord.

"But the doctors put me back together again, and I went on and played two years of college baseball. Then I tricked the scouts again and got drafted by the Pirate organization. From there, I spent six years in the minors, then I got the callup in 1991. I can tell you that my whole life flashed before my eyes in the time it took me to walk to the plate for my one at bat. Every step I took on the way to first base, I was reliving everything that led to my being there. I sometimes think, Those people who study baseball records and know all the stats, they'll see that one line in *The Baseball Encyclopedia*. But they'll never know what it took for that guy to hit 1.000.

"The next year I needed arm surgery. That effectively ended my career as a player. At least as a major league player. The Pirates asked me what I wanted to do, and I told them I wanted to manage. They gave me a job as a player-coach for the Carolina Mudcats, their AA team. So I went back to the minors. My very first at bat as a pinch hitter, I got a single. That meant there was one point for about three days where I was sitting on another 1.000 average. I thought about retiring just so I could be the only person in history to have a career batting average of 1.000 in two different leagues! It would have been a great trivia question. But I couldn't do it. We had some individuals who were hurt, and they needed for me to play, so I went on and finished the season."

His first season of minor league managing nearly behind him, Jeff Banister seems a happy man.

"I'm a baseball person. I don't know what else I'd do with my life. During the winter nights when there are no games, I start getting the itch at about seven o'clock. I feel like I need to be out underneath the lights. This is what I love to do. I can't imagine that anyone has loved the game more than I do. It's brought me back from some pretty bad places. Every time someone told me I'd never walk again or run again, I pictured myself playing baseball. It literally brought me back to life more than once."

I tell Jeff that it's difficult for me to reconcile all of this with the healthy-looking guy I had seen in the batting cage. I wonder if the guys who are playing for him know about his history.

"I don't know," he says simply. "I'd like to think I'm a lot more modest than to expect them to know about my troubles."

But then he adds, "That locker room is a pretty small place. I use it just like everybody else on the team. I change in there. I work out in there. I shower in there. When I get undressed I've got a scar across here, another one here, another one over here that goes all the way to here. And these aren't small scars. They're pretty hard to miss. These guys have to know something happened to me. And some of them may have seen the story about me when it appeared in the news. Some of them know.

"But the way I figure it, everybody has had their own adversity in life. To them, it probably feels as great as my adversity does to me. If hearing about my stuff helps somebody out, then I'm happy to share it. If not, we don't need to talk about it."

After a moment, Jeff says, "Sometimes I think about this and it seems a lifetime ago. Almost like it happened to somebody else. But I can still see all the scars, literally. And every morning when I wake up, my knees feel like they're going to explode. So does my ankle. I've got a crick in my neck from all the surgeries. It doesn't take long to realize that I went through it all.

"I feel like I owe it to myself to make the most of my life and do whatever I can with it. I've been given these second chances that other people have been denied. I've got to make the most of them."

While we're sitting in the dugout talking, a fan approaches tentatively. He's driven up to see the game from Wheeling, West Virginia. Would it be OK if he introduces his four-year-old son to Jeff and takes a picture of them together in the dugout?

"Sure," says Jeff, never revealing the fact that he's just finished reliving some incredibly painful memories. A little blond kid who looks closer to three years old walks shyly up to Jeff and sits beside him. While dad's Camcorder grinds away, Jeff carries on exactly the conversation this dad wants to hear.

"Hey, big guy! You play baseball yet? What you gonna be, a pitcher or a hitter? I bet you're gonna hit about forty home runs a year and bat .300. I hope you play for me!"

Dad thanks Jeff profusely and leads junior off to the van. Within hours, they'll be across the border heading back home. The kid will be fast asleep, and dad will be reliving the dugout moments as he drives south with a story to tell anyone who'll listen.

Among the more enthusiastic fans in the crowd is a family sitting down by the Batavia dugout. They turn out to be the parents and brother and sister of Clippers outfielder Brent Bell. Bell is a twenty-year-old kid from Downey, California, who was selected in the June 1991 draft. He's hitting .246 right now, but it's been a struggle. This is his third year in the organization and the first time he's hit over .200. Although you'd never tell it from watching him play or listening to his family, this is probably a do-or-die year for Bell. If young Brent washes out, his family isn't out of options. There is a younger brother named Chad who already has scouts dogging his every move. Chad is barely sixteen, but he's already a strapping 6′4″.

Steve Bell, who looks like he has a couple of innings of hardball left in him as well, is proud of both his sons. "Chad could probably make it as anything he wants, but I told him to try pitching. That's where the money is. He's looking real good so far."

If everything goes according to plan, Brent Bell will be chasing fly balls in the Clearwater sun, while his kid brother Chad works on his curveball in Martinsville. That's a lot to hope for, but it's not out of the question.

There's another bonus baby walking around in the Welland sunshine. Wayne Gomes was the Phillies' number one pick in the June 1993 amateur draft, and he has joined the Batavia Clippers. Gomes is a twenty year old from Hampton, Virginia, and he has just finished his third year at Old Dominion University.

Gomes is a relatively late arrival to Batavia. There is usually a gap between the drafting and signing of high round picks, during which a period of financial haggling takes place. Everyone breathes a sigh of relief when the ordeal is over. In Gomes's case, it went relatively quickly. The dance only took seven weeks.

There is no doubt about how Wayne Gomes fits into the Phillies' plans. He is a closer. He throws hard and strikes out a lot of guys. In three years of college ball, Gomes has pitched 100 innings and struck out 156 batters. *Baseball America* described him as one of the best amateur pitchers in the country and ranked him in the top three in velocity. Comparisons to Lee Smith are being made, and appellations like "intimidating presence" are already being applied.

"How you handling all of this? Is it driving you crazy?" Gomes and I are talking in center field while he and his teammates shag flies.

"You get used to it," he says. "Everyone told me to expect it. As long as they let me pitch I can deal with it."

While we talk, Gomes makes a couple of catches. He then *rolls* the ball to one of his teammates, who throws it in. Having just spent in the neighborhood of three-quarters of a million on a signing bonus, the Phillies are not about to see their investment evaporate on an ill-advised throw from the outfield. Gomes is getting special treatment. His teammates know it. They may not love it, but they understand that it's part of the system.

I snap a few pictures while we talk.

"Am I going to be in your book?" Gomes asks me. It strikes me as an odd concern for a guy who is being lionized by the press.

"If you don't mind talking a bit."

"Go ahead," he invites me.

"You're looking very serious in these pictures. Can you think of something to make you smile?" I ask.

A grin slips across his face.

"What are you thinking about?" I inquire.

"My family is coming up to see me soon, and my girl is going to be here too." Talk of his girl leads to a chat about musical taste. There isn't much common ground between us. We don't do much better on drinking preferences.

"When my girl and I get together, we're going to drink some Courvoisier, Coke, and Spumante."

"You may not live to pitch your next game," I suggest.

"No, no," he explains. "I won't mix them all together. I do the Courvoisier and Coke. She drinks the Spumante."

Getting back to baseball, I mention the obvious — that being a number one draft pick means that just about every pitch he throws is going to be under the microscope.

"It's not just what I do now," he explains. "Everything I've done for the last two or three years has been under a microscope. It was even worse before I signed."

"You seem surprised by that," I say.

He looks at me for a moment and concedes that he is. "I mean, I knew they'd have a good look. It's an important decision. But . . ." Gomes shrugs in a way to suggest that this level of scrutiny was more than he had bargained for.

"The Phillies don't have a great success record with their first round draft picks," I point out. "Their scouts have been criticized for not doing enough homework."

Gomes looks absolutely blank. Signing with a team isn't like applying for citizenship. You want to become a U.S. citizen, you have to learn about U.S. history. Gomes doesn't seem to know a whole lot about the history of the team he's just signed with. Obviously, it wasn't a priority either for him or the Phillies front office.

Wayne Gomes.

I mention the fact that the last three collegiate pitchers who were the Phillies' number one draft picks all came up with arm problems. First there was Brad Brink out of USC in 1986. Then Pat Combs out of Baylor in 1988, followed by Tyler Green out of Wichita State in 1991. The careers of all these guys have been derailed by side trips to the DL (disabled list) and various surgeons. Arguably, all three pitchers were damaged goods, accidents waiting to happen, when they signed.

"Obviously, they didn't want you to become one more bad example."

"Yeah, I can see that," he concedes.

For good measure, I also tell Gomes the woeful tale of Jeff Jackson, the Phillies' number one pick back in '89. Jackson was a high school phenom when the Phillies selected him ahead of Frank Thomas. Thomas has since become an institution, while Jackson never made it beyond AA before being released. Gomes has never heard of Jeff Jackson. I fill in some of the details, including Jackson's age when he signed.

"Seventeen! Man, I couldn't have dealt with any of this when I was seventeen." He shakes his head. "Seventeen!"

Gomes calls over to Joey Madden, a twenty-two-year-old rookie outfielder standing near us. "Hey, Joey. Can you imagine going through all this when you were seventeen or eighteen?"

Madden is from Richmond, California, drafted out of Cal State. He shakes his head solemnly. "No way," he replies.

"I didn't have the maturity back then," Gomes continues. "I would have messed something up. I wouldn't even have wanted to try back then. Those years in college made all the difference to me."

Someone near us mentions that the Phillies have just traded for Bobby Thigpen. Thigpen was once a star closer for the White Sox, but his career has fallen on hard times. The trade is viewed as a reclamation project, a long shot at best. Nevertheless, Gomes seems surprised, even annoyed.

"What'd they do that for?" he asks. He never says it, but I sense a "What do they need *him* for? They have *me* now." Unlike many guys in the low minors, Gomes is not shy about his abilities or guarded about his chances.

"I'm ready to pitch for them now," he says. I suspect he doesn't just mean Batavia. Reportedly, part of Gomes's deal with the Phillies involved an invitation to the major league camp next spring. Gomes understands that he has to put in his time, but he sees himself on the fast track through the system. I ask him to project how quickly it'll happen. The word "whether" never emerges. It's just a question of when.

"I figure I'll finish the season in Clearwater," he begins.

"Clearwater?" I ask. Gomes has already skipped Martinsville, not uncommon for a college draft pick. But the usual next stop is Spartanburg. *Then* Clearwater, the highest A-level team in the Phillies system. I suggest that maybe if things go well here, there might be a late season promotion to Sparty.

Gomes listens politely and shakes his head.

"Clearwater," he repeats.

P.S. Wayne Gomes and I spoke on Thursday afternoon. Three days later he was promoted to Clearwater. He made his debut the following Monday. He pitched one inning, striking out the side and walking one.

Compared to Wayne Gomes, Jason Abramavicius is anything but a bonus baby. Jason graduated from Florida International University with a combined 20–10 record. His ERA was around 4.00. His name never came up during the June amateur draft.

"I thought I had some chance to get drafted," he tells me. "You know, not in the early rounds, maybe later on. I kept waiting, but it never happened. It was disappointing, but I figured that was that. I was twenty-three years old, out of school and without a job.

"I went back home to Chicago. I was playing basketball in a district league. I got home late one night from a game and there was a message waiting for me from my uncle Bob. He's always been my biggest fan, always looking out for my career. He called to tell me there was a Pirates tryout camp the next morning. He had spoken to one of the Pittsburgh scouts about me and arranged for me to go. The local scout knew who I was. I had been pretty good in high school, so they had heard my name before.

"The next thing I knew, I was at this camp. There were lots of kids there, quite a bit younger than I. About 120 of us altogether. I had a pretty decent day, threw about eighty-seven to eighty-eight miles per hour. That was it. Next thing I know, they offered me a contract. I was the only one. That made me feel pretty good. Also kind of surprised. I signed a contract on Wednesday, and they told me to be in Welland on Friday. So that's how I made the big time."

With that, Jason and I laugh. The "big time" in this case means sitting in the left field stands at 6 P.M., eating a gourmet minor league supper of nachos and cheese.

Despite its humble start, Jason is making the most of his minor league opportunity. In twenty-six innings, his ERA is 3.08. He's struck out twenty-five batters and only walked five. Opponents are batting just .213 against him.

"Actually, my ERA was better than that," he explains. "I kind of got roughed up last night. Before that, my ERA was 1.65."

"What happened?" I wonder.

"I think it's important to pitch inside in this league," he tells me. "I didn't do that very well yesterday, and I paid for it. Other than that, I've been doing well. I have a really good curveball, and I've been changing speeds. I've learned to spot my fastball and change-up."

Tonight is baseball card night in Welland. Everyone gets a free team set. That means the demand for autographs is even greater than usual. Periodically, Jason has to wipe the cheese off his fingers and sign a card. They all come to ask: middle-aged women, prepubescent kids. No one seems immune to this ritual. When our chat is about over, I decide to take a picture of Jason signing an autograph.

"Write slowly," I ask, fumbling to get my camera set up.

"Are you kidding?" he laughs. "Look at my last name. You'll have plenty of time."

When we say goodbye, I tell Jason I'll be watching his career and rooting for him. It's fun to champion a cause like this. In a world of high-priced, highly touted draft picks, here's a twenty-three-year-old nondrafted free agent of whom no one expects a thing. The proverbial long shot. Also, a decent, funny guy with no superstar pretensions. Someone who seems to be watching it happen from inside the system with the same bemused fascination as a fan or

Welland, Ontario

Jason Abramavicius.

journalist. If Jason were listed on the stock market, he'd be what's known as a "penny stock." A speculative gamble, probably trading for between fifteen cents and a quarter, depending on last night's outing. I'd buy a few thousand shares, partly on sentiment and partly on clearheaded reckoning. Then I'd file the shares away and wait a few years.

Jason Abramavicius may not be traded on the stock exchange, but I was in Welland that night, and I got my very own Pirates team set. That means I have Jason's rookie card. It's almost as good as a stock certificate.

Al LeBoeuf almost made it to the Show. The Batavia manager came as close as anyone can, without actually setting foot on the artificial turf at Veterans Stadium. In 1985, LeBoeuf was enjoying a solid season with Portland, the Phillies AAA affiliate. The decision was made to promote him, but before word got through, LeBoeuf was involved in a brutal home plate collision. It tore up his knee and scuttled plans for his promotion.

LeBoeuf played through three more seasons of minor league ball before he finally decided to retire.

"I might have kept playing beyond that point if it hadn't been for my family. It's amazing how unrealistic you can be. Sometimes you need something outside yourself to give you some perspective.

"I'd wake up in the morning, and it would take me over an hour just to fight past the pain and get out of bed. By the time I'd get to the ballpark, I'd have some mobility again and I'd play through the day. It wasn't too bad while I was playing, so I'd figure, 'Sure, I can keep doing this.' I'd forget what I had gone through that same morning. And then it would start all over again. I'd get up and not know if I could make it across the room.

"Finally I said, 'Enough is enough.' It wasn't easy to quit. At least I knew there was a minute there when I was considered good enough to be in the big leagues."

Since retiring, LeBoeuf has worked in the Phillies minor league system. He spent one season as third base coach for AAA Scranton before taking over as manager of Batavia.

I ask LeBoeuf if he has seen the piece on him in a recent issue of *Phillies Report:*

"Not yet," he replies. "How do I come across?"

I tell him the truth. "Like a really decent, caring, hard-working guy."

"I am," he says simply. "I know how that sounds, but the point is, really, what's the advantage of being an asshole or a jerk?"

As that sinks in, he adds, "You ever been to the winter meetings?" I shake my head, no.

"You walk around there and you see famous players, Hall of Famers, and they're scuffling around looking for work. They're out of a job. They'd give anything to get back into baseball, and there's nothing for them. There's not *that* many jobs out there. A guy like me, I've got a nine-year minor league career and the knowledge that I almost made it. That's not much of an edge, when you're competing for work with Hall of Famers. Given those odds, can you see any advantage in being an asshole? I'd rather be known as decent and hard working. That's my edge."

We talk a bit more until we're interrupted by a phone message.

"It's Jayson Stark. He wants to talk to you," one of the Welland staff tells LeBoeuf. Stark is a well-known writer whose columns appear regularly in the Philadelphia *Inquirer* as well as *Baseball America*. I'm curious about what has prompted this call to southern Ontario, although I think I can guess.

"Gomes?" I ask.

LeBoeuf gives me a "What else?" nod.

I'm walking around the Welland outfield during batting practice when one of the Batavia players waves to me. I walk over to number 19, a pitcher named Scott Barstad.

"Didn't I see you about a month ago traveling around the Appalachian League?" he asks.

"That was me," I reply.

"What are you doing *here*?" he wonders.

"Same thing I was doing down there," I tell him. And then I explain about the book. Barstad and I haven't met before, although our paths have obviously crossed.

"I should be asking you the same question," I tell him. "What are *you* doing up here? You were with Martinsville in July."

"Yup," he tells me with a smile. "I was promoted. Three of us. Todd Genke was sent up first, then me and Bryan Wiegandt."

Martinsville to Batavia is more than a lateral move. They're both A-level teams, but the New York–Penn League is a higher level of play than Martinsville.

"That's got to feel good. You guys must have been doing pretty well down there."

"I was doing OK," Barstad explains. "I think it has as much to do with our age. We're likely to get promoted more quickly because we're older."

Older in this case means twenty-two years old. Not exactly over the hill, but also a bit long in the tooth to be competing with eighteen year olds in the Appy League.

Todd Genke adds, "If we're going to make it, we're going to have to start showing them something pretty quickly. At least it's good that they're keeping an eye on us and willing to keep moving us through the system if we play well."

Bryan Wiegandt, the only nonpitcher in the trio, has a slightly different slant on things.

"I'm glad to be here," he assures me, "but it's all moving very quickly. It's still kind of unreal to me. I had finally made the adjustments and was doing pretty well in Martinsville. Now it feels like I have to start all over again. The pitching is tougher here. The quality of play is higher. I guess every time you move up, the league makes new demands on you."

I ask Bryan how he's been hitting since he came up to Batavia.

"Not so great. The first eight games were brutal. Last night I got the game-winning hit in the bottom of the ninth. That really did a lot for my confidence. I'm hoping it carries through for the rest of the season."

Tonight Batavia doesn't need any ninth inning heroics to win. They beat Welland cleanly. In the last of the ninth with two out, Elvis sings "It's Now or Never" over the PA system. There is no response from the Welland bats, and Batavia drives back across the border as winners.

As folks are getting ready to leave, the winner of tonight's fifty-fifty lottery is announced. It turns out to be the general manager, Brian Sloan. Not only has he won, he's managed to corner the season's largest jackpot, $75. There are humorous cries of "Fix!" from some of the regular fans. Even his staff is riding him.

"Will you keep it?" I ask.

"Sure," he says. "It was a fair draw. Anyway, the way things are going here, I don't know where I'll be working next year. I may need it."

St. Catharines, Ontario

"You're not going to see Captain Dynamite blow himself up on this outfield."
—Ellen Harrigan, St. Catharines GM

It may not seem like much to the gender-conscious outside world, but the St. Catharines Blue Jays baseball club is run entirely by women. The general manager is a woman, the assistant general manager is a woman, and the head secretary/office manager is a woman. Three for three in a profession that has not exactly been progressive in the area of gender equity.

"Sure, we've gotten a lot of attention for this," says GM Ellen Harrigan. "*Sports Illustrated* did a story on us, and there's been lots of media coverage. But when you get back to real life here, it's all about running a ball club, not about women's issues."

The club's history is short and sweet. Sometime late in 1985, the Toronto Blue Jays bought the Niagara Falls, New York, White Sox and moved the franchise to St. Catharines, Ontario, where they became the St. Catharines Blue Jays. The "Baby Jays" had their inaugural season the following year and promptly won the New York–Penn League championship. It was a hell of a debut. They also drew over 42,000 fans, which continues to eclipse their present attendance figures, although things have been on a gradual upturn.

The Jays play in Community Park, a nondescript stadium with endless rows of metal benches. It has that eighties look about it: instant ballpark, built to your specifications. Strictly functional, no character. The present park was created in 1987 to replace the wood structure that was here when the Blue Jays affiliate began its tenure in '86. What you see now is a serviceable A-level ballyard that seems devoid of history. But appearances can be deceiving.

The consensus seems to be, "Go ask Jack Rountree if you want to know about the history of this place. He can tell you anything about local baseball."

History of this place? I didn't know St. Catharines *had* any history.

"Oh sure it does," says Jack Rountree, living up to his billing. He's got a nearly photographic memory for baseball, which includes a litany of area stadiums and teams he's played for since his youth.

"This is quite an old ballpark," he begins. "It's been in continuous operation since 1923. I played here that first year. I was twelve years old. I played for the Merritton Midgets. Merritton was a separate town then; it's been incorporated into St. Catharines now. That first year the stands were made of wood. The next year, 1924, they put in steel stands. The park held about six hundred people.

"The field was good, but we had to work hard to make it playable. It used to be a brickyard. Every winter the frost would push up tons of bricks. We had to go around with a wheelbarrow and collect all the broken pieces of brick every spring. Then we'd play on it all season. Next winter the same thing would happen. Another layer of bricks would get pushed up to the surface by the frost. I guess eventually all of them worked their way through. I haven't heard tell of any bricks coming through these days."

Rountree went on to play for a procession of semipro teams in Ontario from his Midget days in Merritton until 1941, when he retired as a player and manager.

"I played here on this field for a team called the Merritton Alliance. We won the league championship in 1930. I went on to play for teams in St. Catharines, Sudbury . . . I played one full season at every position except second base. Even pitched a bit, but they used to want me in there for my bat. Even when I pitched, I'd be out there the next day playing outfield or third base. I had a real good arm. I came up as a catcher, but more often they'd use me at third to take advantage of my arm.

"I had a chance to turn pro back then, and I thought about it. But pro teams in the area were paying $85 a month. I was making better money than that working and playing nights and weekends, so I never made the change. When I look at the salaries today, I just shake my head. I played 'cause I loved it. I can say I would have played for nothing 'cause that's just what I did."

Guys like Jack Rountree are a national treasure. In his ninth decade, he attends games more regularly than most fans a quarter his age. He is a bonanza of local history, but the historians have not been beating down his door. Part of

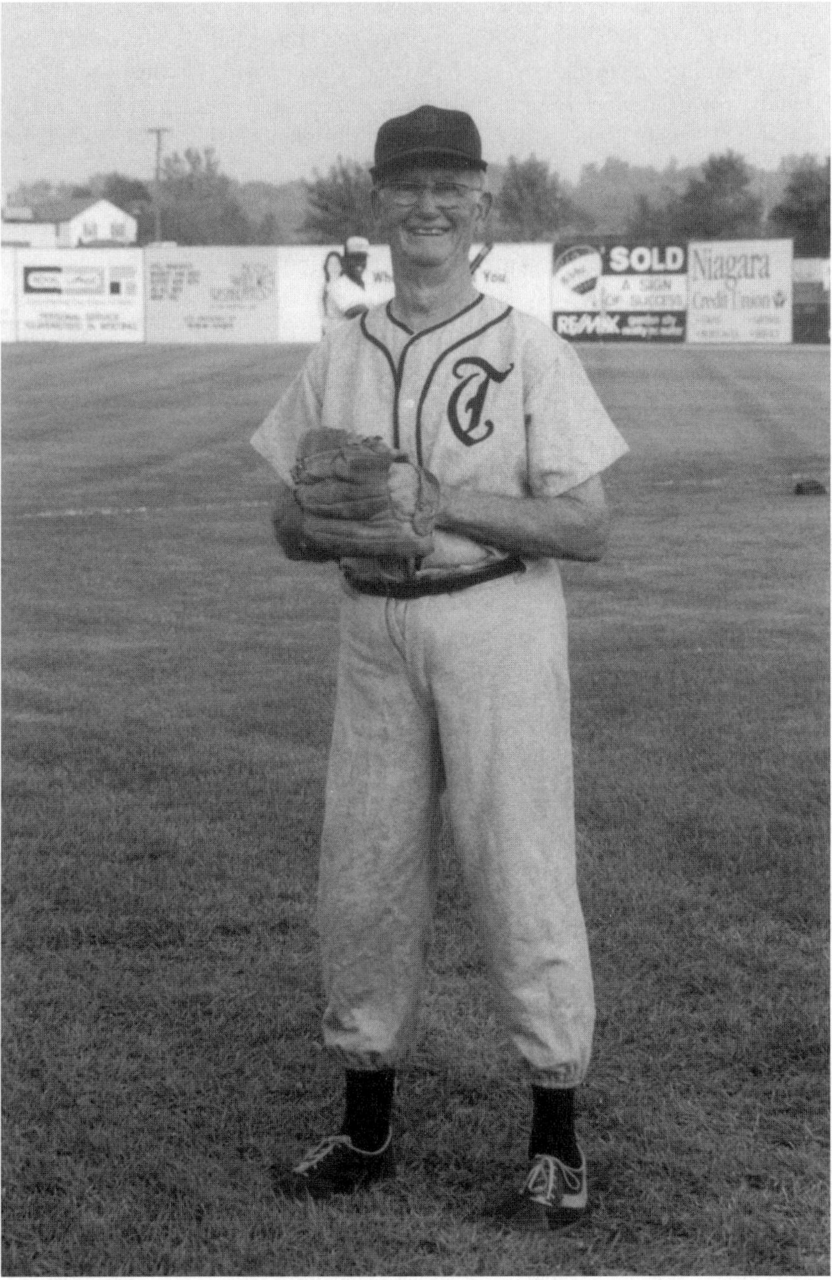

Jack Rountree, ballplayer and historian, on his eightieth birthday.

the problem is that Canada does not yet take baseball as seriously as its neighbor to the south. Substitute the word "hockey" for baseball, and Jack's face would be smiling from the covers of national magazines. If Greensboro, North Carolina's War Memorial Stadium, built in 1926, is "the country's oldest minor league park," what is this unassuming former brickyard where the St. Catharines Blue Jays play?

If you haven't noticed, baseball is a conservative business. Even the game is conservative: it doesn't take to change kindly. Rules are rules. If in doubt, keep 'em the same. There would be considerably less resistance to rewriting the Bible than changing the distance between home plate and first base. Purists still bemoan the addition of the DH (designated hitter) and artificial turf. *In the best interests of baseball* is another way of avoiding change.

If you think the sport on the field is conservative, have a look at front office politics sometime. A surprising number of major league owners still bear a passing resemblance to what central casting would send if you asked for cigar-smoking fat cats from the 1930s. Depression-era bad guys.

Minor league baseball is noticeably better. It's not uncommon to find a local consortium of doctors, dentists, or university professors, guys who never played pro ball but wish they had, joining forces to buy a minor league team. Owners like these are usually a little less profit oriented. Their decisions are a tad more likely to come from the heart than the pocketbook.

Having said all this, the St. Catharines ball club is a real shocker. For one thing, they are not owned by a bunch of local investors or wannabees; they are the property of the parent club: the Toronto Blue Jays. Although that poses some problems, on balance it seems to be a real advantage. There are some things about this club that probably wouldn't happen if local businessmen held the purse strings. St. Catharines is not exactly a progressive or upscale place. It is a decidedly working-class town of about 130,000 folks, located on the Niagara peninsula. By and large, traditional values reign here.

Except at 426 Merritt Street, where the St. Catharines Blue Jays have set up shop. As noted, this is the only franchise in professional baseball with an all-woman front office staff. And they are not, shall we say, cut from the demure, nonassertive fabric of southern Ontario womanhood. These ladies are strong, professional, and funny. They take a lot of kidding and give it right back with a refreshing in-your-face attitude. Happily, all of this seems to be surviving within the strictures of baseball's old boy network.

Ellen Harrigan, the general manager, has been working for the Blue Jays organization since 1981.

"I was eighteen years old, just out of high school. I saw an ad in the Toronto paper for a junior secretary position. It turned out to be the Blue Jays. I didn't really care that much about baseball back then so I wasn't in awe when I went in for the interview. That probably helped me. Other girls might have fainted when they realized who they'd be working for. I just took it in stride. They probably mistook that for confidence."

But that wasn't the only thing that got her the job.

"What probably clinched it was the fact that I was six feet tall," she says. "I was the only applicant who could reach the top of the roster board."

Ellen worked her way from the ranks of junior secretary to administrative assistant to Gord Ash, then Blue Jays assistant general manager, who has a strong hand in player development. In 1988, the assistant general manager position opened up in St. Catharines, and Ellen was offered the job. She graduated to general manager in 1990.

What does it mean to work for a team that is owned by its major league affiliate?

"Oh, it makes a very big difference," Ellen tells me. "The Blue Jays have their own priorities. It's not just here, by the way. The Jays also own their Dunedin club [Florida State League] and are 90 percent owners of the team in Knoxville [Southern League]. They're not as bottom line–oriented as a group of local businessmen would probably be."

So if they're not trying to make a bundle off these clubs, what are their goals?

"The two priorities for this team are image and player development. I spend more time than most GMs working one on one with the players. I do all kinds of behind-the-scenes stuff that a more business-oriented GM probably wouldn't get involved with. The players know this door is always open to them. We get involved with everyday problems. Money matters. Language problems. Even occasional legal problems. We had a rather well publicized case last year of one of our players getting involved with the law. He was in here almost every day. He just needed to talk about it. It's part of my job to deal with all this stuff so when our guys go out on the field, they have their minds free to play ball."

After a pause, Harrigan adds, "I even deal with their parents. I've had mothers on the phone asking me, 'What shall I pack for my Tommy?' I want to tell her, 'Jeez, lady. Just some socks and underwear will be fine. Your kid will survive. He's made it this far.'"

Harrigan also sees some downside to being associated with the Blue Jays.

"This is a community team. If I go to the local politicians and say, 'We need five thousand dollars to do such and such,' I'm less likely to get it because they know we're owned by the Blue Jays. They'll tell me, 'Why ask us for the money? You guys are rolling in money. Look at what you just paid Joe Carter. What's five thousand dollars to the Blue Jays?' It really is hard to function independently as long as that tie to the Blue Jays is so strong.

Former Blue Jays pitcher David Wells with St. Catharines GM Ellen Harrigan (right) and assistant GM Marilyn Finn (left). Photo courtesy St. Catharines Blue Jays.

"We even thought about changing our name, but that sword cuts both ways too. We want this to be seen by the community as their team. That's hard to do as long as the words 'Blue Jays' are part of the title. That logo is very powerful in this part of the country. But we had to face reality; if we became the St. Catharines Whatevers, fan interest would probably drop. As it is, we're averaging about twelve hundred people a game. We need that support. We don't have to get rich running the club, but we have to cover expenses."

Not surprisingly, the tie-in with the Jays raises fan expectations.

"People actually complain when we offer typical minor league giveaways. They see this as a Blue Jays team, and they want the same kind of high quality merchandise they've seen at the Sky Dome. Yes, the name turns them out, but then they expect more. And you hear about it when they're disappointed."

The most noticeable benefit of having the Blue Jays run the show in St. Catharines is the emphasis on traditional baseball. There are still promotions and giveaways, but somehow things are tangibly more dignified, less *hokey* here.

"We try to encourage a festive atmosphere. But unlike a lot of our competitors, we don't run this like a carnival."

What does that mean in real terms?

"It means forget the Chicken, for one thing. Let him make his five thousand bucks somewhere else. It also means you're not going to see Captain Dynamite here. That poor old man is not going to blow himself up on this outfield."

But how pure is pure? Do the Baby Jays employ a mascot?

"Yeah," Ellen concedes. "But even there you'll see differences. The main thing is we do not let him on the field. Whatever he does, he does it in the stands."

And she's right. That night I watch as the mascot greets fans all over the park. He's like a one-bird reception committee. He shakes hands, or claws, with the folks. The kids seem to love him. They follow him all over the park.

The large bird isn't alone out there. Also wandering through the stands is a young woman in very ostentatious formal attire. She is called "Miss Clean." She carries a large plastic sack into which she throws the garbage fans hand to her. The public address announcer makes a fuss over her appearance.

"Folks, Miss Clean is here. Please give her all your refuse when she comes by."

It's a strange ritual. As if begging for handouts, this well-dressed vagrant searches for eye contact with potential donors. All the while, fans seek her out. They call to her and proudly hand over their empty pop containers and sticky wrappers. Her sack grows, the fans smile, and the park stays clean.

"Is that Miss Clean or *Miz?*" I ask her with my notebook prominently displayed. She looks puzzled for a moment but reaches a decision.

"Miss."

A few minutes later I notice another odd St. Catharines feature. The mascot *talks*! With the exception of the itinerant Chicken, most baseball mascots are mute.

At first I think I'm imagining things. The kids hover around him and ask a million animated questions and he *answers* them, in the voice of a nineteen-year-old male.

"He's a theater arts student," Ellen points out, barely hiding her cynicism. "He told us that during the interview. Claimed it would be very useful in establishing the bird's personality. I told him, here's the suit. Just go out and *do* it." She still sees the whole thing as just a bit too much. "I mean, he's got all this training in pantomime, right. And what does he do? He ends up talking to everybody."

Later that night I catch another first for the St. Catharines mascot. Around the eighth inning, I witness the fabled "Dinosaur Toss." Picture a giant bird waddling in front of the first row of seats. In his hand is a large basket filled with small dinosaurs which he tosses into the stands like bridal bouquets. Most of them end up in the hands of kiddies. The adults seem to duck, and the kids are drawn to these things like, well, kids to dinosaurs.

Ellen watches this display, smiling but shaking her head in mild disbelief.

"A buck apiece at the Biway," she informs me.

"Money well spent," I reply.

She nods.

Groupies are a fact of life anywhere there are celebrities. Baseball, or for that matter minor league baseball, is no exception. By 10:30 every night, there are twenty-five or thirty freshly showered young men who are living away from home and are ready to take on the world. They are far too wired from the evening's work to even think about resting. And there is an ample supply of young women from town who would be only too happy to spend the next few hours with them. Like field mice, groupies seem to exist in inexhaustible supply.

Marilyn Finn, the Baby Jays assistant general manager, provides an unusual slant on things.

"Sometime around the eighth inning," she tells me, "go over to the ladies room and stick your head in there. It smells like a whorehouse. You can hardly breathe for all the hairspray and perfume being used."

And it's true. This is a silent baseball ritual, every bit as real as the short reliever getting up in the pen just in case he's needed in the ninth inning. These young women are doing some last-minute touch-up work. They've got to look their best. Soon they'll be lined up on display, like young girls at a dance. They know all the right places to wait. And the players know all the right places to browse. A quiet and effective symbiosis, probably as old as the game itself.

Flowers in the press box? Talk about sacrilege! Nothing better symbolizes the good-natured conflict between traditional male sportswriters and the all-female management of the St. Catharines Blue Jays.

"We thought flowers would look lovely. I mean, I guess it is a *girl* thing to do." Ellen exaggerates the word for emphasis. "But it wasn't that unreasonable. The press box *is* a working environment. Marigolds look nice. We thought it'd give the place a little touch of class."

But class in the press box?

"Well, that's what the guys said too. Like, who needs it? As soon as we put them in, the complaints started. It wasn't 'These things are too feminine.' It was 'We can't see over them!' So we made a deal with the guys. We said, 'Let us keep the flowers and we promise not to put up lace curtains.' They agreed to that real quick! So we thought we had a truce, except it didn't work out too well. The flowers died."

The cause of death?

"Too many cups of coffee and who knows what else got dumped into them."

Today, the press box in St. Catharines remains a largely male preserve. There are neither lace curtains nor marigolds in sight.

Rivalries are not confined to the playing field and the press box.

"We've been running neck and neck with Niagara Falls all year in the standings," Harrigan tells me. "There's a lot of friendly competition between us. You can even feel it in the front office.

"Last week a car drove up, and a guy from the Niagara Falls club runs into our office. He puts a statue of a black cat down on the counter and says, 'This is for bad luck.' Then he jumps in his car and drives away."

The St. Catharines response was brief and to the point.

"I faxed them a message saying, 'Giving another pussy to an all-female front office only adds strength to our numbers.'"

St. Catharines, Ontario

During the last few seasons, the Toronto Blue Jays have begun to do a passable imitation of George Steinbrenner and the much maligned New York Yankees. The Jays have gone to expensive free agent signings as well as "rent a player" trades. These late season acquisitions (e.g., Rickey Henderson, David Cone) have frequently cost the Jays minor league prospects, the very players they have carefully nurtured within their system. This mortgage-the-future approach for instant gains has divided their fans and clouded the emphasis the Jays continue to place on player development.

"Every time I see one of those trades involving someone like Steve Karsay, I have to take a deep breath." Ellen Harrigan shakes her head. "I remember when Karsay pitched here. I remember how good he was and how much work has gone into his development. The Jays really have an incredible minor league system. Most fans don't realize how it's structured. It's not uncommon for major league clubs to use their teams in this league as a testing ground for rookies.

"The Jays aren't like that. By the time a Toronto player gets here, he's usually been through some development elsewhere. The Jays have minor league teams in Medicine Hat [Pioneer League] and the Gulf Coast League. Both those teams are classified below us. The Jays also have two teams in the Dominican Republic. Think about what a difference that makes. You sign some sixteen-year-old phenom out of the Dominican and what do you do with him? Some teams will take this kid with virtually no English language ability and minimal social skills and ship him to play here or in the States. He's unhappy, his teammates may not be thrilled, and you never really get a look at his talent.

"Sure, we have Dominican or Venezuelan players on this team, but they're not raw kids who are over their heads in a foreign country. By the time they get here, they've been in the system for a while. They're a pleasure to work with because they already have professional experience. That just shows you the priority the Blue Jays put on systematic player development. I can tell you a lot of clubs don't share that outlook."

Canadian baseball fans, at least *English* Canadian fans in Ontario, really differ from their counterparts south of the border. As in most things, Canadians are more reserved. In the ballpark, that translates as quieter. During the 1992 stretch drive to the pennant, Joe Carter and Dave Winfield had to engage in a well-publicized campaign to encourage Jays fans to MAKE NOISE! They had a point. It was an eerie experience to sit in the Sky Dome, a sealed chamber, with 50,000 other human beings and hear silence prevail. Polite applause would erupt after a well-executed play, but on balance it felt more like watching a tennis match than a ball game.

Back in the early eighties, Canadians from Ontario were just getting used to baseball. They weren't quite sure of the rules or how to behave. The honeymoon is over. This blushing bride is now wearing a World Series ring. She's been around. But she still isn't so worldly about minor league baseball.

"We've had to go through an education process," says Harrigan. "It's really incredible. So many fans in St. Catharines just don't understand what it means to have a minor league club. They see the Blue Jays logo on the building and on the souvenirs. The guys are wearing Blue Jays suits, but they don't see Joe Carter and John Olerud playing here. They wonder, What's going on?

"The sign outside says Toronto Blue Jays Farm Team, but many of them are still fuzzy about the details. I still get calls from mothers asking if their son can come down and try out. We've been here since 1986, but they still haven't quite got the hang of it. The longer you stay in a town, the better it gets. The key for a lot of them is seeing guys who have played for this team make it to the majors. Then they start to get the picture. They realize it's about development. And development takes time. And not all of them make it. Stuff like that seems to take a while to understand."

It's rare that fans, players, and the front office agree about anything. But in this case, everyone gives me the same advice.

"You gotta go talk to Psycho!"

So I do. Psycho, aka Chad Brown, is easy to find, sitting in the clubhouse watching TV. And he doesn't look like a psycho. He looks like a sweet, all-American kid who might come from a traditional home in the heartland. In this case, the source is Gastonia, North Carolina.

"So you lost your minor league team back home?" I say as we depart the clubhouse for the less-populated bleachers three hours before game time.

"Yeah. You know about that?" He seems pleased that someone has knowledge of his roots. The Gastonia Rangers have moved an hour down the road and become the new wildly successful Hickory Crawdads franchise.

"My whole family has been there. Everybody but me. They keep telling me, you gotta go see it. It's great. But I'm playing up here whenever they go. I'll finally get to see the ballpark this winter when I go back home."

Chad Brown was drafted in the twenty-first round in 1992 and sent to Medicine Hat.

"I was actually drafted before that by Cleveland," he tells me. "But I decided to go to college first. I graduated from North Greenville Junior College. Then I went through the draft again, and the Jays selected me. I'm really glad I took the extra time. I didn't lose anything by it."

Chad Brown, aka "Psycho." Photo courtesy Paul Hutchinson.

Neither did he cut a swath through the rookie Pioneer League that first season, but the Jays promoted him to St. Catharines anyway. Brown has responded to the challenge by becoming the team's closer and a candidate for the Rolaids Relief Award in his league. Through August 25, Brown had a 2–0 record, an ERA just under 2.00, twenty strikeouts in seventeen-plus innings, and nine saves. Opponents were batting under .120 against him. Good as those numbers were, Brown wanted more.

"I set some goals for myself. I wanted fifteen saves, but it's been hard to get them with this team. We've been playing such good ball, we're in a lot of blowout situations, so I don't get credited with a save. I'm just getting innings in. My ERA should be lower too. I've given up four runs all year. They came in one game on two home runs. Every time I pitch, I bring the ERA back down a bit more. I don't want it to stay as high as 2.00."

In truth, a momentary lapse of attention probably cost Brown at least one of those blemishes on his record. Still annoyed at himself, Brown tells me, "We had this game during extended spring training. It didn't really mean anything, but there were some bad feelings and we got into a brawl. There was a whole pile of guys on the field, and my roommate ended up getting beat up by this guy named Ruben Rivera. He got spiked pretty bad. It seemed to be really malicious, and it stayed on my mind. I vowed I was going to get him back somehow. I kept talking about it to everybody in the pen. You know, just looking for my chance. I finally got it. The first time I faced him he hit a home run off me."

"Sounds like you were a little too motivated to be at your best," I suggest.

"I don't know," Chad answers. "I believe it was the Lord. I was talking badly about this guy all the time. I don't think it's right to be like that. I think that home run was my punishment. I don't do that anymore."

And then he adds, "Anyway, the next time I faced him, I struck him out. So it's over. I figure we're even. I really don't think about it anymore, except that home run is still on my record. It's like a reminder for me."

How do traditional religious values fit in with baseball life in St. Catharines?

"Sometimes it's difficult," Chad admits. "Like on Sundays. We have afternoon games. We're supposed to be out here working and I'm thinking, This is wrong. It's Sunday morning. I'm supposed to be in church with my family. After that, we're supposed to go out for Sunday dinner together. Suddenly all that's changed. I was very troubled by that for a while, but I've adjusted. I have a bigger view now. Baseball is my church. The mound is my pulpit."

He looks around the stands and says, "The fans are my congregation. There's music here too. I think this is OK. The Lord understands."

Along with religion, baseball was a strong part of Chad's upbringing.

"My father played in the Pirates' farm system. I'm just carrying on the tradition. Bryan Harvey is from my town also. Another closer. He's older than me, but I know him. We played together, and we talk baseball. I can't imagine not playing ball. I'd play for free. If I got released today, I'd probably go to a ball game tomorrow. It's just part of my life."

So how does this hard-working, clean-cut kid get a nickname like Psycho?

"I'm very enthusiastic out there. A bit wired, you could say. I'm not doing it to show off or show anybody up. I just have a lot of energy."

Indeed. During a typical performance, Brown comes sprinting in from the bullpen as if angry hornets were in pursuit. Once on the mound, he paces around, talking to himself.

"My catcher used to say, 'What? You talking to me?' I'd tell him, 'No, no! Just get back down and catch me.'"

After each strikeout, Brown stalks a counterclockwise circle around the mound. Then he's ready for the next guy. He can barely stand the time between pitches and batters.

"When the batter digs in there, I give him my death stare. I try to intimidate him any way I can. I'm not that big physically, so I look for any edge. I'm only about 5′ 10″, but I always list myself as six feet tall. You'll see it everywhere. I'm hoping some of the guys I have to face will also see it. Maybe it'll help keep them intimidated."

Chad Brown exudes energy. He can barely stop talking or moving. It's all this enthusiasm that has earned him the name Psycho. Mostly, he's viewed with tolerant amusement by his teammates and coworkers. He talks to fans and stadium workers constantly. His GM sees him as a dream come true.

"Whenever there's a promotion to do, an appearance at Canadian Tire or McDonalds, Chad is always first in line. Other guys are hiding under chairs, but Chad is bouncing up and down saying, 'When do we leave!'"

His manager, J. J. Cannon, tells the local press that Brown is a "typical left-hander." Around baseball, that simply means "flaky."

Harry Muir, one of Brown's former roommates, shakes his head and smiles. Muir is as calm as Brown is frenetic. Whoever thought to put them in the same room had a hell of a sense of humor.

"I've never seen him have a down day or take anything slow and easy," Muir tells me. "And he drinks enough Coke to wire anybody. I bet he goes through twelve or thirteen of them a day."

When I see Chad a while later, I tell him, "You need caffeine like a fish needs a bicycle."

He looks comically exasperated. "Who you been talking to? Durso? Muir?"

I confirm it was Muir.

"I suppose he told you about the Sun Drop also?"

I let Chad tell me. Apparently Sun Drop is a soft drink back home that may not even be *allowed* across the North Carolina border. By all reports, it makes Coke look caffeine-free. Needless to say, Chad is a big fan.

"I couldn't believe it. When I got up here, they never even heard of it! I didn't know what I was going to do! I finally started drinking Coke. I never used to back home. Once when we were in Pennsylvania playing Erie I found some Sun Drop in a small store. I bought every one they had, but it didn't last long."

Harry Muir adds another piece to the puzzle. "Did he tell you his mother ships him cartons of Sun Drop?"

But Chad has a better solution to this addict's nightmare.

"See, I'm going to become famous. When I'm a household name, I'm gonna work out some kind of endorsement deal with Sun Drop. They'll feature me in their ads, and I'll be supplied with their product wherever I go. It'll always be waiting for me."

P.S. Chad came in that night in the top of the ninth with the game tied, runners on first and third. He raced in from the pen to the delight of the fans. He struck out the first guy he faced and circled the mound counterclockwise. Then he induced an easy grounder for the force to end the inning. The Jays scored a run in the bottom of the ninth, and Chad got the win.

I went down to the clubhouse to congratulate him, but Chad was emitting a very loud high-pitched noise that probably drew small animals from miles around St. Catharines. It certainly ruled out human conversation. Ten minutes later I checked again, and Chad was a tad calmer. I congratulated him but pointed out he was supposed to be collecting saves, not wins. He agreed and happily told me that sometimes it doesn't go according to plan.

Did Harry Muir and Chad Brown grow up on the same planet? These guys are sufficiently unlike to suggest a species difference. Yet here they are, both twenty-one-year-old men pitching for the same team and standing within ten feet of each other in St. Catharines, Ontario. They must have something in common.

Part of the difference, a *large* part obviously, is cultural. Brown grew up in the rural South, in a culture that rarely selects gray as its favorite color (unless they're talking about the Civil War). Harry Muir is from London, Ontario. Guys like Chad Brown are rarely found in southern Ontario unless they are being paid to entertain.

Harry Muir was signed by the Blue Jays out of high school. He played for the Ontario Provincial Team, then the Canadian National Team. He attracted a lot of attention.

"If I were superstitious," he begins, "I'd think I was fated to be here. I was originally supposed to sign with Kansas City. I had a tryout with them scheduled, and the day before I sprained my ankle really badly. That night I got a call from the guy who was supposed to catch me. He had just broken his leg.

Harry Muir.

So much for the tryout. In the meantime, the Blue Jays called. I didn't even know they knew about me! They told me they had been watching me for years. I was amazed. I was happy to sign."

Muir still looks a bit awestruck. I ask him, "How much of an advantage do the Jays really have in dealing with Canadian talent?"

He shakes his head. "They can get any Canadian they want. It's not even a contest. I grew up being a Blue Jays fan. How could I turn them down?"

Then he reflects, "Kids growing up here are at a disadvantage. Compared to Dominicans and most kids from the States, we barely get to play. I had thirty-two games all season. The rest of the time it was too cold. We just don't get the innings in."

Muir signed with the Jays on March 3, 1991, just days before the ground rules for the draft were changed to include Canadian athletes. His first season was spent in the Gulf Coast rookie league.

"I had a good year there, a 2.23 ERA, and some decent performances."

Harry describes his next season in Medicine Hat as "hectic."

"I put up some awful numbers, but things started to turn around late in the season. I think they looked at how I did in August and decided to promote me.

I felt good about that. It means I've progressed every season. At this rate, I'll be twenty-four when I'm in AAA."

Then he laughs to make sure I don't misread any arrogance in his statement. And he adds, "I'm in no hurry. I'm having lots of fun doing this."

Whether he wants it or not, Harry Muir is about to have his first taste of publicity. He is the "token Canadian" in a documentary about minor league baseball produced by the Canadian Broadcasting System.

"I've heard the CBC will be broadcasting it in early October, right around World Series time," he tells me. "I guess a lot of people are going to see me pitch."

A sheepish grin crosses Harry's face, but it's too late to be nervous. The performance is already on tape.

Shannon Stewart was the Jays' number one selection in the June 1992 draft. That means he's been under a microscope ever since. He's also been subjected to endless media attention. It's fair to say he hasn't enjoyed either. Nor has he been thriving in the system.

Shannon is a speedy outfielder who is projected to steal a lot of bases in the majors. The trouble is, you have to get on base to steal, and Shannon hasn't been doing a lot of that.

In his rookie season for the Gulf Coast Jays, Shannon hit .233. As expected, he showed little power; of his forty hits, thirty-eight of them were singles. But he did score forty-four times on those same forty hits. This year, things have improved somewhat. Shannon's average was up to .261 when I saw him. He led the team with twenty-four steals and was the only position player without an error.

I talk to him an hour or so before game time. He's a quiet teenager from Florida whose reticence will easily be confused with aloofness, just because he's a first round draft pick. That's a shame. The guy is simply shy.

And he's also tired. "I'm really finding it hard to get up for the game every day. Just to push through the tiredness and be ready. It can really be a struggle sometimes. This has been a long season. It didn't start with this league. Some of us also had extended spring training. I've been doing this nonstop since March. Late in the season like this, you start to wear down a bit."

Shannon seems troubled that he's having to push this hard. Something that used to be fun is starting to feel like work. I tell him about my talk with Ron Lockett on the Reading Phillies and how much he wanted me to know that playing pro ball was hard work. Shannon wants to hear about that conversation in as much detail as I can remember.

"Do you go home after the season and get to rest up?" I ask.

"No," he replies. "I have the instructional league. It's not as intense as this with a full game every day. But you still have to put in the hours. There's plenty to do."

That night Shannon plays nine innings of baseball. He maintains his errorless streak and even steals a base. No one in the stands would have guessed how tired he was.

An August visit to St. Catharines during the 1994 season points me in the direction of Mark Sievert, who has just pitched a no-hitter against Utica. Everyone at the ballpark is still talking about it — fans, the front office, and his teammates. When I walk into the clubhouse, guys take one look at me and my camera bag and know immediately what I want. Everyone points to the showers and calls his name. For a moment, the clubhouse echoes with the name "Sievert!!!"

Out of the mist steps the stark naked figure of Mark Sievert, peering into the clubhouse. He looks a bit dazed.

"You want me?" he asks no one in particular. His gaze finally lights on me and he says, "Oh, you want some pictures. You want 'em now?"

"Not unless I plan to blackmail you," I reply. "Why don't you dry off and we'll go outside and talk a bit."

Several moments later I step into the light with this twenty-two year old from Janesville, Wisconsin, an area of the country not traditionally noted for baseball. Sievert has thrown a Blue Jays windbreaker over a T-shirt and some old blue jeans. This is to be an informal photo op. His fair skin, blue eyes, and red hair are in stark contrast to most of his teammates, who are either Hispanic or very southern. Sievert looks like he needs to be shielded from the sun.

The ball club has left the scoreboard unchanged from Sievert's no-hitter. It's a nice gesture: a token of respect as well as a confidence builder.

"Did it surprise you?" I ask.

"Yeah, I guess it did. I've been doing OK. I've struck out a lot of guys this season, but this was different. It was like everything was working. I guess that's what happens when you have a no-hitter."

Actually, Sievert is being a bit modest about his record. Although his ERA is perched around 3.70 (including the no-hitter), he leads the league in strikeouts, and opponents are hitting a mere .218 against him. Sievert's won-lost record (4–4) probably reflects more about how poorly the Blue Jays are playing than anything about his pitching performance.

As we head back for the clubhouse, he says rather softly, "I'm already starting to wonder if it really happened."

I stop and turn around and point to the scoreboard. We look together at the row of zeros on the Visitors line. He nods and smiles as we continue walking back to the clubhouse.

Mark Sievert in the afterglow of a no-hitter.

Despite their admirable philosophy and best intentions, the Toronto Blue Jays may be selling their ownership of the St. Catharines club.

"I know for a fact," Ellen Harrigan tells me, "that the Blue Jays were not soliciting offers for this team. But they've had at least half a dozen serious offers come in. It's made them sit up and take notice. They really didn't see this as an investment situation when they bought the franchise back in '86. But it suddenly has the potential to become that, so they've got a decision on their hands."

Harrigan reflects on everything she's told me about the club's priorities and what makes it special. "I'd rather it weren't sold, of course, but I have to be realistic. It isn't the end of the world if they do sell it. The vast majority of minor league teams are privately owned and still manage to do their part for player development."

Then the bottom line. "There's not a thing I can do about it at this point. My job is to keep things moving for this season. As far as next year goes, we're operating on the assumption that we'll be here. We're talking to our sponsors and advertisers just like we always do. If nothing changes, we've got to have everything in place for the next season. If there's an announcement, then I guess we'll go from there. I'm not worried. This is a good organization. I'm sure I'll land on my feet."

Following the 1994 season, the Blue Jays sold their interest in the St. Catharines club to a group of investors that included former Toronto catcher Ernie Whitt. Beginning in the 1995 season, the club officially became the St. Catharines Stompers.

Ellen Harrigan may have landed on her feet, but they were no longer planted in St. Catharines, Ontario. John Belford, previously associated with the now-defunct London Tigers, is the new St. Catharines GM.

Few things stand still in minor league baseball.

Buffalo, New York

"Let's go rob a bank. They'll never catch us today. All the cops are on the field."
—Pokey Reese, Indianapolis shortstop

If there is a better-looking or more professionally run minor league franchise anywhere, I've yet to see it. It's true that the city of Buffalo isn't exactly the jewel of the North. But somehow the grime and crime and nightly arson haven't penetrated the charms of Pilot Field. It stands like an oasis, bringing entertainment and civic pride to this shopworn city on the shores of Lake Erie.

The Bisons continue to draw crowds that exceed those of several major league teams. And part of the reason is sheer, good old-fashioned hard work. Yes, it's true that the team is enjoying a new affiliation with Cleveland, arguably the best young team in baseball. And it's also true that when I visited, the Bisons were seventeen games over .500. But the franchise doesn't coast on those features. They continue to put on a show out there, every day of the week. The Rich family, who own the Bisons, believe in providing their fans with a lot for their admission dollars. The entertainment goes well beyond baseball.

On a sunny Sunday afternoon in August, the field was so congested before game time, it seemed unlikely that baseball would ever be played there. Before the ceremonial first pitch could be thrown (there seems *always* to be a ceremonial first pitch), the following would have to leave the playing field: two helicopters, fifteen police cars, four honor guards in uniform with assorted flags, a troop of Little League players, the One Hundred Club of Buffalo, and no fewer than three mascots. The Bisons go in for mascots in a big way. First there's Buster, then there's Chip, then there's Micro-Chip. Buster is probably the fiercest-looking of the three, although they look pretty much alike except for size. Micro is just right for the kiddies.

Some of the players are sitting in the dugout, shaking their heads at the chaos on the field.

"Unbelievable," says Tim Costo. He's been with the Bisons all season and has seen his share of Buffalo-style promotions. "Actually," he adds, "if you can believe it, there were more cars out there yesterday. About a hundred of them. It was some kind of Vintage Car Day. But no helicopters," he concludes.

Casey Candaele is also marveling. "I've never seen anything like this in my whole career."

In the visitors' dugout, the reaction is no less obvious. Pitcher Travis Buckley looks at the show of law enforcement out there and says, "What did I do? Is my ERA that bad?"

Shortstop Pokey Reese surveys the fifteen cop cars and two police helicopters and shakes his head in disbelief.

"Let's go rob a bank," he says to me with a big smile on his face. "They'll never catch us today. All the cops are on the field."

In the middle of this, Alan Embree is warming up in the Buffalo bullpen, seemingly oblivious to the chaos surrounding him.

Finally, someone from the Erie County Sheriff's Department comes out and sings an a cappella rendition of the national anthem. As the applause begins, someone in one of the honor guards begins to play taps. This is the cue for the cop cars to head for the outfield exit, the civilians to head for the gate behind home plate, the mascots to head for the dugout, and the helicopters to begin their final ascent. Within minutes, order is restored and somebody yells, "Play ball!"

Today's game features the AAA affiliates of two of baseball's best teams. Kevin Jarvis is a pitcher for the visiting Indianapolis Indians. He's already spent some time with the parent Cincinnati Reds club. Jarvis was up for a while during the '94 season (1–1 in six starts) and pitched for the Reds during the first half of the '95 season. Now he's back in AAA.

"They sent me back down after the All-Star break," he says glumly. Jarvis is lying on the grass doing some stretching exercises. I wonder if having been to The Show makes it doubly hard to be putting in time at AAA.

"Sure," he concedes. "I've had a taste. I'm past the novelty. I don't wonder about it anymore. I know what it's like and I know I can pitch up there. I just want to get back."

In fact, Jarvis is being modest about his performance. On May 10, Jarvis pitched the first complete game of the 1995 season as Cincinnati defeated

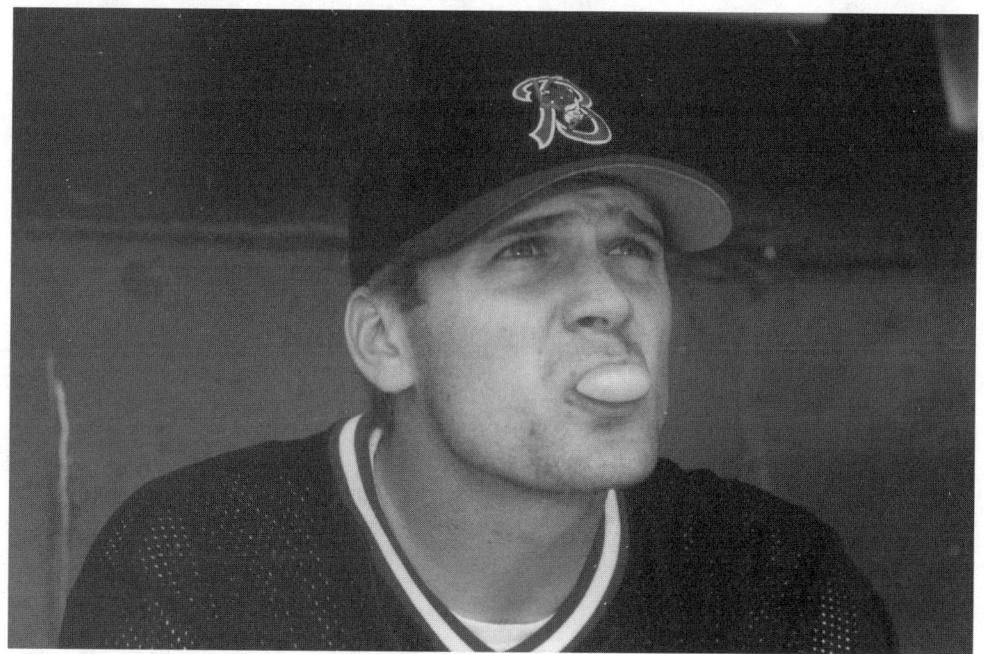

Tim Costo surveys the busy skies above Pilot Field.

Florida on Jarvis's two-hit gem. His reward, barely three months later, is to sit on the AAA outfield grass and discuss his career with me.

Despite the setback, Jarvis is doing well at Indianapolis. But he also knows that because the Reds are also doing well, it will be doubly tough to be called back. And even if he gets the call, he'll probably be looking at fewer innings.

"They're in a pennant race. They're going to use veterans, known quantities. If I were with an organization like the Pirates, I'd probably be in the majors right now, and I'd be pitching regularly. They know they're not going anywhere, and they're willing to give young players a look. It's nice being with a winner, but this is the price you pay."

His exercises over, Jarvis gets up and walks back toward the clubhouse. As he leaves, Jarvis adds, "I'm happy for all their success. I wish them well in the postseason. But I don't want to be watching them on television. I want to be up there doing it with them."

Scott Sullivan, another pitcher on the Indianapolis roster, echoes Jarvis's sentiments. Like Jarvis, Sullivan is having a solid season in AAA but doesn't expect a callup to The Show any time soon. Unlike Jarvis, Sullivan has never pitched in the majors.

"That's the downside of playing for a successful organization. They're committed to winning it all. That means they're likely to bring in free agents rather than taking a chance on somebody untested like me. Nobody wants to play for a loser, but you're more likely to be promoted in a losing franchise. A lot of guys are feeling the crunch down here. It's the same for most of us."

When we finish our little chat, Sullivan is off to chapel. Like most minor league teams, the Bisons create some semblance of a church service shortly before game time on Sunday afternoons. There'll be some Bible reading and some inspirational words from a local minister. Sullivan is checking to see which of the clubhouses or dugouts will be the site of today's service.

Kevin Jarvis walks by, and Sullivan reminds him that chapel will be starting soon.

"Aren't you going?" he asks.

"No, I want to throw," Jarvis replies. "Aren't you going to do some throwing?"

"Not now. I'm gonna go to chapel."

"Well, I'm gonna throw," Jarvis replies matter-of-factly.

Sullivan sits for a moment, then with a vague smile on his face he calls out "Heathen!" as Jarvis heads for the bullpen to work out his arm.

Lloyd McClendon seems to tower over his Buffalo teammates, even when they're all stretched out on the grass. He is, to put it mildly, a big, strong man.

McClendon spent eight power-filled seasons with the Pittsburgh Pirates. Now he's hanging in with the Indians AAA club, not ready to retire yet. Lloyd has been hitting for average and power with the Bisons, although his playing time has been restricted by a sore wrist. He's been on the DL since the end of July, and everyone is hoping that the injury is superficial.

"This is a cruel game," McClendon says. "Things can change very quickly. You've got to have some backup skills or you'll find yourself in a lot of trouble.

"I talk to a lot of high school kids. The truth is, I try to discourage them from playing this game professionally. I've got to be realistic with them. The likelihood of making it all the way is very low. If you're going to try, at least get an education. Prepare yourself for failure. Have something to fall back on. Too many kids coming out of the inner city, they sacrifice everything for this dream. If they make it, great. But most of them don't. And then what?"

Lloyd McClendon.

Lloyd and I talk a bit about some of the A clubs I've visited.

"Oh man, that puts me in touch with what I was like about thirteen years ago. Just a scared kid from Gary, Indiana. All the steel mills were closing. I knew that would be a rough place to have to go back to. I knew I had to make it. I'm glad I did. I was one of the lucky ones. I don't know what I would have done otherwise."

Lloyd McClendon has just suffered another of the defeats that baseball routinely delivers. His name has fallen from the record books. In 1971, McClendon set a Little League World Series record when he homered five times in five at bats. The record stood for nearly a quarter of a century until Lin Chih-Hsiang went to bat for the Taipei Little League team. Like Lou Gehrig, Lloyd McClendon has learned that baseball records were made to be broken.

As Jim Hornung can tell you, the groundskeeper's job is particularly challenging in Buffalo. Not only does Hornung have to undo the wear and tear from that day's baseball game, but he has to patch up the havoc caused by omnipresent promotions. In Buffalo, that can include honor guards, foot races, and helicopters landing in the outfield.

"We've actually kept things working OK here until this last postgame concert. We didn't expect to have four bands performing, and we didn't do enough to protect the field. The outfield got chewed up pretty badly. We'll have to do some resodding. I'm hoping that will handle it."

Along with helicopters and rock bands, Hornung also has to contend with a regular stampede of kids.

"They open up the field to the kids. They come out behind home plate and get to run the bases. They make the most of those few moments out there, sliding and jumping and pretty much tearing up the base paths. The trouble is, we have to rake it down and get it back to playing condition again. Billy Ripken nearly took one in the chops recently. He was pretty unhappy about the condition of the field, but he understands what we're working against here."

A. J. Maloney is taking a well-earned break from his on-field activities. His Buster costume is half on. The head is askew so A. J. can get some fresh air. But the animal paws are still attached, making our handshake a unique experience.

A. J. is recounting the weekly schedule of promotions.

"Yesterday," he tells me, "we had a Turn Back The Clock Day. We do one every year. This time we went back to 1959. The players wore vintage uniforms. All the employees wore stuff like rolled-up jeans and T-shirts, greased hair, the waitresses in the stands wore poodle skirts. There were vintage cars on the field. There were specials at the concession stands; they rolled the prices back. After the game we had a sock hop in the tent, like a theme party.

"Every Sunday is Kids Day. That's what all those Little Leaguers were doing out on the field. Their teams are being honored. Every Friday we have what's called a Bash. There's live music before and after the game. We also have fireworks after the game. Tuesdays are Festival Nights. They usually have an ethnic theme: Polish, Italian, German. Wednesdays are our day game so we have a business person's special. Free fax and cellular phone use. There's a guy who'll cut your hair and shine your shoes in the stands. There's always something going on here. Even baseball.

"Actually," A. J. pauses to reflect, "maybe sometimes they forget there *is* baseball going on here. Maybe it's a little too much. But who am I to talk? Look what I do for a living! In fact, I hardly ever get to see the game here. If I see too much of the game, I'm not doing my job.

"It's funny. I was at a Red Sox game earlier this season up in Fenway. The game was great. They were getting pounded by the Tigers. But there was absolutely nothing going on. It was so *quiet*. Hardly even any music. Maybe a little organ music between innings, but nothing like we have here. No rock &

roll. It seemed like something was missing. I was kind of surprised I reacted that way 'cause I tend to be a baseball purist. But I've gotten so used to what we do here, I just came to expect it."

Today's attendance is announced: 15,663. Not nearly a full house. A threat of rain earlier today probably kept some fans away. Yet I'm sure if I check tomorrow's paper I'll find that the Bisons outdrew more than a few major league games today.

I wander down from the press box, where I've been enjoying the field view as well as a panoramic look at the Buffalo skyline. Down the hall is the TV production center. I've been glancing at the TV coverage in the press box and am surprised to learn that only two cameras are in use. The line director is segueing effortlessly between the two, giving a fluid and revealing look at the field from a surprising variety of angles.

When I get back to the press box, I comment how good the coverage is and ask how many games are televised locally.

"Oh, that's not being televised," several people correct me. "That's just for in-house use. It's called Bison-Vision. We do televise a handful of games, but this isn't one of them."

In-house? This sure seems like a lot of trouble to go to for a signal that never leaves the ballpark. Where does it go?

And people start pointing. First, there's the press box, where I've been watching the overhead monitor. Then some of the corridors outside so the fans don't miss anything when they visit the concession stands. And the executive boxes, don't forget them. This is where the rich folks sit in their air-conditioned boxes and watch the game on TV while it's being played live under their noses.

The Bisons lose a squeaker, 4–3. As promised, as soon as the last out is registered, every kid in the place tears down the aisles and out on to the field. The PA system plays "Born to Be Bad" as the kids hit the diamond. Now is their chance to run the bases. All the pent-up energy from the last two hours gets turned into infield dust. Buster stands on first base, waving the stampeding kiddies to second, where Micro-Chip turns them toward third base. At third, Chip points them home. Many of them slide into home, dust themselves off, and return to their waiting families. They've seen flags, cops, helicopters, and a frustrating hometown loss. All in all, a great afternoon.

Batavia, New York

"They thought I was going to get rich playing here. Can you believe that?"
—Chuck Cox, Batavia catcher

If you so much as look sideways at old Dwyer Stadium in Batavia, one of the locals — even if he or she doesn't work for the Clippers — is quick to remind you that (1) the stadium has been around since the late 1930s and (2) the town is getting a brand-new park next year. It's a good thing. Quaint and historic as it might be, Dwyer Field is a pretty minimal facility.

"As soon as the last pitch is thrown this season . . . actually, we hope it's the last pitch of the *post*season, the wrecking ball will be here. There'll be a brand new park, right on this site next year."

I'm talking with Julia Rogers, who has taken over the GM position temporarily while her father, Brad, is recovering from surgery.

"The field itself will remain the same. We've already spent a million and a half on it. But the stands will be rebuilt and improved. Right now, the stadium capacity is around three thousand. We only draw that on the Fourth of July. Most of the time we average about a thousand or eleven hundred. The new park will hold about the same, but it'll be a lot more comfortable. The clubhouses will also be new. There'll be a batting tunnel to work out in. In case we have a rainout, the players can still practice while the grounds crew works on the field."

One way or another the Rogers family has run the Batavia Clippers since 1984. In her father's first years as GM, Julia sold tickets.

"This was always a part-time job for my dad. He just retired this year, but he's been a science teacher here in town. That meant we needed somebody in the office in May right before the draft and during the peak of our spring training. Since

I was going to college locally and I'd be off for that month, they hired me as assistant GM. That was back around 1989. After I graduated from college, I started teaching. But I continued to come home for the summer breaks so I could work here.

"This year when my father got sick, they asked me if I thought I'd be able to take over the GM's position. I said, yes, I'd be comfortable doing it. I guess I was in training all those years without actually knowing it. Our whole family has been involved with the team for quite a few years. I have three brothers and three sisters, and they've all worked here. My brothers have been batboys or clubbies. One sister is presently selling tickets. Even my mom worked here for a while, helping out in the office. It's really a great arrangement. Whenever somebody was home from college or in town for a while, we could always call and say, 'We're shorthanded. Can you come down and help out?' We've always counted on the family. In fact, we often ended up hiring friends of my brothers and sisters. It's like a giant labor force. This has really been a family business."

I'm wondering why the Batavia Clippers share a name with the Yankees AAA team from Columbus, Ohio. Are there clipper ships in Batavia's history as well? Did Sal ("The Barber") Maglie once clip hair in Batavia?

"No, no, no. Those are very imaginative guesses, but they have nothing to do with our name." Brad Rogers, former GM and official godfather to the Clippers, is about to clear up the mystery of his team's name.

"About sixty years ago, there was a large company in Batavia that made farm machinery. When the stadium was built in 1939, they decided to name the team after the famous equipment that was built here. It was called the Clipper Combine. Anyone who lived in town back then would have understood the name. Over the years, Batavia lost its association with farm machinery, but the team's name stayed the same. Today we have people growing up in town who take the name for granted, without realizing its history. Outsiders like yourself, of course, have no idea."

I ask Brad what's going to happen next year when, along with the new stadium, Batavia gets more deeply involved in merchandizing its logo. Can we expect to see T-shirts with images of clipper ships with a giant *B* on their sail?

"Oh no," he assures me. "I seriously doubt that will happen."

Walking out to the field, I hear the rhythmic cadences of a workout. There's a lineup of fifteen pitchers behind the mound. They're told there's a runner on second and the batter is about to bunt. The pitcher has to field the ball cleanly, check the runner back to second, and throw out the batter. The pitcher throws a fastball to the catcher, and pitching coach Ken Westray rolls another ball back to the mound. The pitcher pounces on it; the catcher yells, "Check two. Throw to one." The pitcher looks the imaginary runner back to second base and throws over to first in time to get the invisible batter. There's lots of enthusiastic chatter and personalized encouragement as the pitching staff rotates through the workout one by one. Nicknames are always used. "Way to go, Fordie" (Brian Ford). "Atta boy, Cow" (Kyle Kawabata).

Fundamentals. They're stressed over and over. Next, it's the grounder to the right side. The pitcher throws a strike. Westray hits a ball to the right side. The first baseman fields it while the pitcher races over to cover the bag. Once in a while, the pitcher is in a better position to field the grounder. He screams, "I got it, I got it!" loud enough to hear in Albany. The first baseman puts on the brakes and returns to cover the bag. "Way to go!" shouts Westray. "Way to *communicate* out there!"

Fundamentals. Workout after workout. Day after day. This stuff has got to become reflexive. If you have to stop and think, you won't make the play.

A day after I watch the Batavia workout, I see a rookie pitcher on the Toronto Blue Jays blow the very same play. Edwin Hurtado has just been promoted from AAA Syracuse. He's been pitching well in his first look at major league hitters. But today a ball is hit to the right side with a runner on first. First baseman John Olerud fields the ball and throws to second for the force. The second baseman pivots to complete the double play but has to eat the ball. Hurtado has forgotten to cover first. He's standing several feet off the mound in front of 40,000 fans watching his infielders instead of being one. He looks embarrassed and frustrated with himself. He literally hits himself on the head with his glove in a universally understood "What's wrong with you!" gesture. Robbie Alomar has to call time and come over to calm Hurtado down. Fundamentals.

Chang Yang Choi is a rarity: a Korean in American baseball. His father also played professional baseball, but he never saw the lights of downtown Batavia. This is Chang Yang's first American season, and he's still a stranger in a strange land.

"He's doing real well," Julia Rogers tells me. "When he first got here he was very shy and uncertain. But we're fortunate. There's a small Korean community in Batavia. Several of our doctors and their wives are from Korea, and they sort of adopted him and helped him get acclimated. Once a month these people meet with other Koreans out of Buffalo and Rochester and they have a huge meal. The men sit down and discuss business and medicine, and the women cook. Very traditional roles.

"These meetings solved one of Chang's biggest problems. They provided him with food. He really didn't like American food. He wasn't used to the kind

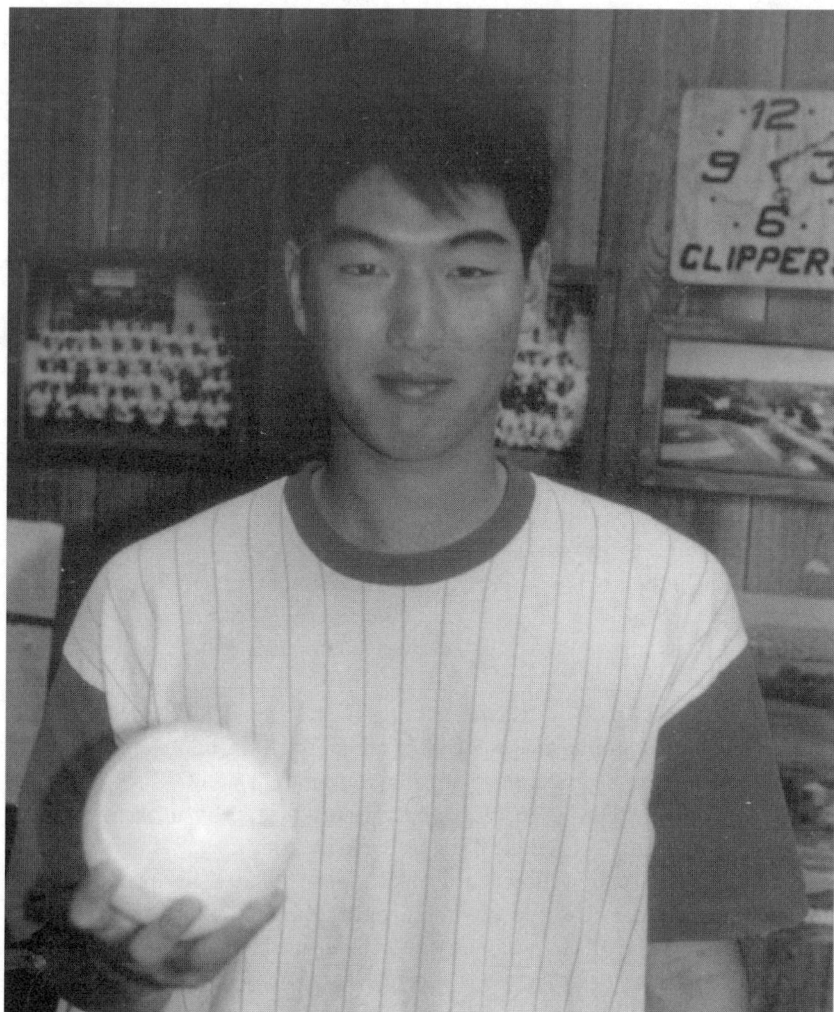

Chang Yang Choi.

of fast food that ball players eat. He just couldn't handle the hamburgers and greasy fries that are a way of life around here. Even deli meats didn't appeal to him. He seems to like seafood; I guess it reminds him of what he had back home. When I saw him during spring training in Florida he was OK because of all the seafood down there. That's all he would eat. Up here, it's been a problem for him. There isn't as much seafood available and, as he says, 'Cost lots.'

"There's also additional pressure on him that comes directly from his background. According to Korean culture, Chang Yang is the oldest child, so he's expected to provide for his family. He's chosen baseball, and it's expected that he will succeed at it. That means bringing his family over here, supporting his parents, and putting his brothers and sisters through American schools. If they want to stay in Korea, then he'll support them there."

For now, Chang Yang is just trying to get along.

"He's beginning to learn enough English to feel comfortable speaking. He's just like any foreign exchange student. He's got all the usual problems, on top of trying to refine his baseball skills and become a big league player."

Things got off to a slow start when Choi hurt his arm. He was worked slowly back into the pitching rotation. Prior to my visit, Choi had only started two games and pitched a total of four and two thirds innings. He was still not healed, and opponents were hitting him pretty well. His ERA was nearly 8.00.

Then things took a turn for the better. While his adopted hometown cheered him on, Chang Yang pitched six innings of no-hit ball against the Hudson Valley Renegades. Being cautious with his tender arm, the Phillies kept Choi on a strict pitch count and pulled him after the sixth inning. He departed a scoreless game to enthusiastic applause. Using body language and what broadcaster Vin Scully has called "pitchin' English," Skipper Al LeBoeuf did everything he could to say, "Good job!" The message seemed to get through. Chang Yang was hot and tired, but he was smiling as he left the field for the clubhouse.

He was relieved by Kyle Kawabata in the seventh. I talked to Kawabata earlier in the day, and he told me that if anybody from this team had a real chance to make it to The Show sooner than expected, it was Chang Yang.

"He's got some wicked stuff," Kawabata assured me. "He can sure get guys out in this league, and I think he'll succeed even higher up."

Unfortunately, tonight Kawabata's skill doesn't match his predecessor's. Taking the mound in the top of the seventh, Kawabata hits the first man he faces. Then he gives up a home run to the second. Choi has barely begun his shower and his perfect game is already lost. Worse yet, the Clippers are down 2–0.

This is the third season in a row I've seen Bo Hamilton. On two previous occasions we've run into each other when he pitched for Martinsville, in the Appalachian League. This is his first season with Batavia, and he's finally starting to fulfill the promise that led the Phillies to sign him as their eighth round pick in the 1993 draft.

Bo has a 5–1 record, with a stellar 2.19 ERA. Opposing batters are hitting a meager .210 against him.

"I'm healthy. I feel good. It makes all the difference in the world," he says,

Bo Hamilton (right) performs unlicensed physiotherapy on teammate Anthony Shumaker.

smiling. "I've also developed another pitch. I'm not just trying to throw everything by everyone I face. I'm becoming a pitcher."

Bo seems to be having fun. The truth is, he always seems to be enjoying himself, even when he isn't thriving professionally. I remind him that the last time we talked was in the bullpen in Burlington, North Carolina.

"That was the night the horse crapped on the field," I add, in case it's still a bit fuzzy.

"Oh yeah! Right over by first base, right?"

"Yeah, that's the horse," I confirm. Just how many horses has Bo seen in his baseball career?

We talk about the game I've just seen in Buffalo, and Bo asks if I visited with Jason Grimsley. Grimsley is a couple of years older than Bo, although both came up through the Phillies system.

"You know, it's really strange," he says. "Jason and I live about ten minutes apart back in Texas. Now we come all the way up here this far from home, and we're thirty minutes apart again. But we never get to see each other. We're in different leagues, and we're traveling to different places all the time. I guess we'll have to wait until we get back home.

"How'd he pitch the last time?" Bo wonders.

I tell him, "Typical Jason game. In the first inning he walked a couple of guys, gave up a bunch of hits, hit some batters, gave up some runs. Then he settled down and pitched a hell of a game."

"Yeah, that's Jason," Bo says. "You saw the right guy."

Chris Gambs is not a happy camper. Drafted in the second round in 1991, Gambs was once considered a top prospect in the Giants organization. Nevertheless, he was left unprotected after the 1994 season and claimed by the Phillies in the Rule V draft from AA Shreveport. Now he finds himself languishing in Batavia in a league that represents a considerable demotion.

"I just couldn't believe I was drafted by the Phillies. First I was in shock. Then I thought, OK, maybe some good will come of it. They must really want me. This is an opportunity to succeed in a new organization. I tried to develop a positive attitude about it. But now, I don't know what to think."

We're having this pregame talk under some rather symbolic conditions. I'm sitting on the grass in the Batavia bullpen in left field. Chris is sitting on the other side of the outfield fence, looking in at me and his teammates. Here's this guy who feels excluded from his team, and we're having our conversation through a chain link fence, with him on the outside.

"Why are you sitting out there?" I ask him.

"I'm supposed to retrieve any balls that get loose or get hit out."

I say nothing, but I'm thinking, This sounds like work for a local kid, not a Rule V draft pick.

"I've got to find out what's going on here," he tells me. "I haven't pitched in over a week. I'm not getting any innings. I feel like I keep getting passed over. My last start went great. No one got a hit off me. You'd think that would count for something. Instead, I'm transferred to the bullpen. Now I'm not even pitching. This is driving me nuts. I feel like I'm in the doghouse, and I don't even know what I did."

But there's a complication, and Gambs knows it.

"This is a bad time to ask. We've been losing a lot. You don't want to go to your manager when he's trying to deal with a losing streak. Maybe I'll talk to our pitching coach. Something's got to happen. I feel like I deserve better than this. I really do."

It's hard not to agree with him, even though his numbers are short of stellar. To date, Gambs has pitched thirty-four innings with a 5.50 ERA. He's struck out twenty-one and walked twenty-two. While far from great, these numbers are not substantially different from his career record. The Phillies had those numbers in front of them when they drafted Gambs, so disappointment and surprise seem a curious response to his performance.

"I've got to decide what to do with my life. If I'm not going to make it in this career, then I want to get on with things. I want to give baseball every chance, but if it's not going to happen for me, then I want to move on. One of the reasons I'm hanging on is I know it was very important to my father. [Chris's father, Craig, played for Kansas City in the mid-sixties.] He died last year. I owe this effort to him. I don't want to quit too soon. But I've got to find out where I stand. I can't go on like this."

This is Chuck Cox's first season in professional baseball, and he's been struggling. At least it looks that way if you check his numbers. If you talk to him, however, you find a surprising patience and maturity.

"I've been working on my defense. I'm putting a lot of time into learning how to be a good catcher. I can't do everything at once. If that means my batting average is going to suffer for a while, then I'll have to let it."

It is suffering. When I meet Cox, he is hitting .164, and he's struck out in almost a third of his plate appearances. A lot of guys would be going crazy, which, arguably, wouldn't do a lot for their batting average. But this thirty-fifth round draft pick from Pasadena, Texas, sees things differently.

"I'm trying to take some pressure off myself so I can relax and learn. That's what I'm here to do. I know I'm not hitting .310 like [second round draft pick] Marlon Anderson. But the fact that Marlon is hitting well means I can relax a bit. I don't have to carry the team."

Cox credits Blake Doolin, a pitcher in the Phillies organization, with helping to shape his attitude.

"Blake has been great for me. He's a bit older than me. He's been a really positive role model. This ability to take things in stride and not panic at the first sign of adversity. These are attitudes that I've gotten from talking to him. He's a pitcher and I'm a catcher, but we're up against similar pressures and demands. All you can do is your best.

"One thing I'm thankful for. I was drafted in the thirty-fifth round. I know that's not a high pick, but I *was* drafted. That means a lot, and it goes beyond an ego or money thing. A year earlier, at the end of my junior year in college, both the Phillies and the Pirates wanted to sign me as a free agent. A lot of people were telling me to grab it while it was offered. But I felt like I could do better. I knew it was a risk to turn them both down, but I went back to school and played another year. And it paid off. I was drafted by the Phillies this June.

"Some people think it's just the money. Yeah, it's true that I got more money than I would have as a free agent. But what's more important is that as a draft pick, the Phillies have a bit more investment in me. Maybe they'll give me a longer look. I'd be afraid that as a free agent, they wouldn't be as likely to ride

Chuck Cox.

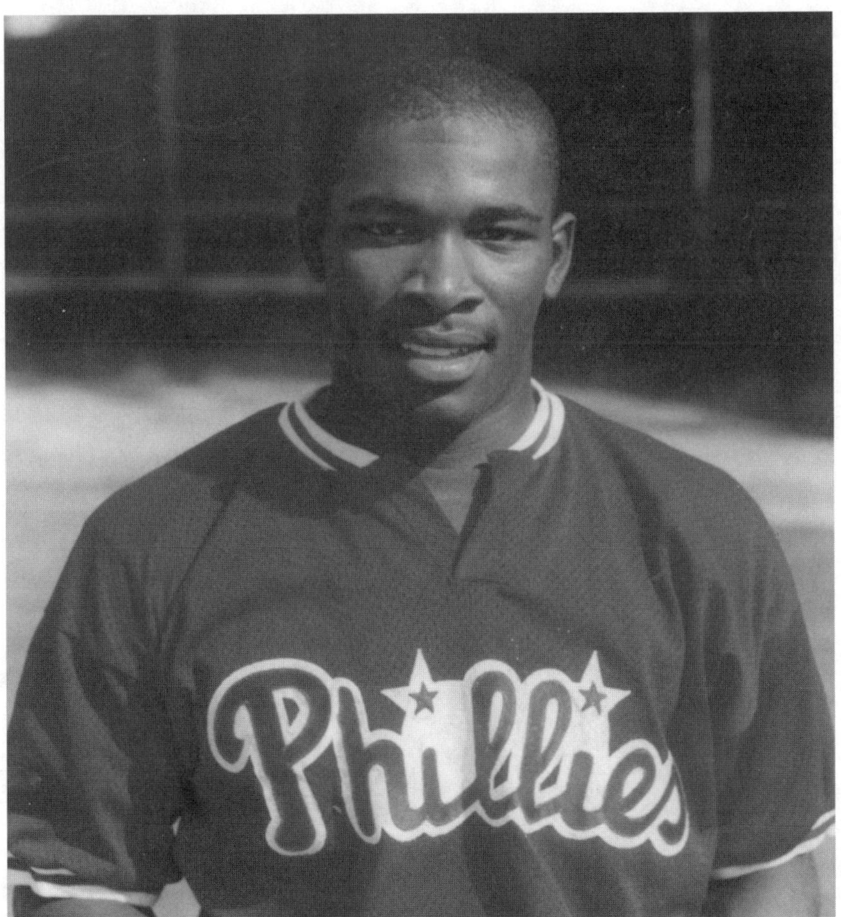

Marlon Anderson.

out a slump with me. I'd just be gone. The more they have invested, the more likely they are to let me develop. I'm going to need that time, and I'm glad that by holding out for another year I'm more likely to get it.

"I really hate the emphasis that people put on money. Even my friends. They had a farewell party for me before I left home. Some of them were saying, 'Boy, you're going to make a fortune now.' They even thought I was going to get rich playing here. Can you believe that? I'll probably end up *losing* money during this season. Could you get along on this kind of meal money? But who cares? This is an important experience, and I'm here to learn everything I can. A reporter from my hometown did an interview with me and

John Cornelius: matinee-idol looks but a game-ending strikeout.

asked me how much I signed for. The truth is, that offended me. I wouldn't ask him how much he got paid for doing the story."

Chuck Cox was hitless that night. But he was working hard behind the plate, trying to incorporate what he's being taught in his first season. At least he can say that this early in his pro career, he got to catch six innings of no-hit ball by a Korean guy who may turn out to be a star.

I spend the bottom of the ninth inning in the stands sitting with Julia Rogers and John Smith, whose son Justin pitches for the Clippers. Smith lives with his family just outside of Rochester, about forty minutes away. John, a former pitcher in the Mets organization, gets to see his son play on a regular basis. He's finding the present Batavia losing streak pretty tough to take.

Julia is cheering loudly and emotionally for the team, the very antithesis of a frosty or detached general manager. She's plainly living and dying with this team, which means the past two weeks have been cruel. The three of us are watching the team lose their tenth straight in typical heartbreaking fashion. The tying run is on third, the winning run on second in the bottom of the ninth. John Cornelius, the team's leading RBI man, comes up with two outs and strikes out. Batavia loses 3–2. Julia slumps forward with her head in her hands. Then she gets up and walks away without a word. The elder Smith and I look at each other and shake our heads.

"When you're going bad, that's about what you can expect," he says. And of course, he's right. What's more, he's seen it both as a player and, this season, as a parent.

I leave Dwyer Stadium and head for my car. I arrived earlier than most folks so I got a prime parking spot, nestled under a tree away from the heat. There's a blue Ford Escort with Maine license plates parked next to me. The back window has been smashed. There, on the back shelf, framed by about five pounds of broken glass, is a brand new New York–Penn League baseball. It's made one journey in its brief professional life: from the hand of Chang Yang Choi toward his catcher, Chuck Cox, at which point its path was interrupted by the bat of a Renegades player, who fouled it off over the stadium roof, where it came to rest on the rear window shelf of a Ford Escort, having first penetrated a pane of auto glass.

Like me, the owner of this Ford knew enough to face his windshield *away* from home plate. But that's where his luck ended. Because he parked approximately two feet to the right of my car, he'll be spending some of his vacation time tomorrow talking to the local Ford dealership. At least the local kids have shown some class. In their tireless search to gather every foul ball in sight, they've chosen not to remove this one from the Ford. It's a hard-earned souvenir for the family from Maine.

Jamestown, New York

"I can barely tell you who the managers are today, but back then it was Stubby Overmeier."
—Greg Peterson, Jamestown historian/fan

Nobody seems to know exactly what a Jammer is, but these fierce-looking little animals appear to live in Jamestown and work in the New York–Penn League. Actually, they're fairly new residents of this lovely town, nestled on the shore of Chautauqua Lake in mountainous western New York.

Until fairly recently, the Expos held fort in Jamestown. Their seventeen-year marriage to the town is quite long by minor league standards. When they departed for Vermont after the 1993 season, the Rich family, who also own the thriving Buffalo AAA franchise, lured the Tigers affiliate from their substandard facility in Niagara Falls to College Stadium in Jamestown. Everybody, from the players to the townsfolk, seems happy with the move.

Jamestown seems to be lost in a time warp. The architecture, indeed the ambience, come from another decade. Admittedly, the local kids, with their skateboards and baggy shirts, are rooted in the nineties, but they seem out of time, zipping down cobblestone streets or past the Jamestown Rubber Stamp Company. Rubber stamps! It's hard to imagine anyone selling them in an era of computer graphics. In all likelihood, this Jamestown business dates back fifty years and now sells laptop computers and fax equipment, yet their sign to the public is still Rubber Stamps. And it seems not at all out of character.

Baseball is not the only attraction in Jamestown. This is resort country, rich in fishing and camping sites. Music and art festivals abound, and the idyllic Roger Tory Peterson Institute, devoted to the contemplation of natural beauty, is located in the hills just behind the ballpark on Curtis Street. It's hard to imagine that the same little town gave birth to Peterson, Lucille Ball, and the Jammers.

Greg Peterson is a lawyer. We're sitting in the covered stands, out of the hot sunshine, four hours before game time. The sounds of batting practice fill the air while I talk to this very dignified-looking man in a suit and tie. Greg begins by outlining the history of Jamestown baseball. Professional and semipro teams have played in this area since the nineteenth century. Jamestown takes its baseball seriously. But until recently, no one has taken its history very seriously.

"We've started writing a book on the history of pro baseball in Jamestown. It goes all the way back to the 1890s. There was a New York and Pennsylvania league back then, and Jamestown won the championship the first year they played in the league. In fact, the Jamestown first baseman back in 1890 was R. A. Kelly. He was a black man, which made both him and the town rather exceptional."

Peterson goes on to confirm that Jamestown deserves its footnote in the history of black baseball.

"The town of Celoron, right outside of Jamestown, hosted the last all-black team in organized baseball. These were the days when traveling black teams would play local white teams. We had a team here called the Acme Black Giants. They were described in the local paper as the Celoron Chocolates. The town had a large amusement park in those days, and the black baseball team was considered part of the local entertainment.

"They were awful," Peterson tells me, dashing any romantic visions of dazzling Negro League All-Stars. "When they finally folded for lack of attendance and lack of success, they probably had a .200 winning percentage."

Jamestown was a charter member of the New York–Penn League when it started back in 1939. Peterson explains, "The team originally played in Celoron, but the field was terrible and the attendance was pretty bad. So the Pittsburgh Pirates bought the team and moved it to Niagara Falls. That lasted one season, and the team was moved back to Jamestown after 1940. The stadium we're sitting in right now was built to entice the team back here for the 1941 season. It's a good thing it was built when it was. The Second World War started in December of that year, and I doubt construction projects like this would have happened once the war began. So we got this stadium at the last possible moment."

It's obvious that the slick facility we're sitting in wasn't built in early 1941. Indeed, Peterson confirms that $2 million in renovations were made in the mid-1980s. On top of that, another $450,000 was spent more recently to meet league standards.

"You can still see where the original scoreboard was," Peterson says, pointing out to center field. But the seats we're sitting in and the roof over our heads are all decidedly modern.

Peterson tells me he's been digging through the archives to find the history of local baseball.

"Actually, when I say archives, I mean a lot of attics in local homes. Once we got word out that we were looking for historical material, people started calling us. They bring us pictures and home movies. We've got photos of Nellie Fox during his first year of pro baseball. He was playing center field here in 1944, back before he was a second baseman.

"We've also found two 8 mm color movies taken here in 1941, the first year the stadium was opened. Unbelievable!"

Peterson is really excited by these discoveries. There is a very enthusiastic little kid buried inside the suit and tie, and he seems to be coming up for air.

"I grew up here. I came to this ballpark when I was a kid in the early sixties with my grandfather. I used to keep score. If you keep score, you tend to get very involved. You remember names. I can recall Jim Rooker, Johnny Eisen, the guys who played in 1962. I can barely tell you who the managers are today, but back then it was Stubby Overmeier.

"I've been a member of the Society of American Baseball Research for several years, and up to now I've been very passive about it. Now I feel a sense of urgency. I've gotten intrigued about oral history. When we had our fiftieth anniversary of pro ball here, I thought, This is it. We'd better start talking to these guys while they're still around. It became an obsession with me: have Camcorder, will travel."

Peterson invites me to join him at the Chautauqua Institute tomorrow for a course called "Baseball in America's Culture."

"It should be great," he assures me. "There's a couple of authors in it, a couple of guys from the *New York Times* who are vacationing in Chautauqua, some corporate guys. We're all obsessed," he says, smiling. "Just like you."

"I'm on automatic pilot doing this work," he continues. "It takes very little encouragement to keep me going. I'm meeting some very interesting people, some old heroes. Occasionally I get an autographed baseball. That's enough to keep me hooked."

"Last month I attended an old-timers game, and afterward I got to sit down with Harmon Killebrew, Juan Marachal, Luis Aparicio . . . Shoot! Me sitting down with those guys! Far as I'm concerned, that's dying and going to heaven. I'm still an awestruck fourteen year old. Doesn't matter how old I am or what I've accomplished. I can still be overwhelmed in the presence of a major league baseball player."

Then he adds, "I'm not sure I'd feel all that with today's players. It's the old-timers. I'm time-warped into the fifties and sixties. Those are the guys who do me in. I just wish I still had my baseball cards."

Peterson and I start talking about our old baseball cards. We laugh at how we were likely to flip superstars or trade them for "common" players, without regard to financial values. I'm groping for the name of an everyday Yankees player, a "common" to compare to Mickey Mantle, and I come up with Irv Noren. I doubt I've even thought of Noren's name in thirty years, but somehow it pops into my head while I'm searching for a nonsuperstar in pinstripes. Peterson looks oddly at me and says, "Funny you should mention Irv Noren. He's not exactly a household name. Did you know he was born in Jamestown?"

I didn't.

Mike Ferguson is in charge of public relations for the Jammers. He is pleased about how well the local fans have accepted their new team after a long association with the Expos.

"It's amazing. They've turned right into Jamestown Jammers fans. Part of it is all the hype. The Rich family organization really got behind this new franchise. There was lots of publicity. 'The Buffalo Bisons present the Jamestown Jammers.' That new logo was really out there for everyone to see. Mike Billoni of the Rich organization really deserves credit. He was one of the first to simply say, 'We're not going to use the parent club's name and colors. We're not going to simply be the Buffalo Pirates or Indians. We're going to have our own identity and our own logo. And we're going to market it ourselves.' All those years the Expos were here, the team logo was just the Montreal M. Now we've got the Jammer, and team merchandise sells like crazy. We had somebody write us from Japan yesterday, saying he wanted to join the Jammers Booster Club. They had seen the logo, and they wanted to be part of it. We've had exchange students from England, France, Italy, Germany in Jamestown before, and we send them away with a T-shirt. They'll take it home and wear it. That's the way your reputation spreads."

Ferguson is evangelical about the role of minor league baseball.

"I want to hook the kids in the audience. I want them to turn into baseball players, or fans, or guys like you and Greg Peterson. To do that, this game has got to be a peak experience in their lives. But the reality is, I can't keep them interested for nine innings. They just don't have the attention span. That's where the rest of the circus comes in. The entertainment, the promotions.

"It's really wonderful at this level. I look at these local kids. They are absolutely in awe of everything. Not just the players, but even the mascot. They are in awe of J. J. Jammer, something we just created. I look at him and I see a uniform with a fifteen-year-old kid inside making five bucks an hour. But the local kids follow him around with their mouths open. They believe in the magic. I think the minor leagues have a special responsibility. Major league ball seems to have given up. They either don't care about or have lost the ability to inspire the true magic of baseball in the next generation. Down at this level, we're still doing it. In a sense, we're the ones who can save the game. These kids still climb over the fence. We actually leave the center field gate cracked open just a little bit so you can spot the kids hanging out.

"I don't come to baseball from a corporate standpoint. I come at it trying to provide the dream for kids. I keep my own family in mind. I've got four kids, including a brand new baby. I want them to have fun when they come here. If everybody on our staff has that attitude and does their job, we'll get where we want to be. The financial stuff will fall in place.

"I was a morning DJ here in town. I got the job because the owners of the team spotted me and said, 'He's just as crazy as we are.' I gave up the radio work. I was going to be the next Rush Limbaugh or Howard Stern. Now I'm arranging apple pie promotions for the local minor league team."

Ferguson is willing to take some risks as far as promotions are concerned.

"The other night we had a promotion that's never been done before. We had eighteen hot air balloons. We called it Sky Jam. Right after the game, we inflated all eighteen balloons. We turned out the lights and they did what balloonists call a nightglow. The flame goes up into the balloon, and they turn into these beautiful Chinese lanterns. The only problem is, when you get eighteen hot air balloons on a baseball field, it fills up real quick. When they weren't inflated, it looked like we'd have lots of room. We just didn't anticipate how big they were. I mean, they're six stories tall! They inflate to two stories wide. We had this one balloon that was scheduled to be on the dugout. It ended up filling up the backstop and went into the press box. We were out there on the field trying to pull this hot air balloon away from the grandstand. We were fortunate there was no breeze. If we had the kind of weather we're having today, it's hard to tell what might have happened."

Despite all this enthusiasm, Ferguson is somewhat pessimistic about the attitude of today's players.

"When our team first got here, the Jamestown Chamber of Commerce had a lunch for them. One of the first things we told them was 'You have an opportunity to change the way people see professional baseball players. Instead of being aloof millionaires, take the time to sign the autograph. If the community asks you to come down to the local carwash and talk to kids, do it.'"

I'm surprised that Ferguson believes that these players need to be convinced to sign autographs and mingle. Won't they naturally enjoy the grassroots experience?

"I'm not so sure," he tells me. "I think kids coming out of high school or college today see the Barry Bonds, the huge salaries, the arrogance. They don't

Rivers Mitchell enjoying a pregame dog.

see nine baseball players, they see nine millionaires. So they're a little more distant. A little less likely to dive for a ball and hurt their bodies and their earning potential."

Ferguson is right about one thing. This is a good time to learn humility. The fact that these guys are making $800 a month, eating hot dogs or Doritos for dinner, will surely help.

It's about 6 P.M., an hour before game time. Players from the Jammers as well as the visiting Utica team are wandering around the concession stands, mingling with the fans, buying their hot dogs and Doritos for dinner. Still wearing their batting practice jerseys, they line up for fries and Slush Puppies along with the locals. There is no distance or pretension here. Uniforms and signing bonuses seem beside the point. Hot dogs and fries have brought these folks together. Barely an hour after this easy mingling, these same players will be on the field performing.

Ty Norman, an outfielder for the Utica Blue Sox, is a bit short of the price of his meal. He shouts over to one of his teammates: "Hey, you got a quarter?" Instantly, a dozen hands belonging to local fans are extending coins to him. His teammate gets there first, and Norman thanks the locals, who nod and slip the change back into their pockets and go on about their business. Several hours later, Ty Norman hits a home run against the Jammers. The same fans who groan in disappointment at Norman's power were more than willing to help fuel it during dinnertime.

College Stadium in Jamestown has a concession called the Arcade. It features the latest in video games, along with a surprisingly well-equipped sports card store. I'm browsing the baseball section, and there, nestled among the superstar display, is a 1989 Topps card of Bruce Fields. Bruce who? By any reckoning, Fields in his Mariners uniform qualifies as a "common," worth at most five cents. But here, Fields's card sells for a dollar.

Bruce Fields is the Jammers' manager. He laughs at the fact that his card is selling for a dollar.

"I thought it was pretty much in the penny range," he tells me.

I suggest that everybody has a neighborhood where his card is worth a buck or so.

"Griffey's neighborhood is a lot bigger than mine," he observes wryly.

The Jammers' program features a full-page photo of Bruce Fields with a brief quote superimposed: "I played in the minor leagues a long, long time . . . You learn to be patient all those years, and maybe you learn how to pass it along."

J. J. Jammer is easily the scariest mascot I have seen. The designers have attempted to combine scary and cute. They don't mix well. This face is mostly scary. When Mike Ferguson talks about local kids being in awe of the mascot, I'm wondering if maybe they're not a little bit terrified. He's even giving me the creeps, and I *know* there's a fifteen-year-old kid inside the costume.

One of the staff interns confides to me that during a visit to a Walmart yesterday, the mascot had eleven different kids in tears. It'll be interesting to see if J. J.'s face gets toned down over the next season. That'll be a lot of T-shirts to redesign. Yet, you don't want the same kids who believe in magic to

Emily Sweet meets J. J. Jammer.

be afraid to come out to the ballpark because there's a monster prowling the grandstand.

Despite everybody's best efforts, attendance tonight is unexpectedly poor. Mike Ferguson, who has invested more effort than most at getting folks to come out, is understandably annoyed. He paces around the press box for a few innings, grumbling to anybody who'll listen. Finally, he can take it no more. He strides down to the radio booth and goes on the air, using his broadcasting expertise to chastise the local fans. This is the audience he wants to reach. They care about the Jammers enough to listen, and they're plainly not at the ballpark. With all the tact he can muster, he reams them out. Maybe he uses too much tact, because he's still pissed off when he gets off the air.

"I mean, hell, we're in the middle of a pennant race. This is a beautiful Tuesday night. If this is all the support Jamestown fans can show, they're going to end up with American Legion baseball here.

"Last week Pittsfield had a home game, and there was a last-minute scheduling conflict. The game had to be moved to a local high school field. I heard they *still* drew about three thousand fans. Back here, everybody knew about tonight's game in advance. The team is doing well. And this is the crowd we get." He gestures to rows of empty seats. "What kind of support is this?"

Ferguson is still fuming when he leaves the press box. I walk out on to the stadium roof above the grandstand. It is a lovely night, and the whole field is spread out before me. The crowd has just been announced at 658. I look out at the stands and do a quick count. I can't even see 300 fans.

Not only does Jamestown broadcast its games, but it has a color man. Two broadcasters is a luxury by New York–Penn League standards.

Actually, Bernie Walsh is not your average color man.

"I grew up in Long Island, New York. I was a Giants fan. I used to go to the Polo Grounds. To this day, I still have a soft spot for the Giants, even though they betrayed their fans back in '58. I still remember the day they left.

"I retired from the FBI last November. I had been with the Bureau for twenty-six years, and I became eligible for retirement when I turned fifty. I loved the job, but I had also had enough of it.

"I was transferred to Buffalo in the early eighties. When I had the opportunity to buy season tickets behind home plate for Bisons games, I jumped at it. I could never do that as a kid living in New York. That's how I discovered minor league baseball. I got totally caught up with the team. I lived and died with the Bisons. Then I started going to minor league games wherever I could find them. Whenever I had to do any traveling, either for my job or a vacation, I always checked for minor league baseball. If there was a team nearby and it was summer, I was there. Everything from Salt Lake City to Welland, Ontario. I've been through about all of the New York–Penn League.

"What I really love best about the minors is the intimacy. You're closer to the game while it's being played, and you actually get to hang out with the players. These guys will talk to you."

Like Greg Peterson earlier in the day, Bernie Walsh seems to be undergoing an age regression.

"I find it incredible that I can just hang around and listen to real baseball players talk to each other. I listen closely to the conversations like I'm expecting to hear some kind of life secrets revealed. Can you imagine, waiting for wisdom in a talk between two nineteen year olds? But I'm finally getting to hear these magic conversations that we all wondered about as kids.

"I fully believed when I was fourteen that I would grow up to be a professional athlete. My level of skill peaked pretty early, so I learned to do other things. But I'm still living that dream when I do this broadcasting. It brings it all back for me. Even as a kid, I used to pretend to broadcast games from my bedroom. My parents used to hear me sometimes and come upstairs to make sure I was all right. Maybe those years of broadcasting from my bedroom helped prepare me for this. Anyway, I can tell you, doing color on the radio like this is a lot of fun. I just love it. Sometimes I sit up here and I think, I can't believe I'm actually here. I'm actually *doing* this."

Erie, Pennsylvania

"When the opposing players start acting like tourists in a visiting park, you know you must be doing something right."
—Bruce Hetrick, Erie PR director

Erie, Pennsylvania, is celebrating its two hundredth anniversary. There are bicentennial signs and festivals galore, which don't quite mask the fact that this city is suffering from an advanced case of urban blight. About a quarter of a million people live here, which, along with another hundred thousand in surrounding areas, is an extraordinary fan base for a single-A team. That's the good news. The bad news is that no one is going to confuse Erie with a boomtown.

To their credit, the town has located its new stadium smack dab in the middle of the downtown area. Bruce Hetrick, the SeaWolves public relations director, admits, "There was originally talk of building the ballpark on the Lakefront. That would *really* have been a showpiece. But the present site was already owned by the city. It was hard to argue with that."

Unlike most stadiums in the New York–Penn League, there's hardly a tree to be seen from home plate. You hit one out of here, and you risk breaking a window in an old office building or a rundown residence. There's no foliage to cushion the blow in Erie.

But forget the city and the location. This stadium is beautiful. In fact, it outclasses most of the surrounding architecture, as well as most ballparks in the New York–Penn League.

"We know we're a bit advanced for this league," admits Hetrick. "But you never know what the future holds. So we decided to aim high and do it right."

Hetrick, who has lived all his life in or around Erie, believes there will be considerable spinoff from having this fancy new stadium in the heart of downtown.

"There'll be some very real effects. Even in the brief time

since we announced the park, I can see signs of revitalization. People are redecorating. New businesses are opening. I wouldn't be surprised to see the inner city start to come back. And this ballpark will have had a lot to do with it."

Despite the best-laid plans, the stadium was barely open in time for the 1995 season.

"We were still applying the last coat of paint when opening day arrived. We didn't even have the phones working. It was a circus here for the first few days. But it's been worth it. We've been drawing incredible crowds since we opened. It's not uncommon to get four or five thousand people.

"I was picking up some of our players at the airport. Chad Hermansen and Garrett Long, our number one and number two draft picks, had just been promoted from the Gulf Coast League. So they asked me how many fans we drew. I asked them what they were used to. They said, 'In the Gulf Coast League, maybe forty or fifty a game.' I said, 'Well, you'll be looking at maybe forty-five hundred a night here.' They just couldn't believe it. That's literally a hundred times what they're used to.

"We're having no trouble attracting fans. For years, Buffalo, which is just an hour and a half away, was a Pittsburgh farm team. So there are a lot of Pirates fans in the area. Plus we get calls from Pittsburgh itself. We just had a call yesterday from some disgruntled Pirates fans. They said, 'We're sick of big league egos. We're coming up this weekend. We want to see some kids who want to play ball.'

"Every day of the week, all hours, there's always people wandering in here. They just want to see the place. They come in, they look around, they find a seat, stare out at the outfield, look around at the stands, then they leave. It happens all the time.

"I'll tell you how impressive this place must be," Hetrick says, laughing. "We had some of the Pittsfield Mets come in this morning and go to the souvenir shop to buy T-shirts and caps with our logo on them! When the opposing players start acting like tourists in a visiting park, you must be doing something right."

Hetrick is walking me around the stadium, and we get to the luxury boxes. There are six of these self-contained universes. Each has been furnished differently, in a way that reflects the personality of the owner. The first suite belongs to a couple of orthodontists. Hetrick guesses they're in their early forties. They've turned their suite into an adolescent clubhouse. Baseball cards from the sixties and seventies line the walls. There are pennants on the wall, along with a vintage Ted Williams ad for Creamy Root Beer. And, of course, there's beer on tap. Are these orthodontists old enough to drink? What's for sure is that they can afford the ten-thousand-dollar yearly fee for the suite. Catering is extra.

The next box is owned by a local law firm. These guys seem to have made it past their adolescence. The furniture is staid, and the surroundings are more "dignified." Scotch and Chardonnay are probably the drinks of choice in this suite. If they run out of potato chips, they can go next door and borrow some from the teenagers.

It's 76 degrees at game time. It's turned into a lovely evening to see a ball game. The vendors add a touch of class, selling Matt Anthony red ale on draft. It's good to see local microbreweries infiltrating the evening baseball crowd. The governor of Pennsylvania has thrown out the first pitch, and now a team of local men, both black and white, who played ball in Erie during the last sixty years are being honored. The crowd is polite, but you can tell most of them have come to see the heroics of guys like eighteen-year-old Chad Hermansen, not a bunch of gray-haired, slow-moving men who played for teams their parents barely remember. Each of the old-timers is introduced to scattered applause, and then the SeaWolves take the field. They are introduced individually as they take their positions. The crowd response couldn't be more enthusiastic if these guys were in the World Series.

In the bottom of the second inning, a blood-curdling howl, "Ah ooooooooo," cuts through the crowd noise. "Now batting for your Erie SeaWolves. Number 45. Charles Rice!" At key moments throughout the evening the cry of the sea wolf echoes through the ballpark. It's become the acoustic signature of the team. The locals have grown used to it, but it's a pretty primal experience for neophytes like me. Presumably, this is the call of a sea wolf, although it's not clear that anyone really knows what one sounds like. Or, for that matter, what it is. Presumably, if one can invent an animal, one can also invent its voice. Still, I'm wondering where this howl comes from.

GM Erik Haag laughs at my question. "When we were setting up the sound system, they gave us a CD ROM full of various effects. One of them was labeled 'werewolf,' so we tried it. It was pretty scary, but we decided to use it a few times and see how it went over. The fans loved it, so we just kept it."

It still gives me the shudders, echoing through the ballpark. Every time they play it, along with the announcement "Your Erie SeaWolves," I keep hearing it as "Your *Eerie* SeaWolves." Both Haag and Bruce Hetrick get a chuckle out of this. It's never occurred to them before.

A moment later the werewolf howls again as third baseman Boomer Whipple is announced. Predictably, the crowd goes wild. Boomer is a very popular player. He's a thoroughly likable, sweet, open-faced kid who looks like a poster boy for the U.S. Heartland. Actually, Boomer comes from just outside

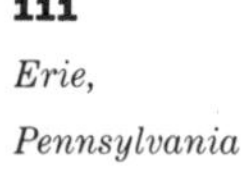

Boomer Whipple.

Chicago. The fans love him, and he returns the attention. He spends an inordinate amount of time talking to kids, signing autographs, just being friendly and available. When he comes to bat, they're in his corner.

Boomer is a pretty decent ball player. He is batting around .270, but more important, his on-base average is around .400. He knows how to walk; in fact, he leads the team with twenty-six bases-on-balls. Sitting around talking to Charles Rice, who is slugging nearly .500, Boomer is taking a little good natured kidding about his tendency to walk.

"Yeah, I guess I do get quite a few walks," he tells me, almost apologetically.

"Don't you see it as a good thing?" I ask.

"Yeah, I guess so," he replies, far from convinced.

"You keep rallies going," I tell him. "Guys like Rice and José Guillen (an outfielder also slugging close to .500) get more out of those long home runs when you're on base. I promise you there's someone in the Pirates organization who's looking at your on-base average and seeing that you have an eye at the plate. You don't just go up there hacking. Those are good at bats."

"You really think so?" he asks. "I don't hear this a lot."

Ironically, Boomer also has twenty-six RBIs to go with his twenty-six walks. *That* he hears about. It ranks him second on the team. And he's not doing it with longball. He seems to have a bunch of well-timed base hits. One more reason the fans love him.

Around the fourth inning, Boomer gets eaten up at third base by a sharp ground ball, and the Pittsfield batter makes it to first. The play is scored an error. Boomer has his head down and is pounding his glove. Suddenly, a voice from the stands cuts through the background noise: "That's all right, Boomer. Don't worry about it. It's not going to matter."

As if on cue, the next batter grounds into a double play, ending the inning.

Chance Reynolds is another crowd favorite. Chance played for the Erie Sailors last season when the town had a team in the independent Frontier League.

"We played at Ainsworth Field, the same place the Sailors played the year before when they were in the New York–Penn League. The field was in pretty bad shape. It might be OK for high school teams, but you didn't really want to be playing pro games there.

"The Pirates signed me as a free agent after last season, and I just came back here to play. A lot of the fans who got to know me over at Ainsworth followed me here to the new park. I say hello to a lot of them before the game every night. It's like coming home."

About an hour before game time, I take a picture of Derrick Bullock in the clubhouse. He is relaxed looking, leaning against his locker.

"What would you like the caption to be?"

"I'm not sure," he replies. "Can I think about it?"

"Sure. Let me know before I go, if you can," I reply.

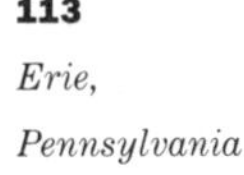

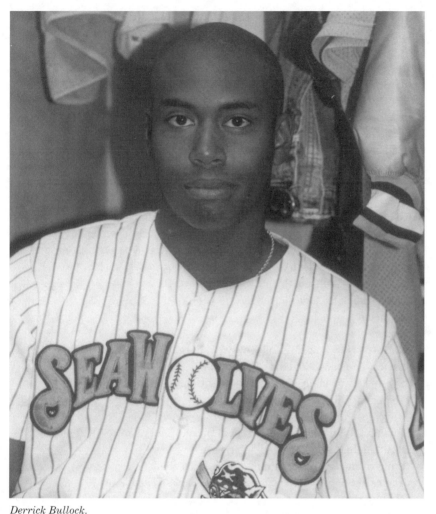

Derrick Bullock.

It turns out that this quiet, reflective man is tonight's starting pitcher. Going into the top of the ninth, he's still in there. Erie is ahead 6–0. Although Derrick Bullock has pitched a hell of a game, he's starting to get hit hard in the last couple of innings. Fortunately, these rockets have been right at somebody. His manager, Scott Little, is going to stay with Derrick as long as he can. He'd like him to experience his first complete game of the season. The young man from Nevada has a fine 1.81 ERA going into tonight, but this is plainly his shining hour. With a six-run lead, he's going to get every chance to finish the job himself.

And he does. At just under two hours, Bullock has a complete game shutout against the Pittsfield Mets. The TV crew rolls on to the field for a postgame interview. The pitcher is both exhausted and elated. He's wringing wet, yet trying to remain coherent. It's a mercifully short interview, and when it's over I walk over to shake his hand.

"Fine job," I tell him. For a moment he looks blankly at me, not sure who I am or what I want. So I add, "I think you just wrote the caption for the picture I took before."

It all comes back, and he nods and smiles. Then he heads off to the clubhouse for a much deserved shower.

I decide to look for the lone Canadian on the SeaWolves. I check out the bullpen, but pitcher Ryan Duffy is nowhere in sight. So I remember the axiom that most pitchers would rather hit than throw. And, sure enough, next to the batting cage is Ryan Duffy hitting grounders out to the infielders.

"So where is Wilksport?" I ask, walking over.

"Oh, it's up in Canada," he says.

"Yeah, but where?"

"Ontario."

I can see this isn't going to be easy. "Where in Ontario? What's it near?"

"Sarnia," he says. "You ever hear of that?"

"Sure," I say. Finally I've got his attention.

"You have? Where are you from?"

"I live near Guelph," I tell him.

"Guelph! My brother went to school there." Duffy has stopped hitting altogether. "Guelph! What are you doing here?"

"I'm writing a book about minor league baseball."

"You're kidding. What aspect of it? The parks? The history?"

"No, the people."

"Just Canadians?" he wonders.

"No. Although I usually make a point of checking in with them. Sometimes it's like a visit from home. We can talk about the economy or the CBC or the politicians."

"No thanks," he laughs. "Tell me about the Canadian guys you've met. I've probably played with some of them."

So I do, and the usual names come up. Andy Stewart and Todd Betts. Troy Fortin and Harry Muir. It turns out that Duffy seems to know all of them, one way or the other. It's like a secret fraternity. When the visiting team arrives, the Canadians find each other, probably using a secret "eh" detector. They catch up on each other's progress, who's making it, who's been promoted, and who's been released.

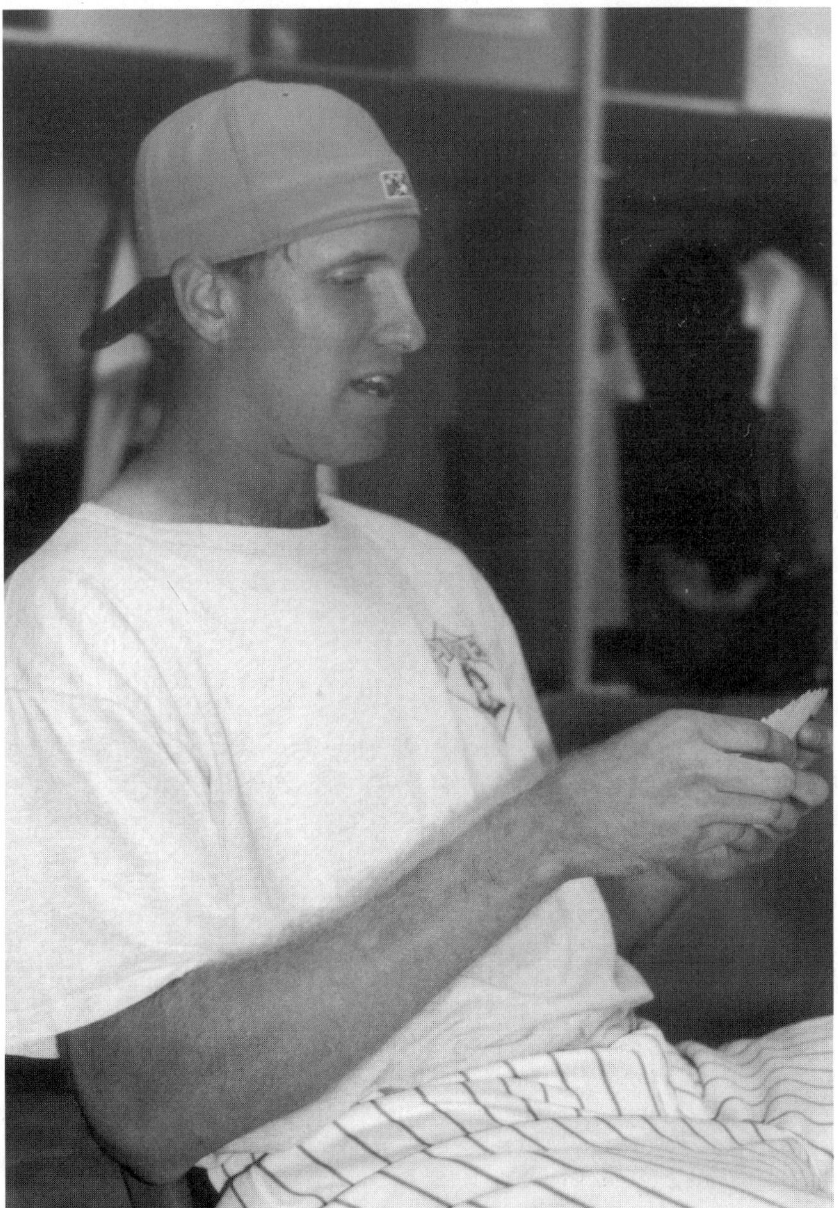

Ryan Duffy.

Duffy's teammates don't see him as a Canadian. He's a pitcher who talks a little funny sometimes. Or a guy who hits some infield practice. Back in the clubhouse, he's involved in a card game I can't begin to figure out. Four of these guys are engrossed in a game that I find as incomprehensible as cricket. I watch them for about fifteen minutes and finally give up. I'm half convinced this whole thing is a clubhouse prank: wait for somebody to watch, then make random moves, all the while pretending something real is going on.

I don't get to see Ryan pitch tonight. We say good-bye in the bullpen, and I promise to call his folks and fiancée when I get back home. Baseball has no shortage of generalizations about ethnic and national groups. Most of them are useless and borderline offensive. Nevertheless, it really strikes me that on a team stocked with exceptionally nice guys, Ryan Duffy still manages to stand out. I suppose if he were from Los Angeles I'd just assume it was *him*. But because he's Canadian, and I can hear all the regionalisms in his speech, I can't help but wonder how much of this conspicuous niceness reflects the national character?

About a week later, I speak to Ryan's father. If anything, this makes it even harder to dismiss thoughts about national character. Maybe it's a combination of being Canadian and coming from a small town. Wilksport has about five hundred people.

I talk with Ryan's fiancée, Sandy. I wonder if she's been to Erie to see where he plays.

"Oh, I can make the trip blindfolded," she says. "It's exactly four and a half hours from here. We're in touch all the time. We must own Bell Canada by now."

Is Sandy a big baseball fan?

"I am because of Ryan, but I didn't really care about it before. The truth is, I had no idea he even *played* baseball until his mother started showing me some pictures about three weeks after I met him. She took out this photo of Ryan playing for Team Canada. He never talked about it. To Ryan, that would be like bragging. And that's something you just don't do.

"I was shocked that he was a ball player. I had no idea. I remember thinking, What have I got myself into? But by then it was too late."

Sandy and Ryan are getting married in December.

"We both know the odds are against him making it. But we agree for now that he has to give it his best shot. It's important to stay healthy and play as well as he can. If he makes it, it'll be very exciting for us. If he doesn't, that'll be OK too. It's probably easier to prepare for failure than for success. Either way, I'll be with him."

Toledo, Ohio

"At this level guys don't care. The harder you throw it, the harder it's gonna come back at you."
—Tim Crabtree, Syracuse pitcher

Ever since television actor Jamie Farr wore his hometown baseball jersey on the set of *M*A*S*H* twenty years ago, Americans have been intrigued by the Toledo Mud Hens. Are they a real team? Do they still play? Did they only exist during the Korean War?

The answers are yes, yes, and no. The Mud Hens are very real, and they started playing long before Corporal Klinger and the Korean War. Although professional baseball in Toledo goes all the way back to 1883, the first Mud Hens team didn't appear until 1897. They were previously known as the Swamp Angels, and they played in Bay View Park, right next to a marshland. During ball games, spectators and players often noticed a flock of funny-looking birds that were identified, perhaps not too accurately, as mud hens. The Swamp Angels were ultimately renamed in their honor. During the next twenty years, the team's name changed several times, but by the time Casey Stengel made his Toledo managerial debut in 1927, the team was again known as the Mud Hens.

The Toledo team has another claim to fame. During the 1884 season, Toledo was part of the American Association, a forerunner of major league baseball. Their roster included two black ball players, brothers named Moses Fleetwood and Welday Wilberforce Walker. Technically speaking, Toledo broke the color line sixty-three years before the Brooklyn Dodgers did in 1947 with Jackie Robinson.

Toledo has always been a minor league city, and the Mud Hens have had rather promiscuous affiliations with major league teams. Such brief liaisons are not uncommon, and, although Toledo has been associated with five teams since

1965, their present relationship with Detroit is long-standing by minor league standards.

Fans all over the world, even those who barely remember *M*A*S*H,* now make casual reference to the Toledo Mud Hens. Being part of popular culture has resulted in a procession of nonlocal spectators every year and a healthy trade in souvenirs: everything from baseball cards and pennants, to jerseys like the one Jamie Farr wore some twenty years ago to get the whole thing started.

The decision to send Klinger a Mud Hens jersey back in 1978 was made by general manager Gene Cook. Cook was no stranger to baseball. Although he had no pro ball experience, Cook did play some outfield in the early fifties when he was in the army. This might not be noteworthy except for the guy who played beside Cook in center field. His name was Willie Mays.

It's hot as hell in Toledo. Plans for a refreshing late morning swim evaporate when I sample the pool and find it warmer than the air temperature.

"The thermostat's broken," the front desk tells me. "It's been heating continuously for a couple of days. The part's supposed to come in today, but nobody knows how long it'll take to cool the water back down."

I head off for lunch in an air-conditioned restaurant on the strip but find it only slightly more refreshing than the pool. The waitress is soaked in sweat and urges me to fill in the customer feedback card.

"I'll mail it for you," she says. "I don't mind about the stamp. If you leave it here, it'll never get through, especially if you complain."

At the next table I see members of the visiting team in their civvies. The one facing me is slightly older, a trainer or coach. I don't recognize his face. The guy with his back to me is a player: tanned and broad shouldered. He wears a cap that says "Hawaiian Winter Baseball League." One more place to go to speed up player development, to make baseball a twelve-months-a-year job.

Their conversation, which is mostly a monologue by the older guy, is masked by talk about sausages and blueberry pie from nearby tables. I'm trying unsuccessfully to eavesdrop. In a sudden lull I hear, "I don't think Greg Myers is such a bad catcher."

And then it's back to the sausage and pie serenade.

Minor league parks can sometimes be hard to find. But not in Toledo. *Everyone* seems to know where Ned Skeldon Stadium is. Once you get within several miles of the park, there are signs everywhere. "This way to the Mud

Hens"; "Mud Hens Park next right." They *want* you to find it. It's an attractive field, located right next door to the Ohio Baseball Hall of Fame.

Like all but the newest minor league parks, this one has a slightly funky side to it. The sign outside has seen better days. "Lucas County Recreation," it proclaims. "Mud Hens vs. Rochester 7 PM." But then the other shoe drops. "Toy Fair July 11. Baseball Card Show Sunday." Like many folks in Toledo, the stadium needs a second job just to make ends meet.

Inside the park, there are lots of friendly people. And there is no shortage of things to buy and people to sell them to you. The circus midway has become a rich part of the minor league persona, and Toledo is no exception. The stadium also exudes tradition. Pictures of Mud Hens teams of days gone by are proudly displayed. The famous and the obscure, all gone to their various rewards. One picture stands out: the aforementioned Casey Stengel, manager of the 1927 Toledo Mud Hens. There's the old perfessor himself, happily ensconced in Toledo while the Bambino was knocking down the fences in Yankee Stadium.

Once the game starts, the local traditions become apparent. As the Mud Hens take the field to rapt applause, the PA announcer chants, "Here come the flock!" The folks love it. There's lots of good-natured cheering, and things never seem to get too serious. The ushers have a pretty laissez-faire attitude about seating, and by the third inning there are kids everywhere, including the unoccupied field level box seats. People seem to like working here. A zany three-piece band entertains fans as they walk through the stadium interior on their way to seats or during a pit stop for a hot dog or beer.

If the sound and fury of minor league baseball become a bit too intense, there is always the Stadium Club. Located one level below the press box, directly over home plate, this "members only" facility is one of the most bizarre places to experience a ball game in the minor leagues. Ahead of you is a panoramic view of the field through a protective window. But there is no sound. Nothing. The attenuation is perfect. Not even the crack of the bat is audible.

The Stadium Club offers a sensational view of a ball game accompanied by an eerie silence: a wide screen baseball movie with no soundtrack. But the silence isn't total; there is the din of nonstop bar talk, relatively little of which has to do with the game. People tell jokes, laugh, flirt, talk business, talk baseball in general while surrounded by this vivid look at a ball game that might just as well be unfolding on a different planet. The room is climate controlled, while down below people swelter in the July humidity. Kids scramble for foul balls and vendors hawk their wares, but not a decibel of it gets through to the Stadium Club.

Like most baseball mascots, Muddy the Mud Hen has gone from support staff to minor celebrity. Bearing an uncanny resemblance to the Chicken (who travels the minor league circuit, doubling attendance wherever he goes), Muddy prowls the Toledo stands with a purple baseball bat, delighting the kiddies and marginally antagonizing the adults. Muddy is as unsubtle a cheerleader as one will find in the minor leagues. Wherever she goes, a small pocket of coerced cheering emerges. Let's Go Hens! (Bam! Bam! Bam! goes the bat on the nearest firm object.) Let's Go Hens! Bam! Bam! Bam!

For better or worse, Muddy has become part of the Mud Hens' image. Not only is she featured in the team set of baseball cards, but Muddy has her very own set of cards. A full package of nothing but the Mud Hen, issued by Big Boy Restaurants. Take the family out for a chicken fried steak, pick up your pack of cards, then come on out to the ball yard and have Muddy autograph the whole pack. Bam! Bam! Bam!

Maybe I caught Muddy on a bad night. When I checked her out a second time, I found the act toned down a bit. I also found a kinder and gentler inhabitant living inside the hen suit.

"I'm thirty years old, but I act like I'm sixteen," Steve Sophis tells me. "I've always liked to entertain and I love kids. For the past four years I was a full-time manager at Meijer's Thrifty Acres. Now all of a sudden I'm out of the business world and I become someone else every night. I really love this. I don't just work at the ballpark. Muddy has become very popular around here. I appear at everything from kid's parties to corporate events.

"The best part of this is seeing how people react to me. Hardly anyone treats me as a normal person when I'm wearing the suit. Kids love it. They hug me, tell me stuff. Major league baseball seems to have forgotten about the kids. The minors haven't. I did a personal appearance at a hospital recently. There was one kid in particular; he was dying of cancer. I made him smile. That made the nurses smile. It made me very happy too.

"Sometimes the youngest kids get a bit scared. Once in a while they'll start to cry when they first see me. Often if I shake hands with their parents they calm down a bit. I try not to leave them scared. Often they'll come back. Sometimes I look up and see them staring at me from across the stands. They're still curious, still not sure."

At the end of the game, Steve Sophis gets out of his hen suit and drives away in a sporty black Celica. The license plate says HENS 7. We both stand there looking at his car gleaming in the Toledo sunshine, and Sophis admits, "It's a pretty fancy car for a chicken."

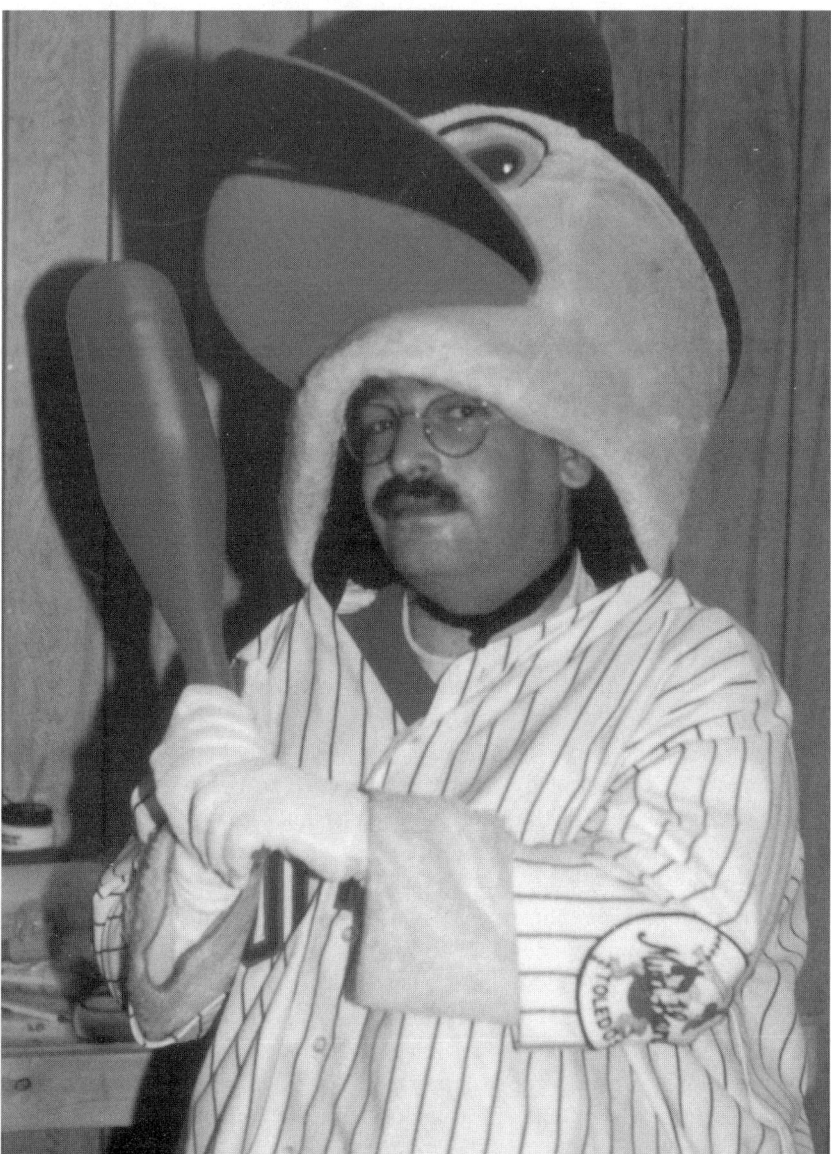

Inside the Mud Hen.

Number 18 walks over to me and asks if I'm taking pictures for the Mud Hens.

"No," I reply, and I mention the book.

"Really? You looking for a story?"

"Sure," I tell him. While we talk, I shoot a practiced glance over to my roster sheet, but no one is listed as number 18.

"I'm Keith Aragon," he says. "I'm here on a fantasy week."

"In the minors? I thought only major league teams have them."

"That's right. But I have a friend on the Mud Hens. So I'm having my own private fantasy week."

Indeed he is. Keith Aragon is a high school physical education teacher from Fort Collins, Colorado. He grew up in La Junta, a small town in the southern part of the state, barely an hour from the New Mexico border.

"You remember Tippy Martinez?" Keith asks me.

"All too well. He's the guy who picked off three Blue Jays in one inning."

"Well, he's from La Junta," Keith proudly announces. "A lot of guys play baseball there."

One of them was Frank Gonzalez. Keith and Gonzalez grew up together and spent lots of time playing ball. Fortunately, Gonzalez is a pitcher and Keith is a catcher. These days, Keith is still catching his friend, only Gonzalez is now in his second season of AAA. With any luck, Frank will end up pitching at Tiger Stadium while Keith will fly back to Colorado and resume teaching high school. He also coaches the baseball team and is quick to note that lots of what he was seeing in Toledo will be translated into his coaching program two thousand miles west.

In fact, the Colorado connection doesn't stop with Gonzalez.

"There's another guy who grew up with us who's also here today. He's on Rochester. Another pitcher. Mike O'Quist."

Both Gonzales and O'Quist had taken the usual path through the minor leagues. It involved more hard work and travel than most fans appreciate.

"Guess I found a pretty painless way to get to AAA," Keith acknowledges.

I wonder if, like most of us, Keith holds on to the fantasy that he'll get discovered while working out with the team. Maybe manager Don Sparks will wander over, shake his head, and mutter, "How'd we miss you? You got one hell of a bat there, son." Or maybe, "You got a rifle for an arm. Ever think of turning pro?" After a week with a AAA team, does Keith believe more than ever that he is good enough for prime time?

"Naw. What it's really shown me is how good these guys are. I see it all kinds of ways. Mostly it's the bat speed that impresses me. You think you're good, then you see these guys hit."

I watch Keith take batting practice. Standing in the cage, facing 70 mph batting practice fastballs, Keith sprays line drives all over the infield. He sends a few fly balls to the outfield, not particularly deep. The crack of the bat sounds good, but most of the hits would have become unspectacular outs during a game.

Still, he is *doing* it. Keith is dressed in a real baseball uniform, taking BP in a professional park. And he isn't embarrassing himself. In fact, he is largely indistinguishable from the other twenty-five guys who are wearing the uniform or running the bases. It doesn't matter that his close friend Frank Gonzalez or their buddy Mike O'Quist might make it to the Show. There is no jealousy. There is only enthusiasm here. And the knowledge that wherever Keith Aragon ends up, no one will ever take this week away from him.

There's a very anxious guy pacing around the press box. Chip Mundy, a reporter from the *Jackson Citizen Patriot*, has been dispatched from Jackson, Michigan, to do a story on a hometown boy who's making good. His subject is Tim Crabtree, who pitches for the visiting Syracuse Chiefs.

"I'm not sure he's here," Mundy announces to anyone in sight. "They had to make a roster move. Somebody had to be cut. I'm hoping it's not Tim."

Mundy is hunting for his man through the press box window, getting more nervous by the minute.

"He's been struggling. Maybe they did cut him."

I have a quick look at Crabtree's stats. A 1–5 record and 6.26 ERA. Struggling indeed. But the Syracuse team ERA is over 5.00, so maybe Crabtree doesn't stand out so badly. Suddenly Mundy hits paydirt.

"There he is! There he is!"

Mundy's excitement stands out. Most of the press corps are pretty neutral. It's been a while since anyone showed this much enthusiasm about anything. Mundy is plainly working on more than a story here. This is a project.

"Tim's a great kid," he assures me. "You gotta meet him. He'll be a great story for your book. We've been following him since before he was drafted by the Jays. He went in the second round in '92, you know. He's gonna make it. I just know it. The whole town is really behind him. I'll introduce you guys after the game. Don't leave town without talking to him."

Mundy is as good as his word. The next morning I call Tim, and we arrange to meet for breakfast. He's traveling with his wife, a semi-unusual arrangement in AAA circles that requires Syracuse to do a little juggling around room assignments.

Tim is far from certain about his future in baseball as we settle into our booth.

When the Blue Jays drafted him out of high school, Tim was a catcher. But

Tim Crabtree. Photo courtesy Tim's mom, Eunice Zakrzewski.

at 6′4″, 205 pounds, he didn't look the part, which must have occurred to the Jays as well. They obviously loved his arm and thought it was being wasted returning pitches from behind the plate.

"I never had any trouble throwing strikes. The problem was learning how to pitch. I had to develop some different pitches. That's not something a catcher worries about. It was a whole different world on the mound. As a catcher, I used to concentrate on calling the game, deciding what pitch to throw in a particular situation. How do you set up this guy to strike him out? How do you mix up your pitches? Once I went to the mound that was no longer my job. I had to learn to turn that over to my catcher and concentrate on delivering what he wanted. I like to believe in my catcher and throw what he calls. That way I don't have to do all that thinking out there. My job is to throw strikes, to pitch to the locations he calls for."

Considering that Crabtree has more experience than most in calling games, it seems odd that he's relinquished so much control to his catcher.

"I think sometimes that's hurt me," he admits. "I don't do as much thinking out there as I might. I can think of situations where I've trusted my catcher more than myself, and it's cost me. Like I might have a good feel for my change-up, and he calls for a fastball. So I throw it, even though I know it's not my best pitch. I've got to start believing in myself more out there. One of my pitching coaches told me, 'If you have a strong sense of what's working for you, or what you want to throw in a particular situation, go with it. If your catcher doesn't call for it, shake him off.' I'm learning to do that more and more."

I suggest to Tim that trusting his catcher makes more sense when the catcher's experience is greater than the pitcher's. Back in A ball, letting the catcher call the show is a bit like letting the blind lead the blind.

"But that's how catchers develop," Tim explains. "The Blue Jays had a policy two years ago, when I first came into the organization, that in A ball you weren't allowed to shake a sign off. The catchers called the game. In AA, they changed that to where the pitcher could call his own game. In AAA, of course, you can shake off any time you want to."

I ask Tim about his background.

"I come from a small town. I think I'm the first guy from Jackson who's played pro ball in about thirty or forty years. On top of that, I came from the smallest high school in the district. I really feel the support. It's like the whole town is behind me. It's especially strong when I come here to Toledo. It's only an hour away so it's like a homecoming. So many people I haven't seen in a while come down to see me play.

"After I was drafted in '92, I went to St. Catharines for the short season A league. Halfway through that season, they called me up to AA. I jumped into pro ball with both feet. I was originally slated to go to Dunedin in my second season, but when I did so well at AA, they just let me stay. I skipped a lot of A ball."

Other than helping his ego, is there a downside to moving through the ranks so quickly?

"I had some rough patches in AA last season. The first half was particularly bad. I had a nine-game losing streak at one point. But then, the second half I just turned it on. I went 8–1 with a 2 something ERA in my last ten starts. We went into the Southern League championship, and I beat Greenville 2–0 on a two-hitter. So, yeah, it's been a quick ride through the system, especially for me, since I really didn't know how to pitch when I started. But I think I'm learning a lot more this way than I would be if I were dominating in some A league. Here, if I don't have it together, I'm not going to last an inning. I'm under great pressure to learn."

I think about Chip's anxiety in the press box and wonder if Tim would be devastated if he were demoted to AA.

"No, it wouldn't be the end of the world if they sent me back to Knoxville for a while. Especially since they're trying to turn me into a closer. They just took me out of the starting rotation twelve days ago. It's because of Duane Ward's shoulder injury. They don't know if he's ever going to pitch again. When they drafted me, they saw me as a short man. The only reason they had me starting was to get a lot of innings in. Now they've said, 'You've done enough starting, you have enough experience. We're going to throw you into the bullpen as a closer or setup man. Let's get you some experience there.'

"And it is different. I didn't expect it to be, but there is a big difference! You have to throw strikes right off the bat, you have to challenge hitters. You can't let people get on base 'cause usually you're in a close ball game. You're not starting with a clean slate. You've got a narrow lead and you've got to protect it. It's not the time to make any mistakes."

How did Tim feel about making the switch from catcher to pitcher?

"At first I was disappointed. Even a little hurt. I thought I was pretty good behind the plate, and they weren't giving me a chance to show what I had. But then I thought, Why not try it out? I trusted my coach's judgment. So they put me in the bullpen and I liked it! It seems like all I did was grab the ball and go out there and throw it over the plate. It seemed too easy, but before I knew it, I had eight saves. Then one of our starters got hurt, so they put me in the rotation and I went 8–2. We went to the Big Ten Championship and I beat Illinois to put us into the final round. We lost to Minnesota, but it was a great thrill. '92 was a hell of a year for me! Everything was moving so fast. One week I was in the playoffs; the next thing I knew I was pitching for St. Catherines.

"When the Blue Jays signed me, I was a pitcher. Even though I was twenty-two, you could say I was a real young pitcher. I had barely had a full season on the mound. Before my senior year, the last time I pitched was Little League.

"I was getting scouts calling me all the time. They all wanted to know if I was going to sign or I was going to go back for my senior year in college. I was telling everybody that I wanted to sign, I wanted to play professional ball. The day before the draft, the Cleveland Indians took me out to lunch. They told me, 'We've got two picks in the first round. We're going to take this kid out of college named Paul Shuey. And you're going to be our second pick.' And I was thinking, Fine. That's OK with me. It sounded like a definite thing. A lot of other scouts expressed interest, but they didn't know what would happen. So I expected to go with Cleveland.

"Then something happened. Either they lost that second pick in the first round, or there was some kind of mix-up. But all they got was Shuey. Before they could get around to choosing me in the next round, the Blue Jays had their selection, and they picked me. It was a complete surprise. I had been at home waiting for the call with all the photographers there. I was wearing a Cleveland hat. When the phone rang, the voice said, 'Hi, this is so and so from the Toronto Blue Jays, and we've just selected you.' So I threw my Cleveland hat off, and I noticed my little nephew was wearing a Toronto hat. I put it on real quick, and the flashbulbs started going off."

Tim's journey to professional ball was almost derailed before it started.

"When I was coming out of high school in my senior year, I was in a delayed entry program to go into the Marine Corps. It was all set; I had taken my physical, passed my exams. When I graduated, our team went to the regionals, and we won. Then we went to the state championship, and we won that too. At that point, I finally got scouted by Michigan State when we were in the semifinals and finals. Up until then, I hadn't been scouted by anybody because I played for such a tiny little school. I was eight days away from going into the military. My friends in high school threw a going-away party for me. They had a big cake that said, 'United States Marine Corps' on it. In that eight days after we won the state championship, Michigan State signed me to a scholarship. I had to call my recruiter up and tell him the whole situation.

"So much of my life seems like it's based on last-minute events. If we didn't go to the state championship, I never would have been scouted. If I hadn't gone to Michigan, I wouldn't been drafted by the Blue Jays. Who knows what would have happened? I would have gone into the Marines. I was designated for the Terrorist Reaction Force, which meant at the time I would have been involved in Desert Storm. How many of those guys came home, and in what kind of shape?"

Now that he's established himself as a pitcher, Tim's forte remains his fastball.

"I've been clocked in the mid-90s. Last week in Columbus, I topped out at 97 mph. We had a one-run lead, and I threw a 97 mph fastball to Russ Davis, and he hit it over the left field wall. He hit it like it was a batting practice fastball. That's what amazes me. At this level, guys don't care. The harder you throw it, the harder it's gonna come back at you. Back in high school, you didn't see guys throwing that hard. If you did see guys in the 90s, it was a rarity. And you didn't see many batters catch up to that fastball. Here, it seems like everyone can hit it. The fastball is the easy thing to hit. It's all the breaking stuff that gets guys out at this level.

"Hitters hate movement on a fastball. I seem to have a natural sinker. I get a lot of ground balls. Toronto likes that about me as much as they like my velocity. A hard thrower who throws a sinkerball is pretty important to them. I also throw a slider change-up. I was using all my pitches when I was starting, but now that I'm in the pen I'm concentrating more on the fastball. On sheer velocity, my fastball might be in the top 5 percent of what you find in the big leagues. But there's obviously more to it than that. I'm still learning how to pitch.

"I'm in AAA this season because I had a decent spring. I also pitched well in the Arizona Fall League last year. That's a tough league because everybody sends their top prospects there. It helps to have a couple of coaches who like you and stick up for you. It makes a lot of difference when someone in the organization says, 'I want this guy on my team. I think he can help us.' Bob Didier, our manager, did that for me. Last year, Garth Iorg, our manager in AA, did it as well. When I was slated for Dunedin in single-A, Garth stood up for me and said, 'I've seen this guy pitch. I want him on my team.'

"I've seen the SkyDome once. Back in '92 I won the Webster Award. Toronto picks the outstanding player from each of its minor league teams, and I was selected for St. Catherines. So I got the run of the SkyDome for the weekend and got to experience Toronto. It was awesome. Incredible. That's someplace I've definitely got to pitch.

"It's just a question of learning how to pitch out of the bullpen here in AAA. Once I get comfortable with that, the Blue Jays will give me a chance. I really believe that. When that happens, I hope I make the best of it."

I ask Tim if he didn't make it to The Show, whether he'd stay in AAA just for the love of playing the game.

"I was talking to my wife about it just this week. I don't think I would. People romanticize this life-style, but I don't really enjoy it so much. I want to get to the big leagues, where money will compensate for the life-style, 'cause I don't even believe that the big league life-style is so great. You're on the road a lot. You're away from your family, your friends, your hometown for six, seven months a year. You're traveling all over, living out of a suitcase. That's not for me. I'd miss my wife. I'd want to settle down, have a home, have some kids, watch them grow up, be a regular fatherly influence.

"I have a bachelor's degree in criminal justice. My wife is going to graduate with a Ph.D. in psychology. I'd probably be more willing to stick it out in AAA if I only had a high school diploma, but there are other options for us.

"If I don't make it in baseball, I'd pursue a career in law enforcement. I'd be a cop or maybe join the FBI. My father is a cop; so is my closest friend and his father. I really like the way they command respect in the community. There's something really important about that to me. The uniform and the respect. That's what impressed me about the Marines also."

"Not unlike a baseball player," I suggest to Tim.

"I hadn't thought of that," he admits. "It is kind of the same thing, isn't it?"

If Tim Crabtree is right about throwing straight fastballs not being a ticket to the major leagues, then Carlos Delgado is living proof that you can't build a career hitting them. The Blue Jays highly touted prospect started the 1994 season with Toronto in a powerful blaze of glory. Delgado's most famous moonshot came in the SkyDome when one of his missiles nearly shattered a window of the Hard Rock Cafe, stunning customers almost 500 feet from home plate. For a brief moment in May 1994, Carlos Delgado was the toast of the town. Within weeks, major league pitchers had figured him out. He became just another flash in the pan. By June 9, the party was over. Delgado went limping back to Syracuse, his tail between his legs. The totals for his brief 1994 career included nine home runs and twenty-four RBIs, but his average had plummeted to .215. Worse yet, the at bats were becoming embarrassing. Delgado was as shell-shocked as the mercenary collectors who had stockpiled his rookie cards.

"It's still a treat to play with a guy like Delgado," observes Tim Crabtree. "Just to watch him walk up to the plate and know he has a chance to hit the ball 500 feet. Carlos just needs to get aggressive again. After what happened, his confidence level has come down. Last week I saw him take a few first pitch fastballs right down the heart of the plate. Last year he wouldn't have done that. He would have hit them 460 feet. When he gets aggressive again, look out!"

In the meantime, Delgado is making the most of his return to AAA. Trying to put a positive spin on the demotion, the Blue Jays are emphasizing the need for Delgado to develop his catching skills "while he regains his batting stroke." Here in Toledo he seems to be doing both. During batting practice, Delgado routinely launches them off the Food Town sign, high above the 395-foot marker in right center. I'm watching him next to the cage with Robert Perez. We're both shaking our heads. When it's Perez's turn, he fouls a couple off and then nails one to the deepest part of the outfield. It hits the Official Mud Hens Time sign, right as the clock shows 5:12. Perez leaves the cage with a big smile on his face. As he walks by, he says to me, "Drink some water! It's very hot out here. You ought to have a cap on your head."

Then he walks over to the dugout and gets himself a big drink. When I look over several minutes later, he's still smiling.

A bit later, with the temperatures still well into the nineties, Delgado crouches behind the plate. Time after time, he pounces on balls rolled by his coach, picking them up and firing them down to first or out to second base. The sweat rolls off him in layers.

Carlos Delgado (left) and José Lima.

"It looks like a little more work than playing left field," I sagely observe.

"No shit," he retorts.

Just before the game, the drill over, Delgado is in better spirits.

"Sure I'm smiling," he says to me. "I'm always smiling." Delgado is hanging out with his buddy José Lima, a pitcher for the Mud Hens. In just two months, Lima will be a bigger story than Delgado, a prediction few would have made in mid-June. With Tigers general manager Joe Klein sitting in the stands next to Sparky Anderson, Lima puts together a no-hitter against Pawtucket. Impressing everyone in sight, Lima caps his performance by remaining at the ballpark long after his teammates have left, honoring every last request for an autograph.

"You know me," he explains. "I'm always like this. How can I say no to these people?"

Columbus, Ohio

"It can drive you crazy listening to all these rumors."
—Kyle Abbott, Scranton pitcher

Cooper Stadium in Columbus, Ohio, is a clean, well-managed operation. When things run as well as this facility, you get the feeling that it's effortless. It isn't. There are a lot of people here who know their jobs and do them well.

The '92 season marked the 100th year that professional baseball has been played in Columbus. The Columbus Clippers, the Yankees AAA affiliate, are contributing some glory to that tradition. The team has won consecutive Governors' Cup Championships in the International League. The local fans have a lot to be happy about, and over 600,000 of them showed up at the ballpark in 1992.

The Columbus ritual for showing enthusiasm might be the gentlest in all of baseball. The Clippers have their own theme song that gets played over the PA system periodically.

> Columbus Clippers, our team is number one.
> Columbus Clippers, our fans are half the fun.
> No matter who they're playing,
> They'll always play them well
> Columbus Clippers, ring your bell.

When they hear that "ring your bell" line, all the regulars take out their cowbells, which have been dutifully brought from home for just this moment. The sound of five thousand cowbells ringing in unison takes some getting used to. It's not something you're likely to hear outside of Columbus, Ohio.

Despite their allegiance to Columbus, the loyalties of most fans are split by regional preferences. Talk to someone in a downtown bar, and they'll tell you they root for the Clippers, but they're also either a Reds or an Indians fan. Cincinnati and

Cleveland are near enough to attract a lot of attention. Some fans even follow the dreaded Yankees, not because they have any love for New York, but because so many of the players who have come through here end up playing for the Yankees. In AAA, the turnover can be very fast. Last week's center fielder in downtown Columbus can be patrolling the outfield next week in the house that Ruth built.

When the aptly named skipper Stump Merrill comes bolting out of the dugout on to the field, the fans get on him a bit. It's kind of hard not to respond to his physical presence. But it's good-natured kidding. There is plenty of respect as well for the ex-Yankee manager who is now in his seventeenth season in the organization.

During one of my visits to Cooper Stadium in June 1993, Mark Hutton is the starting pitcher. Hutton is a 6′6″, 225 pounder who wants to be the first Australian to pitch in the majors. He missed his chance for that distinction earlier in the year, when Graeme Lloyd joined the Brewers staff. The night I see him pitch, Hutton seems all but unhittable, beating Scranton 13–2 on a four-hitter. The seats behind home plate are stocked full of scouts from various organizations. Every time Hutton lifts his right arm to deliver a pitch, at least a dozen radar guns and stopwatches are perched and ready to do business. Within three weeks of my visit, Mark Hutton is promoted to New York. On July 27, he becomes the first Australian credited with a major league win.

Sitting inconspicuously among the scouts are two guys in their early twenties. Unlike most of the scouts, they seem interested in what the Scranton pitchers have to offer tonight. Their names are Mike Williams and Paul Fletcher. Both are starting pitchers on the Scranton roster, and it's their job to keep an inventory of their teammates' performance.

Within two weeks of this evening, both Williams and Fletcher have been called up to pitch for Philadelphia in the middle of a pennant drive. Such is life in AAA. Fletcher's career turns out to be brief, but Williams spends considerable time for the next several years commuting between Scranton and Veterans Stadium, earning him the nickname "Turnpike Mike." During an injury-ravaged 1996 season, Mike Williams becomes a regular member of the Phillies pitching rotation.

Pitching help isn't the only thing to come from Scranton this season. A fresh-faced kid named Kevin Stocker is playing shortstop for Scranton. Stocker was the Phillies second round draft pick in the June 1991 draft. He's got a flashy glove, although, like most of the Red Barons, he's not exactly having a banner year at the plate. During my visit to Columbus, Stocker is hitting around .230 with little promise of possessing a major league bat. The front office has wisely decided that Stocker needs at least a full season at AAA before making the final step of his journey to The Show. Stocker is playing under no pressure and is probably as surprised as anyone when barely two weeks later he finds himself the Phillies' starting shortstop. Word is, the Phillies have grown weary of the present cast of characters. The devils they know include Juan Bell, who has just been run out of town on a rail, as well as Mariano Duncan and Kim Batiste. Duncan and Batiste can hit a bit but represent too great a defensive liability for what is starting to look like a pennant-contending club. After watching a particularly harrowing evening of infield frolics, GM Lee Thomas decides the time has come to promote Kevin Stocker. The general message is: I don't care if he hits .150. We've got enough bats on this team. We need his glove in there. And so, without much fanfare, Kevin Stocker becomes a major leaguer, and Scranton goes scrambling for a shortstop.

The gods of minor league baseball are shining on Kevin Stocker. Rather than hitting his weight, he surprises everyone and bats .324 in his rookie year, eclipsing even his best minor league campaign. Instead of cowbells ringing in his ears, Kevin Stocker has a World Series ring to show for the 1993 season.

Also sitting behind home plate, charting pitches and munching on the ubiquitous meal of corn chips and cheese, is Scranton pitcher Kyle Abbott. Abbott is a good-looking guy, although none of his publicity pictures show him in the relatively thick glasses he wears off the field. He could pass as a philosophy major at USC, rather than a professional athlete.

Abbott is best known to baseball fans for his 1–14 record for the hapless, injury-ridden Phillies of 1992. A year later, when things were soaring in Philadelphia, Abbott is pitching for Scranton.

"I don't know," he sighs. "They got a pretty good look at me last year. There's been some movement this year, but I haven't been one of the guys called up. I guess we'll see what happens in September when the rosters expand."

Abbott admits that maybe his best chance is with another organization.

"I'd love to pitch for the Phillies, but I keep hearing these rumors. Every day there seems to be some kind of deal cooking with another team. It can drive you crazy listening to all these rumors. I just try to pitch the best I can and take care of the things I can control."

The following year, the rumor mill stopped, and Kyle Abbott went off to pitch in Japan. In some far-off reaches of the universe, he may still be considered a prospect. In most other places, a lot of the shine has rubbed off his star.

Canton, Ohio

"Oh, no! All the work I've done. All for nothing!"
—Tony Mitchell, Canton outfielder

Like its namesake, Thurman Munson Stadium is not going to win any beauty contests. But neither is it shy. This sheet metal monument to Ohio baseball is pretty easy to find. I take Interstate 77 south, pass the exit for Lovers Lane (so help me!), and in about twenty miles the ballpark rears up on my left.

It's 99 degrees as I pull up, shortly before three o'clock. The vendors are starting to set up their wares, and the sounds of batting practice are audible from the parking lot. The stadium itself is a curiosity. Unlike most parks, the best seats are not at field level. The front row is located about six feet above the playing field. This "sunken field" has a distancing effect. You get used to it, but most fans who have been to other parks notice it immediately.

Something else you can't help but notice is the noise level. As in most stadiums that feature metal stands, seats, and walkways, the fans here have learned to express themselves with their feet. During moments of peak excitement, the sheer amount of stomping that goes on in Canton probably wakes up kiddies across the West Virginia border.

Canton, Ohio, has attained a certain notoriety among country music fans and historians for being the location of "the show Hank Williams never gave." Williams died in the backseat of his limousine en route to Canton on New Year's Day in 1953.

Nearly half a century later, Canton seems more interested in baseball than country music. The city has been part of the Eastern League since 1989 and has been a Cleveland Indians affiliate since its birth. This is a working-class area, and baseball draws well. The Canton club took in over 273,000 fans last season, which ranks it eighth among twenty-eight AA franchises in all of baseball. Not bad at all.

The community is well catered to by the Indians' management. Fans turn out not just to see baseball but, as in most minor league towns, to see a *show*. The night I visit is Western Auto Night. That means we get to see a muscle car drive around the field carrying the kind of smiling, waving cargo that sends most self-respecting feminists screaming for the exits. Fast cars and purty women. This display of heartland values is followed by a pregame parade of Little Leaguers from Akron. I don't recall any giveaways, although I may have missed a free carburetor for the first five hundred fans. On an earlier visit to Canton, I came home with a batting helmet. This season, if you time your visit right (as many locals do), you can return home with anything from a free T-shirt to a baseball glove. Not a bad deal for a four-dollar ticket.

Local historians will tell you that while the modern era of minor league baseball may be new to Canton, the town's baseball roots go back over a hundred years. In 1890, a regular season major league game between Pittsburgh and Cleveland was transported to Canton's Pastime Park field. The game was a big draw, as Canton native Cy Young (he of pitching award fame) started the game for Cleveland.

In 1902, a major league game between Cleveland and Boston was again played in Canton. This time, the Indians took their game south to Canton in order to circumvent the Cleveland blue laws which prohibited them from playing baseball on Sundays. Canton was unencumbered by such morality. An overflow crowd of 6,000 fans flocked to Mahaffey Park, which literally collapsed under their weight. No one was seriously hurt, although a section of bleachers was destroyed.

The final major league game on Canton turf occurred in 1903. Again, the crowd was beyond the capacity of Mahaffey Park, despite repairs to the previous year's damage and the addition of extra seats. Not only did Boston beat Cleveland this time, but local fans were disappointed when Cy Young, who had since been traded to Boston, never showed his face during the game.

In its brief history, the Canton franchise has managed to generate its share of memorable moments. Some of them have been immortalized by Bill Nichols in the Canton program, which, at 108 pages, is one of the slickest in AA baseball. Highlights from the past six years include pitcher Jeff Shaw's 1989 tantrum after he walked a batter unintentionally. Shaw turned his back on home plate, stomped to the rear of the mound, and angrily kicked at the grass. Unfortunately, his kicks were better aimed than his fastball. They triggered the water sprinkler, which, to everyone's surprise, erupted into life. It took the novice ground crew nearly twenty minutes to stem the tide.

Canton must have wondered if its 1991 season was jinxed when the sky-diver they hired to deliver the ball for the ceremonial first pitch not only missed the mound but, to the amusement of several thousand fans and players, missed the entire stadium.

Nichols also reports the kind of tale that easily slips into legend. Like many minor league franchises, the Canton Indians occasionally allow fans to sing the national anthem. On one evening a "rather full figured woman" stepped forward to deliver her rendition. She performed admirably, but then, rather than ending her performance, she kept adding verses. Apparently, nobody knew what to do with this rather large woman singing an endless version of the national anthem. Players milled around while she continued her patriotic exhibition. Finally, an inspired fan yelled out, "The game can't start until the fat lady stops."

Brent Horvath has been with the Indians for three years. He played some baseball at Ohio University but soon realized that he'd better look elsewhere for a career. He's found one with the Canton club as director of media relations. In everyday terms, Horvath is the middleman between the players and the outside world. He sets up interviews, prepares daily handouts for the press box, and arranges speaking engagements and player appearances in the community. In the brief time Horvath has been with the club, he's noticed some changes.

"This year's team is fun to work with. These guys are young, and you can see that they're having fun. They like to do stuff in the community, like talking to kids, signing autographs. It's easy to coordinate things with them.

"Last year he had a lot of older guys on the club. They'd already been to AAA or the Show. More of them were on their way down than up. That made a big difference in attitude. Don't get me wrong, they were good guys, but they didn't have the same enthusiasm for community work that this year's club has. That made my job a little tougher."

So I settle down in the dugout to meet some of these young, enthusiastic guys. One of the players I want to talk to is Antonio Mitchell. I don't know anything about him personally, but I've heard about a rather impressive feat of his on the field. There's a light tower down the left field line. The tower looms about 130 feet above the 340-foot sign. One of Mitchell's home runs has hit the transformer box at the very top of the light tower. My high school geometry is a little rusty, but I make that to be a 365-foot shot that was rising into the Ohio night when it encountered an unyielding metal object.

"Did you really do that?" I ask Mitchell.

Tony Mitchell.

"I guess," he shrugs. "That's what I've been hearing." He looks a touch uneasy about it.

"Did you see it go out?" I wonder.

"No. I never did. I had my head down when I hit it. I knew it was out, but I had no idea how far it would go. I could hear from the crowd that something had happened. First they were cheering, then they got quiet. By the time I looked up, it was gone."

I get goose bumps hearing him describe the crowd reaction. I've been part of it. I remember seeing Fred McGriff hit one out of old Exhibition Stadium in Toronto. As soon as he made contact with the ball, we all knew it was gone. The crowd started to yell and scream, but within a couple of seconds, we all got very quiet when we saw what was happening. The ball traveled over the fence in right center and was still rising when it found the darkness outside the park. It landed somewhere in the Canadian National Exhibition that lay just beyond the ballpark. There was an eerie silence in the stands for a moment, then a wave of applause began to emerge. I don't think McGriff saw that one go out either. He was probably asked about it by the press after the game and was probably just as ill at ease with the questions as Mitchell.

Once we get beyond his heroics, Tony Mitchell is more comfortable talking.

"I grew up in Detroit. I went to high school there, and I was a pretty good ball player. I was going to get drafted in a very high round. I even heard I might go in the first round. Then right before I graduated, I stopped into a convenience store one night with a couple of friends. Just went in, you know, to buy some soda or something. There was a robbery while we were there, and I ended up getting shot in the arm. I remember thinking, 'Oh, no. All the work I've done. All for nothing.'

"I finally healed and ended up being drafted by the Pirates anyway, although I went in a lower round than I would have otherwise. Up till then, everything had come easy to me. Getting shot meant I had to work hard to recover, to be good again. I learned the value of work, which I really didn't know up until then."

Mitchell spent his first two seasons with the Pirates at Bradenton in the Gulf Coast League. After nearly hitting .300, he was promoted to Welland in the New York–Penn League, then to Augusta. There, he began to show signs of the power that scouts had predicted. In the middle of the 1992 season, Mitchell was traded to the Indians along with John Carter in exchange for Alex Cole. Switching to the Indians' Columbus affiliate in the Sally League did nothing to dampen Mitchell's fine season. He finished second in the league with twenty-three home runs. A month after being traded to the Indians, Mitchell enjoyed a particularly sweet moment when he went three for five against his former teammates at Augusta, including a solo home run and a grand slam. That night, Mitchell didn't have his head down.

"I'm a very intense player. I'm a lot better now than I used to be, but I still don't take the game lightly. When I was a kid I used to go home and cry after my team lost. It was almost impossible to console me. It meant so much to me. I used to think, It's my fault! What could I have done differently?" Mitchell pauses for a moment. "I've at least learned one player can't take all the responsibility for everything. You can contribute, but there are eight other guys out there."

The most obvious thing you want to ask "Pork Chop" Pough is how he got his nickname. But I've been warned.

"Don't bother asking him," Brent Horvath has told me. "He won't tell you."

So I stay off it. Clyde Pough and I have a pleasant chat. We talk a bit about life in Florida, where he's from. We talk about his team. We talk about the weather. Then he sees my copy of the Canton *Media Guide* and he's curious about what it has to say about him. Like many players I've met, Pough rarely gets to see the stat sheets and media handouts that press are routinely armed with. I've grown used to getting extra copies of stat sheets to leave in the dugout or bullpen while players swarm over them. Pough's entry appears on page 29 of the Canton guide. He shares the page with Cesar Perez, a pitcher who came over from the Yankees in 1992. Perez hasn't had a bad season in pro ball, but he's suffering through some injuries right now. He's just as eager to see the guide, and the two of them sit in the dugout staring at their joint page like a couple of school kids sharing a comic book.

When they're through, I talk to Pork Chop about the fine season he's having. He's presently hitting .313 and is second on the team in home runs, behind only Tony Mitchell. You'd think that kind of performance would be routine to a guy who was the Indians' number three selection in the June 1988 draft. Apparently it hasn't been. Pough's career average coming into the 1994 season is .258 with not much show of power. Suddenly, this year, everything has changed.

"I'm finally starting to hit like I should have. It seems so easy! What was wrong with me?" With this, he turns to me, making the question more personal than rhetorical. "Why didn't I do this before?" He seems genuinely baffled, yet pleased that things have finally turned around. "It's so simple," he continues. "I can't believe it's taken me six years to hit like this."

That night, as if to dramatize his point, Pough gets a couple of hits, including one that clears the left field fence. I wish I knew the answer to his question. The unspoken fear behind it is, if this surge can start out of nowhere, it can stop just as quickly. It wouldn't be the first time.

Before we finish talking, I decide to take my chances.

"How'd you get your nickname?" I venture.

"I don't talk about my name, man," he informs me, smiling all the time.

Raymond Harvey has a great attitude. Many people believe that the work ethic in baseball is dead. I don't believe that in general, and it's even less applicable in the minors. Most guys I meet are working their asses off looking for a break. It's rare to find anyone, even a high round draft choice, taking anything for granted. If they do, they don't do it for long.

I think about all of this as I'm talking to Ray Harvey. Here's this big, likable guy from California who went to college for four years expecting to be drafted. But it never happened.

"The funny thing is, I could have been drafted in high school as a pitcher. But I didn't want that. I decided to go to college instead. By then, I had become an outfielder/first baseman. And the call never came. I figured, OK, I'll live with it. So I applied to graduate school, and then I got a letter from the Cleveland Indians. They weren't drafting me, but they did invite me to a

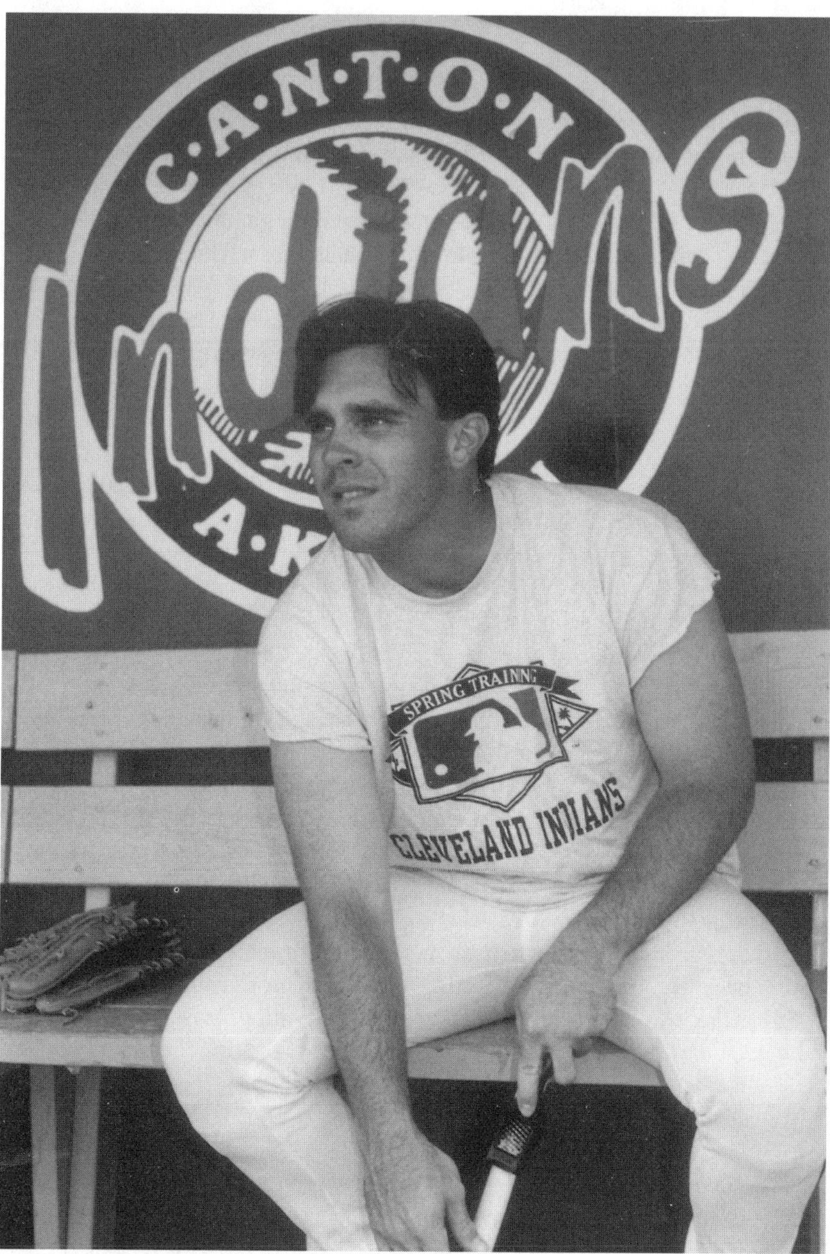

Raymond Harvey.

tryout camp. It's the kind of deal where you have to be invited. I suppose that's better than walking in off the street, but it's not as good as being drafted.

"So I decided to go. It wasn't like I had given up on the idea of playing ball. I had already been to five tryout camps where I lived in Nashville. But I never made it. I kept coming up empty. So I figured, what the hell. The Indians camp was in Orlando. I drove down there and had my best tryout ever. It was unbelievable. The first day I hit a home run. The second game I had two doubles. Everything went right. I got signed right then and there and invited to spring training in '91.

"I did well and was assigned to Columbus in the Sally League. They were taking a chance placing me so high in the system. They let me skip rookie ball altogether. But by then I was twenty-two years old and I had four years of college ball under my belt. I played a full season in Columbus and did well enough to start the next year in the Carolina League."

Actually, Harvey's first season was better than just OK. He hit .280 with ten home runs and seventy-nine RBIs. He maintained his average the next year after being promoted to Kinston (.284), although his power stats were off (two home runs and forty-five RBIs). One of those two Carolina League home runs was particularly memorable to Harvey.

"I hit my first home run in '92 in Durham. It hit the bull, but because I was on the opposing team, the bull didn't do any snorting and tail wagging. It still felt good, though. I loved playing in that park. The clubhouse was very small, but the atmosphere was great."

In 1993, Harvey's stats in Kinston were virtually identical to the previous year (.284 BA/3 HR/39 RBI), although he seemed overmatched during a brief promotion to Canton. The 1994 season has been a different story altogether.

"I'm not just an add-on with this club," he told me. "I'm playing every night. I'm in the lineup. I'm getting my chance."

Harvey was hitting .294 when we met, and there were signs the power was coming back. He looked upbeat, sitting in the dugout, shaving bat handles.

"If I make it to the majors, I'll know I did it myself. I clawed my way in. No one helped me."

Like most teams in the Eastern League, both Canton and tonight's opponent, Reading, broadcast all their ball games both home and away. In fact, tonight's game is being televised in the Canton area as well. I visit with Steve Degler, who's been the radio voice of the Reading Phillies for as long as I've been touring around the Eastern League.

This is a full-time job. Degler is there for all seventy-one road games, as well as an equal number of home games. He travels on the team bus and knows more about these players than he could ever tell on the radio. When we sit down together, he fills me in on a long list of team developments. Reading has been playing appallingly bad baseball, and there is a huge amount of player movement. In the last week alone, there have been promotions, demotions, retirements, and free agent signings. It's a fascinating litany of what are undoubtedly milestones in the lives of these young athletes.

Broadcasting is not a glamorous job. Degler has all the inconvenience and discomfort of eight-hour bus trips with little of the glory or fame afforded to AA players. On top of that, his working conditions are usually less than ideal. When Degler, the Reading bus driver, and I sit in the cubicle assigned to visiting broadcasters, we have to leave the door open for space and air. The temperature at game time still hovers in the nineties, and there's no air conditioning in sight. At one point, a fan sitting directly in front of the booth decides to stand up and stretch. He is apparently unaware that he is blocking the view of a play-by-play announcer in the middle of an inning. Degler has few options short of banging on the window and hoping the fan gets the message.

Somewhere around the fifth inning, the AP news wire in the booth starts humming, but it is spewing out something other than the latest score updates. This is the moment when O. J. Simpson has begun his legendary car chase along the L.A. freeways. Since Simpson once played football, the Associated Press has decided that this event needs to be chronicled on the sports wire. And so, like his counterparts all over North America, Degler begins to read the bulletins over the air.

Within the next half hour, the plot thickens considerably. The contents of O. J. Simpson's suicide note have now been made public, and they are beginning to emerge over the sports wire in this little broadcast booth in Thurman Munson Stadium. While Reading makes a pitching change, Steve Degler pulls the sheet off the printer and begins to read the text of Simpson's suicide note over the air to the listeners back in Reading. He's doing his job. It's news. This is a radio station. It's even, in somebody's eyes, *sports* news. What is doubtful is whether Simpson, at the height of his despair, could have guessed that his words would find their way three thousand miles east to the lips of a minor league broadcaster who, in turn, would transmit them back to folks in Reading, Pennsylvania, who had tuned in to hear how their Phillies were doing this evening.

Charleston, West Virginia

"It's like we know we're gonna lose. We just don't know exactly how when the game starts." —Robert Walker, catcher, Boys' Summer League

Interstate 77 south out of Canton winds its way through some mighty beautiful country. Sixty-five miles per hour seems just the right speed to enjoy the scenery and still get where you're going. In my case, the destination is Charleston, West Virginia.

The farther south I get, the more colorful the exit names become. Closing in on Charleston, I pass places called Tuppers Creek Road, Gold Town, and Skitter Creek. Even the franchise fast food stops have names like Pit and Git. I've been through Charleston maybe a dozen times before, always on my way to somewhere else. Today all that will change. Charleston is home to a minor league baseball team called the Wheelers. Tonight I intend to see them play the Columbus Redstixx at Watt Powell Park.

Charleston is the capital of West Virginia, and you can see the shiny roof of the capitol from the interstate. On a sunny day, its reflective gold surface is almost blinding. The only sports-related thing I recall from traveling past Charleston is a roadside marker for the birthplace of NBA superstar Jerry West. West was born in one of the little hollows ("hollers") that dot the lush countryside. West has never been a hero of mine, and I've never bothered to track down his ancestral home, such as it is. First baseman John Kruk, who *is* one of my heroes, is also from West Virginia. But he's from Keyser, in another part of the state entirely.

I find my motel fairly easily and head out for the ballpark. Watt Powell is a fairly typical-looking Sally League park. Charleston has been in the league since 1987, and the team has been a Cincinnati Reds affiliate since the 1990 season. When I arrive, the parking lot is unusually empty. In fact, the ball park is ominously quiet for this time of afternoon. I figure maybe batting practice starts a little bit late in Charleston.

I walk inside and the place is deserted. The field is empty, the concession stands are locked, and the offices are closed. Something is plainly wrong. Finally, I see a couple standing by one of the exits. I walk over to them and ask about the Wheelers game tonight. They look utterly blank.

"I'm pretty sure the Wheelers are out of town," the husband tells me. Was I here for the high school game? If so, I've just missed it.

No, I tell him. I'm here to see some minor league ball. They don't know a lot about that. In fact, they were just leaving after watching their kid's game, which started around one and finished about half an hour ago. Maybe I should check with someone else.

I walk back out to the parking lot and spot a father with two kids in uniform. I repeat my question to him, and he confirms what I've just heard.

"Oh, the Wheelers are out of town. No doubt about it. The local leagues are using the park while they're away."

I'm thinking, this can't be! My trusty *Baseball America* directory has never let me down. Charleston is plainly home to Columbus, according to the notes around which I've choreographed my trip. Just to be on the safe side, I'll go double check. All the while, I'm expecting two bus loads of ballplayers to come rolling up, go scrambling for their clubhouses, mumbling "Sorry we're late" as they brush by.

That's what I hope for. Instead, I discover the error of my ways. What I vaguely knew has come back to haunt me. There are *two* Charlestons in this league. I'm in the wrong one. The Charleston Riverdogs, a team from South Carolina, is indeed home to the Redstixx tonight. The West Virginia team is on the road several states away playing the Capital City Bombers.

My immediate reaction is disbelief. Then I start to laugh. What the hell. If life hands you a bowl of lemons, make some lemonade. Today happens to be perfect weather for lemonade. Something good is going to come of this.

If I'm going to be philosophical, I might as well do it in the dugout. So I go over and sit down, out of the 95-degree heat, in the deserted Wheelers dugout. I'm still sitting there looking philosophical when I hear the unmistakable sound of cleats on concrete. Before long, three teenagers have joined me in the dugout. We introduce ourselves and sit looking out at the field.

We go through an unusually polite "who am I and what am I doing here" exchange. I tell them why I came and how I screwed up the schedules. They're quite impressed by the book. They've never met anybody who's written a book, and they have all kinds of questions. Being on the road, traveling to different towns, meeting people all seems very exotic to them. They ask me

Left to right: Jimmy LaLonde, Robert Walker, and Scott Wolfe: the Boys' Summer League at its finest.

about different ballparks and cities, both major and minor league. One of them tells me that he has an uncle who played pro ball a *long* time ago. Images of the Cincinnati Redstockings are dancing in my head when he drops the other shoe.

"Yeah. My uncle played back in the sixties." I reluctantly conclude that this young man's idea of ancient history includes the 1960s. Why not, I suppose? He wasn't even born yet. He probably also thinks of Woodstock as medieval music.

It turns out that the relative in question is Lew Burdette, who used to play for the Braves. Pretty damn good pitcher, as I recall. Of course, he would have lost something off his fastball by the time my young friend first met him at a family picnic in the 1980s.

The dugout gradually fills up. These guys have a game at six o'clock. It's the Boys' Summer League, for sixteen-to-eighteen-year-old kids. They're here an hour and a half early to get some practice in. They can use it, Robert Walker assures me. He's the catcher, and he admits the team hasn't been playing too well lately. His teammates Scott Wolfe and Jimmy LaLonde agree with him.

"We really suck," Scott concludes. What seems to be happening, they all agree, is that even when they're winning, something goes wrong in the field, then something else, until it all unravels in a hurry.

"It's like we know we're gonna lose," Walker explains. "We just don't know exactly how when the game starts."

Scott agrees. "Other teams have stopped taking us seriously." They all nod.

Like most ballplayers I've met, Scott is superstitious. He has decided to do something *radical* about all of this. He has shaved his head. With unerring logic, Scott sees a connection between his hairstyle and his performance.

"I have about three hits so far this whole season. Maybe it'll all change now since I've cut my hair off."

A couple of team coaches arrive closer to game time. Roger is Scott's dad. He's been coaching local teams for about eight years. He loves baseball and gets a tad frustrated with the sloppy play and lack of concentration by his team. Part of his frustration is a natural reaction to what's happening on the field. Part of it is more personal.

"I really love baseball. I was very good when I was in high school . . . kind of a local hero. The Reds scouted me, and I got invited to go to Gary, Indiana, where they had a AAA team. They wanted to have a look at me. It was a great opportunity."

Then he pauses and looks out at the field. "But those were the sixties, you know? I was doing drugs pretty heavy back then, and I just didn't go. I just never showed up. It's the biggest regret of my life. It's that simple. I'm pretty sure now I could have made it. But I'll never know."

Roger adds the punchline matter-of-factly. "I finally got myself straightened out. But by then no one was scouting me."

A couple of decades later, Roger tries to stay upbeat while the kids he's coaching boot ground balls, miss the cutoff man, and swing at balls several feet out of the strike zone. Sometimes it isn't easy to be a coach.

I want to take some pictures of these kids. I know it's a must as soon as they change into their game jerseys. Teams all over North America are sponsored by local businesses, everything from car dealers to plumbing supply stores. Here in Charleston I may have blundered into the only baseball team in North America that is sponsored by a private detective agency. Right across their shiny black jerseys are the words Gene Sigman Investigations.

Visions of *The Rockford Files* and bad private eye movies are dancing in my head. And none of the images meshes particularly well with grassroots baseball. But no one here seems to share my sense of the bizarre. None of the kids thinks it's particularly unusual that a private eye is backing their team. They wear their uniforms unselfconsciously, and not even the opposing players take any note of the sponsorship. They're probably distracted by other things, like the lousy defensive show my guys are putting on.

I remain struck by the image of a low profile profession emblazoning itself across nine teenage chests on a baseball diamond. So I decide to talk to Gene Sigman before I leave town. Sigman, it turns out, is a local guy who made good. He was a cop back in the late sixties for about five years. Then he went off to university and got a degree in criminal justice. He started Gene Sigman Investigations back in 1982.

"The city gave me a successful business," he tells me. "I thought it was time to give something back."

Why baseball? Partly it's because Sigman played some ball himself in high school. But there's more.

"I figure if you keep a kid occupied, you keep him out of trouble. These teams can keep you mighty busy during the summer. It's not just the teenagers. I also sponsor a Little League team. Might as well start them out early with good habits."

Sigman seems like a guy who keeps pretty busy himself, so I wonder if he ever gets to see the Wheelers play.

"Yeah," he laughs, "about two or three times a year I go out with some friends to see a Wheelers game. We sit out in the left field bleachers and split a six-pack. It's about the only time I drink all year. A beer out at the ballpark still feels good once in a while."

Back in the Senior Boys League, the game goes pretty much as predicted. The Sigman Investigations team takes an early lead, then fritters it away with sloppy play that seems to snowball. Physical errors lead to mental errors, and before you know it, the team is behind and heads are hanging everywhere.

I'm surprised to find myself caring. I've been traveling all over, watching a ball game a day strictly for the sake of seeing baseball played. Here, where it arguably means least, I find myself caring about the outcome of this contest and its players. Nothing historic is happening here. Records are barely being kept. The final score will probably end up as a line of agate type in a West Virginia newspaper and no more.

Nevertheless, I care about these kids. I'm not sure what I am to them. Someone who obviously likes them but, more importantly, a stranger from a far-off place with an exotic life-style. I've already signed one kid's glove and been asked to touch a few bats for good luck. Even though my magic doesn't seem to be working, they keep coming back for more. When I finally pack it in around the sixth inning, I get an official team cheer and copious thanks for coming to see them. Even the coaches are shaking my hand. I don't need to be thanked. The day in Charleston has become special in its own way. And none of it would have happened if the Wheelers had been in town like they were supposed to be.

Princeton, West Virginia

In the name of the Father, the Son, and the macaroni salad.

Princeton, West Virginia, is a small town. If you're driving in from somewhere in the Appalachian League, you're probably headed west on Highway 460. Just look for one of those unforgettable road signs that dot the rural South: this one says "Possum Hollow Road." If you're driving in from the outside world, you're probably motoring along Interstate 77. At speeds in excess of 60 mph, you might miss the Princeton exit altogether and with it a singular look at minor league baseball.

When you get to town, you wonder whether Princeton can support a Burger King, much less a minor league team. In truth, the population is around 7,000, which qualifies Princeton as the smallest city in the United States to host a professional baseball team. In 1992, its closest competitor in the puny population sweepstakes was Pulaski, Virginia, which had been affiliated with the Braves for ten seasons and won the Appalachian League championship in 1991. At the end of 1992, however, the Pulaski Braves packed it in and moved to Danville. As of 1993, Princeton had won the "smallest city with professional baseball" contest without a fight.

Finding the ballpark is hardly an issue. Not only does everyone know where it is, but the lights are visible from just about anywhere in town. Every evening at 7:05, the joint is jumping. It is magically converted to a timeless scene from middle America: a concert in the park, a clown, a midway, happy faces, kids laughing. It is literally all there, as if someone had suspended the Appalachian poverty and multicultural turmoil of the nineties. Everything is on hold as long as the Princeton Reds are in town.

I visited Princeton twice: once during the off-season, and again at the start of the '93 campaign. The ballpark had really been spiffed up in the interim. The Reds play on what was the high school baseball field. Up until this year the park still looked like what it had been. It was almost a tad embarrassing. This year, things were different. The most noticeable addition, along with a slick paint job, was an outfield wall full of advertising signs. It's amazing how much the garish patchwork quilt of local ads has become part of the ambience of minor league baseball. Without it, the park looked too clean. Too much like what it had been: a high school field.

The Princeton team are relatively new kids on the block in the Appalachian League. They've been here since 1988 and have finally settled into an affiliation with the Reds after serving the Pirates and Phillies and spending time as a "co-op team," a sort of nonsectarian incubator for several big league teams. During 1990, when the Princeton Patriots were a co-op team, fans were sometimes treated to the sight of future Phillies playing themselves. Not only was the Princeton squad stocked with a number of Phillies hopefuls, but they competed against Martinsville, another Phillies affiliate in the same league. On days like that, the locals watched what looked like an intersquad game. Such oddities obviously haven't hurt attendance. At its worst, in 1991, Princeton drew a respectable 25,000 fans in this short season rookie ball league with about thirty home dates.

The Princeton Reds are unusual in several ways. First, they are run as a nonprofit organization. Yes, they're trying to draw as many fans as possible and keep them happy and entertained. And, yes, they want to sell all that lovely space on the outfield signs, not to mention as many season tickets as possible. But, ultimately, they've got to break even. That same money is going to get pumped back into the organization.

Having said that, Princeton is also unusual in its league because it employs a full-time general manager. Jim Holland is there to keep the seats painted and filled, the fans happy, and the players housed and fed. Short of pitching batting practice and pinch hitting, he does it all. General managers in the minor leagues bear little resemblance to their counterparts in The Show. They are typically young, underpaid, and energetic. They are expected to do, not to delegate. Doing includes everything from selling tickets to raking the infield. Minor league GMs are not above selling hot dogs, delivering prizes to the lucky fan with scorecard number 1486, and unplugging toilets after double headers. They do not sit in air-conditioned offices and talk to other GMs about trades. In fact, they rarely sit.

Jim Holland is a wiry man who appears to generate enough energy to heat and light most of Princeton. When we first met shortly after the '92 season, he was preparing for another round of meetings with local merchants. Business sponsorship is an essential part of minor league success, and Jim was working with his strongest suit ever: a second-place finish and a fresh renewal of Princeton's affiliation with Cincinnati. The latter was particularly important. Local fans were becoming disenchanted with the procession of faces and uniforms in the brief history of their team.

While working for a nonprofit organization takes some pressure off him, Jim still works overtime along with his battalion of unpaid "boosters." They are geared to making this park both physically and psychologically comfortable for players and fans. The comfort takes many forms — a fresh coat of paint on the stands, new seats for the paying customers, an Astroturf logo for the on-deck circle, and separate bathrooms for the players and fans. Imagine going to a New York Yankees game, having a few beers, and finding yourself standing next to Don Mattingly (still in uniform) using the men's room. This may be ludicrous or unthinkable in major league baseball, but it can and does happen in the minors.

The minor leagues are about player development, not championships. In fact, it is not uncommon for the major league team to promote players just when they are needed most by their minor league affiliate. Nevertheless, Jim could not conceal his pride in showing me the trophy Princeton had won in defeating league champion Bluefield, their closest neighbor and longtime Oriole affiliate, in a special playoff staged for local fans. Pride is pride, whether played to the tune of a million-dollar network contract or a local West Virginia trophy.

What do you do if your mascot, in this case Roscoe the Red Rooster, is ejected by an irate umpire? This can happen in the minors, where mascots and PA announcers occasionally exceed the bounds of propriety in expressing their home team sentiments. On a warm night, *no one* is beyond ejection. When his mascot is given the heave-ho, there is no point in the GM pouting or complaining to the league president. With the true soul of a carny operator, Holland turned the situation into two nights' worth of entertainment. On the first night of his suspension, Holland had the big bird appear on the far side of the center field fence, safely beyond the jurisdiction of the umpire, waving to the thousand or so delighted fans. One night later, just as the game was due to start, a patrol car drove on to the field. Guess who emerged from the backseat, proudly showing off the manacles on his feathered hands?

Fred and his daughter Ashley have showed up unexpectedly in Princeton, all the way from Hamilton, Ontario. Fred loves minor league baseball, and Ashley is starting to. At least she seems to be enjoying having all those cute young guys in uniform autograph her baseball. Fred tolerates the attention to Ashley but is feeling rather angry with the gods who control the location of teams.

"Can you believe it?" he asks no one in particular. "I live in Hamilton, and we spend half the year in Myrtle Beach. I used to be in heaven going to see games in both places I live: the Hamilton Redbirds and Myrtle Beach Hurricanes. Now, all of a sudden, both teams are gone. No more baseball in either place. Just like that. Here one season, gone the next. I mean, what are the chances of both those teams disappearing like that? What am I supposed to do now?"

Short of moving to Princeton and taking his chances with the Appy League gods, none of us has an answer. In truth, the minor league team shuffle is a very popular dance. Mind you, having *both* teams in your life disappear at the same time seems a bit extreme. It's a good thing that Fred and Ashley didn't pick up and follow their beloved Cardinals from Hamilton to Glens Falls, New York, where they relocated the next season. Within a year, Fred and Ashley would have been back on the phone to Allied Van Lines, as the Cardinals moved again, this time to Augusta, New Jersey, where they became the New Jersey Cardinals. Same league, new city.

"If the lucky number on page 23 of your scorecard is 2684, you're the winner of a five-dollar gift certificate to Taco Bell."

There is a scramble as pages turn, followed by a squeal from the general admission section.

"We have a winner! Keep waving so we can find you."

A minute later, GM Jim Holland bounds up the steps and hand delivers a certificate good for $5 to a happy teenager. That voucher will probably buy a filling meal. I can't help thinking that same five bucks probably wouldn't let you sniff a burrito at the SkyDome in Toronto.

Hometown batboys live in a special universe. They get to dress up in the team uniform, and the players treat them like a cross between water boys and little brothers. On the whole they work hard and have a grand time. They know all the players by name and even get to exchange high fives after home runs are hit.

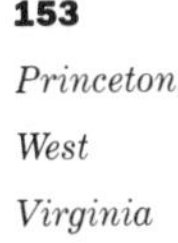

Roscoe the Red Rooster does his job under the watchful eye of Kevin the Enforcer.

In Princeton, this season's batboy is Jonathon Alvis. He's a tough, stocky little kid. The longest conversation we had went like this: Me — You gonna be a catcher one day? Him — I *am* a catcher. End of dialogue. About an hour before game time, we work out a routine in the Reds' bullpen. I stand on the mound and fire him my best stuff, which doesn't seem to be opening any eyes in the bullpen. As soon as he catches me, Jonathon flips the ball to one of the pitchers sitting in the pen, who dribbles the ball in front of the plate. Jonathon then pounces on it like a feral cat and fires me a rocket, presumably nailing an imaginary runner who is trying to take possession of the pitcher's mound. I apply the imaginary tag. The guys in the pen nod in approval. We repeat this ritual about thirty times until it is time for the *real* pitcher to warm up. Unfortunately, this is as close as I've come to pitching in the minor leagues.

The Princeton mascot has an unusual distinction. Unlike other giant birds or mythical creatures who roam around the stands during baseball games, Roscoe the Red Rooster has a protector. It's not altogether clear that he needs one, but wherever Roscoe goes, so does Kevin Sharp. Kevin is a big, warm-hearted guy who looks like he'd be comfortable on the back of a Harley. He's known locally as "The Enforcer." Presumably if someone in the stands ever thought of blindsiding Roscoe and collecting a sample of feathers between innings, he'd have Kevin to deal with. You mess with Roscoe, you mess with Kevin.

It's kind of stirring to see this giant rooster prowling around the grandstand with a rather large, imposing-looking gentleman patiently following him. Like the best Secret Servicemen, the Enforcer never seems to restrict Roscoe's movements, but he is always within sight to throw himself on a live grenade should some zealot from Bluefield have treason in his heart.

So how much does Kevin get paid for putting his life on the line? Not a farthing. Like the rest of the Princeton boosters, Kevin just loves being there. When I meet him about two hours before game time, he is playing catch with his daughter.

"She might be the first woman to play in the majors. You never know. Even if she doesn't make it, she can tell her kids, 'Your grandfather caught for the Princeton Reds.'" He pauses for emphasis. "Truth is, I never really caught for them during a game. What I do is during fielding practice every day, I stand out here and take the throws coming in from the outfield. Then I flip the ball back to the guy hitting them out. So technically, I figure I'm catching for Princeton."

I, for one, see no reason to disagree with the Enforcer.

I've been watching this kid for about ten minutes, and I'm far from convinced he's seen his seventeenth birthday yet.

"No way to know for sure," the GM confirms. Nevertheless, whatever his age, this guy is scooping everything in sight at second base.

Later, I ask his name. "Jhonny Carvajal," he says. Actually, he says "Johnny," but the roster sheet reveals the unusual spelling.

"How much?" he asks me, presumably referring to the pictures I've been taking.

"Dinero?" I reply, somewhat taken aback. He must think I'm a free-lance photographer selling his wares.

"Sí," he confirms.

"Nada. But I might want to use one in my book."

"Está bien," he assures me. "¿Cómo no?"

We both know that by the time the book comes out, Jhonny might be a phenom second baseman for the Cincinnati Reds or their AAA club. Or, perhaps more realistically, he might be back home in Venezuela looking for nonathletic employment and playing in pickup games on the weekend. One thing for sure: he won't still be playing rookie ball in Princeton, West Virginia.

Most Appalachian League teams feature a liberal mix of American and Central or South American players. Sometimes the ratio gets close to fifty-fifty. Players from the States come from a wide range of backgrounds: rural and urban, rich and poor. Third World recruits are almost uniformly small town poor. They also tend to be a little younger than their U.S. counterparts. Guys aren't drafted out of universities in the Dominican Republic.

Nothing separates the cultures more vividly than a pitstop for food during one of the bus odysseys that are a staple of minor league life. One look at the Salisbury steak or luncheon buffet brings groans and sarcastic humor from most of the American players, especially the urbanites. On the other hand, a well-stocked buffet table may be like a vision of Nirvana to a kid from San Pedro de Macorís.

A coach tells me, "For some of these kids, it's like going to heaven without having to do the dying part."

I see a middle infielder cross himself in front of the glutinous dessert display. Is so much chocolate pudding literally his for the taking? A Venezuelan player tells me that even if he is cut from the team, he is going to visit Shoney's one last time with an empty suitcase. T-shirts and underwear he can always replace back home. But boundless macaroni and cheese? Fried chicken? Jello? Only in Los Estados Unidos.

Bluefield, West Virginia

"Mister! Would you buy some Cracker Jacks from me?"
—Stadium vendor, Bowen Field

Like most things, distance is relative. Because I'm on my journey, I think little of driving three hundred miles to see a ball game. But folks who live in Princeton rarely drive twenty minutes down the road to see a game in Bluefield. It's even less likely now that Princeton has its own team. And the people who schedule Appalachian League games treat these neighboring towns as if they were time zones apart. It's not uncommon to have home games in Princeton and Bluefield on the same night. Twenty minutes might as well be two hundred miles.

At a sportscard show in Princeton, I ask a dealer if he stocks a Bluefield team set.

"No," he says. "We only carry the home team."

"But Bluefield is just down the road," I protest.

The idea seems alien to him.

"I guess so, but it feels far away," he replies. "I never go there. I see all my ball games in Princeton. I was there once, about seven years ago. As I recall, it was quite nice."

A debate is going on when I enter the Bluefield Stadium office. Who was it, *Baseball America* or *Sports Illustrated*, that voted Bluefield the second most beautiful baseball park in America? Or was it the third? One look around and you knew the details weren't important. Whoever and whatever it was, they had it right. Bluefield is a jewel.

Bowen Park celebrated its fiftieth anniversary in 1989. Not a lot of ballparks in the minors, or anywhere for that matter, are in their sixth decade of service. In truth, it's not Bowen

Opening night ceremonies in Bluefield.

Field that catches everyone's eye. The best you can say about the old stadium is that it's still standing. There's lots of concrete around, which shouldn't surprise anyone, since the wooden version of this ballpark burned down some time ago. There seem to be a lot of old-timers around the stadium, and they love telling stories. It's not clear whether they're putting on a show for the newcomer who's writing a book or whether all this reminiscing goes on every day. But, in the brief time I visit with them, I hear a lot of "Where were you when the ballpark burned down" stories. In Bluefield, this event may rival Kennedy's assassination as the landmark event used to reckon time.

I also hear a lot of name dropping.

"I remember Stan Musial playing here. He was a pitcher then, with Johnson City. But he was too good a hitter, so they told him to stop pitching."

Everyone's seen somebody famous hit one out. "Boog Powell," one guy says. "Danny Cater." "Andy Seminick." "Darryl Strawberry." They all nod at mention of Strawberry's name.

The locals aren't exaggerating. Bluefield has been in the league since 1946, and a lot of very famous people have played here. Some excelled right from the start. Cater led the league in hits, home runs, and RBIs for the Johnson City Cardinals in '58. Boog Powell, playing for Bluefield, was the RBI king in '59. Tony Oliva hit a mere .410 for Wytheville in '61. A young-looking guy called Donald Baylor led the league with a .346 average for Bluefield in '67. His manager was Joe Altobelli. Kirby Puckett, of the Elizabethton Twins, led the league in hits, BA (.382), runs, and total bases during the '82 season. That's the

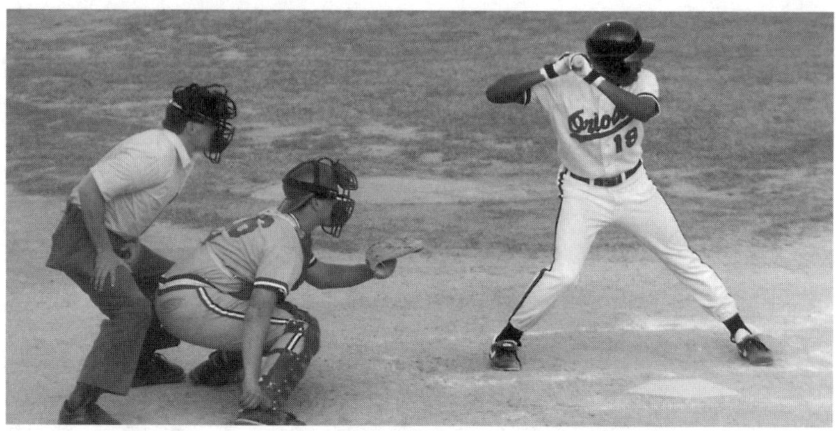

Center fielder Kimera Bartee ready to line a single to left field.

same year Dwight Gooden of the Kingsport Mets pitched for the All-Star team. The list is virtually endless.

It is also rich in names like Thomas O'Connor, Jack Shupe, or Mark Corey, who literally tore up the Appalachian League and went nowhere. Corey, in particular, played for Bluefield in 1976 and led the league in batting (.400), hits, runs, triples, home runs, and RBIs. Many Appalachian League stars never survived the transition to full-season A ball. Some made it to AA and foundered. It's the ones who became stars that catch attention, but there are far more cases of rookie league phenoms who are now farming or pumping gas. No doubt their families and beer-drinking buddies have heard all the tales.

Good ball players pass through everywhere, but what really makes Bluefield unique is its setting. You know this is special as soon as you drive into the parking lot. Bowen Field is surrounded by an absolutely breathtaking wall of green. The stand of trees behind the outfield fence makes an almost unimaginably beautiful backdrop for hitting. People talk about it reverentially almost everywhere I go: fans, journalists, especially players. All over the Appy League, even beyond, players love to reminisce about it. They'll tell you not just how pretty it was but how good it was to hit against.

"I never saw the ball so good as in Bluefield. It looked like a beach ball coming in against those trees." From both a practical and artistic point of view, Bluefield is a standout.

Twenty-year-old Bluefield center fielder Kimera Bartee, playing in his sixth Appy League game, has himself a fine evening. While I watch, Bartee goes two for three at the plate, walks twice, scores four runs, and drives one

Irresistible sales force at Bowen Field.

in. But getting on base is only half the story. Once he's there, the man is hell on wheels. On this lovely Friday evening in Bluefield, Bartee steals five bases, making him ten for ten so far this young season.

"There's no substitute for speed," his manager, Andy Etchebarron, tells the local paper after the game. "Bartee really knows how to run the bases."

It certainly looks that way so far, although a lot of challenges lie ahead in Kimera Bartee's career.

One of the quaintest parts of seeing a game in Bowen Field is the vendors. Wherever you go, other than Bluefield, an army of adults wanders through the stands hawking food and souvenirs. In some places, they even take orders like waiters in a restaurant. Teenage vendors, guys in their thirties, forties. In some parks, the vendors and ushers are pushing sixty, maybe more. In Bluefield, the vendors are kids. Even little kids. They're cute in a scruffy, entrepreneurial way. I haven't bought a box of Cracker Jacks in over thirty years, but all that changes in the third inning of Bluefield versus Johnson City when I feel a tug at my sleeve.

"Mister," she starts. Who could say no? I had obviously been spotted as a nonlocal. The ploy works like a charm. The kids are acrobatic, bounding over rows of seats. They work hard and are surprisingly adept at keeping track of money. Not that they need to be; who could think about cheating one of these kids?

But there's another side to hiring kids as vendors. In the seventh inning when I *really* wanted a bag of peanuts, I had to go get it myself. There wasn't a vendor in sight. I found one of them, now dressed in civvies and indistinguishable from all the other nine year olds in the park.

"What happened to the peanut girl?" I ask.

"She quit for the night. She already made twenty dollars. That's good money!" he explains.

Maybe not in New York, but in Bluefield, for sure. Especially if you're nine years old. In fact, most baseball-related things are cheaper here. Tickets, scorecards, even baseball cards. Down the road in Burlington, North Carolina, a set of team cards sells for $7. Back in Bluefield, depending on the year, sets cost $2 or $3, and if you buy several, the friendly souvenir man might throw in a couple more for a buck apiece. It's card collectors' heaven.

The Bluefield Orioles have an advantage. Their parent club has an affiliate in the Gulf Coast League, which means maybe a quarter of their team has one season of pro ball behind them before they ever play "rookie ball." Add to that the fact that maybe fifteen of these guys had spent part or all of the previous season in Bluefield or played some college ball, and this team has a bit of experience under its belt. Put them up against a team of seventeen- or eighteen-year-old rookie draft choices and you'll see what overmatching is all about.

The *Bluefield Daily Telegraph* puts local baseball where it belongs: on the first page of the sports section. The headline the next morning is "O's Bounce Back to Deck Cards 9–3." They are obviously talking about Bluefield and Johnson City. The game highlights include a brush with disaster as Matt Riemer is credited with an inside-the-park homer when the Johnson City center fielder runs smack into an unpadded outfield wall and knocks himself out cold. There are some tense moments waiting for him to revive. Johnson City contributes another highlight when they field two players wearing number 26. At one point, catcher Joe Wallace (number 26) is at bat while Hector Ugueto (also number 26) takes his lead off second base. You don't see that a lot in pro ball.

Calvin Maduro, the starting pitcher, is from Aruba. Appalachian League dugouts usually look like a branch office of the United Nations, but someone from the island of Aruba is still an oddity. This team also has an Australian (Myles Barnden) and a Yale graduate (probably as rare as an Aruban) named Bill Asermely.

Ken Reed, a catcher/first baseman from Hamilton, Ohio, is another pleasant surprise. Reed wants to know about the book I'm writing. When I describe what I'm doing, he comments, "That sounds like *Stolen Season*." He's absolutely right, but I'm doubly impressed to find someone in the minor leagues who is actually reading David Lamb's wonderful journey through minor league baseball.

"You look surprised," he observes. I am.

"It's a great book. I'm just up to the section on Bluefield. I can't wait to read it."

So here's a guy, standing in Bluefield, *playing* for Bluefield, who can't wait to read what someone else had to say about his life and times.

Lots of players seem interested in what I'm doing, and some even promise to "look for it" or "buy it." But on the whole, my guess is that books about baseball sell to fans, not players. Last year, I offered my copy of Don Drysdale's biography to Don McCormack, manager of the Reading Phillies. I had just finished the book, and it was lying on the front seat of my car. I figured it would break the monotony of those long Eastern League bus trips. McCormack politely refused it, telling me, "I don't read sports books." Then he suggested that maybe Phil, the bus driver, would like it. I can only hope he didn't read it during those same long journeys.

Of everyone in sight, Robert Miller seemed most likely to be the man in charge.

"Are you the general manager?" I ask.

"Nope," he responds. "I'm the team doctor."

"An Appy League team has its own doctor?"

"This one does," he says. And we introduce ourselves.

When he learns that I live just outside of Toronto, Miller is particularly pleased.

"I'm *from* Toronto," he says. "Grew up in Cabbagetown."

The only two people in Bluefield, West Virginia, with ties to Toronto have just found each other.

"What in the world are you doing here?" I ask him.

"Isn't it beautiful?" he replies. "I love it. I came down to visit for a year. That was eleven years ago."

Dr. Robert B. Miller has put down roots. His ear, nose, and throat clinic has two offices, one in Bluefield and one in Princeton, the other baseball town just down the road. And he really is the Orioles team doctor. He proudly shows me the clubhouse, which includes a sports medicine area that would be impressive at the AA level. I get the whole Canadian tour, which includes personal introductions to the real GM, as well as manager Andy Etchebarren and pitching coach Jeff Morris. It also includes a seat for the game in Robert B. Miller's personal, name-plated box seat. With a view of the trees.

Durham, North Carolina

"This is a very low tech bull." —*Cathy Sokal, Belle of the Bull*

Ask the average American to name a city associated with minor league baseball and you're likely to hear Durham, North Carolina. Sure, most of that has to do with the movie *Bull Durham*, but it is more than Kevin Costner and Susan Sarandon that put Durham on the baseball map.

In reality, Durham has had minor league baseball, on and off, since 1902. Durham Athletic Park was built on its present site among the downtown warehouses in 1926. The original structure was destroyed by fire in 1939 but quickly rebuilt with concrete and steel in time for the following season. With surprisingly few modifications, that structure still stands.

There is probably no experience in all of minor league baseball quite like seeing a game in Durham Athletic Park. For sheer, off-the-wall funkiness, Durham has eclipsed the competition. Some of this might be subliminal spillover from the movie, but not all. The place just seems to exude a flaky irreverence that even Hollywood couldn't inspire.

If you look beyond baseball, Durham is hardly an idyllic setting. Like Greensboro, its neighbor to the west, Durham is a tough place. It has tried very hard to change its image from a hard-edged tobacco town to an upscale part of the Research Triangle. To be sure, Durham has more than its share of professionals. Stand up in a movie theater and call for help and you're as likely to find a neurosurgeon as you are an auto mechanic. If you take the long view, an aerial photograph would reveal some lovely homes, a fine university, and lots of good restaurants. There are some unmistakable signs of counterculture here too. Folks came to Durham in the sixties and put down roots. They and their kids still live and work here.

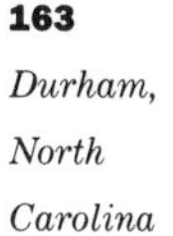

Durham Athletic Park.

But you can also get robbed or killed in Durham more easily than in a lot of American cities. The tough part of the city gets written about in the morning paper because it's where most of the crime takes place. As far as most affluent whites are concerned, that part of town might just as well be located on the moon. They rarely go there, unless they're driving their maid home or visiting the ballpark.

The truth is, I'd move to Durham in a minute. I'd risk the crime and whatever else the city council doesn't want you to know about, because Durham is a beautiful and loopy place to live. And part of that appeal for me, undoubtedly, is the Durham Bulls. It's not the *team*. As we all know, minor league teams change every year. Rather, it's what goes on at the ballpark. If all that sounds a bit rhapsodic, here comes the punchline. They're moving. As of the end of the 1994 season, the Bulls will have played their last game in Durham Athletic Park.

Why, you might ask. Who'd be crazy enough to pack up and leave all that tradition? It's not like the roof is falling in. Or is it?

Unfortunately, the roof *is* starting to sag. I talk with Al Mangum, the Bulls general manager. Mangum joined the team in 1991 when Capitol Broadcasting bought the Bulls from Miles Wolff, thus starting what many locals describe as the "business era" of Bulls baseball. Mangum may not be a structural engineer, but he is as close to the day-to-day operations of the ballpark as anybody. He sees things a little differently from the starry-eyed tourists and journalists who come to do a story on the Bulls.

"There's a lot of romance surrounding this ballpark. Ever since the movie, this has been everyone's idea of baseball tradition. How could anyone take this quaint old place and build some sterile glass and steel tomb out by an interstate? I wish I could tell you how often I hear that question.

"First of all, that's not what we're doing. Neither the sterile, characterless place nor the location. We're building in town. Barely a mile from here. And the same people who designed Camden Yards in Baltimore are going to do our park. They know we're trying to preserve the intimate atmosphere we have now. I'm absolutely convinced the new park is going to be a great place to play ball or to see a ball game."

"But isn't this one?" I reply, not surprising Mangum with my question.

"No. If that sounds cold, make the distinction between someone like yourself who comes in for a few days and only sees the romantic side of things. You don't worry if some of the plaster is falling down. That's just part of the charm. It's a very different situation for someone who works here. A vendor, or secretary, or ball player. They're going to see this place in less romantic terms. We have one of the worst facilities in the country for visiting teams. Even for our own team. The clubhouses are substandard. Players and coaches who have been around know how marginal this old park is. They're not looking for romance. They want adequate rest rooms and a decent clubhouse. They'll have that in the new park.

"From an outsider's point of view, things here may look OK. But it's really all done with mirrors. This is just not a workable facility anymore. Something had to be done. The amount of money it would have taken to get this place up to standards is just beyond what anybody would consider investing. It would literally be cheaper to tear it down and start over again."

"And what will become of the park. *Will* they tear it down?" I inquire.

"No. It will stay what it really is best suited for. Kids will play here. High school teams, area leagues, things like that. For those purposes, it's just fine."

Al Mangum has a difficult job. He gets to face a procession of awestruck writers and tourists who keep asking, "How can you do this?"

"Keep an open mind," he replies. "We think you'll be impressed."

There are only about a dozen people in the stands when I arrive at 3:30 in the afternoon before a night game. It's over 100 degrees on the field, and the Bulls are taking infield practice in their team shorts. They look more like the Commonwealth soccer team than an American baseball team.

Out in the right field bleachers, a big guy is sitting by himself. He looks like he'd be at home driving a tractor. There aren't many of us around, so we introduce ourselves. His name is Wayne, and he's driven here with his eleven-year-old boy all the way from Oklahoma. I observe that it seems a long way to come

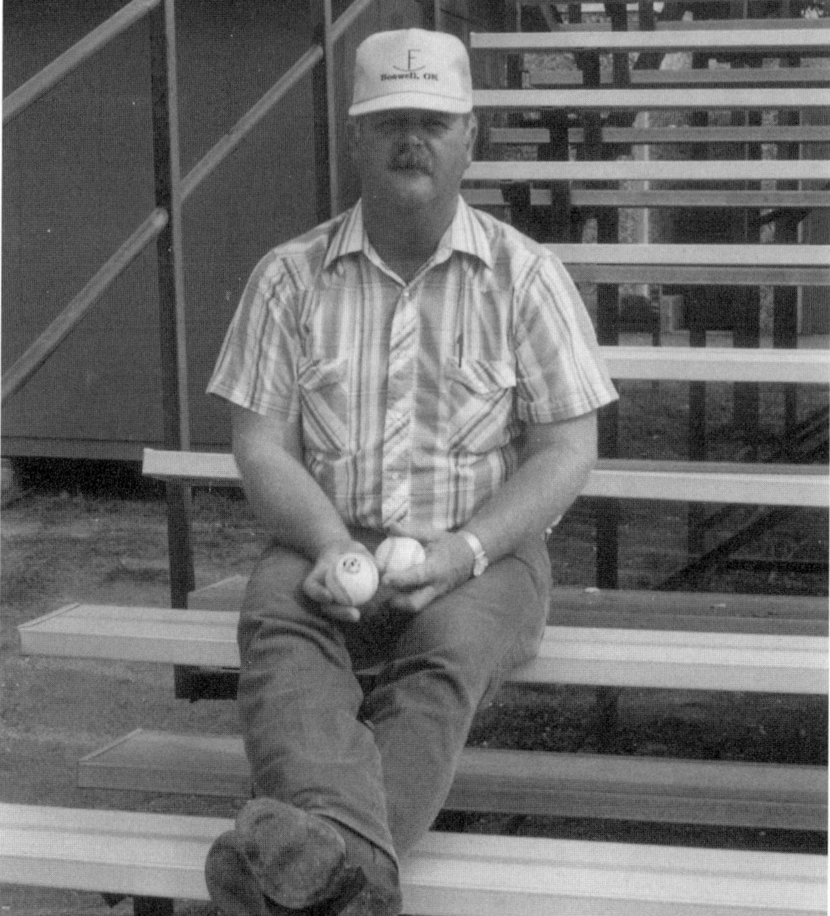

Wayne Sample, all the way from Boswell, Oklahoma.

to see a ball game. He acknowledges that and tells me, "I always wanted to play pro ball but I never really had a chance. Don't even know if I was good enough. But my daughter married a boy, and he *is* good enough."

Wayne nods out to right field, where 6′3″ Dirk Blair is throwing the ball around with his teammates. Blair pitches for the Bulls. He's having a decent season so far, a 3–2 record with a 3.62 ERA.

"He's improved every year he's played," Wayne tells me. "This is his third year playing in the Braves farm system. I think he has a real chance."

Wayne has made the thirteen-hundred-mile drive with his son, who has never been to a pro ball game. A couple of hours before game time and he's already having the time of his life. Every few minutes he reappears with a fresh baseball in his hand.

"These guys keep hitting them over the fence," he says excitedly. Then he scrambles away to wait for the next treasure.

Wayne tells me, "I run a farm back home. We grow peanuts and raise cattle. First time I've taken some time off in years. I left it with my daddy to run while I'm gone. He's eighty years old. It used to be his. I'm sure he can keep it going while I'm off watching some baseball."

After some reflection, Wayne gestures toward right field and says, "I guess I'm living my dream through him. That's not so bad, is it?"

I tell Wayne I can think of a lot of worse things to do than watching your son-in-law play ball.

It's about an hour before game time, and I'm getting hungry. Do I bother driving into town, or is there some decent food at the park? I ask the locals, and the verdict is unanimous. Try some of Dillard's barbecue.

Barbecue at a ballpark? Why not? When you're in Durham, anything is possible. Dillard's stand is located all the way out in left field under an awning. The ballpark isn't that big, but you're still not going to stumble into this concession unless somebody points you.

I arrive to find James Dillard setting things up. He's got barbecue sandwiches with slaw and ribs ("Buck a bone"). I tell him I'll start by trying some barbecue, only to realize I've left my wallet in my car. Not to worry, James tells me. Have whatever I want. We can settle up later. I'm grateful for the offer, and the barbecue is delicious. I go in for a couple of ribs, and they're fine too.

While I'm sitting around talking to James, the sky suddenly turns dark, and a wind picks up. A torrential rain comes out of nowhere. A couple of folks are talking about a "tornado-looking sky." The grounds crew races out and struggles to cover the infield while the wind whips up the tarp. The whole scene has a primal quality. If Pavlov is right, I'll be checking for storm clouds next time I smell barbecue.

In the middle of the deluge, a couple of local kids scramble through the fence and start sweet-talking James. Before you know it, both of them are eating barbecue sandwiches and watching the rain with me. A couple of concession workers from across the park come in for cover, and they too end up with some ribs. I've been here about half an hour now, and I still haven't seen James take in a penny.

"How do you stay in business?" I ask him.

"Oh, I never worry. It all works out. I know you'll be back, and those kids, what was I going to do? They asked me for a slice of bread. How was I going to

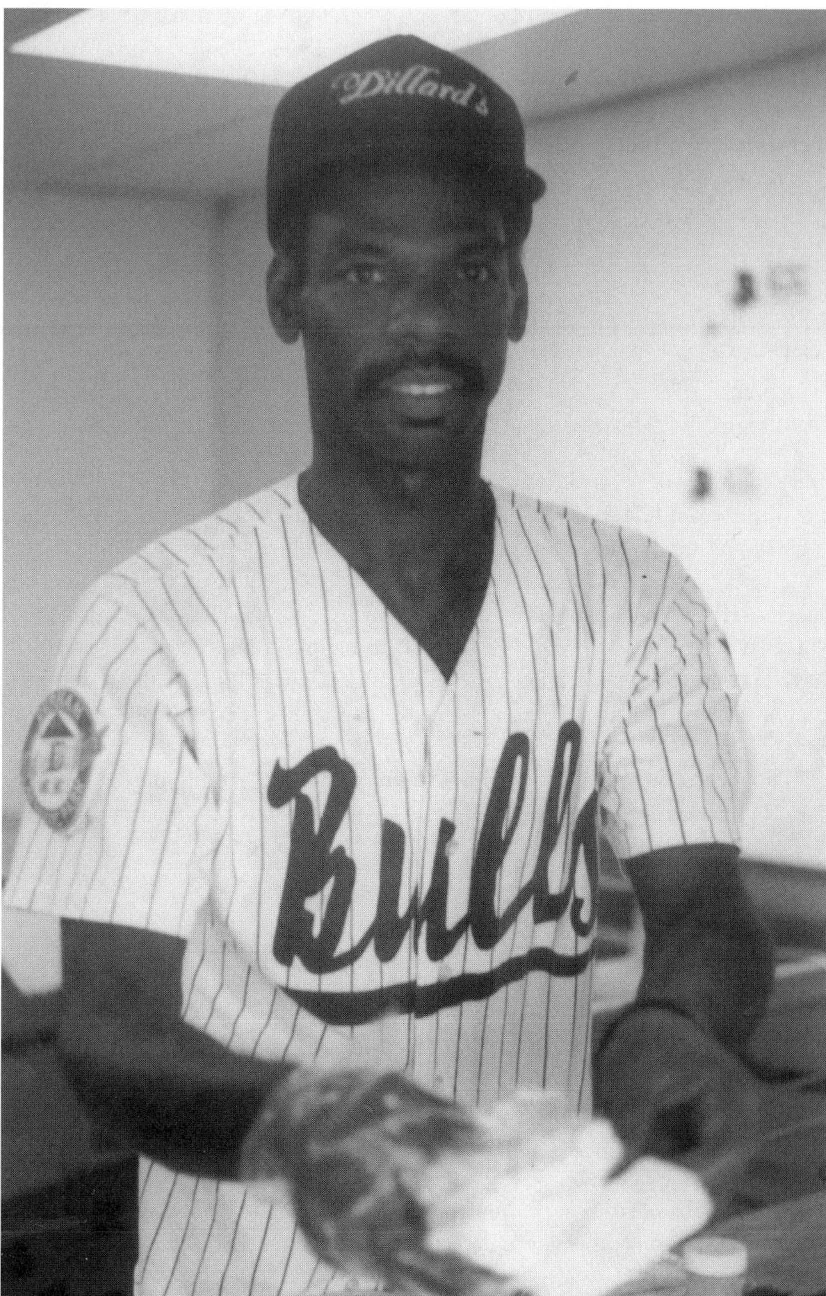

James Dillard: barbecue at the ballpark.

send them away with a slice of dry bread when I've got all this barbecue here? Besides, I know where they live. It's a rough place. I'd just as soon they don't have to walk back through there any more than they have to."

What's happening here? Is Dillard's Bar-B-Que a social agency or a business?

"Oh, we're a business. We do fine. My daddy started the restaurant down on Fayetteville Street back in '71. Everybody knows about us. People come to Dillard's from all over. Even people who never come to east Durham come by for our cooking."

How do you go from family restaurant to ballpark concession?

"That's a very special story," James tells me. "This is our first year. We are the first black-owned business to operate in the ballpark. This is a bit of history here, and we got in just under the wire. Just before the move.

"We don't really make a lot of money with this concession. In fact, sometimes it's a break-even situation for us even on a good night. My daddy is very much a bottom line kind of man. He's not sure all this is worth the effort. I keep telling him we're meeting new people, broadening our base. People will come to the restaurant who never heard of us before. They'll try our catering business. I see it as an investment. I guess we'll see what happens next."

I visit with James every day I'm at the ballpark, and when I'm ready to leave Durham he sends me home with a jar of Dillard's Bar-B-Que sauce and a laminated copy of a story that appeared in the *Durham News & Observer* earlier this year.

"That was on page 1. It's all about our restaurant coming out to the ballpark. My daddy was very proud of that. He had those copies made up."

The headline reads "Make way, hot dogs. Here come the ribs!"

A very imposing-looking cop walks over to me and asks to see my camera.

"O God, he thinks it's stolen!" flashes across my mind. But my paranoia barely has time to get off the ground. The cop is simply curious about my lens. He's just bought a 28–200 mm zoom. Great for surveillance, he explains.

He's a large black man, doubly impressive with the .38 strapped to his hip. Ideal for intimidating drug-crazed felons. But what's he doing at the ballpark? Mainly, he seems to be keeping ten-year-old kids from leaning over the chain-link fence in left field.

"You kids be careful, now. You could get hurt." This from a guy who looks like he'd be at home apprehending axe murderers.

A bit of overkill, I suggest.

He nods. "The Bulls hire eight off-duty cops every game. I'm not sure they need them. It has more to do with local laws about security for gatherings of this size. It's a pretty easy job. Hardly any trouble. Mostly it's just some fan who has had a few too many beers getting into an altercation with someone. People come here to have fun."

He's been on the force for twenty-two years. "What will you do when you retire?" I ask him.

"That's easy," he replies. "Sell real estate."

Down closer to home plate is an equally imposing-looking guy. This one is not in uniform, and, as far as I know, he isn't packing a gun. He is wearing slim-fitting jeans and slick-looking snakeskin boots. And on his finger, big as life, is a World Series ring.

People are giving him a lot of space. He has a whole row of seats nearly to himself. I may be imagining it, but there seems to be a deferential silence around him, and people are definitely shooting sidelong glances his way.

I figure, what the hell. Everything else in this town seems to be a story, so I go sit next to him. He doesn't react. I introduce myself and tell him what I'm doing here, and he nods. Nothing more. I look right at him, violating yet another social taboo. This guy is a special case. And he sure does look familiar.

Finally, I can stand it no more. As unawkwardly as I can, I ask, "Should I know who you are?"

He shakes his head "no."

"Are you a player?"

"No." Then after what seems an eternity, he adds, "I'm a scout." And to prove it, he flashes the stopwatch he's been using to time the pitcher's deliveries and moves to first.

"You work for the Braves?"

"Oakland."

"You here to look at anyone in particular?"

"No. We're always collecting information for future trades. Things like that."

He tells me he's covering the Carolina League this year. He did the Sally League last year.

Meanwhile he sits there. Cool, aloof, trim, and sharp. Chewing tobacco, spitting, and never once hitting those fancy snakeskin boots. The World Series ring, which I honestly believe has gotten larger since I sat down, seems to be reflecting every available bit of light in the park.

I ask him if he enjoys his job. He looks directly at me, maybe for the first time.

"It's a job. I don't find it thrilling. Your job isn't supposed to be enjoyable. It's what you do."

If he were anybody else, I might tell him how much I disagree with that view. But I instinctively know this is not a time for debate.

For a while longer we sit in silence. Other than his name, which I don't *dare* ask, I seem to have run out of questions. I go on watching the game while he clocks runners and takes notes. Silent, efficient, minimal.

Finally, in the top of the seventh inning, with the score tied 4–4, he gets up and leaves.

"Enjoy the game," he says pleasantly, with not a trace of sarcasm.

I did. But who was that masked man?

I realize rather belatedly that part of what makes the Bulls games unique is the style of their PA announcer, Bob Guy. The most obvious feature, the one that gets imitated by fans all over the park, is his use of "Attention! Attention!" before every announcement. Guy manages to drop the first syllable almost every time. What's left are numerous calls of "Tension!"

But that's the obvious part. What really starts to get to me over several days is the structure of Guy's announcements. I'd never thought about it before, but there are rules, or at least expectations, about how ballpark messages are supposed to sound. I've been to maybe forty or fifty different parks in my life. I've grown used to hearing something like "Now batting for Elmira, number 22, Bill Jones." Adding "third base" is optional, but it usually comes after Jones. It's part of the cadence of the game.

You'd think it was a capital offense to break these rules, considering how universally they're accepted. In Durham, of course, they're broken all the time. This is what you're likely to hear on any Wednesday evening in Durham Athletic Park. An exact quote: "Now batting, number 35. Steve Hinton. He's the Blue Rocks' first baseman."

Hold on, Guy. You can't say stuff like that! It isn't normal. It's too . . . *conversational*. It's too *friendly*! You're supposed to sound official, like Charlton Heston, imparting divine wisdom through the PA system. You sound like my Uncle Bob. Everybody's Uncle Bob. I begin to wonder, did the expression "Bob's your uncle" get started in Durham Athletic Park?

Like most people, I got my first look at the mechanical bull when I saw the movie *Bull Durham*. I also carry two very popular misconceptions: First, that the bull has been part of Durham Athletic Park forever, or at least since the "early days," whenever they were. Second, that the bull was operated electronically from the press box or from some kind of master control center. I was wrong on both counts.

To begin with, the mechanical bull didn't exist before 1987. It was created for the movie. But it so captured the quirky, low budget side of minor league baseball ("Hit bull, win steak") that it became a case of instant tradition. Six years later, the bull is still wagging its tail and snorting smoke.

And how does he do it? It turns out there are no microprocessor chips and electronic impulses involved. What we have instead is the "Belle of the Bull," a very flesh and blood lady, perched high above Durham Athletic Park behind the plywood bull, operating a pulley, valve, and switch.

"This is a very low tech bull," Cathy Sokal tells me with a big smile. "People are usually surprised by that. It's just me up here doing all of it. I keep my eye on the game, and when one of our players gets a good hit or makes a nice play, I let the bull act up a bit."

We're talking during a Sunday afternoon game. When one of the Durham players hits a double, Cathy grabs the lever and gives several well-practiced tugs. The bull obediently wags his tail. A few batters later, an RBI is Cathy's cue for some mechanical snorting.

"Don't be startled," she warns me. "This is pretty loud."

With that, Cathy turns the handle on what looks like a large scuba tank. The bull snorts audibly, and smoke escapes from his nose. The crowd loves it.

"The eyes only show up during night games," she explains, but for my sake Cathy flips the small switch several times anyway. A pair of red eyes flashes into the Durham sunshine, even if hardly anyone in the park notices.

"So how did you get this job?" I ask.

"I lucked into it," Cathy answers, using a phrase I was hearing quite often on my journey. People seem to feel genuinely fortunate to be working in minor league baseball.

"A friend of mine was doing it, and when he had to leave, he told me about it. I've been here ever since."

"So is this a career?"

"I hope not!" she tells me. "They pay me twenty bucks a night. I think a day job might be a good idea!"

Although Cathy has a degree in landscape architecture from the University of Illinois, she's not on a career path to make her rich.

"I've been working as a gardener. That's how I got this tan. I lead a pretty simple life."

During the games, Cathy is surrounded by kids. She is a pretty appealing target for them. Along with the pleasure of hanging out with her, they get to operate the bull ("There probably aren't many kids in Durham who haven't made this tail wag"). The kids also know there's a ready supply of peanuts and bubble gum that Cathy keeps for visitors. The back of the bull is covered with little comics taken from bubble gum wrappers.

As entertaining as the bull is from the front, I leave knowing that the show behind the bull is even more enjoyable.

Cathy Sokal, Belle of the Bull.

"Hey!" shouts Tom Smith by way of introduction.

The Wilmington right fielder has been looking away from batting practice in the direction of the mechanical bull. Actually, what's caught his eye is not so much the bull as the lady who works it. Smith figures he can avoid injury by splitting his attention between fly balls and the Belle of the Bull.

"How you doin'?" he asks.

Cathy waves back, smiling. He isn't the first visiting player to express interest.

Smith presses a little harder, and Cathy good-naturedly waves him off.

"How old are you?" he asks, a bit puzzled at why this isn't working better.

"Old enough to be your mama," Cathy laughs, holding up four fingers on her right hand to signal forty. Actually, she hasn't yet had her fortieth birthday, but rounding up by a few months seems useful right about now.

Smith shakes his head in mild disbelief. He's willing to stretch some boundaries (after all, he's a young athlete on the road), but this may be a bit too much. Still, he's enjoying the encounter, even if it's headed nowhere.

A quick check later in the afternoon finds Tom Smith still doing some mild surveillance work in the direction of the bull. He's lost some of his initial ardor, but he hasn't quite packed it in yet. Maybe a few diving catches in right field will help turn the tide.

Whether or not Tom Smith has seen the movie *Bull Durham*, he's destined to find out that Cathy is not looking to reenact the role of Annie Savoy to his Nuke LaLoosh. It's going to take more than some casual repartee in right field to make this bull wag its tail and snort smoke.

Like Cathy, Leisha Cowart is thrilled to be working for the Bulls. Leisha is director of public relations and promotions.

"That's a fancy title, but the truth is I would have scrubbed floors to work here. I didn't care. I was teaching English in high school in Florida. I needed a change.

"My parents asked what I wanted for my birthday, and I asked if they'd send me to the baseball winter meetings in Miami. What a great present. I went there determined to get a job in baseball. The Bulls were advertising for a receptionist. I took it. It didn't matter what I did. I'd have said, 'Fine. When do I start?'

"The first year I was a receptionist. I did what they told me. When this PR position came up, I told them I could do it, and they hired me. It's a lot of work and it's not a lot of money. But that doesn't matter. Some days when I'm

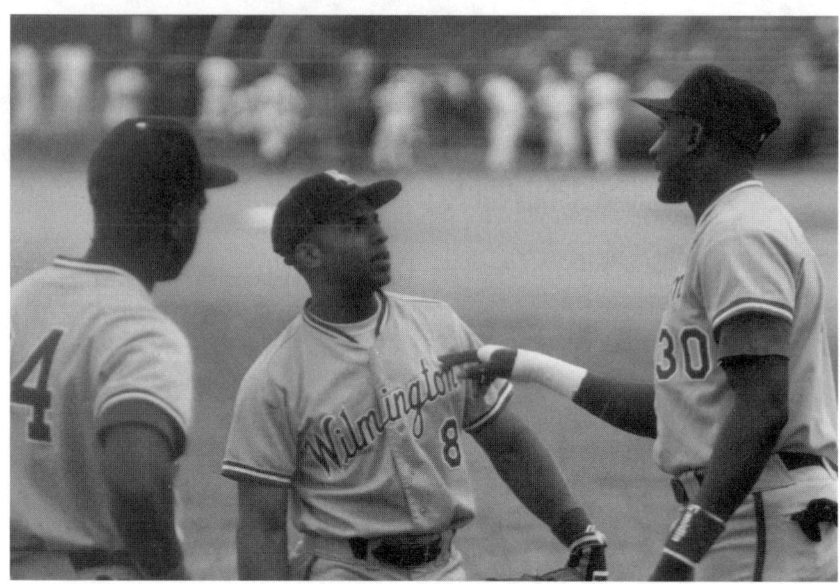

"Listen to me," Tom Smith tells Raúl Gonzalez. "Tonight you're *paying for the pizza!"*

stressed or overtired, I just stop for a second. I listen to the crack of the bat out there and I know why I'm here. It's all worthwhile."

This afternoon, Willie Stargell is in town to throw out the first baseball and sign some autographs. Also on hand is former Negro League star Buck Leonard. Leisha is busy getting everything set up. It all goes smoothly, but behind the scenes there is a flurry of activity. There is Stargell's pregame speech, then the ceremonial first pitch, and all the photographers. Then the tent out back in the picnic area, where Stargell will sign autographs during the game. Leisha is there, seeing that it all goes according to plan. She isn't scrubbing floors, but she sure is working up a sweat.

In addition to worrying about the crowds surrounding Stargell and company, Leisha also has to attend to a daily ballpark ritual. Like many minor league teams, Durham sends each player out to his position escorted by a youngster. They stand together, separated by about three feet, ten years, and more hero worship than you can measure. It's a moment these kids, most of whom are already in Little League, will never forget. They'll always be able to say, "I once stood next to Dominic Therrien at third base before a game!"

Depending on Dominic's fate in the Braves' minor league system, years from now this boast may be greeted by a wide-eyed "No way!" Or perhaps an indifferent "Who?"

Most ballparks, both major and minor league, use music to punctuate events and choreograph crowd response. Very few places still use a live musician to do it. Virtually all musical cues are now prerecorded. There is a service to provide them, from the bugle call that leads to "Charge!" to the "We will, we will rock you!" that accompanies pitching changes by the visiting team.

Somewhere there must be a history of the use of music in ballparks. My own experience started with Ebbets Field in Brooklyn. The musician's name was Gladys Gooding. I can still hear the corny skating rink organ playing everything from the national anthem to between-innings serenades. These days there is a lot of variation in how anthems are performed. Sometimes they're live. I've heard everything from choirs and brass bands to a cappella vocalists. More often, they're recorded. I've heard scratchy old 78s that sound like they come from a yard sale, as well as progressive vocal ensembles recorded in digital sound.

Durham is among only a few parks that still use live music whenever they can. That means a real musician with some knowledge of the game and a keyboard patched into the PA system. The man at the keyboard in Durham is named Mike Mulligan. Why does he do it? Is he getting rich?

"Are you kidding?" he laughs. "I play in a band. On a bad night we make $800. But I love playing for the Bulls. It's fun to be here. I do this whenever I can. I don't think it's the money. I get paid $20 a game."

Another $20 disciple testifies.

On my third visit to the ballpark, I comment to Bob Guy, the PA announcer, that I haven't seen a manual scoreboard like this one in years. It's true. Even the most marginal, low budget minor league parks have electronic scoreboards controlled from the press box. They usually come with a prominently attached corporate logo, telling you that Pepsi, Miller beer, or the Marlboro Man have bought their way into the fans' hearts and lungs.

In Durham, the scoreboard has a catwalk below it so a kid can run along and hang up new numbers every half-inning. Sometimes the kid gets a small round of applause. Maybe he also makes twenty bucks a night, although the work is less skilled than running the bull or playing the organ.

How can Durham get by with such an old-fashioned arrangement, I ask.

"Oh, this scoreboard is electronic," Bob Guy explains. "It works fine. We just learned that the fans really get a kick out of seeing the numbers hung up manually. It's part of the atmosphere. We actually paid extra to have the hooks installed so the kid can go out there like that. Everyone seems to like it better this way. It's kind of old-fashioned."

Right-handed pitcher Jerry Koller is sitting in the stands behind home plate when my friend and I sit down. I'm always amazed at how young these guys look in their street clothes, operating the radar gun the day after they've pitched.

My friend is kind of new to all of this. She's just discovering the joys of minor league baseball, and Jerry is patiently fielding all of her questions. He's not really satisfied with how he pitched last night, although it was good enough for a win.

"I know I didn't have my best stuff. I guess you should be happy when you're not at your best and you win anyway. But I want to pitch better than that."

Jerry had not yet turned eighteen when he was drafted in 1990. He was a high school kid from Indiana.

"It seemed like every game I pitched, there were scouts in the stands. I'd lift my arm and ten radar guns would go up. I got used to it early. By my senior year, I didn't even notice they were there."

Jerry spent his first two years knocking around the Rookie League. His first season in the Gulf Coast League was an eye opener. Fifty innings pitched, forty-five strikeouts, and a 2.12 ERA. He didn't fare as well the next year in Idaho Falls, but Jerry hit his stride in Class A Macon during the 1992 season: 133 innings pitched with 114 strikeouts. Good control and a stellar 2.37 ERA.

"That season got me to Durham. This is an important year for me. I've got to see if I can keep it going."

So far, things were not going according to plan. Jerry's ERA was around 4.50, and opposing batters were hitting over .290 against him.

"My won-lost record is still OK, but that's because we've been scoring some runs when I pitch. I've got to keep working at it."

Work he did. The next two days, Jerry was throwing on the side under the watchful eye of pitching coach Matt West. He wasn't scheduled to pitch; he just wanted to get some work in. Jerry was out there throwing hard and listening even harder. West seemed to have a lot to tell him. Over the next couple of starts, Jerry went 1–1 and lowered his ERA marginally. A month and a half remained of Jerry Koller's season, and a lot could still happen.

In contrast to Koller, there's a new guy on the Bulls who seems to be making his mark in record time. Hiawatha Terrell Wade did not begin his professional life as a high profile draft pick. He was signed out of a sandlot tryout camp in South Carolina when he was a gangly eighteen year old. True to form, he struggled for his first two years in the organization.

Suddenly everything has started to come together. Wade has been just called up from Macon, a good sign that he's raising some eyebrows in the organization. The attention is well deserved. Earlier in the season, Wade pitched an eighteen-strikeout game for the Macon Braves. In his first two games with the Bulls, Wade's strikeout totals continue to impress. In thirteen innings Wade has already whiffed fifteen batters in the Carolina League.

Terrell Wade is scheduled to pitch a big game on Sunday, the Fourth of July. It's big because Willie Stargell is there, along with a lot of press and scouts. The house is packed. It is also hot as hell — at least 95 degrees at game time with a humidity that makes it feel like 120.

Terrell Wade doesn't seem to mind any of that. Throwing at speeds that probably match the temperature, Wade appears unhittable. At least once he gets going. In the first inning, Wade gives up a home run to Wilmington's Andy Stewart, who is in the throes of a twelve-game hitting streak. Those are the last runs the Blue Rocks score.

Pitching coach Matt West has a great quote in the next morning's *Herald-Sun.* He calls Wade "a closer type who can close for eight or nine innings." Over the course of 7 1/3 innings Sunday afternoon, Wade strikes out fifteen batters. It's almost embarrassing. Later that day, lounging around the Red Roof Inn, the Wilmington Blue Rocks do not look like happy campers.

"That guy is very good," right fielder Tom Smith says to me, shaking his head. "I wouldn't be surprised if he makes it."

Durham fans are as quirky as their ballpark. One of their trademarks is providing sound effects when opposing relief pitchers warm up. It's really quite funny and novel enough to upset the composure of an unsuspecting pitcher.

In the bottom of the eighth, Wilmington brings in reliever Chris Eddy with a man on base. Eddy starts taking his warmup tosses, and the fans cut loose. Every time he throws, the stadium reverberates with an ascending "Woooooooooo!" When his catcher returns the ball, they give him the other half: a descending "Wooooooooo!" Within two pitches, the crowd has it timed perfectly. The effect is hilarious, although Eddy and his catcher probably fail to see the humor.

Poor Eddy never gets his rhythm going. The first thing he does is try to pick the Durham runner off first. On his second attempt, he throws the ball away. The runner scampers to second, and the crowd goes wild. They are feeling *powerful* in an evil kind of way. Eddy then turns his attention to batter Vince Moore, and his first pitch hits him. The crowd again goes wild. Out comes the manager.

"Now pitching for Wilmington, number 16, Dario Perez."

Perez raises his arm for a warmup toss, and five thousand voices echo all around him.

"Woooooooooo!"

Burlington, North Carolina

"In high school I was hitting .470. I'd settle for half of that right now." —Richie Sexson, Burlington first baseman

There is something about the crowd noise that stands out during my first night in Burlington. It doesn't register until I hear it again the second night and go to investigate. There, off in the two-dollar seats behind first base, sit three ladies raising a very distinctive ruckus. To begin with, they are not here to cheer for the Burlington Indians. They are Martinsville fans, and, during periods of relative silence, they are cheering for the enemy.

"Come on Josh!" "Get a hit, Manny!" "Hit one for me, Jeffrey!" Their choice of players might be enough to distinguish them. But it is also *how* they cheer. The vocal cadences and clapping remind me of nothing so much as a southern Baptist service. These ladies are baseball fans, all right, but they are also having church! Right out there behind first base!

This unselfconscious show of support is greeted with smiles or indifference by neighboring fans. The wonderful thing about baseball is that a wide range of expression is tolerated. Cheering somebody on, cussing somebody out, hurling praise or insults: it's all permissible. People come to a common area by themselves or in groups, and they shout their wishes and opinions to perfect strangers. Then they go home tired and happy and carry on within the rules of polite society. The ladies from Martinsville are no exception.

"We drove down here to see them play. We wanted to show them our support," Tarsala Johnson tells me proudly.

Their presence reminds me of a basic fact about baseball, be it major or minor league. Relatively few blacks attend games. Per capita, there are far more black players than fans. In fact, there are some nights when there are more black players on

The Martinsville cheering section (Kiki, Dorothy, and Tarsala, left to right) on the road in Burlington, North Carolina.

the field than black spectators in the stands. That simple fact saddens and surprises me. Historically, black Americans have supported baseball. Negro League games drew respectable crowds. Even informal barnstorming teams supported themselves during hard economic times. Many of the towns I've visited have sizable black populations. Yet the crowds were almost exclusively white. Surely the issue isn't economic. The cheap seats in most parks range from two to three dollars. No more than a video rental. Half the price of a movie. Whatever the reason, it's a damn shame.

More Americans are likely to visit Burlington for a day of factory outlet shopping than to watch a baseball game. Nevertheless, minor league baseball is not new to the area. The present franchise has been part of the Appalachian League since 1986. The season most locals remember is the 1987 campaign, when the Indians drew a record 76,653 fans and won the league championship with a 51–19 record. Pretty impressive stats, but by next year it was back to real life and a fourth-place finish. It is impossible to build a dynasty in the Ap-

Night baseball in Burlington, North Carolina.

palachian League, where player development and vertical movement through the organization are what it's all about.

The history of baseball in Burlington is actually a little stranger than most. The town had a team in the Carolina League back in 1945, although they played their games in a park in nearby Elon College. In 1952, they moved headquarters to a park in Graham, a neighboring city. After eight seasons, the Burlington team had yet to play a game in their own hometown.

Following the 1958 season, the town of Danville, Virginia, lost its team in the Carolina League. The owners of the now vacated Danville ballpark offered to sell it to the city of Burlington for the bargain basement price of $5,000. The only catch was, the ballpark had to be moved to Burlington. Over the course of the next year, the park was dismantled brick by brick and trucked south to Burlington. The new/old park opened in time for the 1960 season and housed a Carolina League team until the end of the 1971 season. Professional baseball in Burlington remained dormant from then until the present Cleveland affiliate began play in 1986.

As if to make up for lost time, the crowds in Burlington Athletic Park are noisy and enthusiastic. They led the league in attendance last season, and every time I've visited almost all the thirty-five hundred seats were occupied. As they usually do in similar circumstances, the fans have learned to use the acoustic properties of the sheet metal stadium to express themselves. There's a whole lot of stomping going on.

The Indians' first baseman usually draws a reaction from the crowd. He's tall—the media guide lists him at 6′6″, but that may be a slight understatement. First base is where you want all that height, especially in the Rookie League, where errant throws from across the diamond are on frequent display.

His name is Richie Sexson. In both manner and appearance, he reminds me of another first baseman—Blue Jays All-Star John Olerud. Coincidentally, both men are from Washington. Richie is from a town called Vancouver.

There are two other guys on the Indians named Richard, but neither Mr. Lemons nor Mr. Ramirez is likely to answer to "Richie." Mr. Sexson does. Richie is eighteen years old. A couple of weeks ago he was going to high school. Suddenly, he finds himself playing pro ball. You might wonder how he's finding the transition.

"This is a long way from home. I've never been to North Carolina before. I went to New York once. But that was with my parents."

"How tough is it to play in this league?"

"I can't believe the pitching here. In high school I never saw anything but a fastball. Here guys throw curveballs. Even with 3–0 counts. They change speeds. This is really something. In high school I was hitting around .470. I'd settle for half that right now."

That night, Richie takes a .185 average into the game. When I see him a week later, his average is down to .167.

"At least I'm not striking out. I'm making contact. They'll start dropping in for me."

He might be right, but this is undoubtedly a rough time. The minor leagues draft players who have been considered good, even exceptional, for as long as they can remember. For many of them, this league may be the first time they've experienced being mediocre or worse.

I look up from a very entertaining conversation and see a horse on the field. The truth is, I have no idea why the animal is there. I was talking to some of the players in the visitors' bullpen, and before I know it the game has started and I'm trapped, out of uniform, on the playing field. But right now, no one is likely to pay much attention to me. I'm a hell of a lot less interesting than the horse, who is slowly making his way around the bases, from third to first.

The PA announcer says something to explain why this is happening. There's some polite applause and scattered laughter and utter shock in the bullpen. It takes something pretty special to shut down the obscene conversations and

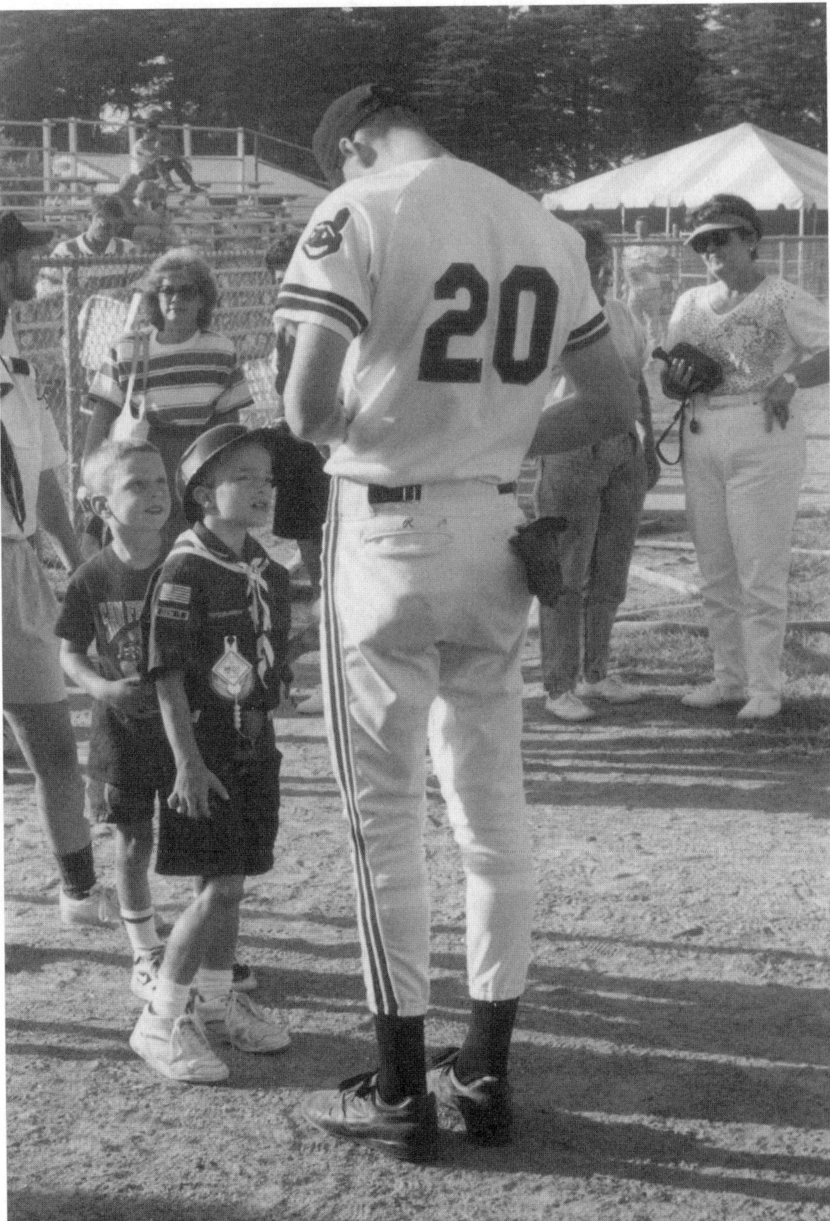

Burlington first baseman Richie Sexson obliges the local kiddies.

verbal abuse that are the staple of bullpen life. The horse has succeeded on all counts. We're all looking at each other and the horse in silent disbelief. Even relative to some of the minor league promotions these guys have seen, this ranks as a strange moment.

The horse finally makes his way to first base, but instead of turning right and heading for home plate and the exit gate, he takes a sudden interest in the visitors' dugout. Needless to say, he's getting a bit of encouragement from the players and coaches who are gathered there. Halfway over, the inevitable happens. The horse stops and does what well-fed horses do. Only they don't usually do it in the first base coaching box.

The laughter begins to escalate through the stands like a ballpark wave. You don't have to be at field level to see what's happened. The Burlington players are laughing too hard to take the field. The first baseman is particularly unhappy with this turn of events. What if he has to track down a pop fly off to his left? Where will he step?

Finally, the umpires call time. There is a moment of confusion as the grounds crew scrambles out with some makeshift farm implements to collect the aftereffects of this equine promotion. No doubt the GM is wondering why he ever agreed to tonight's entertainment. The grounds crew does its job and leaves to ceremonious applause. The umpires check the condition of the field and decide that it is usable, and play is resumed.

Conversation in the bullpen comes back to life, and there seems to be a gleeful consensus that this is the first horseshit delay that anyone has ever seen.

If you're a member of the working press in Burlington, you'd better be in good physical shape. At least, if you want to use the press box. The next time you're in a ballpark, look to see where it is. Their location is fairly standard, although the amenities vary somewhat. In the Appalachian League you don't expect much. I certainly didn't expect a nosebleed, which is what I risk climbing a flight of metal stairs and following a catwalk across the roof of the grandstand. Once inside, I experience the closest thing to a cool breeze I have felt in two days in Burlington in late June. It is lovely up here.

I have risked life and limb on that outdoor staircase to visit with Burlington broadcaster Andy Young. Not many Appy League teams broadcast their games, home or away. Young does all of the Burlington games. That means he works under some very primitive conditions. In Princeton, he shares a tiny wooden coop with a very zealous PA announcer. In Burlington, he has some space to himself but has his notes scattered to the four winds every time he opens the back door for cross-ventilation.

Young keeps up a constant commentary. There aren't two seconds of dead air in all the time I watch him work. He is adept not only in describing what he sees but also in filling the time between plays. You don't realize how much "down time" there is in baseball until you sit in the press box with a mike in front of you. Some might argue that those silences are part of the natural rhythm of baseball. Most media persons don't see it that way. Dead air is dangerous. It's got to be consumed. Young fills those spaces with background. ("José was a fourteenth round draft pick back in '91" or "Frankie hit fourteen round trippers for Susquehanna Junior College before being drafted.")

Since he began broadcasting as a student at the University of Connecticut, Andy Young has worked all over the States.

"I was here in North Carolina back in '89 and '90. Then I went off to the Florida State League and did the Vero Beach Dodgers games for two years. This season I'm back with the Indians."

Where will all this lead?

"I always wanted to be a big league announcer, but now I don't know. I'm starting to like minor league ball more and more. There's something about life down here that you can't duplicate in the majors. I'd like to get into the higher minors eventually. I wouldn't mind slightly better working conditions and living above the poverty line."

The Burlington Indians are owned by Miles Wolff. Wolff is the kind of owner associated with, in the immortal words of Bowie Kuhn, "the best interests of baseball." Many baseball owners are investors or businessmen. Others, probably fewer, are baseball men. Wolff is one of the latter. This is not to say he is a registered charity but that he brings a real love of the game to whatever he does. His former employees speak of him with respect and affection, long after the financial ties have been severed.

Wolff is the former owner of the Durham Bulls and is the founder and publisher of the biweekly *Baseball America*. The masthead on that publication says it all: "Baseball news you can't get anywhere else." Its emphasis is decidedly minor league. One token of Wolff's involvement with the Burlington Indians is their souvenir program. It looks absolutely nothing like a program you'll find anywhere else in the league or, for that matter, anywhere else in baseball. Its size and format look suspiciously like a copy of *Baseball America*.

Whether or not Wolff can bring the kind of alchemy to Burlington that he dispensed in Durham, North Carolina, remains to be seen.

I've yet to visit a minor league park that doesn't feel obliged to entertain fans between innings. Never a dull moment. Bingo, on-field contests, giveaways — anything to keep you in the park. In Burlington, I encounter my first sample of "Name That Tune." The evening's selection is an excerpt from Dion and The Belmonts' immortal "Teenager in Love." I don't see many contestants scrambling for their free pair of tickets but, looking at the crowd, I'm not surprised. I doubt that a whole lot of these people were even *alive* in 1958, when Dion was breaking hearts. There are some older fans out there as well, but they probably missed Dion altogether the first time around.

Promotions, a staple of minor league business, range in Burlington from the usual hokey fare to one eye-opener. A couple of local fans stand in the third base coaching box and spin around in circles ten times, then race each other to the third base bag. When the gimmick works just right, both contestants become comically dizzy and fall all over each other trying to find third base.

"You ought to see it on weekends when they've had a few beers," one of the fans tells me. "It ain't pretty."

Unfortunately, I miss Burlington's big-time promotion by several days, failing to see Bob Feller throw out the first ball. A visit to a local collectibles store before I leave Burlington helps put the event in perspective. While browsing through stacks of baseball cards, I chat with several teenagers who probably qualify as heavy duty collectors. They seem to know every active player, although more in terms of the value of their cards than their present performance. A mention of the forthcoming promotion draws a blank from all of them.

"Who's Bob Feller?" they say in unison.

The Phillies minor league roving instructor show has come to Burlington. Two of its stars are here: outfield instructor Jerry Martin and pitching instructor and substance abuse counselor Dickie Noles. Both Martin and Noles are survivors of the drug wars of the seventies and eighties.

Martin is a tough-looking guy from South Carolina. He had a decent big league career that began with the Phillies in 1974 and ended with the Mets a decade later. Martin played for five different teams and has earned the title "journeyman" in its most respectable sense. He carries a career .251 average and has played in over a thousand big league games. Ironically, he is best known, at least to Phillies fans, for a game he *didn't* play. During the Greg Luzinski era, Martin was the perennial late inning defensive replacement in left field. There was a critical moment during game three of the 1977 National League championship series which Martin is no doubt sick of contemplating. For some reason, manager Danny Ozark failed to make the usual late inning switch. It led to a highly predictable defensive glitch by Luzinski, a lost ballgame, and, arguably, the pennant.

"If you'd been in the lineup in '77," I begin when I meet him, and Martin completes the thought, "I'd be wearing a World Series ring today."

It wasn't exactly keeping him up nights, but the incident strays across his mind from time to time. If it doesn't, there are always guys like me to remind him of it.

The one obvious thing Jerry Martin and I have in common when we meet is living out of a suitcase. Someone standing near us happens to ask what day it is, and Martin and I both look blank. It is a simple, almost humorous thing to share. The notion of "Tuesday" is useless information. For both of us, today is "Burlington." Likewise, Wednesday will be Greensboro for me and, perhaps, Spartanburg for Martin.

Dickie Noles, like Jerry Martin, is a product of the Phillies minor league system. He came through several years after Martin and, consequently, does have a World Series ring. By now, most of the world has shared an image of him knocking George Brett down with a pitch during game four of the 1980 series. Noles, too, is a tough guy.

Noles is in camp not just to teach brushback pitches. That is a sidelight of his mission. Noles has become the Phillies' roving ambassador of a clean, drug-free life. This, of course, raises a few eyebrows among Noles's former teammates and carousing buddies. One, who works for another organization, took news of the pitching instructor part with equanimity but nearly fell over laughing when I added the part about teaching a clean life.

"Just like he lived, right?" was his sardonic verdict.

But Noles makes no bones about his past. In fact, he uses it and himself effectively as a negative role model. He is the walking embodiment of a reformed sinner. It's one thing to hear a "live right" message from a wimpy, Bible-toting teetotaler. It's another to hear it from Dickie Noles. It may be too late for Dickie Noles to get it right, but there are hordes of fresh-faced kids just radiating innocence and vulnerability. Noles wants to get to them before the devil does. He may not be as seductive, but he sure as hell can get in a few punches before the devil works his slimy ways on these young 'uns.

Noles conveys all the fervor of a southern Baptist preacher. No one will accuse him of being lukewarm. In fact, his intensity is almost embarrassing. I have the sense he'd carry on with his mission if the Phillies would just cover his gas and meal money. But they're doing more than that.

"When I was playing, no one talked to us about this stuff," he tells me. "I don't know if I would have listened, but no one was talking about things like this. Booze and beer were accepted parts of the game. Now that's changing. And we're not just sending the message about substance abuse to major league players, we're doing it here in the minors. Even down in the rookie leagues."

Dickie Noles in his own way tries to counsel young men about the foils and snares in the life of a professional athlete. Managers and coaches I talk to all seem to give Noles A for Effort. But some of the players, especially the younger ones, are giving him mixed reviews.

"He's very intense," one guy tells me. Another looked hard for a word, then settles on "energetic." One of the Martinsville players simply says, "He scares me."

Noles exudes missionary zeal. There is almost an aura surrounding him — a purpose. He does not deliver pallid, lackluster sermons. He makes eye contact and lets the fire and brimstone fly. Messages about drug abuse are obviously timeless. You don't need to show ID to buy cocaine. The alcohol part of the sermon is a bit ironic here since most of the Martinsville Phillies are too young to buy a beer after the game.

Noles's message isn't confined to substance abuse. He also preaches the gospel of commitment and toughness. Again, he is a hell of a role model. Before their game with Burlington, one of the Martinsville pitchers is sitting in the bullpen looking absolutely green. He's been sick all morning and has barely made the team bus to the park. The kid looks like he wants to crawl off somewhere and die. Noles has singled him out for an impromptu sermon.

"You can't just sit there like that," he begins. "You've got to be committed to this game. You can't think about being too sick to pitch. When they need you, when the call goes out, you have to be ready."

"But I'm really sick," the kid protests weakly. "I've been throwing up all morning."

"You know where I was two days ago?" Noles cuts him off. "I was in my hotel room sick as a dog. Some kind of virus. I was shitting and throwing up all day. But let me tell you something. If I was still pitching and the call came, I would have been out there. You have to be ready and eager to pitch any time, anywhere. Even if I'm on my way to the toilet and the call comes. I'm going to be thinking about how to get this guy out. You're a pitcher. That's what you do. It's a commitment and it comes first. Feeling sick doesn't get in the way of a real commitment."

Noles continues his mind over matter sermon. The kid looks awful. Not only does he feel sick, but now he's ashamed. But maybe Noles is getting through to the rest of them. At some level they know being here in Burlington is a golden opportunity. It can end at any moment, and they'd better not blow it. The trouble is, for many of them, success has always come easily. Now, here's a guy telling them they have to work at it. Make it such a high priority that they'd try to strike a guy out while they were losing their lunch. It seems crazy, but looking at Dickie Noles, they know *he* would.

"He still scares me," one of them says.

Several weeks later I get a different verdict from pitcher Scott Barstad, who heard Noles talk in Martinsville. Barstad has since been promoted to Batavia, and we're talking about Noles, standing around a thousand miles north of the Carolina sunshine.

"I thought he was great," Barstad tells me. "I could listen to him for hours. He's really entertaining and you just know he's telling you the truth."

Teammate Todd Genke agrees. Like Barstad, Genke heard Noles preach back in Martinsville, before his promotion to Batavia. But there's an obvious difference between these guys and most of Noles's Martinsville audience. Both Barstad and Genke have had their twenty-second birthdays. They may have been young, but they remember Noles as a player. Maybe too many of the Martinsville Phillies were barely learning to walk when Noles was busy knocking Brett on his ass.

Batavia manager Al LeBoeuf also has no doubts about the value of Noles's visit.

"He did us before he went down to Martinsville. I can't say enough about him or his message. Even if he doesn't get through to everyone, he's out there trying. He doesn't just talk to baseball players, you know. He takes his program to community groups, schools. He's on the go nonstop. In fact, I know he's so successful he has to turn down requests. And knowing Dickie, I can imagine how much that bothers him."

More power to the Phillies. Not many teams employ a spiritual guidance counselor who can throw a mean brushback pitch. Still, there is something vaguely troubling about Noles's message. It is the Protestant ethic gone wild. *Work hard, pray hard, prey hard.*

When the Milwaukee Brewers obtained pitcher Graeme Lloyd from the Phillies at the start of the '93 season, they became the first major league team to field an all Australian battery (catcher Dave Nilsson is also an Aussie). Australia threatens to become another hotbed of baseball talent on the international market. At present the Australian baseball league has eight teams, every one of which has an affiliation with an American major league team.

Although the Cleveland Indians are not one of those affiliates, they do have Australian talent in their farm system. They come by it quite honestly and rather easily. Anyone can draft an Aussie. It's as easy as that. Australian players, at least at this point, are not affected by the rules of the amateur draft. The situation is basically a free-for-all. Out of this unrestricted embarrassment of riches came catcher Mike Moyle. Mike was spending his second season with the Burlington Indians. It's not customary to spend two seasons in a rookie league, but Moyle is an exception.

"I was just getting started last year and everything looked great. Then I had to have surgery on my shoulder. Just like that, I was out for the season."

So Mike Moyle went home and went through the painstaking, frustrating process of rehabbing. Finally he was back to full strength, so he boarded

Unlucky Burlington catcher Mike Moyle: all the way from Australia for a broken hand.

the plane for his second shot at the Appy League. He was not yet nineteen years old.

"I got here, I thought, Fine. Everything's OK. I'm going to make up for lost time now."

The first three games were fine. He had nine at bats, got two hits and a walk, scored a run. Then he put on his catcher's gear for the fourth game. It was his last. When I met Moyle he was sporting a very unhappy look and a large cast on his hand.

"Am I jinxed or what? I mean, how many things can go wrong? My parents flew over to see me play. Now they get to look at a cast. Even if this heals in a month, we'll be into the middle of August. The whole league is over the end of August. How much playing can I do?"

I see Moyle three times. Not surprisingly, he looks more despondent each time. He looks for things to do. He sits in the stands one night, hangs out in the press box another. He runs laps tirelessly while his teammates take batting and infield practice. But the frustration is starting to show. He is talking a lot about Australian football games, which are being shown once a week on ESPN. He is probably the only person in Burlington watching them.

"I wish they'd just send me home. What good can I do here?"

The next time I see him, Burlington is "thinking about it."

The last time I see Moyle, he seems relieved. "They finally agreed to send me back. I'm flying out on the 16th. I'll be home in time for the football playoffs. That'll be great."

Moyle is right about one thing: his hand can heal as easily in Perth as it can in Burlington. So can his morale. But what would Dickie Noles say?

My second day in Burlington, I walk over to Ray Rippelmeyer, the Martinsville pitching coach.

"Your guy pitched a hell of a game last night," I say. "You can tell him he sure impressed me."

"Why don't you tell him yourself?" Ray says, gesturing to the player standing next to him.

"You Bryan Lundberg?" I ask.

He nods somewhat shyly.

"Then I get to tell you in person. You really did pitch a fine game last night. Most of these guys looked completely overmatched against you."

"I was getting my change-up over," Lundberg tells me. "That makes everything else look better."

He's right, and seven strikeouts in six innings tells the tale. Guys who can change speeds are deadly in this league. Most pitchers are drafted because they have live arms. But a fastball will only get you so far. This is a league full of fastball hitters. Sooner or later you have to develop some other pitches in order to survive. You do this at the same time the opposition is learning to hit curveballs. It's Darwin at work in the Appy League. Natural selection in all its ruthless splendor. The road out of these towns is figuratively strewn with bodies in uniform; mostly those players who never learned to throw or hit more than a fastball. Lundberg isn't going to have that problem. He's already one up on his opponents. There will be other selection pressures working on him later on, but for now he's doing well. Rippelmeyer wishes he had a roster full of guys pitching like this.

About half an hour later, Lundberg, circulating among his teammates, is taking drink orders in the bullpen.

"Let's see . . . that's two Cokes, one Sprite . . ."

And off he goes to fetch the drinks. I intercept him on the way.

"I don't believe this," I tell him. "After the game you pitched last night, *you're* getting the drinks? These guys should be bringing you champagne."

He laughs and tells me this is a customary day-after-pitching ritual.

It makes sense since there's no way he's going to have to work today. But it still seems kind of anticlimactic.

"What would they have you doing if you had lost last night?" I inquire.

"Running laps," he says and heads off to get the drinks.

During tonight's game, Burlington gets its revenge. The Indians are all over Martinsville pitching. I watch several innings from behind home plate, which puts me right next to Bryan Lundberg, now dressed in civvies and working the radar gun — another "day after you pitch" ritual. As usual, I'm struck by how young he looks out of uniform, although Lundberg is on the brink of his twenty-second birthday. That makes him almost an old man by Appy League standards.

We sit there watching the carnage together. The Martinsville pitchers he's charting are getting shelled. The fans love it, especially those who were around last night when the guy sitting next to me humbled them.

Around the fifth inning, the Phillies bring in a pitcher called Jackie Rife. Rife is a West Virginia high school boy who had his eighteenth birthday two days ago. Tonight isn't giving him cause for celebration. He has absolutely no control out there. He can't get anything over, even the fastball. The details are fuzzy: there's a hit batsman or two, walks galore, guys taking 3–0 and even 3–1. He leaves with the bases loaded and three runs already in. At some point, it becomes so bad that even the Burlington fans stop getting on him. By the time Rippelmeyer arrives with the hook, the score is 12–2.

I look at Lundberg, and he just shakes his head.

"You know, the first time he pitched, he struck a couple of guys out. He looked OK. The second time, his control just vanished. It was sort of like this, but not as bad."

The whole episode is even worse than Rife knows. About ten minutes before he takes the mound, who should show up in Burlington but Del Unser, the head of player development for the Phillies minor league system. *The* head man in the entire organization. The very first thing he witnesses as he settles into his seat is Jackie Rife's hapless performance. Talk about timing. A day earlier and Unser gets to see Lundberg, a budding star in the system, mow them down. Tonight he gets to watch Rife's nightmare unfold.

Greensboro, North Carolina

"This kind of stuff never happened to me when I was on Capitol Hill."
—Jerry Burkot, director of PR

Greensboro, North Carolina, is not the garden spot of the South. True, it has some lovely sections, and the university adds an unmistakable touch of class. But the city also has a tough underbelly and some seemingly intractable Klan activity. In the middle of all these mixed blessings sits the oldest minor league ballpark in the country. It is the home of the Greensboro Hornets, soon to become the Greensboro Bats, self-proclaimed "baseball's hottest team." There is something to be said for the appellation.

If it weren't for all the reminders, you'd never know you were sitting in an old stadium, much less the oldest. A lot of time and effort has gone into upgrading this facility, and it shows. The seats are comfy, the paint is bright, the field is well kept, and the sound system is state of the art. The Hornets also have a standard issue mascot. To their credit, management has resisted the temptation to name him "The Green Hornet." Just about every night, this bright red giant hornet called "Bomber" races some lucky kid around the bases. Not surprisingly, the mascot hasn't won yet. Kids are treated well here. On Tuesday nights, members of the Knothole Gang get in free.

Adults are treated pretty well also. For collectors in the crowd, the Hornets publish one of the best souvenir programs I've seen. It is slickly produced and loaded with entertaining features and just about everything an info-hound could want to know about the franchise, past or present. It's called the *Grand Stand*, and for two dollars it has to be one of the best deals in memorabilia.

There is another Grand Stand at War Memorial Stadium. This one doesn't come in the form of a program. It is a sports bar out in deepest left field. What the new owners of the Hornets have done is transform the worst seats in the house into the best. If it were indoors, you'd think of it as a trendy sports bar. One of those places with twenty brands of beer and nonstop wide-screen ESPN. Here, you can put your feet up, enjoy that schooner of Richert's Red, and look down at the left fielder's back. Feel the breeze, hear the crowd, and taste the suds. Right below the Grand Stand, you can bathe yourself in tradition. The seats are original equipment from Yankee Stadium and Connie Mack Stadium in Philadelphia. While you're watching today's Hornets, you can daydream about how many rear ends have predated yours watching yesterday's Yankees or Phillies.

War Memorial Stadium is really a piece of history. To begin with, the war they're memorializing is the Big One: World War I. This place was not built to commemorate Vietnam, or Korea, or even World War II. The stadium was built (sans sports bar) in 1926, although the Greensboro team didn't formally occupy it until 1930. The team was called the Patriots back then, and they belonged to the St. Louis Cardinals. The park actually had lights back in 1930, four years before Cincinnati made history by playing the first night game at Crosley Field. During the 1940s, Greensboro's team was affiliated with the Red Sox, a partnership that stuck until the late fifties. In 1958, it was the Yankees who began stocking the Greensboro roster with talent. One of their early prospects was a pitcher named Jim Bouton, who probably earned greater fame as the author of *Ball Four* than as a player.

In 1961, the fickle gods of minor league baseball arranged yet another marriage for Greensboro, this one to Houston. The teams stayed together until 1968, at which point minor league baseball vanished from the Greensboro scene for the next decade. During the Vietnam era, America's priorities turned elsewhere, and baseball's popularity dwindled. In North Carolina, a state that once hosted forty-six professional baseball teams, the list shrunk to three. Greensboro was not among them.

In 1978, baseball returned to Greensboro and never looked back. That 1978 franchise cost $12,000, a figure that wouldn't cover a week's worth of beer and vittles at the Grand Stand. It was considered a risky investment at the time. Since 1978, the Reds, Red Sox, and Yankees have played musical dugouts with Greensboro. The most recent allegiance is often referred to as the Don Mattingly era.

Part of the pleasure of coming to War Memorial Stadium is walking through the concrete inner sanctum. This is plainly the oldest remaining part of the park. It looks staid and hardly prepares you for the ultranineties interior. The inner walkway contains a chalkboard on which tonight's starting lineups are posted, along with the league standings and attendance figures for last night's game. Most franchises update this information in a daily press package for a handful of working journalists. Greensboro posts it in chalk for the fans.

The attendance figures are certainly something the franchise can be proud of. The Greensboro Hornets play in the South Atlantic League, and they've led the Sally League in attendance for fourteen years in a row. They probably won't this season because of competition from the new Hickory franchise, but their gate receipts are nothing to sneeze at. The night before, following an absolutely torrential rain that drove me back to my motel room, 2,200 stalwarts showed up at the gates. By the end of June 1993, Greensboro had inched its way to 100,000 fans. Spartanburg, the Phillies affiliate in the same league, had barely passed 30,000.

Like most minor league teams, Greensboro is not above using nightly promotions to increase fan interest. The Hornets seemed to be using a slightly more ambitious and wider-ranging set of themes. They had most primitive impulses covered, from fireworks, to music groups (the Impressions, Elvis imitators), to laser displays, to the exceptionally well endowed Morganna, who has found a new career appearing at Businessmen's Specials. For the wee ones, there was a Ninja Turtle night, and for everyone, the Famous Chicken, roving ambassador of mindless mirth, was putting in an appearance as well.

Fueled by all this success, Greensboro is actively thinking about a move to AA ball. Their biggest problem will be getting some more seats installed and finding a way to park a few thousand additional fans. Parking, rarely a problem in earlier days, is becoming a major annoyance. In any case, it is clear that Greensboro is a supportive hometown. All the games are broadcast, and the *Greensboro News and Record* treats the Hornets as front page news. Unlike many minor league towns I visited, you don't have to turn to page 3 in the sports section to read about last night's game.

You might remember Jerry Burkot. In fact, for a while back in May 1993 it was hard to avoid him. He did the talk show circuit, made the headlines, even had his picture in *Baseball Weekly*. Jerry is the Hornets' director of public relations. He certainly did his best to provide his team with national recognition. All he had to do was get ejected from a game in handcuffs.

What crime, you might ask, was serious enough for public shaming? In this case, Jerry expressed his disdain for a called third strike by playing the theme from *The Twilight Zone* over the newly furbished public address system. Umpire Jim Reynolds decided there were limits to the abuse he was prepared to take, so he tossed Jerry. Actually, he sent the batboy to toss Jerry, who was safely nestled in the press box during this upheaval. On the way, the batboy ran into team owner John Horshok, who, sensing the public relations bonanza at their doorstep, got into the act. By the time it was over, our man Jerry stood cuffed, a sheriff's deputy at his side, a big smile on his face, and flashbulbs popping all around.

Jerry was still laughing about the story when I met him a month later.

"This kind of stuff never happened to me on Capitol Hill," he reflects.

Jerry Burkot spent the last ten years or so in an office building in Washington, D.C., working first as a government press secretary and later as an international lobbyist. Like a number of other people I met, Jerry had fled the joyless pressures of the real world for a career in minor league baseball.

"This is my office now," he says, putting his feet up on a table in the press box.

"No more glass office building. I took about a thirty-five-thousand-dollar pay cut to come here. Can you beat this?" he asks, looking out at the Hornets taking batting practice on a sunny day. As he speaks, first baseman Nick Delvecchio launches one into the afternoon sky. The guys patrolling right field just watch.

"I don't get to keep my feet up like this all day," Burkot assures me. "In fact, a lot of the days are eighteen hours long. But the pace is slower and I'm surrounded by baseball. That's worth the pay cut right there."

The idea that the Greensboro Hornets are "Baseball's Hottest Team" may be a bit of hype from Jerry Burkot's well-practiced pen, but this is certainly a team rich in prospects. If I were a baseball card investor, I'd buy a stash of '93 Hornets team sets and squirrel them away somewhere.

The aforementioned Delvecchio can do more than hit them out in batting practice. Like Jerry Burkot, Delvecchio has graced the pages of *Baseball Weekly* recently. Nick's appearance, however, came under the heading "Minor League Player of the Week." That honor came on May 12, 1993, after Nick's batting average rose to .373, to go with seven home runs in the early season. One of them, an April 18 moonshot in Charleston, was estimated at 500 feet. Other than his credentials, there is something else unique about the 6′5″ Delvecchio. He just graduated from Harvard with a degree in history. There aren't too many Ivy League folks prowling around the South Atlantic League.

Delvecchio isn't the only member of the Hornets who is drawing media attention. Shortstop Derek Jeter has "Yankees shortstop of the future" written all over him. He was the Yankees' first round pick in the June 1992 draft, an honor that brings a fair amount of pressure and media scrutiny as well. This might be a tough assignment even if Jeter were a twenty-two-year-old college graduate, but he isn't. Jeter is barely eighteen, drafted out of high school in Kalamazoo, Michigan. So far, he seems to be handling it all in his second professional season. When I visit Greensboro, Jeter is hitting .322 and knocking in his share of runs as well. But he is making a ton of errors in the field. As I watch, Jeter fields a tough chance in the hole, then uncorks a throw that sails into the fourth row behind first base. Even Delvecchio's fully extended frame can't bring it in.

The Hornets are also hot on outfielder Matt Luke, who has a specially painted section of the left field fence labeled in his honor. Unlike Jeter, Luke hasn't made an error all season. He is a big kid, a little heavier than Delvecchio, although his power stats haven't yet matched Nick's. His ticket to the Bronx is probably on a slower train.

An unheralded part of the Hornets' team has been outfielder Kraig Hawkins. Hawkins has struggled with his offense and seems stuck in the .220 range through two years of professional ball. Local observers will tell you, "Nobody works harder than Hawkins." When they announce batting practice, Kraig is the proverbial "first one out there and last to leave." Getting on base is particularly important in Hawkins's case.

"He's probably the fastest kid in the whole organization," Jerry Burkot tells me. "We've got to find a way to get him on base."

The night I visit, Hawkins has a couple of hits, including a line drive double in a critical situation. I thought the cheers for him were especially loud.

By far, the lion's share of media attention, at least in the summer of '93, has been focused on a twenty-three-year-old pitcher from California named Ryan Karp. Last season in the New York–Penn League, Karp didn't raise too many eyebrows. About the best thing in his pitching line, other than a one-hitter, was a penchant for strikeouts. This season in Greensboro, Karp has come into his own. When I visited, he was trying for his record-breaking fourteenth consecutive win. His 13–0 record was drawing strong press attention, and the Yankee front office was starting to focus on events in Greensboro.

Karp left that night after pitching seven strong innings. He had struck out ten Macon Braves, most of whom took a called third strike and walked away shaking their heads. Karp dearly deserved to win, but he didn't. He left on the winning side of a 3–2 score, with the game in the hands of reliever Joe Long. The first batter Long faced buried one in the right field stands. The irate fans threw the ball back, a practice common in Wrigley Field but all but unknown in the minors. With the score now tied, it was Long's game to win or lose. Predictably, Greensboro scored the winning run in the bottom of the eighth, and Long got credit for the win. Karp seemed calmer about the verdict than most fans and just about everyone in the press box.

Ryan Karp has an easygoing temperament that seems ideally suited to the pressures of professional baseball. The excitement in the Karp family is largely provided by Ryan's wife, Josette. It is hard not to like her and even

Ryan Karp.

more difficult not to enjoy her style. Josette normally operates the scoreboard message center at War Memorial Stadium. Normally means every night except when Ryan pitches. On those nights, you wouldn't want Josette in front of a computer terminal. She paces, frets, and shouts encouragement, mostly in Spanish, to Ryan's teammates. The night I visit, the broadcast team has decided to put a mike on Josette and share her enthusiasm with the radio audience. It is a delight to listen, even though 95 percent of what she shouts eludes what is left of my high school Spanish.

After the game, Josette calls her parents to tell them what has happened. Her enthusiasm seems undaunted by Ryan's no-decision. The rapid fire Spanish narrative is punctuated by English phrases like "forty-man roster" and "14 and 0." Apparently some things need no translation. Before she leaves the press box, I wish Josette well. Although she is absolutely fluent in English, I can't resist the chance to dust off my high school language training.

"Buena suerte en Nueva York," I say sincerely and proudly.

In essence, Josette replies, "Gracias, but we ain't there yet."

In most ballparks, when the last out is recorded, the fans head for the exits. In fact, the exodus usually starts before that. Minor league teams in small towns draw working families who often start filing out around the seventh inning. By 10 P.M. they've had their evening's entertainment and they want to be home. Time to pay the babysitter, put the kids to sleep — whatever it takes to prepare for the next morning.

There is plenty of that in Greensboro, but there is another tradition here. The Grand Stand, that outdoor sports bar in left field that has been jumping all night, gets even busier when the game ends. Now, it seems, a whole new bunch of folks want to party. The customers from game time are still sampling the microbrewery product. Some of them are still talking about the game. Others have turned to more social pursuits. About twenty minutes later, a new group of patrons arrives. They are young, freshly showered, casually dressed men. The Greensboro Hornets are through working for the day and have come to party. They mingle casually with the fans. Women flirt, guys make small talk. I'm standing at the bar with some of the team and a guy walks by, smiles, and says, "That was the best 4–6–3 double play I've seen in a long time."

"Thanks," the infielders say in unison, and the guy moves on. Here in Greensboro you can watch your team play, then have a beer with them after the game. It all feels very natural. Even Kraig Hawkins, who refuses half a dozen offers of beer, stays to chat for a while.

About ten minutes later a Karaoke contest is starting. Contestants line up to sing the vocal track from their favorite record. For a few precious moments they can close their eyes and become Elvis, Tina Turner, or John Fogerty. Some of the contestants are quite entertaining; some are godawful. A few of Derek Jeter's teammates try to coax him onstage to perform with them. He refuses and stands his ground against some intense coercion. This is clearly one eighteen year old who can handle pressure.

I look up and there is Jerry Burkot, no longer worrying about media relations, doing as fine a version of Elvis as I've seen all night. He gets an enthusiastic hand for rendering "Burning Love." As I leave the park in search of a late dinner, it is after 11 P.M., and Burkot and two Hornets have agreed to judge the finalists in the Karaoke contest. Everyone seems to be having a grand time. It is hard to believe, as I walk to my car, that a ball game took place here earlier this evening.

The Greensboro Hornets are not owned entirely by businessmen. Or at least conventional businessmen. One of the owners is a guy who just happened to play for the World Champions '72 Athletics. Tim Cullen started his big league career with the 1964 Washington Senators. He was later traded to the White Sox before finishing his career with a World Series ring in Oakland. Although he has remained active in the Major League Baseball Players Association, Cullen was out of the game for nearly twenty years.

"I became involved in investment banking," he tells me. "I was successful, but I missed baseball. Now I'm around it every day again."

Cullen and I have our little chat standing in the Grand Stand watching the last of batting practice. Behind us, the bartenders and servers are stocking up and getting ready for tonight's game. They are wiping off counters that contain carefully protected vintage sports memorabilia. Among the items is Tim Cullen's 1967 Topps card. He hasn't changed that much.

Life in the press box gives you a whole different slant on a ballgame. I used to think that decisions by the official scorer were divinely inspired and chiseled in stone. They're not. Midgame, a tough play by the third baseman is scored an error. An inning or so later, someone casually asks Ogi Overman, the official scorer, "Did you give so-and-so an error on that play last inning?"

Ogi is the sports editor for the *Chatham News* and publisher of the North Carolina *Piedmont Ballpark News*. He could probably score this game with his eyes closed, but he's willing to listen.

"Yeah. I thought he should have had it." Then the crucial invitation: "Didn't you?"

"No way. Even if he got to the ball, there's no way he would have thrown what's-his-name out."

The seed of doubt has been planted.

"What d'ya think?" he asks, looking at me. Who the hell am I? A visiting writer Ogi has been chatting with for the past half hour. But I'm there and I have an opinion.

"I can't see him making the play either. I'd give so-and-so a hit."

And so he does. The scoreboard operator is notified, the box score is adjusted, and history has been altered. An up and coming third baseman has an error expunged from his record. Maybe the difference between nine and ten errors for the season could mean a promotion to AA next year. A struggling batter has one more hit on his record. Maybe his average goes up to .270 from .263, and someone in the front office thinks that .270 ain't half bad. Maybe he's worth a second look after all. On the other hand, it could add a run or two to the pitcher's earned run line for the night (it didn't in this case). Small talk in the press box affects decisions that affect statistical summaries, which affect perceptions and careers.

We've spent a couple of hours together walking through the ballpark and talking about baseball and life, but Charlie Atkinson, beat writer for the *Greensboro News and Record*, who normally covers the Hornets games, will not be working tonight. Someone else, with less experience, will cover for him. And what cosmic event has kept Atkinson from what he does best? Another ball game. No, not in Yankee Stadium, but down the road from Greensboro. Charlie is on a local team, and they have a game tonight. Charlie's team comes first.

"Normally there's no scheduling conflict. But there was nothing I could do tonight. It's a question of priorities. I'll try to get back for the last couple of innings depending on how my game goes."

But Charlie's game goes long, and baseball on the field takes precedence over baseball in the press box.

We're sitting in the press box, and a younger reporter goes out for a cold drink. He comes back with a pack of Score Select baseball cards. There is some mild interest as he opens it and looks through the contents. Nestled among the B. J. Surhoff and Vince Coleman cards is a Derek Jeter rookie card. First Round Draft Pick is stamped in gold across Jeter's picture. Look out the window, and there he is playing shortstop. Back inside the press box, Jeter smiles up from his card.

"I'll trade you my job for that card," says one of the older guys.

"You mean it?" the card owner asks.

"Yeah. The card and it's yours."

Jeter changes hands and the older guys says, "I was thinking of quitting anyway. I'll call what's-his-name in the morning and let him know you'll be coming by."

It seems pretty bizarre at the moment, but five years from now, I wonder who will have gotten the better deal?

As of August 25, 1993, the services of Bomber the Hornet were no longer required. The team formally announced that they would become the Greensboro Bats, effective next season. It was not clear whether their new name had to do with small flying mammals or wooden implements. The team logo, which includes both images, does little to resolve the confusion. Presumably, Greensboro's new mascot will fly in from center field, knock his opponent unconscious with a Louisville Slugger, and draw some blood from an exposed jugular vein.

Hickory, North Carolina

"He's the only catcher I ever knew who could sit on his ass and pick a guy off second base."
—Catfish Hunter, speaking of Paul Casanova

In 1993, just about everyone in North Carolina baseball is talking about the new franchise in Hickory. If it isn't the park itself, it's the crowds they're drawing.

On the way to the stadium, I stop at a Waffle House for breakfast. They've got signs all over the walls. "Serving you good food fast is our pleasure," says one. I ask for a no-smoking section and meet my first taste of overt hostility in North Carolina.

"We don't restrict our customers' freedom," the waitress informs me.

"How about that?" I ask, pointing to the large sign over the cash register that says "No Firearms Allowed on Premises."

"Guns can kill you!" she announces, looking exasperated.

I try to avoid straight lines like that, so I leave this bastion of traditional values and find alternate eating. Then it's on to confirm these reports of Nirvana in the Carolina mountains.

L. P. Frans Stadium, home of the Hickory Crawdads, is located in one of the loveliest parts of the state, surrounded by a sea of Carolina pines. This is a decidedly out-of-the-way setting for a ballpark. You don't get here without a car and some forethought.

But that's not stopping many folks. As of the end of June 1993, with the season barely two months old, Hickory has already drawn 129,000 fans, eclipsing perennial leader Greensboro by over 35,000. Their opponents tonight, the Spartanburg Phillies, have drawn 31,000 to date.

"It's not just the town," Ed Shepherd tells me. Ed runs a computer graphics company and does some scoreboard work for the Crawdads. "There's only about 30,000 people in Hickory. But there's about 750,000 people living in the Unifour area, within a thirty-mile radius of where we're sitting.

"And it's not just the numbers," he continues. "This area has a tradition of supporting local teams. Doesn't matter what they are. High school, college. Hell, girls basketball games sell out!"

Ed makes it clear that Hickory was ripe for a franchise.

"It's been thirty-three years since we had professional baseball here. If you can call it that. We had a Class D affiliate for the Washington Senators back in 1960. For one year! People were ready for this."

"Don't forget the '54 Rebels," someone adds. The Rebels, it seems, were the only baseball champs to come from Hickory. They won their title in a rather unfortunate way. The team was in first place on June 21, 1954, when the Tar Heel League folded. No need for playoffs.

Other guys in the press box have picked up our conversation and are joining in. You'd expect them to be jaded. Even though they're professionals, they seem impressed by the response the Crawdads have drawn.

"The franchise sold $100,000 worth of merchandise before they had a team. All they had was a logo," one writer tells me.

Another adds, "There were fourteen hundred season tickets sold before the team had a name!"

"There's a waiting list right now for outfield signs," someone else points out. I'm convinced. The folks in and around Hickory, North Carolina, have signed on with this team. They are not going to give it up without a fight.

And what kind of team do they have? Hickory is the Class A South Atlantic League affiliate of the Chicago White Sox. Through the end of June, Hickory is dead last of fourteen teams in the Sally League in batting (.229) and next to last in team ERA with 5.24. Not much to cheer about, but you'd never know it sitting around here.

By the end of their inaugural season, it's clear the Hickory Crawdads are far more successful in the stands and concession booths than on the field. The Crawdads draw a league pacing 278,000 fans and flog memorabilia in record quantities. On the field, however, the team finishes forty-one games behind the first place Savannah Cardinals, with a deplorable 52–88 record.

There is a brief moment when Hickory fans think they may have died and gone to heaven. During Michael Jordan's well-publicized attempt to become a major league ball player, it is suggested that he might have to start his career in the *low* minors. Could that mean Hickory? When the verdict is finally in, Jordan's abortive baseball career begins no lower than AA. It is Birmingham, Alabama, rather than Hickory, North Carolina, that will reap the benefits.

Tonight the Spartanburg Phillies, who are not exactly tearing up the league either, are in town. The bus pulls in around 5 P.M. and parks behind the ancestral home of the Elmer Winkler family, who have generously donated the land for the Crawdads' stadium. This wooden shack needs to be either razed or spiffed up a bit and a historical marker placed. But no one seems to notice. It's just another tumbledown old house, not exactly a rare sight in North Carolina. Of course, you don't often see one just steps from the entrance to a brand new baseball park.

Inside that park, there is activity everywhere. The sound of power tools fills the air. The park is still under construction. Nothing major, of course, and by game time all the evidence will be tucked away. Two and a half hours before game time things are bustling. Ushers, all well into their sixties and beyond, are wiping down the brand new seats. Bright colors abound. Even the old seats, ceremoniously reclaimed from Comiskey Park in Chicago, have a fresh coat of green paint. Leann Rossi, my guide through the park, is thrilled to have these old-time seats. She grew up in Chicago, and this feels like a touch of home. Leann is one more person I've met on this journey who was happy to give up better-paying employment in the outside world for a job in minor league baseball.

The Hickory crowd is very vocal but almost childlike in their enthusiasm. Maybe they're out of practice after all these years without baseball. They "oooo" and "ahhh" in response to just about anything: infield pop-ups, called strikes. It'll probably wear off after a few seasons, but for the moment it's sort of like being at a game with thirty-five hundred nine year olds. Surprising, but not altogether unpleasant.

Around the third inning, I head to the souvenir shop to pick up some T-shirts. I've got a shopping list on this trip, and it includes some Crawdads merchandise. There is a line waiting to get *in* to the souvenir shop. Right now, it's busier than the hot dog stand. Inside, I meet a guy from Tucson. He couldn't care less about the Crawdads' fortunes or developing prospects, but he sure does want some souvenirs. He knows when he gets home, he's going to look cool as hell in his Crawdads T-shirt. Strangers will approach him to ask questions about Hickory, and he'll have a story to tell.

"This is a great league for merchandising," Ed Shepherd tells me earlier. I can see his point. Like the Crawdads, most teams have enticing logos and a full line of merchandise. Still, this seems an odd way to go about minor league business. No mention of great hitting or pitching prospects. Instead, management is focused on how many T-shirts and caps they can sell.

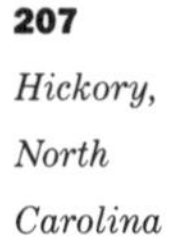

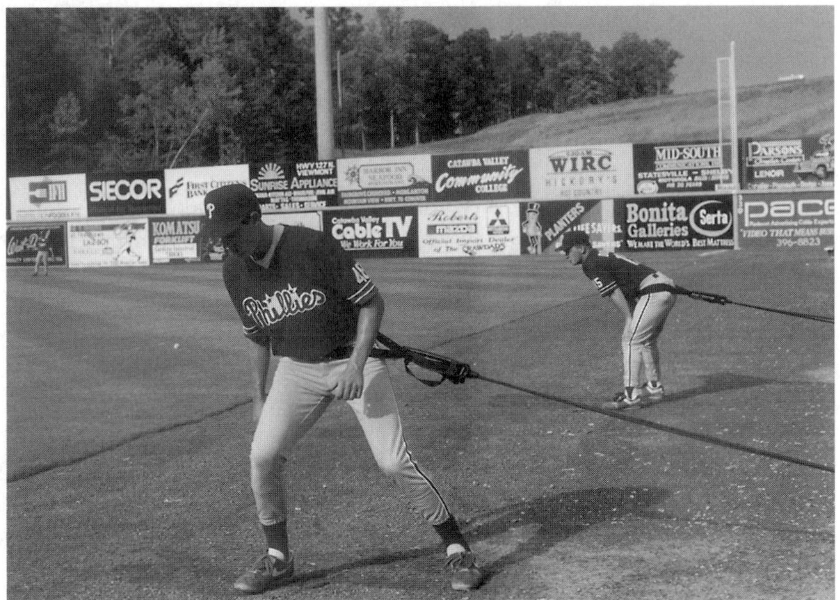

Phillies in bondage: pregame stretching in Hickory.

In contrast, the neighboring Appy League features unimaginative tie-ins with the parent franchise: the Bluefield Orioles, Burlington Indians, Princeton Reds, Danville Braves. Yet there is something to be said for that approach too. Seeing these small-town teams and unknown faces wearing the actual uniforms of the Baltimore Orioles, Cleveland Indians, Cincinnati Reds, and Atlanta Braves brings the local action that much closer to the big time. The game takes on a greater reality. It is no longer just a local sandlot contest featuring unfamiliar names. This is the real thing. Just look at it! These guys are decked out in the team colors of the Orioles, the Reds, the Braves . . . For fans who have seen or rooted for the parent team, there is an undeniable Pavlovian element to seeing these team colors flashing in the Appalachian sunshine. And like most Pavlovian processes, the appeal may not be rational, but it is strong.

Later in the game I wander out of the press box and sit by the visitors' dugout. I find myself next to a guy named Tim Rask who's driven down here from Iowa. Tim is also making a journey through minor league baseball. We compare itineraries, and it looks like we've been following almost the same road map, moving about two days apart.

"I've just about given up on major league ball," he tells me in a lament I'm hearing more and more frequently. "It's beautiful down here. How can you beat this? Great seats, fair prices, lovely park, a beautiful night . . ."

I find it hard to argue with him, especially when the alternative is the overpriced big city charms of the SkyDome in Toronto, my nearest big league city.

Around the seventh inning, Spartanburg brings in reliever Steve Nutt. The announcement draws scattered hoots and guffaws from the crowd. I wonder what happens on nights when Nutt relieves starting pitcher Sean Boldt?

One year later. Hickory is no longer the new kid on the block. The Crawdads are an established team in the Sally League. They've hosted this year's All-Star game just days before my visit. Today, they're home to another recent addition to the league: the Hagerstown Suns. L.P. Frans Stadium still looks spiffy a year after its opening. If anything, some of the rough edges have been smoothed over. Like new cars, baseball stadiums also seem to have a break-in period.

I'm sitting just before game time in the Crawdads bullpen with Richie Pratt, a left-handed pitcher from Hartford, Connecticut. Tonight, we're being treated to a very ornate version of the national anthem by a local woman enjoying her two minutes in the spotlight. Pratt salutes reverently but leans over and whispers, "I hear it every day, so I'm getting to like 'em short and simple."

After the minispectacle is over, Pratt softens his previous comment.

"Hearing it still gets to me. It reminds me that I'm really making a living doing this. I love being here. North Carolina is beautiful: the mountains, the lakes. It's just beautiful. When I was in high school, I was too intense. I was developing high blood pressure. I needed a way to unwind, to unstress myself. I've found a balance down here. Playing ball like this, it's very easy to get into bad patterns. We play mostly night games. We get back home around 11 P.M. Sometimes I'm too wired to sleep. I watch TV, mostly the sports news. I can be up till two. Then I sleep in until noon. Wake up, and it's back out here at 2:30. It's all baseball. Playing it, seeing it on TV, dreaming about it.

"I'm trying to break that pattern. Now I try to get to sleep by midnight, get up at nine. Then I go out to the lake. All I do there is sit and relax. It's a break for me. It helps me cope with all the pressure here."

Pressure? What pressure? Unfortunately, it seems that under all the shiny paint and well-oiled machinery of this new franchise, there's some discontent. It may not be obvious to the fans in the box seats, but down here at field level you don't have to dig deeply to uncover it. The Crawdads are still drawing well, but since the All-Star break, they're 2–5, which places them dead last in

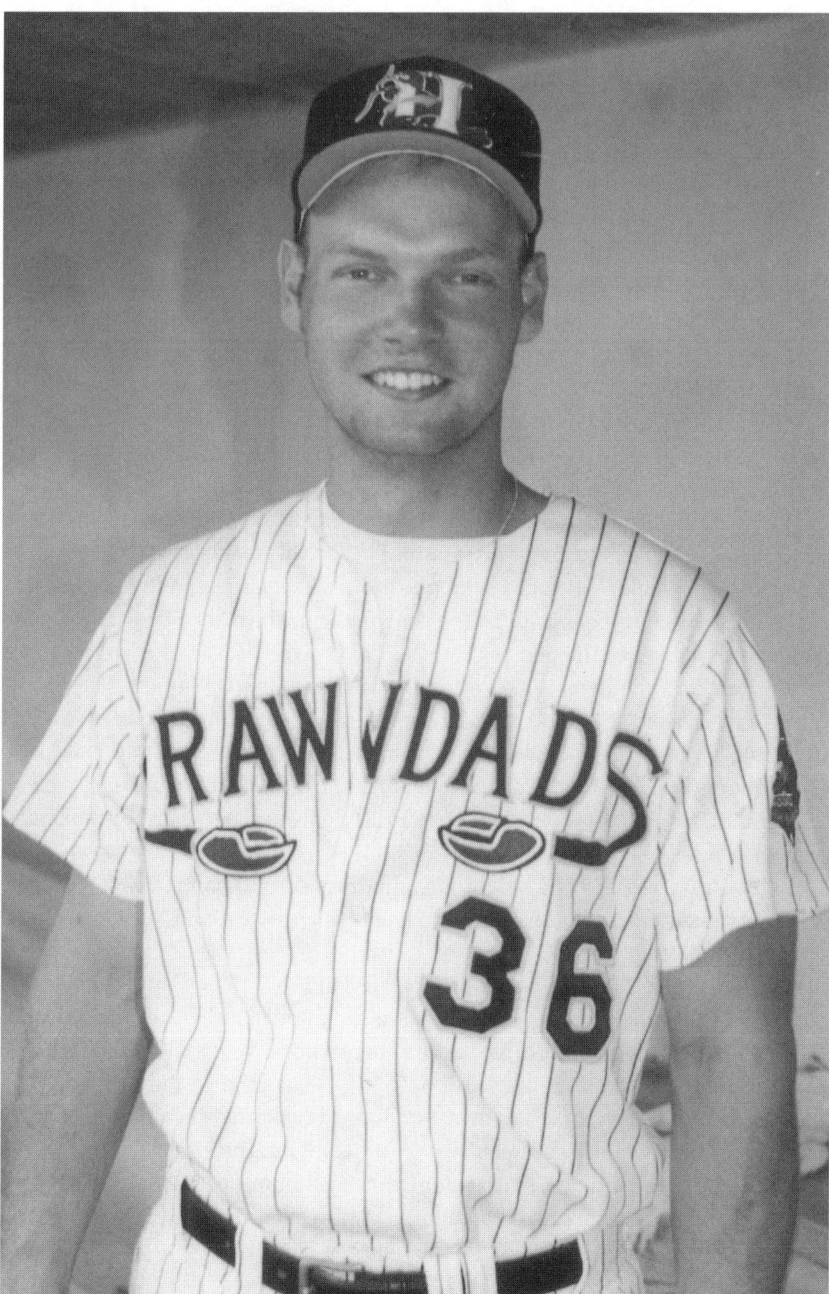

Richie Pratt.

the Sally League Northern Division. Worse yet, the slide didn't start after the break. The Crawdads have an 8–17 record in the month of June, which includes a nine-game losing streak. Like it or not, that kind of performance begins to take its toll.

"The truth is," Pratt observes, "I've seen less and less team spirit since I moved up from high school. There was less in college, and there's even less here. There's concern about individual stats, nightly performance, promotions. There's fear. Competition."

Players sitting near us are listening to the conversation and nodding. One of them interjects, "I'll tell you how bad it is. I've seen guys change the numbers on the radar gun. You know, shave a few miles off someone's fastball."

Other guys nod. It apparently isn't an unknown occurrence.

On the surface, Richie Pratt's season is going well. There's nothing in his numbers to suggest a problem, yet earlier today he's been moved from the starting rotation to the bullpen.

"The rumor in the clubhouse was that they're moving me up. I mean, I'm a ninth round pick. I'm twenty-three, a bit old for this league. Taking me up to the next level wouldn't be out of the question. I haven't been pitching badly. I lost my last two decisions 1–0. So the coach calls me into his office and tells me they're moving me to the pen.

"I'm working the demotion over and over in my mind. Why did they do it? What does it mean? Should I have my agent call them? Maybe it doesn't mean anything."

I point out that in A ball, moves to and from the pen don't necessarily mean the same thing as they do in the Show. Pratt concedes the point, but his mind is still racing.

Richie Pratt seems like a bright guy, more reflective than many of the players I've talked with. But how do Hickory coaches respond to his personal style?

"Last year I had a bit of a reputation," he concedes. "They thought I had an attitude. It's really not true. But I'm not a high school kid either. I have a degree in engineering. I want to know why things work. When a coach tells me to do something his way, I'm likely to say 'Why?' That's the wrong answer. They want to hear 'Yes, sir.' Just like in the military. I hope their evaluation of me is changing. I don't want to be seen as uncoachable. I'm really not."

Finally, Pratt concludes, loud enough for his teammates to hear, "One thing about the minors, there's no communication. Everyone's in the dark."

Heads are nodding up and down the bench.

"You've got no power. No control."

This is starting to sound like a southern Baptist service with amens coming from the bullpen congregation. These guys keep hearing all the usual pep talks, all the "There's no *I* in *team*" speeches, but it doesn't seem to be having much of an effect. There's overt grumbling on this team. Evidence of petty rivalries and competition is not hard to find. Thankfully, not all the annoyances are internal. As a group, they seem peeved with a story about the Hickory Crawdads that appeared in the June 16 issue of *Rolling Stone*. No one on the bench has anything good to say about it.

"That guy was so full of shit."

"Can you believe it? He comes down here for five days, with his leather coat . . ."

For some reason, the author's wardrobe stirs up a firestorm of anger. He's just a slick, smartass New Yorker who flies down here, breezes in and out of the ballpark, and comes away with an understanding of baseball, the South, North Carolina, you name it. A condescending puff piece for pseudosophisticates, with these guys as the butt of the joke. They're not happy. Interestingly, John Quirk is among the chorus of dissenters. Quirk's ERA may be twice that of Richie Pratt, but Quirk is from the Bronx. That qualifies him as a New Yorker. Yet he doesn't seem any happier with this piece of urbanite trashing than his rural teammates.

The team seems to be in a collective bad mood. Yet, it's hard to believe the blame lies solely with them. Something is not working according to plan. The stadium is beautiful. Management is professional. But under these photogenic new uniforms are some pretty unhappy players. They're looking out for themselves, and some of them are starting to look over their shoulders. They act, in the words of Satchell Paige, as if something might be gaining on them.

The contrast in the visitors' dugout is striking. The Hagerstown Suns are coming off a first-place finish prior to the break and have begun the second half with a 5–2 record, the mirror image of the Crawdads. They are confident and upbeat. Sure, these guys are watching their own numbers, but, hokey as it sounds, there really seems to be a sense of team here. Maybe it's as simple as the fact that the Suns have been winning. But there is something else. There have been almost no roster moves on this team. The Blue Jays organization is very consciously trying not to break up this unit. They want these guys to experience playing together as a winning team. Right now, the Suns have all kinds of prospects. Arguably, they are the strongest team in the Blue Jays minor league system. Rather than plundering this pool of talent, however, the front office is resisting the temptation to tamper with it.

The downside of all this teamwork and camaraderie is keeping some guys in the Sally League who deserve a midseason promotion. Is this enough to cause dissension? Not according to pitcher Harry Muir.

"It's not the end of the world as far as your career goes. There's nothing to stop them from moving you two steps from here next season. Some guys who have played well here will probably go straight to Knoxville [AA] without a season in Dunedin [high A Florida State League]. So it all works out."

Guys like Muir seem to take genuine pleasure in hearing about the successes of former teammates. Maybe it's Muir, maybe it's the organization he plays for. Whatever it is, this esprit de corps seems to be every bit as contagious as dissension.

Peter Fisch worked for the Carolina Mudcats for four years before coming to the Crawdads as their assistant GM. He followed his former team from Columbus, Georgia, to their new home in Zebulon, North Carolina, before making the move west to Hickory.

Fisch is still buzzing in the aftermath of hosting the thirty-fifth annual Sally League All-Star game. The Crawdads turned the event into a week-long festival, complete with car races, country music shows, and farm machinery displays. Amid all the glitter and noise, the event that has grabbed hold of Fisch's imagination is the Legends of Baseball game held the day before the All-Star contest.

"The old-timers game was really the highlight for me. It was fascinating, just amazing. The stories I heard . . . We were afraid these guys would get here and just go off in little cliques, the former major leaguers in one corner and the career minor leaguers in another. We weren't sure they'd have anything to say to each other, but we were completely wrong. Everybody seemed to find something to talk about. If they hadn't played together in the minors at some point, they knew someone in common, or they had played together in winter ball. There were so many memories, so many stories. A baseball historian should have been here recording everything, taking it all down.

"At one point Catfish Hunter was talking to our batting coach, Paul Casanova. Cassie was an All-Star catcher for the Senators in 1967 and played with the Braves until 1974. I asked Hunter if he remembered playing with Casanova. He told me, 'Sure, Cassie is the only guy I ever knew who could sit on his ass and pick a runner off second base. He had a rifle for an arm.'" The word "rifle" started some of them reminiscing about playing winter ball in Venezuela and how there were often guys sitting in the dugout with rifles on their arms, literally. They used to sit at either end of the dugout just in case there was trouble in the stands.

"It was a thrill meeting the major league players we invited, but the thing that really got me was some of the minor leaguers we had here, especially the ones who never made it out of Carolina ball. I can't tell you how much those guys appreciated being remembered and honored like this. It was overwhelming. Many of them are retired now, some work in construction, one of them works in a hardware store . . . They just couldn't believe that anyone remembered that they played for the 1954 Hickory Rebels or the Marion Marauders or the Statesville Owls. Some of these guys hadn't seen each other for thirty or forty years. It was a very emotional time.

"The afternoon before the old-timers game we had the Colorado Silver Bullets play here. They've gotten a lot of media attention as the only all-women professional baseball team. Unfortunately, they haven't been doing too well on the field, as far as wins and losses go. In our game, they got no hit and lost 3–0. But those ladies were ecstatic! They only lost 3–0 as opposed to 19–1. They've been in a lot of blowout games, which I guess has been embarrassing for them. Losing 3–0 seemed to mean a lot to them. It's the first time I've ever seen a no-hitter where the losing team was grateful.

"We invited Bob Feller as part of the Legends of Baseball game. A lot of these career minor league guys thought, Here's my chance to bat against Bob Feller! This one guy lined out, and when he came back to the dugout, he kept saying, 'I lined out against Bob Feller!' Actually it wasn't that much of a joke. Feller is in his late seventies, but he can still get something on it.

"Feller is an interesting man. When he first got here, he was kind of sour, just treating it as one more promotion, another 'Bring Bob Feller in and exploit him' job. Some people describe him as being rather bitter. He often talks about how he didn't make the money today's players make. He's very unhappy about that, about the injustice. But the longer he stayed here, the more he got into it. He began to see we really wanted him to be part of the whole thing. He pitched an inning in the Legends game. By the last day, he was in a great mood. It was good to see that change in him.

"The first time you do an old-timers game, it's rather difficult. Coordinating it, finding all the players . . . But things turned out so well that we've decided to make this an annual event. Next year it'll be a lot easier. We'll just send out invitations, and these players will come back."

I wonder if Peter Fisch knew how rich the area was with former players.

"All North Carolina is like that. People say there's a Hardee's restaurant at every stoplight in North Carolina. Back in the forties and fifties there seemed to be a minor league team at every stoplight. When I was with the Mudcats, everyone talked about someone they knew who played professional baseball — an uncle, a cousin. All you have to do is invite one or two and the word spreads. You can barely stop it. We probably haven't even scraped the surface. I know next year will be even bigger, especially when word gets out that we treated everybody so well."

Fisch is turning into a historian of local baseball.

"Just look at the faces in these old team photos. You can see a difference in their eyes. Everything about them seems so different from today's players.

These guys were having fun. They weren't so career oriented. They look kind of ragtag — uniforms falling apart, the stadiums have chicken wire to keep the crowds back. These were different times to be sure.

"I was going through some old newspapers about baseball in the area. In 1936, the Giants came through Hickory to play an exhibition game on their way back from spring training. It was a big deal here; they used to let the schools out so the kids could see the game. There was a story about Mel Ott sitting around talking to the locals before the game. Apparently, he enjoyed meeting one of the local kids, and years later, when he was in the war, Ott met a guy from Hickory. He asked him if he knew this kid.

"The next time Ott came through Hickory was after the war, in 1946. The local paper tracked down the kid and arranged for them to meet. Ten years later and they had a reunion. Stuff like this just doesn't happen anymore. When I was with the Mudcats, we had Barry Bonds come down on a promotion for the Pirates. He was nice enough and signed autographs, but it was never clear he even knew he was in Zebulon, or gave a damn if he did.

"Some of the oldest parks still standing give you a sense of what it was like back then. Our first year in Zebulon, before the stadium was ready, we played about half a season in Wilson, North Carolina. Wilson had a team in the Carolina League back in the sixties. Rod Carew played there in 1966. That park still had the Negro bathroom standing. It's used as a storage shed in right field now. Just walking in to watch a ball game, you'd never know what it was. But you ask one of the locals and they'll tell you. It's hard to even envision that today in a minor league park. But it was everywhere.

"In Columbus, Georgia, you can still see the rail they used to separate the whites and blacks. I met this old peanut vendor who had worked in that park for about forty years. He can show you exactly where the railing used to be in the outfield stands. He will never set foot on the far side of that line anymore because he used to have to stay behind it. The separate gate for blacks and the separate bathrooms are still there too if you know where to look for them. I'm sure it was the same in Hickory as in any southern town. The only difference is we don't have any stadiums still standing to remind you of how it was."

Asheville, North Carolina

"I felt that working at Pizza Hut was stifling my creativity. So I decided to become a bear full time."
— Chris Broaddrick, aka Ted E. Tourist

The terrain leading to Asheville is so lush and overgrown that most of the motel and restaurant signs bordering Interstate 40 have become unreadable. The corporate logos and house specialties have been engulfed by a sea of foliage.

Driving along the highway, I hear a menacing noise off to my left. At first it sounds like a flat tire slapping against the road — wap, wap, wap. I can't tell if it's coming from my car or a neighboring one. Either way it sounds like trouble. Then I see the source of the noise, and I have to laugh in relief. A dog is barking at me from the bed of a pickup truck in the next lane. Woof! Woof! Woof! come his indignant barks. The territory he's defending so aggressively is moving along a North Carolina interstate at 70 mph. But no matter. This yellow Labrador is prepared to challenge all motorists from the safety of his truck bed.

It's hard to be cynical about the beauty of this region. Surrounded by the Blue Ridge Mountains, Asheville is the very embodiment of a tourist town. The economy has reached out to embrace the influx of visitors who arrive each spring and stay through the fall. Motel rooms are hard to come by, and they go for nearly twice the rate as accommodation in neighboring towns.

Yet, beyond its craft festivals and nature walks, Asheville is a real city. The drive to the ballpark along Highway 70 puts you on Tunnel Road. On the near side of the tunnel, it's all fast food and motels against a backdrop of majestic mountains. Pass through the tunnel and it's as if you'd come through a worm hole in outer space and landed smack dab in an urban center. Asheville has a skyline! There's a real city here, waiting quietly on the far side of the tunnel. This is where residents of Asheville (there are about 40,000 of them) transact the business of their everyday lives. Most tourists may never cross over this barrier, but you've got to do it to get to the ballpark.

Like Durham and Greensboro, Asheville has basked in the glory of the film *Bull Durham.* It was in this town that Kevin Costner, aka Crash Davis, finished his minor league career playing for the Tourists. According to film legend, Crash hit his record-setting final home run in Asheville. The Tourists front office proudly displays the uniform Costner wore when filming the scene in Asheville.

What was left of old McCormick Field got hit by the wrecking ball following the 1991 season. New McCormick Field emerged the following year. It is an impressive facility for minor league baseball. Everyone associated with the franchise takes enormous pride in their reborn park. A lot of thought and planning went into its design, from the striking roof lines to the imposing brick facade outside. It wouldn't take much to set up a AA franchise in Asheville should the wheels ever start turning.

As is often the case, this slick new park sits on the skeleton of its predecessor. Once again, we have a strong contender in the "oldest minor league baseball park in America" sweepstakes. In this case, the Asheville Tourists have played ball in some variant of McCormick Field since 1924. According to research by Bob Terrell, the Asheville Skylanders (soon to become the Tourists) christened their new field on March 27, 1924, when they beat Weaver College 13–5. A week later, with the paint on new McCormick Stadium barely dry, the Skylanders knocked off the Detroit Tigers 18–14. If nothing else, that exhibition game provided a piece of trivia that will live forever in the hearts of Asheville baseball buffs. The thirty-seven-year-old player-manager of the Detroit Tigers hit the first home run ever recorded at McCormick Field. His name was Ty Cobb.

Cobb was not the only baseball legend to leave his mark on Asheville history. The following year, when word of Asheville's spiffy new park spread to the major leagues, the Yankees and Dodgers agreed to come to town for an exhibition game. The date was set for April 7, 1925. But by the time the train arrived at Asheville station, a major problem had arisen. The Yankees' biggest star, Babe Ruth, had fallen ill on the trip from Knoxville and collapsed when he exited the train. Fans swarmed around the Bambino as he was carried off to a local hotel.

The game went on as planned without the Babe, and fans were treated to a 16–8 Yankee victory. But when the northbound train left that afternoon, there was one less Yankee on its passenger list. Babe Ruth remained in Asheville under treatment of a local doctor for what was described as the flu. In this pre-electronic world of news transmission, rumors flew faster than data. Ruth was widely reported to have died in Asheville, a possibility that would probably have eclipsed Cobb's home run in the annals of local baseball trivia.

Actually, organized baseball in Asheville predates McCormick Field by over fifty years. Accounts still exist of games played as early as 1866. In the early twentieth century, Asheville fielded teams in the Southeast League, the Appalachian League, and the North Carolina League until World War I depleted the region's manpower. The modern era of Asheville baseball arguably begins in 1960, when the Tourists signed a working agreement with the Phillies and competed in the Sally League. In 1961, the club changed its affiliation to the Pirates, an arrangement that lasted until 1966. Over the years, the Reds, White Sox, Orioles, Rangers, and Astros have been parent club to the Asheville Tourists. Their present affiliation with the Colorado Rockies began in 1994.

Whether it's the mountain air or the beckoning 300-foot fence in right field, quite a few batters have followed Cobb's example and hit baseballs out of McCormick Field. Not surprisingly, steps have been taken to reduce the number of objects flying out of new McCormick Field. The right field fence has now grown to include four tiers of advertising signs. The barrier extends almost 40 feet above field level.

"That's the highest wall in the minors," assistant GM Gary Saunders tells me. "It's second only to the Green Monster in Fenway. Nothing cheap is going to fly out of here," he says.

Just then, the Spartanburg bus arrives, and the Phillies start lining up for batting practice. Within minutes, their shortstop, Manny Amador, launches one in right center. Jon McMullen, the Spartanburg power hitter, shakes his head and tells me, "I don't like playing here. It's beautiful and everything, but it's too easy to hit one out. It shouldn't be this easy."

Gary Saunders is in his second year as the Tourists' assistant GM.

"I'm having such a great time here. This is almost too good to be true."

Saunders can barely contain his enthusiasm about his job. He's on his third story before I can grab a tape recorder or notebook.

"I did a little catching when I was in high school and junior college. I discovered I wasn't good enough to make a career out of it, so I majored in communications and advertising and tried to stay close to baseball that way. Early

Jon McMullen.

on, I was still reacting to a lot of this job like a fan. My first year, I was working in the Cardinals organization. I'd see guys like Bob Gibson or Bake McBride come through and I'd be in awe. It was an effort to stay cool. One day I'm in the office and a guy comes in and asks to use the Xerox machine. I look up and know immediately it's Dwight Evans!

"You're Dewey Evans, aren't you?"

"Yeah," he says. "Can I use the Xerox machine?"

He admits he's gotten better. "But I still bring some of the fan to this job. I don't know if I'll ever lose that entirely."

I wonder how Gary ended up in Asheville.

"I got offered this job at the winter meetings. They said, 'Let us fly you out and show you the town and the park.' One look at both and I was hooked. I called my wife that afternoon and told her to start packing. We're moving to Asheville. It was that simple. They must have known that when they flew me down. Just look around. This place sells itself."

I see his point.

"People talk about progressing though an organization. Maybe that's good for a player, but I wouldn't want to do it. I'm happy being in the minors. I get to do everything and see everything here. If I were suddenly promoted to the major league club, sure I'd be flattered. But my whole job would change.

Everything is compartmentalized up there. I'd have one responsibility. I'd miss all the other stuff that comes with the job here. At this level in the minors, you're expected to know it all and be part of it. I've sold chicken sandwiches and done PA work when our regular guy couldn't be here, and I've been on the grounds crew. I'm even involved in designing the program. Look at this," he says, extending the Tourists' 1994 program to me. "Seventy-six pages. That's exceptional for this league."

Like most of the GMs and assistant GMs I've met in the minors, Gary puts in some long hours. Technically, he may be working for less than the minimum wage. But that's not the way he sees it. Most front office staff I've met in the minors are either single or divorced. The job puts too many strains on most relationships. But Gary has found an ideal solution.

"My wife works here too. She's part of the organization, so she understands what's going on. Her official title is 'merchandising director.' Eileen has a background in retail, so she's brought a lot to this position."

That's putting it mildly. I thought the Hickory Crawdads were running a classy operation with their souvenir shop; I was impressed by the Toledo Mud Hens' mail order business. But nothing prepared me for the Stadium Store at McCormick Field. The Asheville Tourist logo is getting a major league workout. It appears on everything from bumper stickers to jerseys, from coffee mugs to quartz watches. The days of selling a few pennants, T-shirts, and baseball cards in a booth by the hot dog stand are history in Asheville. They've got a full-fledged country boutique here. You can pick up some Tourist brand apple honey, try some pecan apple butter, or — and I swear this is true — buy some Ted E. Tourist label Chardonnay or white zinfandel. A wine list to go with your batting helmet! A local artist named Steve Millard designed the Tourists' bear logo. I wonder if he had any inkling of how widely this bear would travel.

Every Tourists T-shirt comes with a sticker saying *Authentic Bear Wear*—Purchased at Historic McCormick Field. Just looking at it makes me want to sip some Chardonnay.

Like most minor league clubs, the Tourists depend upon promotions to draw fans.

"We'll always get the diehards," Gary Saunders explains. "Nothing can keep them away. But there are a lot of marginal fans out there. They can't decide whether to watch *The Simpsons* or come out to see a ball game. You have to create a bit of a carnival atmosphere to draw them. When one franchise discovers a good idea, word usually spreads to other markets. There's no reason to keep a good idea to yourself. We're really not in competition with anyone else except TV or the movies. Even our closest competitor, Hickory, can help. It pays for us to create a rivalry with them and publicize it. They're just over an hour away. Playing up the competition between our teams will help attendance for both clubs."

Along with the usual promotions, Gary has brought some novel touches to Asheville baseball.

"We give away free haircuts on Tuesday nights. Right there on the roof of the Tourists' dugout. Brought three barbers in here and had customers lined up. It was a strange sight, hair flying everywhere. We did it between 6 and 7 P.M., right before game time. You could get a ball game and a haircut for just the price of a game. Not a bad deal. All the time we did it, we only ran into one problem. One guy in the stands complained that he got some hair in his beer. We gave him a fresh beer, and he was happy."

Speaking of beer, Gary describes his biggest success story.

"We started a promotion called Thirsty Thursday. It was usually a slow night, so we advertised beer for a buck. That's really a great deal. They get a 22-ounce beer. Word spread, and we started packing them in here. It's become the most popular night of the week. Doesn't matter who's playing. We might average about fifteen to eighteen hundred people normally. Last Thursday we drew thirty-one hundred. The idea became so popular locally that we had to copyright the name. Local bars were starting to borrow it to draw in customers. Cost us about fifteen hundred dollars to do it, but now if there's any infringement, we just send them a copy of the legal work and remind them the name is protected. The problem usually stops right there."

Gary and I continue chatting as he takes me through the clubhouse facilities.

"This used to be the home dressing room in the old park, so until the new visitors' clubhouse is built, we just turned it over to them. By comparison, it looks awful. But we still get a lot of managers and coaches who have been around this league telling us that even this is better than what they see at other parks. Kind of makes you wonder."

We get to the visitors' shower, and the tour grinds to a halt.

"Yeah, this is a bit odd. I figured you'd want to know about this," Gary says. What lies before us is a tile shower of every conceivable color and pattern.

"You wouldn't want to be in here if you were hung over. I think what happened is when this was being built, the local tiler told them, 'Look, I can do this real cheap if you don't have any particular style in mind. That way, I can use up whatever tiles I have left over, and I'll give you a real good price on it.' It probably sounded like a good idea at the time, but they didn't figure on just how many styles he had in stock. I doubt there's anything like this in all of baseball."

"Who's that guy out beyond the right field fence?" I ask, pointing to a lone character who appears to have climbed down from some mountaintop to watch batting practice.

"Ah, that's Grizzly Adams. His real name is James. He works here as a ball shagger. A lot of people call him the Mountain Man. He hangs around and retrieves anything that goes over the fence. Then he comes in the next day with a sack of balls and sells them back to the club for a dollar apiece. He's the only one that'll go back there. The underbrush is very dense; I don't know how he gets through it in places. And there's all kinds of snakes back there. We're glad to have him."

James, it turns out, is quite glad to be here as well.

"I been doing this since I was twelve," he tells me. "I'm fifty-seven now. I was born and raised in Asheville. Been here all my life. I love coming down here. I watch the balls fly out of here. Don't try to get them right away. It's too dark back there. I come back the next day with my sack and my pole. I'll get most of 'em. I don't miss very many. I got twenty-four last night."

And the snakes?

"Oh yeah," he laughs. "They're out there all right. They love to sun right beyond the foul pole."

I ask James if the plants give him as much trouble as the animals.

"There's some rough stuff growing out there. Poison ivy, briars, thorns . . ."

I'm not dressed for the tour he offers me, but I do examine some samples growing close by.

"This is what's back there," he says, pointing to a harmless-looking fernlike plant. Using his stick, James exposes the stem, which contains spikelike thorns extending nearly an inch from the stem.

"They can get you pretty good," he says.

About an hour later, I'm talking with visiting clubhouse manager Tony Fischer. Fischer has an immense collection of baseball memorabilia and is bursting with tales. He loves to surprise his listener with unexpected facts.

"Yeah, everybody knows about Ty Cobb hitting the first home run here," he says. "But did you know that Rocky Marciano played his last pro ball game here before turning into a professional fighter?"

I tell him I didn't even know Marciano was a ball player.

"Oh yeah," he nods. "He was drafted by the 1948 Cubs. Very few people know that."

I admit to being one of them. Then Fischer drops the other shoe.

"I saw you talking to James out there. He telling you about all the baseballs he pulls out of that woods? Well, that's true, but that's not the whole story. I bet he didn't tell you the rest, did he?"

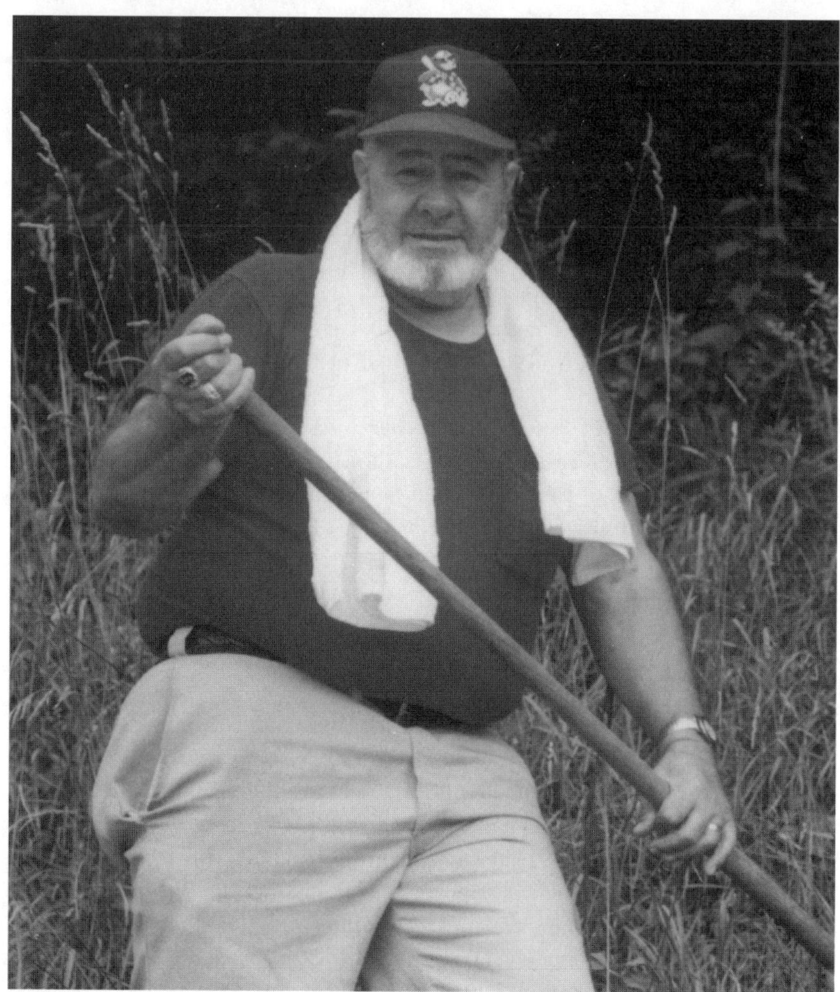

James, the Mountain Man: battling snakes for errant baseballs.

I guess not, I concede.

"James may be a mountain man, but he's also a businessman. He'll go out to one of those donut stores and buy a bag of day-old donuts for thirty-five cents. Then he goes down to the bullpen and trades with some of those guys. It's nothing for them to slip him a ball or two during the game in return for a donut. That's a pretty good return on his investment. A bag of day-old donuts gets him another handful of balls he can sell back to the club. He doesn't have to fight snakes for everything in that sack of his!"

John Thomson is due to pitch for the Tourists on Sunday night, so tonight (Friday) is his turn to chart the game and use the speed gun. Usually pitchers in this role sit anonymously in the stands behind home plate. In Asheville there is a special table located rather conspicuously in the walkway right behind the first section of seats. Thomson shares the table with his counterpart from the Spartanburg pitching staff, as well as several scouts with briefcases and radar guns of their own. Fans tend to give them a wide berth.

I find a chair between Thomson and New York Yankees scout Steve Chandler, who is working his way through a mound of peanuts that could double Georgia's economy overnight. Thomson is from rural Louisiana, a tall, thin redhead struggling to grow a mustache. He's 6′3″ and might weigh 175 pounds on a humid day.

"I've weighed the same since high school. I have no idea how to gain weight. Nothing I do seems to matter, although the good thing is I don't seem to lose weight either. I don't even think three big meals a day would make a difference."

After a pause, he adds, "I'm sure not going to find out on fifteen dollars a day for meal money."

John and I agree that this is a beautiful place to be working, although he is quick to add, "When I first got here back in April, it was ugly as dirt back there. None of the trees had blossomed yet. We went on a road trip for ten days and came back and everything was in bloom. It was kind of like magic."

I mention that I wouldn't have guessed Thomson's home state from the way he speaks. He seems pleased and tells me that some of his teammates from California, that arbiter of good taste, have started to get on him about his accent. I again tell him that I've heard lots of accents in the past month, and his is hardly a standout. After a moment, he tells me, "I guess I'm not surprised. I used to take speech classes. I learned how to enunciate. They also helped me to be more open with people. I used to be very shy. I couldn't even have done this," he says, referring to our conversation.

I kid John about the perils of being a pitcher drafted by Colorado, which plays in a notorious hitter's park.

"Yeah, I know," he tells me. "I thought about that. But they must have seen something they liked. They drafted me in the seventh round. I think they look very carefully to see whether the pitchers they draft throw fly ball outs or grounders. They stay away from guys who give up a lot of fly balls. I guess they figure some of them might go flying out of Mile High Stadium. When I pitch, a lot of guys ground out. I'm sure they knew that. Just recently I pitched in Charleston, West Virginia, and beat the Wheelers. The next morning the

John Thomson.

headline said 'Wheelers Ground Out.' I thought that was great. I wondered if I should send the Rockies a copy of the paper."

John Thomson seems in no hurry to make it to the Show.

"I don't really think about it. I don't have any kind of timetable for myself. Maybe if you forced me to answer, I'd say one year at every level, but even then, what's the rush? I love playing. Just being here has a special meaning for me. People back in my hometown told me I'd never make it. First they said I'd never play college ball. Then they told me I'd never play pro ball. I wasn't big and strong enough. They even said I wasn't good enough. That hurt, but it really peaked my motivation. They weren't trying to motivate me; they were just putting me down.

"Even my high school coach. He told me, 'You'll never make it. You'll never be a pitcher.' I remember that. I remember how I felt. I was angry, but no words were exchanged. I guess partly I believed him. But it also motivated me to try even harder. Just recently I saw him. He asked how I was doing and I said, 'Fine. I'm pitching pro ball.' He said, 'Good,' like it was no big deal or no surprise to him. A part of me wanted to remind him what he had said, but I didn't.

"I'm still very tough on myself. I'm trying to learn that you can't be perfect all the time. That's a real struggle for me. I can get very down on myself for the smallest mistake."

I look at John's pitching line through the end of June. He's got an impressive 2.80 ERA, and in sixty-one innings he's struck out fifty-three people and walked eighteen. In short, those are numbers to kill for in the Sally League. But John isn't sure. He points to the "Opponents Batting Average" column and suggests that his numbers are comparable to those of a less successful teammate who is being hit for a .284 average. I look carefully and see that John's line is actually .224, a sixty-point difference. John shrugs, as if to say, ".284, .224, what's the difference? I still give up hits."

"Is that what you mean by being tough on yourself?" I ask and get a sheepish nod back.

Our conversation is interrupted during the seventh inning stretch by one of Asheville's nightly rituals. Each game, one fan — man, woman, or child — is selected to lead the singing of "Take Me Out to the Ball Game." The fan is planted on the roof of the Tourists' dugout and given a cordless mike. Tonight, our fearless leader is a little kid. He may not even be four years old, but he's funny as hell. He's into the first line before the usher can even get the microphone into his hand.

In some ways, this little kid is the opposite of John Thomson. On the one hand, there's not a trace of shyness. He's having the time of his life on the dugout roof. On the other hand, this kid could really use some elocution lessons. He sings in a curious dialect that suggests his English was learned phonetically. Words are transformed, syllables are dropped, but the net effect is recognizably "Take Me Out to the Ball Game." The fans are loving it, and when he's through, the kid is greeted by thunderous applause. The place simply erupts with laughter and good-natured cheering. It's unlikely the kid even associates this standing ovation with what he's just done, although his parents are drinking it in. Earlier in the day, the assistant GM has told me that sometimes this singing gimmick works and sometimes it doesn't. It's hard to imagine a more successful episode than the one I've just seen.

When it's over, with the crowd still buzzing, John turns to me with a big smile and says, "There isn't a band on earth that could have accompanied that kid."

He's absolutely right. The kid has violated every musical rule there is, from tonality to meter. He barely even spoke English, yet it still worked. So much for perfectionism.

These days, most teams have a mascot. But how many mascots have a master's degree in divinity? Meet Ted E. Tourist, aka Chris Broaddrick. So what's a nice guy like this doing in a bear suit?

"It's real simple," Chris tells me, starting to strip away his street clothes in order to make the transformation for tonight's game. "I was living in

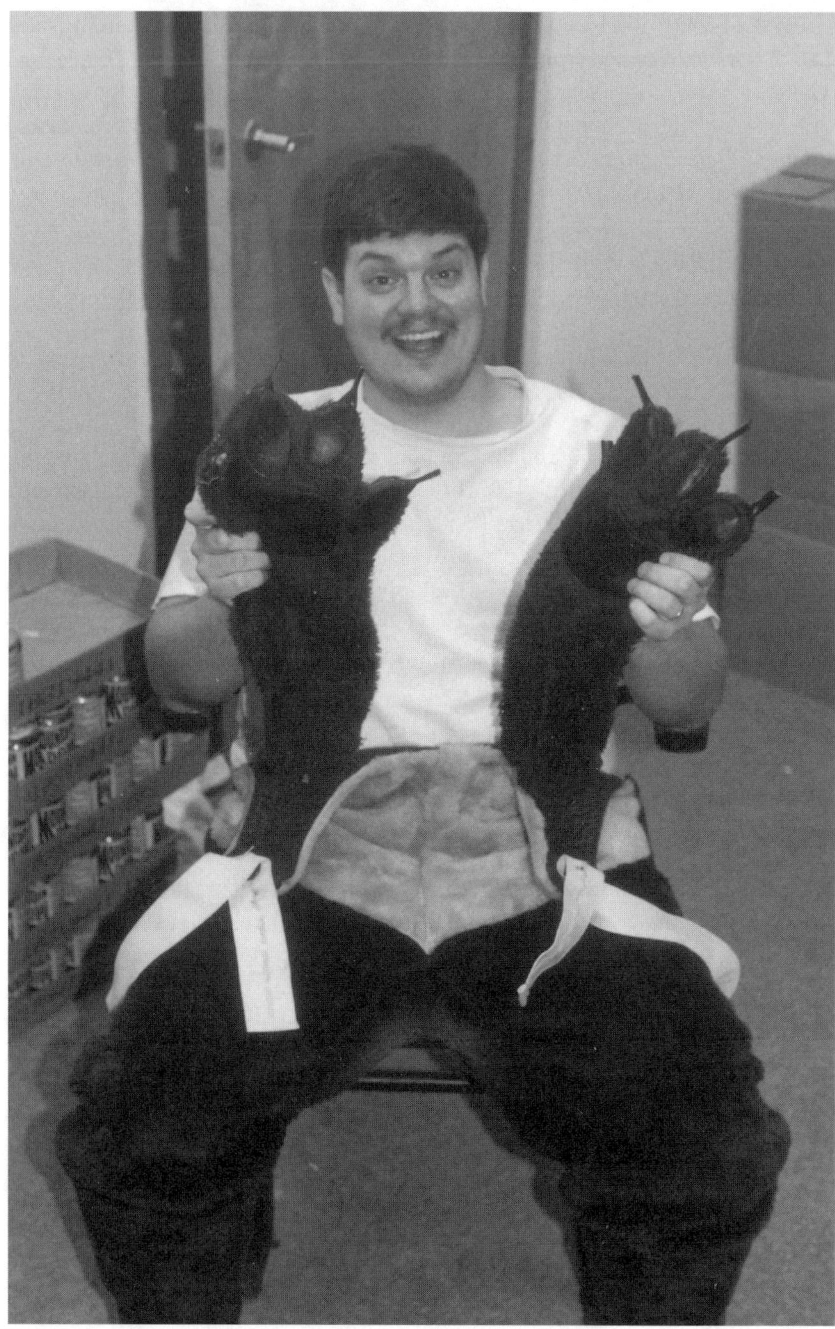

Chris Broaddrick, aka Ted E. Tourist.

Mississippi and I lost my job. So I decided to come back home to North Carolina. I was out job searching one day and I drove by the park here. When I left, this was still old McCormick Field, wooden bleachers and all. I was just in awe when I saw what it had become. So I just walked in and said, 'You guys need a mascot, don't you?' And Gary said, 'Yeah, as a matter of fact, we do. We've been thinking about that.' And it just went from there."

But what is it about Chris that made him think he'd be good in a bear suit?

"Well, I can be extremely funny. I love to joke around and amuse people. And I'd been to a couple of other ball games where they had mascots, and I remember thinking, I can do that. In fact, I can do a lot better than that! So I went about proving it here. I started with an exhibition game this season, and I've been here ever since."

Looking around us, I point out that nobody is going to starve in this dressing room.

"Yeah, there's quite a lot of food in here. That's mostly because Ted E. Tourist has just gotten corporate sponsorship. Nabisco sponsors the bear! So there's all kinds of crackers and goodies. They come in by the boxload. Late in the game, I take my suitcase, the one with all the stickers on it, and fill it with goodies. The kids know when they see that suitcase, the food can't be far behind. It's just one more reason to keep your eye on the bear!"

I ask Chris if he has a day job.

"Well, I did," he says rather slowly. "But I quit. Today was my last day. I was a manager at Pizza Hut. I was in charge of the luncheon buffet. But I felt like working at Pizza Hut was stifling my creativity. So I became a bear full time."

I wonder if Ted E. Tourist does any preaching during his nightly gigs at the ball park.

"No. Absolutely not," Chris assures me. "I don't talk. Talking breaks the line between fantasy and reality. When I'm out there, I'm Ted E. Tourist. But if I talk, I'm just a guy in a bear suit. The only exception I've made is when I see someone I know who doesn't recognize me. Like I'm part of the Asheville Community Theatre Group. Sometimes I see someone from the group here, and they have no idea who I am. So I might lean over and say, 'Hey, I was in *To Kill a Mockingbird* with you.' That usually gets a reaction!"

I wonder if Chris is here for the kids or the adults.

"Mostly the kids," he concedes. "It's important to keep the kids coming to the ballpark. That lets the adults come as well. The adults get to see a ball game, and the kids stay entertained. A family night out."

Indeed, of the sixteen hundred people in attendance tonight, it seems that fully half of them are under twelve years old.

"Of course, that would be very different on Thirsty Thursday. That's not a big kid night. But adults get involved with the mascot also. Like I'll have a guy come over to me and say, 'Hey, see that guy sitting over there. I work with him and today's his birthday. Could you go over there and mess around with him?' So I'll go over and sit in his lap and mess up his hair, and then everybody makes a big fuss over him. But mostly it's kids. They just go crazy. Last night was special because I got my first baseball card. It's part of the Tourists' team set. I guess it's kind of like my rookie card. All the kids wanted one, and I was giving them out and signing autographs all night."

I wonder if the response is always positive.

"With the real young kids, you get one of two reactions. It's either adoration or sheer terror. Some of them just can't deal with a giant bear walking around in a Hawaiian shirt hugging people. You can see them trying to work it through so they won't be so scared. They'll say stuff like, 'Hey, those claws are just a glove. I can see your arm up there.' You can see them trying to convince themselves. But the little ones, especially, they're still not sure."

How about the guy in the bear suit? Does Chris ever get spooked by any of this?

"Actually, the one thing that bothers me is when I get swamped. I guess it comes with the territory, but sometimes I'll get maybe fifty kids swarming around me, and I can't move. I don't like that. I have a couple of waitresses here I'm pretty good friends with, and when they see that starting to happen to me, they come over and help. They move the kids back, you know, and say, 'OK, everybody get into in a straight line.' Then I can move again."

I point out that Chris is not a very typical guy. Neither your average bear nor your average preacher.

"No," he says. "I don't do things the easy way. I've had a lot of jobs, done a lot of things. I think mostly I'd like to teach. I do some substitute teaching around here in high school. I also do a little preaching. When one of the local pastors is out of town, I'll get a call asking if I can fill in. I enjoy that too, but mostly I see myself as a teacher.

"One of the things I like most about this job is the changes it makes in me when I get into the bear suit. I get to be a different person. I can do different things when I'm wearing that suit. It's OK to walk up to someone and hug them. They let a giant bear do that; they even enjoy it. But as a real person I could never get away with most of the things I do.

"It's strange. After the game, I have to come down from that plateau. Nobody runs up to hug me or touch me; nobody wants my autograph. I'm just a normal person again like anybody else. Nobody recognizes me. It's really a comedown."

Differences in team chemistry, so apparent in Hickory, North Carolina, are again on display in Asheville. Phillies pitcher Tyrone Swan seems quite happy with his team's winning ways. The Sparty Phils are in first place since the All-

Star break. Swan leans down (he's 6′7″) and tells me, "We've been hearing that they're going to leave us alone to play. There's not supposed to be a lot of player movement for the rest of the season. That lets us concentrate on being a team and finding ways to win."

A policy like that may be great for team chemistry, but it puts a limit on career mobility. How do the Phillies feel about sacrificing promotions for victories? I have a brief chat with Jon McMullen, a first baseman who is leading the club in home runs and RBIs, along with hitting .300. McMullen, if anyone, is a prime candidate for midseason promotion to a higher level of play.

I begin by observing that the team looks a lot looser than the last time I saw them.

"Sure we are," he says. "We're winning. It's easy to be loose when you're winning."

"And it's easier to win when you're loose," I observe.

Having jointly discovered the secret of life, I ask Jon how important winning is to him at this level. Would he put it over personal advancement?

"Are you kidding?" he asks me. "I'd take a playoff ring over a promotion any day." There is a clear touch of "How can you even ask?" in his voice. I think about my experience talking to some of the Hickory Crawdads, and it almost makes me reply, "You don't want to know."

Nate Holdren, the Tourists' DH, began the season by hitting a home run. Then he went into a prolonged slump. I comment that his are pretty lean numbers for a designated hitter, and assistant GM Gary Saunders says to me, "I don't think he'd even be this good if it hadn't have been for the pizza."

And so I ask, "What pizza?"

And this is the story I am told.

"Nate was mired in a slump. Just couldn't buy a hit. So one day he comes up, and while he's in the on-deck circle, one of his teammates calls to him from the runway behind the dugout, 'Hey, Nate! There's some pizza back here.'

"Now Nate's a big boy. We've got him down as 6′4″, 240 pounds. And you know these guys aren't getting much in the way of meal money. So Nate hears about the pizza and he can't resist. He slips out of the on-deck circle, runs into the clubhouse, grabs a whole slice of pizza, and comes back out to the on-deck circle, figuring he's got some time to finish eating it.

"Wouldn't you know it, on the very next pitch, the guy lines out. And there's Nate, with a whole slice of pizza hanging out of his mouth. He's not sure what to do, and the umpire is calling over for the next batter. So Nate crams the whole thing into his mouth. He can barely fit it in, much less chew it or talk. He wipes his hands on his uniform and stands in. God knows what's going through his mind other than getting this over with as quickly as he can.

"He swings at the first pitch and sends one out of here, way over the fence. A look of relief crosses his face as he trots around the bases. Then he races back to the dugout, where he can finally sit down and chew his slice of pizza, which has been sitting in his mouth uneaten all this time. And ever since then, Nate has been starting to hit again."

As if to punctuate the tale, the night I'm there, Nate hits one out.

Do assistant GMs lie?

After the game, I leave slowly, not wanting this lovely July evening to end. The Tourists have just held on to win a 5–4 squeaker. Fans are milling out slowly. The mascot is among them in his civvies, an anonymous man with a smile on his face. The concession kids are leaving to enjoy what's left of a Friday night.

Before I get into my car, the last person I see is James, the Mountain Man. He spots me and walks over to wish me a safe journey and remind me to send him copies of the pictures I've taken of him.

"Just address them to the Mountain Man, care of the Tourists," he says. "They'll know who I am."

I promise to do so, and we finish our good-byes. The last image I have is of a bearded man with a sack, like some latter-day Santa Claus, trudging up Buchanan Street, disappearing into the North Carolina night.

Danville, Virginia

"We have more of a football team here than a baseball team."
—Carper Cole, Braves assistant GM

A bit of the lyric from "Wreck of the Old 97" comes back to me as I head into Danville.

It's a mighty rough road, from Lynchburg to Danville . . .

Someone ought to tell Johnny Cash that the road has been fixed. In fact, a lot of things about Danville have improved. I'm told it was the last capital of the old Confederacy. Things have changed on that front as well. The day of the ball game, I go for a swim at my motel and share the pool with two black kids. I even give an impromptu swimming lesson to a little girl named Princess. Old Jeff Davis would have rolled over in his grave.

The new Danville Braves play at American Legion Post 325 Field. That's not the catchiest name in the Appalachian League, so most folks refer to the stadium in terms of its location: Dan Daniels Memorial Park. It's a gorgeous, if somewhat out of the way, spot for baseball. Like the new Hickory facility, this park is off the beaten track. The city is operating a shuttle service from one of the downtown malls to the ballpark. You have to *plan* to come here.

To be honest, the destination is worth the travel. Baseball set among rolling hills and Virginia pines. In fact, baseball isn't the only activity in these woods. There are hiking trails and swimming pools dotted throughout. If your sense of direction fails you, you can find those old-fashioned signposts with arrows pointing in different directions. The ballpark is posted among arrows pointing to Doe Run Trail and Turkey Trot Trail. This is a different universe from Yankee Stadium or the SkyDome.

Last season the Danville Braves played in Pulaski. They came in dead last in the Southern Division of the Appy

League, a cool twenty-three and a half games out of first. Attendance matched the team's performance. The flight from Pulaski was spearheaded by Tim Cahill, who also runs the Martinsville Phillies, just a half-hour drive from Danville. It's fair to say that Tim has brought baseball to the area.

And the area has responded. Assistant GM Carper Cole tells me proudly that season tickets were sold out in hours.

"There's a waiting list now. The place is packed every night."

He must be right. The Danville Braves are leading the league in attendance, averaging over twenty-five hundred fans a game. At the other end of the curve, Elizabethton is barely drawing six hundred fans a night.

"We've signed a five-year agreement with the Braves," Tim Cahill assures me. "We've really brought a first-rate facility to Danville. This is unquestionably the finest park in rookie ball. In fact, some of what we have here, like the dressing rooms, are the best in A ball."

Carper Cole adds, "It's not just because the park is new. A tremendous amount of planning went into this. It's much better than you'd expect at this level. The players love it."

Cole exudes enthusiasm. He's just graduated with his M.A. degree in sports management. How did he get this job?

"I lucked into it," he explains, echoing a familiar sentiment.

About two hours before game time, I'm wandering around talking to people and snapping pictures. All of a sudden, I'm surprised to see a team racing on to the field. No announcement? No national anthem? What kind of place is this? Worse yet, this is a bad-looking team. They're going to get creamed in the Appy League.

Indeed they would. What I had blundered into was a softball game between two local banks. Tonight, along with their families and friends, these folks will be in the stands watching the pros do it. But for now, on this very same turf, they get to play several innings of softball. My immediate reaction, which I never entirely get over, is to see this as sacrilege. This is a *real* ballpark. Professionals play here. How can you desecrate it, even risk damaging it, with a bunch of amateurs? For the sake of filling a few extra seats at night, you let *clowns* play on this hallowed ground?

OK, maybe this is a bit harsh. I keep reminding myself that one of the things I love about minor league baseball is its connection to the local community. And who do you think is out there playing softball? I've also learned the hard way that scheduling local softball games two hours before *real* baseball is hardly confined to Danville.

The softball show is just about what you'd expect. Overweight loan managers huffing and puffing their way to first base. Worse yet, actually making it there, because an equally out of shape shortstop boots their slow roller. Lots of laughter, very little hitting, virtually no defense. In short, a splendid day. Late in the game, the left-fielder chases a long foul ball into the bullpen and makes a running catch, crashing into the fence. He's not hurt and gets up to cheers of "Sign him! Sign him!" Tomorrow there'll be bruises and aching muscles galore. It'll be a hell of a day to get a mortgage in Danville.

Just before the game, assistant GM Cole looks out at the Danville Braves and tells me, "You could almost say we have more of a football team here than a baseball team."

Cole points to rookie outfielder John Reece. "He's likely to get drafted by the NFL next year. He's not the only one. Jamie Howard is a quarterback from LSU, and Jason Shelley is a wide receiver from Washington. Both of them could be drafted by the NFL in three years."

Returning to baseball, Cole tells me, "In general, we have fewer draft picks on this team. A lot of these guys are in their second year. That kind of gives us an edge."

He's right. About two-thirds of the Danville team has played at least a year of pro ball. Still, Cole assures me, "Anyone with more than a fastball is going to cause trouble in this league. These guys have a lot to learn about hitting curveballs and change-ups."

The Braves are playing the Burlington Indians tonight. I've been seeing a lot of the Indians lately. I saw them play in Princeton, at home, and now in Danville. One of the guys I've been particularly impressed with is third baseman Todd Betts. Betts has four home runs coming into tonight (he's one behind the leader in this short-season league). I've seen him hit two of them, and he hits another one tonight. Obviously, Betts thrives when I'm in the stands. So does catcher Todd Johnson, who hits two home runs tonight. Maybe I'm just good for guys called Todd. Or maybe it's because Betts and I live in the same part of the world, less than an hour apart in Ontario, Canada. The trouble is, after tonight, Todd Betts is on his own for a while. I'm heading back north, and he has about two months of Appy League pitching to face.

If minor league baseball has a fault, it's that it can't keep quiet for very long. Like a hyperkinetic carnival barker, it can't bear even a minute of silence. It's got this compulsive need to entertain, to fill all the spaces, to keep talking. I've come to expect it between innings. Maybe it all started with television filling in the ninety-second gaps with commercials. Once fans became used to that, how could the ballpark let them down? Got to fill that dead air. Can't have folks thinking or talking to each other! So we have lucky number scorecards and lucky ticket stub giveaways.

Now it's getting worse. The trend is no longer confined to *between* innings. In Danville, I saw my first touch of noise *during* the inning. It's called baseball bingo, and I should be quick to point out that, like the amateur softball games, this practice is not confined to Danville. I just happened to run into it first in Dan Daniels park. I've seen it since, and I fear I'm going to see it again.

The way it works is simple. You buy a scorecard for a buck and a half, and, aside from all the usual stuff, you also get a bingo card. It comes stapled to the official Taco Bell Baseball Bingo page, which explains it all. So you're sitting there, enjoying the game, and let's say the right-fielder grounds out. As he's walking back to the dugout, the PA announcer suddenly says, "N-33." A minute later, the shortstop hits a double. You're leaning over to discuss the play with your friend when the announcer blurts out, "I-25."

You see how this goes? Every possible outcome, or at least about seventy-five of the most common ones, have been given a code on your bingo card. So pretty soon, you forget about the grace of the game, about individual performances or highlights, and you concentrate on what's really important: winning a few bucks or a free burrito. For all intents and purposes, you might as well be sitting in a stuffy church basement, not in a beautiful new park watching a ball game on a lovely night in July.

Martinsville, Virginia

"I'm just eighteen. What could be better than this life?"
—Bobby Estalella, Martinsville catcher

Compared to Danville, Martinsville, Virginia, is a small town. If Martinsville has a central downtown core, I've never managed to find it. Martinsville is one of the most *horizontal* towns I've ever seen. It has clusters of buildings and malls galore, but nothing reaches for the sky. A second-story man would starve in Martinsville.

Tim Cahill, the GM of Danville, is also the man behind Martinsville baseball. He was still the GM on my first visit, but an increasing commitment to getting the new Danville facility off the ground led him to delegate the Martinsville GM job to Lee McDaniel. There aren't a whole lot of GMs in the Appy League who have seen their thirtieth birthday, and McDaniel is no exception.

The Martinsville team has been affiliated with the Phillies since 1988, their first year in the league. Unlike other franchises that were overwhelmed by initial support, the local response to the Phillies developed gradually. By 1991, their fourth year, Martinsville led the league in attendance with nearly 73,000 fans — not bad for a ten-week season, or a town of barely 18,000 people.

"The size of the town cuts both ways," Cahill explained to me. "On the one hand, it's impressive to draw that many fans from such a small population base. It tells us we're doing a good job marketing the team and providing entertainment. On the other hand, it's a bit easier to draw when you're the only game in town, so to speak. There just isn't a lot to do in Martinsville."

The first time I visited with Cahill was during the off-season. He was relaxing a bit (if minor league GMs ever relax) after the '92 campaign and shared some of his frustrations.

"The local fans would love a winner. It's hard for them to understand that winning teams in the minors are usually an accident. The Phillies front office doesn't care if we have a winner in Martinsville. What they want is player development. What that means for us is losing a player at the very time he can do us the most good. Just when a guy is starting to hit consistently or pitch like a winner, he gets noticed by the front office. That usually means he gets called up, either to Batavia or all the way to Spartanburg. That's great for the guy's career, but the local fans are disappointed. The team suffers, and a local hero is gone."

That situation was at its worst during the '91 season, when the Martinsville Phillies were in the middle of a pennant race as late as mid-August, only to blow it by losing eleven of their last fifteen games, including their last six in a row. To make matters worse, their late season collapse repeated itself in the '92 season, when Martinsville lost sixteen of its last nineteen games.

"That was pretty hard to take," Cahill remembers. "The fans were really upset. Even Roly DeArmas, our manager, was visibly frustrated. Last year we lost some good pitching when Larry Mitchell and Sean Boldt were promoted, and the offense suffered when Stan Evans was called up. In the '91 season, there were several injuries, but the thing that really hurt us again were guys getting called up. We lost three of our top starters, Dominic DeSantis, Joel Gilmore, and Ricky Bottalico. Up until then, we had one of the best rotations in the league. Suddenly it was gone."

Cahill's account was echoed in an article published at the time in the *Martinsville Bulletin*. Just in case anyone missed it, the piece was reprinted in the 1992 souvenir program. It appeared almost like an apology, saying "Yeah, we know you're frustrated. We were frustrated too. Here's why it happened. There wasn't a whole lot we could have done." The only irony was the somewhat ambiguous headline used to frame the piece in the program. It said, "PROMOTIONS RUINED FINISH FOR PHILLIES." When I saw it, I wondered how an appearance by Max Patkin or the Famous Chicken could have screwed up the team's won-lost record.

The Phillies play in what used to be called English Field. It was recently renamed Hooker Field in honor of the Hooker Furniture Company, which contributed to stadium renovations. It is a serviceable park, but it needs more than a name change. Then again, nothing is going to look very good after a trip to Danville.

Today the Braves are in town. Like me, they have driven about half an hour west to Martinsville for the game. "The battle of Highway 58," tonight's scorecard proclaims. Nothing like local rivalry to increase attendance. A half-hour bus trip is something to be treasured in minor league ball. If these guys are lucky, they'll get promoted to AA so they can ride these same buses for eight to ten hours at a time. Something to look forward to.

I arrive about four hours early for tonight's game, only to find things in full swing. The parking lot is jammed, the stands are full, and the joint is jumping. How have I managed to screw up reading my schedule?

I walk through the gate, look out on the field, and whammo! Like Yogi Berra once said, Déjà vu all over again.

A bunch of happy, middle-aged folks are romping around the field, booting grounders, dropping fly balls, and generally having the time of their lives. The Phillies, or for that matter the Braves, are nowhere in sight. Today is Sara Lee Knit Products day at Hooker Field. Everyone who works for the company is admitted free. So are their families. From what I can see, that's a lot of people. And they don't seem to have trouble finding things to do or buy.

I ask a couple of folks if the Sara Lee they work for is the same lady who bakes cheese cakes, but no one seems to know. Folks from Martinsville think of Sara Lee as a kindly old lady with knitting needles in her hand. I'm from up north, where we see her as the queen of high caloric frozen desserts. No telling if these two Saras are kin, much less the same person. The ultimate corporate image: She knits! She bakes!

Long about 5:30, the softball winds down and the real athletes show up. A couple of Phillies start appearing in the dugout as if by magic. Then the Braves' bus pulls up. I've seen both these teams before in other venues, so there's time for some greetings and performance updates to go along with the introductions.

Ramon Henderson, the Phillies manager, and I stand watching the last of the softball crew disappear into the stands. He watches it smiling. I'm still shaking my head in disbelief.

"Is it just this league?" I ask him.

"Oh no," he says. "It's all over. I've even seen it in AA."

Henderson doesn't seem bothered at all. It's part of the rules. It just means you get a later start and maybe miss batting practice. Or maybe the mound or the infield are a little chewed up. Maybe it means an extra hour's sleep. That can be a godsend.

The only thing Henderson doesn't want to miss is fielding practice.

"We made seven errors last night. We can't afford to take a day off," he observes.

Managing in the rookie Appalachian League requires some special skills.

"A lot of these kids are barely eighteen," Henderson reminds me. "Some of them haven't been away from home before. I'm a cross between a coach, a father figure, and a baby-sitter. It's all part of the job."

The last time I saw Dana Brown, he was playing second base for the Reading Phillies. Dana was drafted by the Phillies in 1989 and made his way through the farm system from Batavia to Reading in three years. Sometime after the '91 season, which is when I last saw him, the Phillies must have concluded Dana had gone as far as he was going as a player. But they saw other potential.

"I was really stunned when they retired me. I was just twenty-five. I wasn't having a bad season. But they brought in this other guy, Pete Alborano, to replace me. Then they ended up letting him go too. So there I was, out of a job. I was really bitter. It was very hard to take.

"I was trying to figure out what to do, whether to try to stay on in baseball. Then I got another call from the Phillies. They offered me a job coaching. I couldn't believe it."

Dana still looks surprised, even though this is his second season coaching for Martinsville.

"I knew I should be honored, and I was. I mean, here I was, just twenty-five, and they want me to coach! So I agreed to do it. But it's been an adjustment, you know? It's easier now. But at first, I'm thinking, I can still play. This is crazy. Even now, I still haven't got playing completely out of my system. I know I have to accept where I am and what I'm doing."

Dana is working with outfielder Dell Allen when we start talking. Gradually Allen and several other players drift away. Either they aren't interested or it is getting a bit too personal. It seems to mean a lot to Dana that I've seen him play. None of the guys he is coaching are old enough to have known him as a player.

"Hey, come here!" he says, calling Dell Allen back. "This guy has seen me play! In AA, right?"

I nod my head.

"Tell him!"

"It's true," I say to Allen. "I saw him play a bunch of times when he was with Reading. He could hit, and he had a decent glove too."

Dana is eating it up. "See! I told these guys, but they don't believe me. All right!"

Dell Allen is watching me closely to be certain I mean it.

At twenty-six, and in his second season with Martinsville, Dana Brown is one of the youngest coaches in pro baseball. I think about Vicente Javier, who coaches for the Princeton Reds and can't be a lot older than Dana. Maybe younger. Last week I had kidded him about being Stan Javier's kid brother. He told me he was Julian's father. He is, of course, neither, but he has good rapport with the Hispanic kids on the Princeton team. The difference is that

Javier is quick to tell me he knows he is no longer good enough to play. Dana is also a good coach, but he hasn't yet come close to Javier's resignation. That will take some time.

Bryan Wiegandt is a recent arrival in Martinsville. I recognize the name on his uniform because I've seen his brother Scott pitch for Reading. I ask Bryan where he was drafted from.

"I wasn't," he tells me, which guarantees that whatever he says next is going to be an unusual story.

"I went to college in Kentucky, same as my brother," he begins. "My coach told me I'd probably go, but not till the later rounds. I waited and waited, but I never got picked. It was really disappointing. I'd been hoping for it so much, and I was pretty sure I'd get called. So then what do you do? Give up completely and get on with your life, or give it one more try? I knew I had to give it another shot. Just to be sure.

"So I went to a tryout camp. They can be real weird. Sometimes there's a bunch of older guys there, like thirty-five or something. They just can't give it up. But my competition there was real young. Teenagers. Anyway, I hit the ball pretty well that day. Showed them something. Next thing I know, I'm down here. Just like that.

"I got my wish, but what a change! The pitching! The bats! Wood! You got to hit it just right. The sweet spot is only a couple of inches. I was used to an aluminum bat. You hit the ball anywhere and it just flies out. I'm also having to adjust in the field. I'm usually a second baseman, but when I got here, they took one look at me and told me I didn't have the range of a middle infielder. So they made me a third baseman. I've worked so hard for this, how could I say no? Trouble is, after a few days I was throwing my arm out. I've never had to make throws like that before, hard stuff across the infield. I had to take a few days off just to rest my arm. I was afraid to take the time off, but they were good. Told me to take my time."

Bryan's arm came back, and within several days he is handling routine plays from third base. The last time I see him, though, he is struggling at the plate. I watch him face a tough Danville pitcher, taking one too many close pitches and failing to produce in a critical situation. He is visibly shaken and carries the frustration with him onto the field next inning. But Wiegandt's manager, Ramon Henderson, is sticking with him, giving him a chance to play through the tough spots and learn. That's what rookie ball is all about. I like Bryan, but I'm not overly optimistic about his chances when I leave Martinsville.

Two weeks later I hook up with Scott Wiegandt in the Reading dugout. Scott knows who I am before I speak. Bryan had told him all about our meeting. He has also filled Scott in on his stats for the two weeks since I've been gone. Things have been going well. Bryan had a couple of three-hit games and raised his average to over .300. He is starting to put it together.

"He got it all from his good-looking older brother," Scott proclaims. I have brought some photos of Bryan in his Martinsville uniform, and Scott passes them around the Reading dugout. He can't seem to stop smiling.

If you're over thirty-five, you may remember Ray Rippelmeyer. If you're over thirty-five and a Phillies fan, you certainly will. Ray was the Phillies pitching coach during the highlight years of the seventies when the team was frequently in contention, if not in the playoffs. He also pitched for the 1962 Washington Senators, but you *have* to be a fan to remember him for that.

Ray has some strong feelings about trends in the use of pitchers that will not endear him to a lot of today's fans or managers.

"I hate the way people have gone overboard with the role of closer. I'm all for letting a guy finish what he started, if he can. If you need to go out and get him, that's one thing. But pulling a starter just because it's the ninth inning and you have some guy sitting in the pen who makes three million bucks . . . I can't see that. I was lucky with [former Phillies manager] Danny Ozark. He and I saw eye to eye about when and if to change pitchers. I'm not sure how many managers I'd get along with today."

One way or another, Ray has been around pitching for a lot of years. He is knowledgeable and patient, an unbeatable combination for a minor league coach. He also has a fatherly manner that makes him ideal for the rookie Appalachian League. Ray has a son playing for the Greenville Braves in AA. He manages to keep an eye on the Southern League results while tending to his crop of rookies at home. After coaching the likes of Tug McGraw and Ron Reed, the old master is now giving advice to a whole new generation of talent who were toddlers when the Phillies entered the '76 playoffs.

I wonder how tonight's game is going to go.

"We're playing Danville, and they have a roster full of guys with some kind of minor league experience. I've got about fifteen guys here who have never played an inning of pro ball. They're full of potential, and some of them can be real good before it's over. But at the moment we're at a disadvantage here."

He's right. If the major league affiliates cared more about won-lost records in the low minors, they would pay more attention to inequities in how rookie league and A-level teams were stocked. But Ray rightly points out that even if it's mostly about development, confidence should be targeted along with physical skills.

"If you're consistently overmatched, it's hard to develop confidence," he concludes.

Pitching coach Ray Rippelmeyer counsels rookie prospect Rich "Catnip" Hunter.

Later in the game, I get a firsthand look at Ray going beyond the letter of his job description. Along with paying inspirational visits to the mound and deciding how much punishment to allow a starting pitcher to endure before sending for help, Ray is also entrusted with damage control. After a really brutal outing, I catch a glimpse of Ray standing off to the side with his hands on the shoulders of an eighteen year old who has just surrendered more hits and runs in one inning than he may have in a year of high school. Ray just talks quietly to him. I can only guess at what he's saying.

Players expect to see photographers on the field. Even in rookie ball, they have learned to just go about their business. They assume you're from the local paper, and if you need something, you'll ask for it.

Once in a while, a player checks with me to see who I am and what I'm doing. That usually leads to a conversation since "I'm writing a book on minor league baseball" is a fairly unusual reply. Some guys, perhaps dumbfounded, nod and leave it at that. Others don't.

"What's it about?" they want to know. That I can tell them.

The tougher questions are "What's it called?" and "Am I gonna be in it?" One guy was bowled over by the fact that I was working on a book and didn't yet have a title.

"How can you write something if you don't know what it's called?"

I told him it was like making a baby before you had a name for it. That was apparently close enough to his life experience to stop him in his tracks.

One of the guys who asks what I'm doing is Martinsville catcher Robert Estalella. Bobby had played a good game the previous night, both hitting and catching, and I tell him so. He thanks me, and we get into a little chat. Not a minute into it, I start thinking, What a great attitude this guy has! Here he is saying things that someone twice his age might try to instill in a young player. But here he stands, all of eighteen years old, sharing these thoughts with me.

Bobby is from Dade County, Florida. Miami, the roster says. He was drafted out of high school, but he decided to spend one year in college first.

"I'm really glad I did that," he says. "It made a lot of difference to me. It's making everything here a lot easier."

I ask how he feels here. Is he homesick?

"No. Not at all. I love to travel. I'm meeting new people, seeing new places. All of it for free," he laughs.

Then he considers. "Maybe it's not exactly free. There's a lot of work here. *Hard* work. Every day. But I love the challenge."

How does this compare to the baseball he's played before?

"In high school, they used to intentionally walk me all the time. Here they challenge me. They come right after me. I love it!"

Here's a guy basking in the idea of a level playing field. He's been taken from an arena where he was obviously better than the competition. He intimidated his opponents to the point where they walked him rather than deal with his bat. Big fish in a small pond. Great for the ego, right? Maybe for a while, but not any more. Now he is surrounded by all the other big fish, the intimidators from all the other ponds. And he is almost wringing his hands with the glee of anticipation.

Most coaches are former players, and they'll tell you that the average guy doesn't appreciate his playing days while they're happening. They'll tell you it's only later that you look back and see how great these years were. I'm almost ready to accept that as human nature when Estalella says to me, quite un-

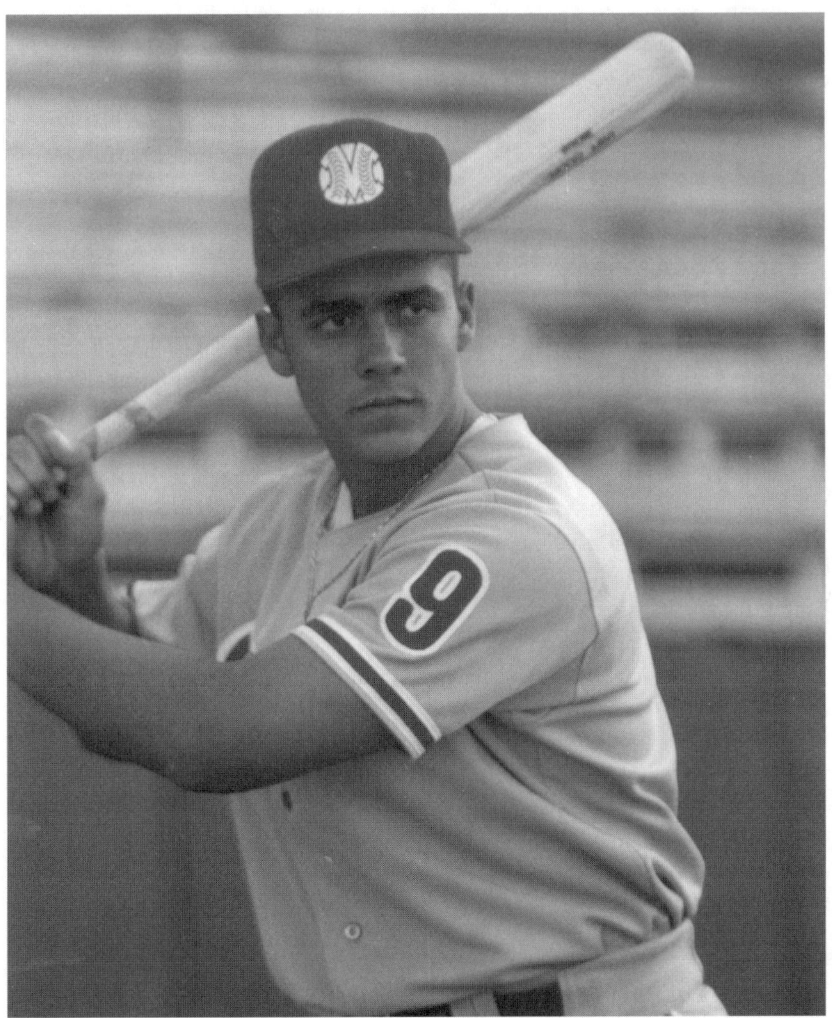

Future catching star Robert Estalella.

prompted, "I'm just eighteen. What could be better than this life? I'll go home soon enough. I'll see all my friends. It'll be like I never left. But for now . . ."

Although he never mentions it during our initial talks, Estalella has quite a baseball pedigree. His grandfather Roberto, after whom he is named, was a successful major league player for nine seasons with the Philadelphia Athletics, Washington Senators, and St. Louis Browns. The elder Bobby Estalella was a center-fielder whose career totals (.282 BA/.383 OBA/.421 SLG) can be a source of both pride and inspiration to his grandson.

In a number of recent interviews, Bobby has begun to discuss the influence of his grandfather, as well as his father, Victor, whose baseball dreams remained unfulfilled because of the Vietnam War. Bobby remembers seeing his grandfather's picture on a baseball card when he was a kid and thinking, I'd love that to happen to me. Technically speaking, it already has, due to the magic of minor league card sets. But Estalella's wish of seeing his face on a major league card may not be far away.

A visit to Martinsville a year later reveals a couple of interesting guys out in the bullpen. The roster sheet says Kenny Reed is 6′6″, 175 pounds. Somehow I doubt it. Maybe with his spikes on and a pocket full of baseballs Reed might weigh 175. The roster sheet also says he's nineteen years old. Maybe they reckon time differently in Rolla, Missouri, where Kenny is from.

"Yeah, I know I look young," he concedes. "I can't wait for the day I don't hear that anymore. Maybe someday when I'm old I'll stop hearing it. Like when I'm thirty or something. I know it's because of how skinny I am."

"Hey, tell me about it," says Jason Boyd. "Everyone I meet here keeps telling me I look like a shortstop." Boyd, a right-handed pitcher, is officially listed at 6′2″, 165 pounds.

"If you figure out a way to gain weight down here, let me know. I'll do it," Boyd offers.

"Not on fifteen dollars a day meal money, you won't. Not the way you guys work," I say. "You'll be lucky to hold what you got."

Both Reed and Boyd look glum.

"Hey, you guys are pitchers." I'm trying hard to bail this out. "You're not catchers or power-hitting DHs."

"Yeah, but it's about stamina too. I don't have any spare energy." Kenny Reed is serious. "If I don't gain some weight, I doubt I can have a pro career, no matter how well I pitch."

I'm trying very hard not to do a "When I was your age" routine here. But it's true. Reed is six inches taller than I ever was, but inch for inch I wasn't an ounce heavier when I was nineteen.

"Kenny, I can guarantee you're going to gain weight. Whether you like it or not. Whether you work on it or not. It's just gonna happen."

"I hope you're right," he says solemnly. "And I hope it happens soon."

Other than body mass, I wonder how it feels to be here in the Appy League. Tearing a page from the Estalella upbeat philosophy book, Kenny answers, "Oh, I love it. The truth is, I can't believe they're paying me to do this. I'm happy down here. I'm not homesick at all. This is fun! I mean, they're paying me to play baseball! I'd do this for as long as I could. If I could make a living in

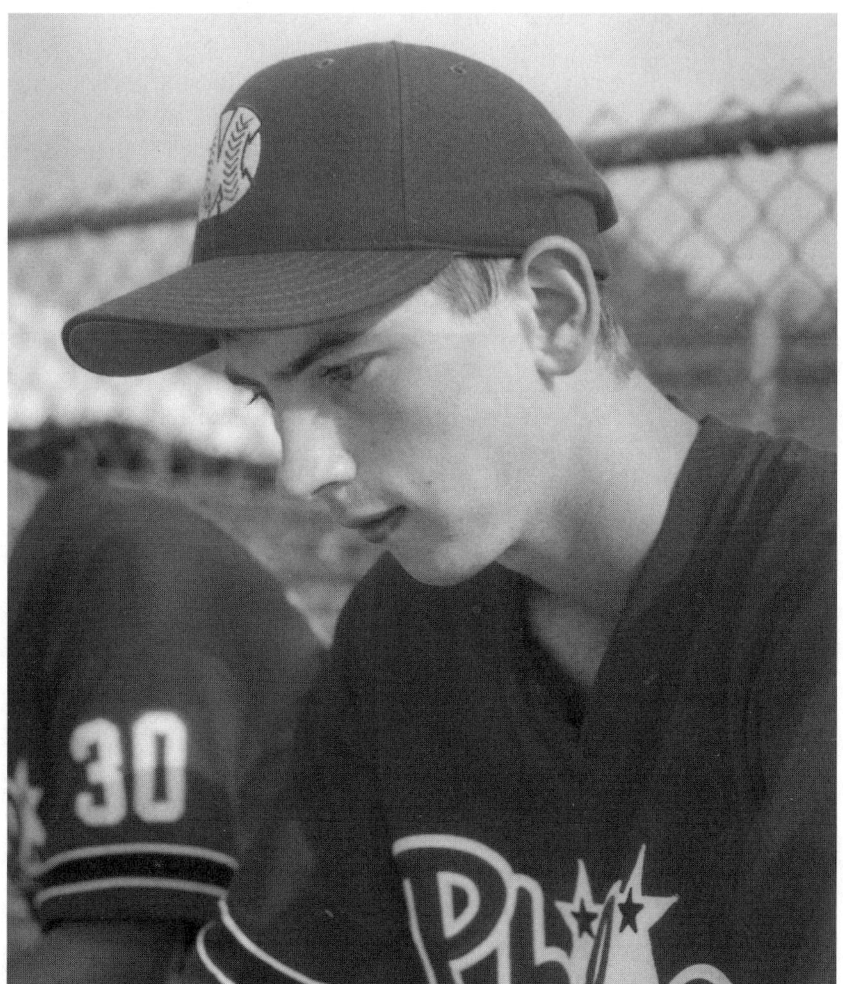

Kenny Reed.

AAA, I'd stay there even if I knew there was no chance of making it to the majors. Just to get paid for playing baseball, I'd just keep doing it."

Boyd, who has been taking in all this enthusiasm, speaks quietly a moment later.

"I don't think I'd go that far. At some point you have to start thinking about your future. As long as there's hope of making a career out of this, I'd stick with it and do what it takes. But I'm not sure I'd want to be a career minor leaguer."

"You think you have a real chance?" I ask him.

"Yes!" he replies immediately. "So do the Phillies. I was 29–1 in high school and 22–4 in junior college. That tells you something. And I actually pitched better than my record. That one loss in high school," he begins.

"Let me guess. You got beat 2–1."

Boyd freezes. "How did you know?" he asks slowly. "Seriously, how did you know that?"

"I don't know," I tell him.

And it's the truth.

I'm sitting next to an older guy in the Martinsville stands who obviously knows baseball. Between discussing the plays and groaning at the misplays, Vic tells me about his background.

"I played some minor league ball back after the war. I was with Elmira. We were a farm team for the St. Louis Browns. After I got out of the army, I was looking for something to do, you know. Playing ball seemed a lot better than working. We didn't get paid much, but it sure was a lot of fun. There were a lot of guys in my situation. One of the guys I played with was Pete Gray, the one-armed guy who played for the St. Louis Browns during the war years. He was good.

"After I stopped playing, I became an umpire in the New York–Penn League. In the early fifties, we used to have these barnstorming teams come through Elmira. Major leaguers would get together and tour after the regular season. Guys were doing it just to make some extra money. They were also having a lot of fun. I remember teams with Gene Woodling, Eddie Waitkus, Gil MacDougal. Those were really good times."

Somewhere around the fifth inning, Vic has to leave. His daughter is flying into Greensboro, and he has to drive down and pick her up. We say good-bye, and I'm thinking this is exactly the kind of experience you can have talking to a stranger in a minor league ballpark. It seems everybody has a story. Now that I think of it, Vic *looks* like a retired umpire.

Bobby Estalella sits on a folding chair outside the Martinsville clubhouse, his hat turned around in rally-cap fashion. He is meticulously shaving the handle of his Louisville Slugger.

"Anything for bat speed," he smiles at me as I pass him and move toward the clubhouse.

I walk up to a young, lanky guy.

"Paul Hamilton?"

"It's Bo," he corrects me politely. "I tried to tell them that for the roster, but they put Paul down. Everybody calls me Bo."

"Drafted out of Cleveland High School?" I continue.

"Cleveland, *Texas*," he corrects me.

I tell him I doubt anybody is going to make that mistake once they talk to him. Bo is as Texas as they come.

"I was drafted number eight," he says proudly.

"How you doing so far?" I ask him.

"I'm not. I started the season on the disabled list. My elbow was sore. They said, "Shut it down till it feels better.' They didn't want to take any chances."

"Guess they think a lot of you. Last thing they want to do is risk your arm."

"Yeah, I know," he sulks. "But I'm going crazy. I'm dying to pitch."

"What kind of stuff you have?"

"I got a ninety-two-mile-an-hour fastball and a couple of different kinds of curves." Then he brightens up.

"I was 9–2 in high school. Every time I pitched there were about fifteen different scouts out there."

All the way from Cleveland, Texas, to sit around in Martinsville, Virginia, and wait for his elbow to feel better. A lot to ask of an eighteen year old.

Bo, along with several of his teammates, is signing autographs for fans, who are milling around the field during a special pregame promotion. One of the requests comes from a young brunette. She is strikingly pretty in a barely pubescent way, and heads are turning as she walks slowly between the seated players. But she's probably no more than thirteen or fourteen years old. No matter how sweetly she smiles, some kind of internal restraint has to keep these guys from offering anything more than their autograph. That's no small demand on their resources. Most of the Martinsville players are lonely, far from home, and no more than four years older than this pretty young fan.

I continue my walk to the clubhouse. There, posted prominently on the wall in both English and Spanish, is a further reminder that self-discipline is the order of the day. Along with professional baseball's rules about gambling is a boldly lettered warning: DO NOT ASSAULT THE UMPIRE! Just in case that isn't clear enough, the next line adds: KEEP YOUR HEAD! I check the rest of the small print, but there's nothing there to remind these novice players laboring at the lowest rung of professional baseball to keep their distance from all the adoring fourteen-year-old girls they're likely to meet on hot summer nights in the small towns of the American South.

As I leave Hooker Field, I notice one lonely cop standing near the gate. It's a bit unclear whether this is his beat or he's off duty and picking up a few bucks working for the Phillies. In either case, it isn't a lot of security. At least, compared to Durham, it isn't.

"Nothing ever happens here," he tells me. "Folks are just having a good time."

Bristol, Virginia

"Find this boy a uniform. And try not to give him number 26. We already have three of those."
—Boyce Cox, Tigers GM

Highway 460 west into Tennessee is a rolling, divided four-lane road with suburban houses perched alongside in clusters. As I pass them on my way to Bristol, many have yard sales going on. This must be a cottage industry around here since it's Monday afternoon, barely after twelve, and lawns are filled with clothes racks, outgrown running shoes, paperback books, and a sea of melting vinyl.

I drive past the exit for Marion and recall that one of the old-timers in Bluefield mentioned a farm team from Marion. It's long gone now, part of the growing litany of former franchises and ballparks abandoned to high school and Little League teams. The old-timers in Marion would be glad to tell you about the heroes they saw play here — guys who batted .340 one season or knocked more than a few into the Appalachian night. Maybe one or two of them made it to The Show. More of them found they couldn't hit AA curveballs. But for a few unforgettable moments there seemed no limit to it: the potential, the adulation, and the local girls.

On Highway 19 into Bristol, the gas stations reflect the local priorities. The price of regular unleaded gas is barely visible. Even diesel gets second billing. The big draw here is kerosene, sold by the gallon. Around Abington, it's going for $1.09.

Until now, my luck with the weather has been pretty good. All that changes as I approach Bristol. It doesn't matter which side of State Street I'm standing on (Virginia on one side; Tennessee on the other). It's going to rain here. The locals tell me not to worry — "It's just what we need to cool things off." But I'm not so sure.

It turns out to be more than any of us bargain for. This is no paltry rain shower that cancels tonight's game between the Bristol Tigers and Elizabethton Twins. No siree. The front page of tomorrow's *Herald Courier* features a photo of a car plowing through bumper-high water and the headline "Thunderstorm Cuts Power, Floods Streets."

"An isolated but intense thunderstorm wreaked havoc with Bristol's electric and cable systems Monday, causing flash flooding and numerous fender benders." So says the front page the day after I hope to see a ball game in Bristol.

Boyce Cox, a Bristol native, has just celebrated his seventieth birthday. Now that his days working for the post office are behind him, he is free to pursue his baseball fancies. Boyce has been president and GM of the Bristol club for the past fourteen years. He was elected Appalachian League Executive of the Year in 1983, 1988, and 1992. Sometimes the job is a pain in the neck, but he's still having fun.

"They couldn't pay me enough to do this job. This is hard work, and there are some long days here. But the truth is, if I didn't have this to do, I'd be climbing the walls at home. There's a limit to how many times you can mow the yard and tie the tomatoes up. In fact, I don't like doing either one of them."

Boyce is not taking home a paycheck. The time and expertise he provides are donations, to the city of his birth and to baseball. I point out that he's giving quite a lot of service away.

"I'm not doing it myself," he protests. "I've got thirty volunteers."

I persist. He's doing no less than what others in the league do for a full-time salary.

"Well . . ." he drawls. "You know, a thank you, a pat on the back makes it all worthwhile sometimes. It's too bad they're so few and far between."

A curious number of Bristol's front office staff have connections to the postal service.

"Aside from me," Boyce explains, "we've also got a former postal inspector, an ex-postmaster, and a guy who's still working for the post office."

What is it about the mail that brings all these men to baseball? Boyce thinks for a moment, as if he's never considered the coincidence. Then he says simply, "We like to be outside, I guess." Then he adds seriously, "I've loved baseball all my life. I played some when I was in my teens. Back in World War II. When they couldn't get older guys to play, then I got to play. I kept at it, all through the war. After the war, too. I played semipro in the area until I was in my thirties.

"I had a coach who played professional ball. He was a catcher named Cy Perkins. I asked him once, 'How can I tell when it's time to quit playing ball?'

GM Boyce Cox.

And he said, 'When it gets to be work.' And that's just what happened eventually. So I quit and I went to work for the post office."

But now he's back to baseball, although Boyce's playing days are over.

"Now I'm trying to run this team and keep people coming out to the ballpark. These days you have to be giving something away to put fans in the seats. We have giveaways every night. Something's happening every half-inning. I've had them call the day of the ball game. They didn't ask who we were playing but what we were giving away."

Jim "Red" Phillips, a retired postal inspector, also works in the front office. He's proudly showing me what the Tigers will be offering on Merchant's Night, scheduled for June 29.

"Look at all this stuff we got here. A guitar, a basketball, a case of Pepsi, T-shirts, ice chests. We had over two thousand people here last time. Where's that picture we got, Boyce? People really come out for this."

I'm sure they do. Admission is free. They get to see a ball game, and more than a few of them go home with some kind of prize, although only the lucky ones will be claiming a canned ham. Up in New York, David Letterman gives away canned hams to his sophisticated audiences, and they laugh in urbanite satirical glee. In Bristol, it's no joke. These folks are taking dinner home from the park, and nobody's laughing.

DeVault Memorial Stadium is named after Chauncey DeVault, who was both a Bristol resident and president of the Appalachian League. The stadium dates from 1969, the first year of Bristol's affiliation with the Tigers. Both have lasted a long time.

At the start of the 1994 season, the stadium received considerable and costly renovations. Some of the meagre profits from the Tigers operation went toward the cost, but the city contributed the lion's share. As Red Phillips explains, "They have a vested interest. We have a real hot shot baseball program in Bristol. The Bear Cats won the state championship in 1981, '83, '92, and '93. They wanted a real good place to play, and they get to share this facility with us."

Boyce goes even further.

"We do everything we can within reason to make this a first-class place to play ball. We're nonprofit. Every penny gets pumped back into this facility. The field, the clubhouse, the lights, the washrooms. You name it and we've either upgraded it or have plans to."

The results show, yet Boyce is annoyed that not everybody appreciates the quality of DeVault Stadium.

"There's still criticism out there. Little things. It's not the Tigers organization itself. It's not like they send an inspector down here. But some of the coaches, the guys who have been to the big leagues. Some of them think they're still there. You hear stuff about the mound. The bullpen. The base paths are too soft. Anything less than what they remember of the big leagues is just not good enough for them. I wish they'd look around the league and see how good they have it here."

English and Spanish are the languages of choice in the Appy League. You don't tend to hear much Japanese spoken. Except in Bristol.

"I think the Tigers have some kind of deal worked out," Boyce explains. "The Japanese send over a couple of players for the season. This is the third year we've had them. I don't think they're prospects in any formal sense. They're just here to develop. At the end of the season, they go back to Japan and play there. This year we have a pitcher, Tomo Adachi, and a catcher, Kazu Shiotani. They also sent us a coach from Japan. His name is Shegay Takahashi. He not only trains them but also helps them get along with the language and the culture. They're a long way from Japan."

"There's guys coming and going from this team all the time. The season's just started, and we just lost a catcher for Jamestown." Boyce Cox looks at the roster. "Cardona. He's gone. Moving up. And we've got to get out to the airport later 'cause there's three new ones coming in. Hagge, Smith, and there's one other guy. What's his name, Red?"

Red Phillips rustles through a pile of paper on the office desk but comes up empty.

"It's here somewhere," he frowns. "We'll recognize him at the airport. You can usually tell."

Later, Kirk Hagge, all 6′5″ of him, arrives from California.

"You've had a big day," I say to him as he stares out at the field. He shakes his head and says, "You're not kidding. I've been up since three this morning." Then he looks around, nearly turning 360 degrees.

"It's *beautiful* here," he concludes, like a kid who's never seen the mountains before.

Boyce walks with us to the clubhouse and yells in, "Find this boy a uniform. And try not to give him number 26. We already have three of those."

Number 26, actually one of three number 26s, is Elvis De La Rosa, a nineteen-year-old catcher from the Dominican Republic. I'd love to ask him how he got his name, but I don't trust my Spanish. I'm sure I could get my question across to him in some form, but even if this young man could explain the depth of his parents' attachment to the King, I doubt my Spanish on the receiving end is sufficient to pick up all the nuances. Anyway, I'm pretty sure I already know the answer. It's not like Elvis is without fans in Central America. The thing is, the Elvis in Bristol was born in 1975, two years before the King died. It's not like Presley was at the peak of his career in 1975. More likely, he seemed like a pretty overweight, debauched specimen to be naming your son after.

Obviously, that didn't stop the De La Rosa family. Neither did it slow down the Peñas, whose son Elvis plays for Asheville. In fact, earlier in the season, when the same Elvis Peña played for Portland in the Northwest League, he had a teammate named Elvis Jimenez. Twenty years after the King's death, a

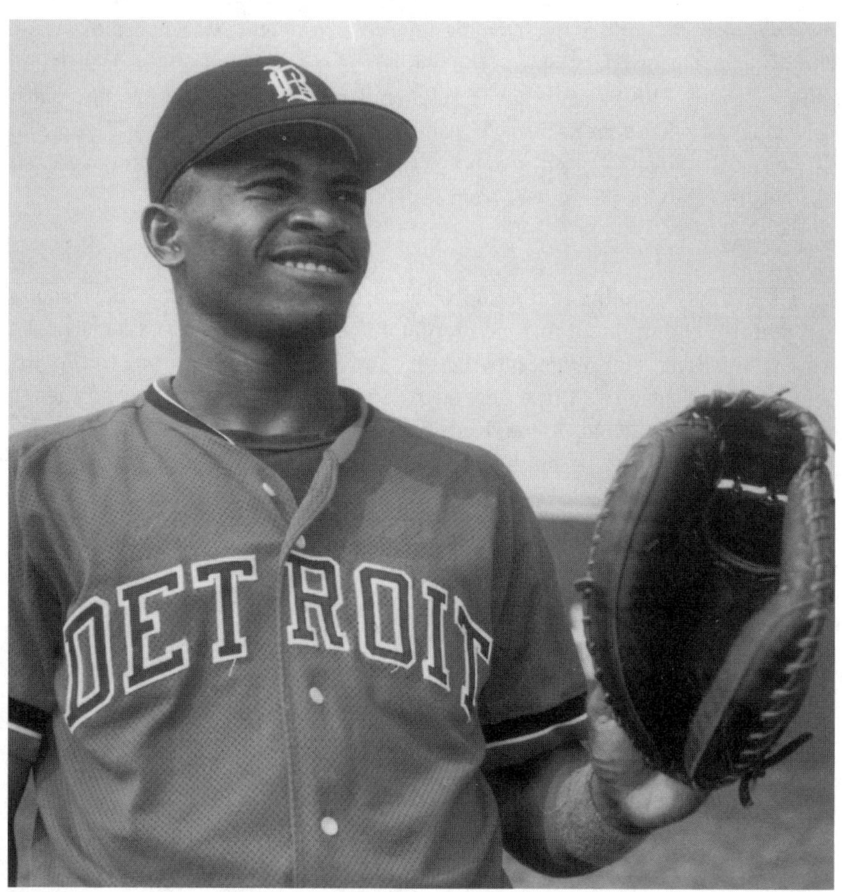

Elvis De La Rosa.

new generation of Latino players named Elvis is starting to make its way through the minor leagues. If any of them becomes a major league star, there will be yet another generation of players named Elvis whose parents will probably never have heard the original Elvis sing.

By five o'clock it's pretty clear that this weather is not going to break. The rain is becoming heavier, and the sky has turned ominously dark. The phone is ringing every minute with a question about the fate of tonight's game. The visiting team is here, everything is ready, but Boyce is shaking his head.

"I think we're gonna have to bite the bullet," he says. After conferring briefly with the umpires, Boyce returns. "That's it. It's official. The game is called." He gets up and walks toward the office door, only there's really no place to go. It's raining even harder now, as if the sky were waiting for final approval to really let it rip. Several of us take turns answering the phone, saving Boyce having to repeat the same sorry message.

Within minutes, it is raining incredibly hard, erasing any lingering doubts Boyce or any of us had about his decision. Thunder and lightning have now joined the parade. Midway through this show, it occurs to me that I've left my car windows partly open. If this rain ever breaks, I'm going to make a run for it just to be certain.

About ten minutes later, there's a visible reduction in the downpour. The sky about twenty miles from here looks absolutely clear. It seems that Bristol has been singled out for this storm. Boyce offers me an umbrella that's left over from a similar experience last season, and I begin my dash to the parking lot. I'm nearly there when the sky opens up again. The car window was open, but not as much as I feared. Certainly not worth this exposure to the elements. I slam the door shut and huddle in the car. Lightning and thunder are all around me. Water is running through the parking lot in sheets. The car is steamy hot, but if I open the window to breathe, I get soaked. There's no telling how long I'll be sitting here. My papers and camera are back in the office. Even if I wanted to leave, it's doubtful the roads are passable.

And so I find myself sitting in the Bristol Tigers parking lot at ten minutes to 6, trapped in what was supposed to be a passing shower "just to cool things off." I figure, even an hour of this and there's going to be some serious flooding around here. On the radio, I've got a station from Kingsport, Tennessee. WGAC, Topgun Country. Needless to say, the weather is fine in Kingsport. The station is promising free admission to the Kingsport Mets series against Bluefield for anyone who turns in last year's telephone book. The fan turning in the most phone books wins a free telephone. Sitting here in the rain, I wonder if there is any limit to minor league promotions.

By 7:00, the rain seems to have stopped. I walk back to the office to pick up my camera and papers. Boyce is closing up for the night. The phone is still ringing intermittently, and one or two stragglers are showing up at the ticket booth drenched. The Elizabethton team has boarded their bus and gone home. All that's left are two guys from the press box, Boyce, Red, and I, and tonight's umpires. When we get to the parking lot, nobody seems to want to leave. I end up in a conversation with the umpires, who unexpectedly find themselves with an evening on their hands.

Ken Ratliff and John Conley are a team. Like all Appalachian League umpires, they work and travel together. Only these guys are a bit different. They are the dreaded "local umpires," the nonprofessionals who now work side by side with the pros. At the start of the 1994 season, in one of its pointless cost-cutting moves, major league baseball sliced more deeply into its support of the minor leagues by reducing the number of umpires per game to two and — in cases where there were already two umpires, as in the Appalachian League — instituting a local crew to work with the four professional crews in an area. Presumably in any five-day cycle, a team will see four professional umpiring crews and one pair of amateur umpires, such as my friends in the parking lot.

Needless to say, there has been much concern expressed by management and players alike. I've heard comments like, "These local guys will ruin the game."

"They won't be able to control the situation."

"No one will show them any respect."

"They won't know the rules."

"They'll do the best they can, but the players and managers will run all over them."

On paper, these seem like reasonable concerns. Talking to Ratliff and Conley, I'm not so sure. To begin with, both these men are in their forties. That makes them nearly twice the age of most professional umpires I've seen in this league. At the least, they're likely to have more, not less, experience.

Another thing I immediately realize is that "amateur umpire" does not mean the guy who runs the local hardware store, whose kid plays Little League, who now gets a chance to put on a blue suit and officiate a "real" game. Ratliff and Conley have professional training, every bit as extensive as the regular crews.

"I piddled around for years," says Ken Ratliff. "I played hardball and I played softball. When it came time to earn a living, I turned to the family business. My dad had a candy shop here in town. When he had a heart attack, I came back and took over for him. It's a good job. I make candy in the fall, and then I'm off the rest of the year.

"All this time, I had wanted to umpire. So with all this free time on my hands, I finally said, 'I'm going to go to umpiring school.' So that's what I did. I enrolled in Joe Brinkman's school. I told them when I got down there, I don't want to do it for a job. I just want to learn to do it right.

"Boy, was I in for a treat. I never knew how much work it would be. And did my legs get sore! I thought when I left here I was in pretty good shape. Forget it! I could barely move the first week. The second week it was a little better, but I still hurt. And let me tell you, the two-man system is hard to learn! You're moving all the time. Your mind doesn't wander out there. I really worked hard, even though I knew I didn't want a job when it was over. And they knew that, but they treated me the same as everybody else.

"One of the guys I went to school with was Ron LeFlore. You remember him from the Tigers? Well, Ron was down there trying to get a job. He still wants to be in baseball. I don't know if he's going to make it as an umpire, but he sure did make good barbecued ribs. I was also down there with Lenny Dykstra's brother Kevin. He's got a chance. He made the cut. There were also some Korean guys there. They were going to work in the Olympics. It was tough for them. Baseball is an American game, which means it has to be called in English. They not only had to learn all the rules and positions like everybody else, but they had to learn enough English to call the game.

"There were 182 of us in the class at the start. Maybe only three or four of us weren't looking for a job. These people are really serious. It's kind of scary. They come from all over and they quit their jobs. Some of these guys are thirty, thirty-five years old. Professional baseball isn't looking for people that age. They want people who are nineteen or twenty years old when they're starting. It makes sense to have them so young. There's quite a waiting period until you get to the big leagues. You can afford to do that a lot easier if you're in your early twenties.

"One guy I met was a schoolteacher. One was a car dealer from Las Vegas. They think they're going to take this course and instantly become professional umpires. They don't realize that out of 182 candidates, 14 of them are going to go on to extended training. And even *those* don't know that they're going to make it. Those aren't very good odds. And these people have quit their jobs before they even got there!"

The bleak picture painted by Ratliff is only half the tale. Even if someone defies the odds and gets a job in minor league umpiring, what does he have in store? After years in A ball, he might get promoted to AA. That important promotion will carry with it seasonal work at about $2,200 a month and $16 a day meal money. If one considers long hours, hard travel, and meagre pay part of an investment in the future, remember that only 1 or 2 percent of minor league umpires ever make it to the major leagues.

John Conley's story is similar.

"I went to Jim Evans's umpiring school out in Arizona. We had seventy-five Americans and twenty-five Japanese in my class. Unlike Ken, I really was there to get a job. I didn't think my age would be a problem, but by the time it was over I knew I was wrong. I was too old. In my class of seventy-five people, I finished second in the class and first in the field, and I still didn't make it. It had everything to do with my age. They really do want you from the time you're out of high school until you're twenty-four, so you can come up with the ball players. You're working side by side with the players, developing at the same time. They don't want guys in their thirties and forties just starting to develop.

"I learned a lot out there. I thought I knew a fair bit about umpiring when I enrolled, but they taught me a whole lot. And I brought it all back here. I'm a better umpire because of it. I do these games, and I'm in line now for the NCAA World Series."

I wonder how Ratliff and Conley feel about all the criticism surrounding the use of amateur umpires in this league.

"We heard all that," Conley says. "About how it was a slap in the face of minor league baseball. I just don't see that. They did lots of checking before they hired any of us. That tells me the league really takes it very seriously. They're not just throwing anybody out there. If everybody was screened as much as I was, this league is in very good shape.

"I'm forty-four years old. I've been calling for about twenty-five years. When I put my blue on, I go out there and do the very best I know how to do. Ken and I are in a position to do a very good job for this league. Maybe even better than some of the guys who are just starting out. We're twice as old as some of them. We got past all the jitters long ago. We're way ahead in terms of experience, and that's got to count for something."

We finish talking and I ask Conley if there's anything he wants to add.

"Yeah," he laughs. "I'm happy. I'm just happy to be here."

"I can see that," I tell him, joining in the laughter. "I only wish we had a game to watch tonight. I'd love to see you guys work."

"Well, I'm sure you'll catch up with us if you keep traveling this league," he says.

It's clear from this conversation that these two umpires bring as much and probably more expertise to their job than the younger "professional" umpiring crews. Perhaps the debate about amateur crews was simply uninformed. Or perhaps it masks a deeper reality. Just as this is a league for player development, tolerant of on-field mistakes that lead to professionalism, so is it a league for umpire development. The question was never about competence or control. There are lots of amateur umpires out there who can bring both. But if they are used, where would professional umpires develop?

The minor leagues are there to develop both players *and* umpires. They're both going to make mistakes, and one can only hope they make fewer of them as they near the upper levels of professional baseball. One expects perfection in major league baseball players and umpires. Where will they start developing it if not in this league?

If the goal were simply to develop ball players, the Appalachian League would be full of forty-four-year-old umpires with twenty-five years of experience behind them. But it isn't, which is why it's not uncommon to find a guy calling balls and strikes who hasn't yet blown out twenty-one candles on his birthday cake.

Elizabethton, Tennessee

"Just bop on down and big league it a little bit in front of the kids."
—Ray Smith, Twins manager

I hate mispronouncing names. It's pretty easy to do when you're on the road, meeting scores of new people every day in towns you've never before visited. Some folks, like Jim Czajkowski, a pitcher for the Colorado Springs Sky Sox, prompt a moment's reflection. I wince at the ones that seem easy but end up being minefields. Mike Quade (manager of the Scranton–Wilkes Barre Red Barons) is actually Mike *Quad-dee* to those in the know. The Mike part is easy.

The names of towns can also be tricky. If I were traveling in Wales, I'd take my time before asking directions to Aberystwyth. But it's places like Cairo, New York, or Lima, Ohio, that get you in trouble. I've learned never to assume you're in Egypt or Peru. The locals have managed to transform the former to *Karo* (as in syrup), and the latter to an Italian citrus fruit: *Lime-a*.

So what do you do with Elizabethton? It seems pretty straightforward, but with five syllables, there's a few ways you can go wrong. I decide to ask when I'm still outside of town. I figure there's no sense embarrassing myself in front of the locals. My best guess is E-LIZ-a-beth-ton, just like the woman's name, plus "ton." Needless to say, that's wrong. But by the time I cross the city limits, I've got it down just like a resident, although no one is likely to confuse me with the mayor. Nevertheless, I can ask, "How long have the Twins been in ElizaBETHton?" or "Are there any good restaurants in ElizaBETHton?" without wearing my alien costume.

It turns out there aren't a whole lot of locals to offend by mispronouncing the name of their home. This tiny place in northeast Tennessee, right near the North Carolina border, seems the last town you'd expect to find a professional baseball team. But, then, that's the Appalachian League. Somehow, the world of strip malls and endless vistas of Days Inns and Arby's has bypassed Elizabethton.

Without trying, I end up smack dab in the center of downtown. Traveling this circuit, I haven't even *seen* a downtown in days. It's easy to forget that these little southern towns used to have centers, with courthouse squares and soda fountains and dry goods stores, long before commerce was drawn to the periphery by the interstate.

It's Thursday morning at 11 A.M. and I have the place almost to myself. Commercially speaking, that's probably not a good sign. But the streets are clean and the storefronts are picturesque, as if Universal Studios had created a set for a 1940s movie. People say hello to you on the street, and it is plainly impolite to pass someone without greeting them in some fashion. About the only concession to reality is the downtown cinema. It's now vacated in favor of a few video rental places.

There is one trendy-looking antique store run by a couple of women who sound like urban transplants. I'm guessing that they saw the quaintness and have moved here to be part of it. Tourists will love browsing through their three-story emporium; locals, I think, will give the place a wide berth. But tourists in Elizabethton?

Farther down the main street I find a baseball card shop. Curiously, it does not carry minor league cards.

"There's no call for them," the shopkeeper tells me. Her husband can tell me more about it, but he is presently out trying to find lodging for a couple of young ball players who have just arrived in town to play for the Twins.

"Nice boys," she assures me. "They're staying at the hotel." Then she adds, "That's not right." This latter observation comes with a shake of her head that seems to imply, "Hotels are for strangers. These young men have come to play for our town and should be treated not so much as celebrities but as native sons. The sooner we can get them out of our hotel and into our homes, the better."

Beyond the baseball card shop, I pass by Brumit's Sports Shop. This is a storefront to treasure. Covering all the essentials, Brumit displays baseball equipment, hunting licenses, taxidermy, and Bibles. A Twins baseball jersey hangs next to an elk head, whose glassy eyes are forever frozen on the holy scripture. More than any other merchant, Brumit seems to have found the pulse of life in Elizabethton.

From where I've parked my car, I can see a small river running through town. I walk down and find myself surrounded by another picture postcard come to life. I figured they stopped making scenes like this fifty years ago. This little river has a grassy bank, where you can sit and feed the ducks who swim in the gentle water below. To the right is a covered bridge, built in 1882 and still functional. Behind the riverbank and the lunchtime duck feeders is a tree-lined street with houses so perfect and in such good repair that they seem, again, like a Hollywood mock-up of simpler times. Yet, people seem to live here. I walk up and down the street, snapping some pictures, and encounter several tourist families doing the same thing. The covered bridge and its historical marker seem to be the drawing card. It's not exactly a crowd, but, apparently, I'm not the first one to discover this place.

I sit down by the riverbank and begin to feed the leftovers of my take-out breakfast to the ducks. There are about half a dozen people sitting along the bank. They're all men in their twenties and thirties, and, frankly, they don't seem like the kind of people who'd be feeding ducks at noon. Nevertheless, we must be kindred spirits if we've all found our way to the same riverbank to share our food with these ducks. But these guys look like, do I dare think it, something out of *Deliverance*. I make some small talk with the guy nearest me, and it goes fine. But I'm still thinking that these can't be tourists. They look backwoods, even a bit menacing. My nearest neighbor has small eyes that seem to be focused very far away. Even though we're all members of the duck-feeding brotherhood, I find myself feeling uneasy. I'm starting to check my camera bag and my wallet.

I don't like these feelings, and I'm getting even more uneasy with the fact that I'm having them. These guys have done nothing to provoke them. Finally, despite an inner protest, I get up and drift away. It's time to check into my motel, which can't be far. I walk over to an older man standing in the shade. He's wearing what looks like a postman's uniform, so I figure he'll be a good source of directions. We greet each other and exchange pleasantries. Both the ballpark and motel are nearby, and he's happy to direct me. Then as an afterthought he says, "You know who you're sitting with over there?"

I look back at my duck-feeding partners, who seem a bit less menacing when you can't see their faces.

"No," I reply, disowning any trace of paranoia.

"Them is inmates," he replies matter-of-factly. At that instant, and not a moment sooner, I see the Tennessee Department of Corrections on his uniform. Then I also see the firearm leaning against the tree. And the holster on his hip.

"What are they in for?" I ask.

"You name it," he smiles. "This is a work furlough," he explains. "They're building a gazebo out here by the bridge. It'll be nice for folks to sit in the shade and have their lunches."

And they'll never know who built this quaint little structure, I think.

As I leave, the least-*Deliverance*-looking of the prisoners comes up to me and asks, "He tell you who we were?"

"Yup," I say.

"What do you think?" he ventures.

For some reason, all traces of fear have gone. I'm feeling nothing but camaraderie at this point. I shake my head and say, "It's gotta be better than sitting in a hot cell all day."

"Yeah, it is," he concedes. "But we're out here at 7 A.M. and don't go back till 4. It gets pretty hot out here too."

"At least you got the ducks," I offer, but it seems pretty lame. We shake hands good-bye, and I go off in search of my air-conditioned motel.

The Comfort Inn isn't quite ready for me when I show up. They had a full house last night and are expecting another one today. What am I missing, I wonder.

"It's the rhododendron festival. People come from all over every spring. You ought to go up into the mountains to see them. It's really quite beautiful."

I'm vaguely tempted, but I have a date with Joe O'Brien Field and the Elizabethton Twins. Following my can't-miss directions to Riverside Park, I turn down the main street until I see a giant hot dog sign. Then I head down the gravel road in search of light towers, the most reliable landmarks in a baseball journey. I park near the field, windshield pointed away from home plate, another survival strategy I've learned on the road.

The closer I get, the more vivid the sounds become. There is nothing more distinctive than the sound of batting practice. But in Elizabethton, something else has been added to the mix. The community swimming pool is located just over the right field fence. Hundreds of screaming kids frolic just beyond the outfield grass. Standing outside in midnineties heat, I choose between two self-contained summertime universes. Into the ballpark I go.

The first thing I see when I walk onto the field is a picture-taking session. Like most fans who grew up collecting baseball cards, I've always wondered how it was done. Here it is happening before my eyes.

Mark McIntyre is a free-lance photographer from Greensboro. He's working for Procards, one of the pioneers in the minor league baseball card business. Procards has recently been bought by Fleer, but they still pretty much go about their business, churning out minor league team sets all over the United States and Canada. Most of these will be consumed within twenty miles of their respective ballparks, but some will end up in the hands of collectors and dealers who have never set eyes on places like Elizabethton, Tennessee. It all depends on how much "star potential" someone sees in a particular player. When Michael Jordan graced the Birmingham Barons with his presence, there were more Birmingham team sets sold all over the world than ever changed hands within the Birmingham city limits.

McIntyre has his equipment set up on the pitcher's mound when I arrive. One by one, the players go through their pitching motion, encouraged by the photographer to keep their movements as fluid as possible. His camera is fast enough to stop the action. Each sequence begins with a "mug shot," a static pose of the player holding a hand-lettered sign with his last name.

"It's strictly for ID purposes," McIntyre explains. "It's too easy to confuse these guys. If I do four towns, that's about a hundred players and maybe four or five shots of each. The ID shots take all the guesswork out of it, just in case something gets lost."

I notice that McIntyre seems to be putting a lot of creativity into his work. Based on the quality of some of the team sets I've seen, I had just assumed it was routine to herd a whole team through in an hour, with no thought whatsoever to varying one or two standard poses.

"A lot of guys probably work that way," McIntyre concedes. "They'll just get a local photographer to take a few hours away from his portrait business. He doesn't know a thing about baseball and just marches everyone through the same hackneyed poses you've seen on cards for twenty years. I try to do something different. I like to try to reflect the personality of the player as much as possible."

Why does McIntyre go to all this trouble?

"You've got to remember that for a lot of these guys, this will be their first professional card. They want to have something they can be proud of, to give to their families. You know it's going to go back to the uncle and the aunt and the mom and dad. They're going to be signing it for little kids. I always try to ask them, is this your first card? You can see the excitement when they tell you, yes! Try to get my uniform number or my leg kicked up high. They'll tell you what they're proud of.

"Sometimes I see another photographer just lining up these players and working his way through the line. I think, oh man! Take some time with it. These kids have done something to get this far. Let it show in their cards. Make it show that they're each special. Even if you're in a rush, it doesn't take that much time. Let a guy carry two bats on his shoulder if he's a hitter. Then as you're taking his picture, say something about the thirty dingers he's going to hit this season. You get that little extra smile on his face.

"In some cases, I get real interested in a guy. I'll follow him around the field and take some action shots as well as the more posed ones. I keep a file at home, and if I get a call from some publication like *Baseball Weekly*, I'm ready for them."

The team seems to enjoy being photographed. There's a lot of good-natured kidding off on the sidelines, which accounts for some of the unrepressed grins and curious expressions you've seen on minor league cards. The players also like the obvious personal attention McIntyre is giving them. They didn't expect to be asked whether they'd rather be pictured with their glove or with a bat. There's a lot of individuality here, and it seems to be working its way onto the Elizabethton Procards set.

I catch up with two of the Twins pitchers who have just been photographed and march them out of the near-one-hundred-degree heat into the dugout. Matt Leach is from Rockland County, New York. Darren Fidge is from Adelaide, Australia. They may have a lot in common at this moment, but they've come from very different places to get here.

"I signed out of Long Island University in Brooklyn," Leach tells me. "The same scout who signed Rod Carew and Frank Viola signed me. I got drafted in my junior year in college by the Cardinals, but I turned it down. I went back to school and got my degree. This year I got drafted in the twenty-fourth round by the Twins."

Leach is twenty-one years old, which means that come July, the Twins will have to make a decision about his career. There is a limit to how many players over age twenty-one a team can carry on its roster in the Appalachian League. Leach may be moved either up or down.

"It depends on whether I'm struggling or not," he says, rather matter-of-factly. "If I am, I'll go down to the Gulf Coast League. If not, they can keep me here or move me up."

Darren Fidge won't be under the same pressure.

"I'm only nineteen now. I just graduated from high school. I was seventeen when I first signed."

Leach and I both look at him, so he adds, "That's twenty-five in Australian years." When the laughter subsides, Fidge continues. "I signed as a free agent out of Australia. We're not eligible for the draft yet. I've heard that's going to change. It'll probably have to; there's so many guys being signed out of Australia now. There's some really great players back home."

Australian prospect Darren Fidge.

I wonder what it is about these two pitchers that got them a pro contract.

"It's hard to know with scouts," Leach observes. "Some guys put up great numbers in college and don't get signed. Other guys end up with contracts without outstanding records. My numbers were OK, but I think they liked the fact that there's a lot of natural movement on my fastball. I've also heard that I have an 'effortless motion.' That's the kind of stuff that can get you signed. Plus Darren and I are both big. He's 6′3″ and I'm 6′4″. They tend to like that too."

Fidge agrees. "They saw pretty much the same thing in me. They told me I had a good body to develop velocity. A good live arm. They also liked the fact that I threw strikes. I didn't hardly walk anyone when I was in high school." But then he adds, "There's a big difference between a high school fastball and what it takes over here. In high school, I used to throw in the high seventies and strike out fifteen, sixteen guys a game. Over here, I couldn't get it past anyone at first. I had to learn to throw other pitches. I'm still learning."

I point out that culturally speaking, both guys are a long way from home. Leach has the advantage that phone calls to home are cheaper, but in most other ways rural Tennessee is an alien culture.

"That's true," Leach acknowledges. "We had our first run-in with the Carter County sheriff the other day. We found out you can buy fireworks legally here."

Fidge is laughing. "They're illegal in Australia. You can buy them *anywhere* down here!"

"We were lighting some off," Leach continues, "and we met the sheriff. I think he just wanted to make sure we weren't drinking, and we weren't. We told him we played for the Twins. I think he could tell we weren't from around here. We were parked in the middle of the school field lighting off skyrockets. I don't know how many people from Elizabethton do that! The sheriff was laughing at us and just told us to be careful.

"The only thing that makes it feel at all like home around here is cable TV. That's pretty universal. I'm sharing a townhouse with Paul Pavicich, another pitcher on our team. We haven't had time to do much exploring yet."

Fidge, on the other hand, is getting a deeper taste of southern hospitality.

"I'm living with a local family," he tells us. "About eight miles from here. It's up in the hills. There are three of us living there. I think the family is kind of set up for doing this. We have the whole basement. There's a kitchen down there, a microwave, a private bathroom. There's no TV, but they have a video game for us."

The Twins season is just beginning, and so far the team has only traveled to Bristol.

"I had a pretty rough start in this league," Leach admits. "Opening night, I came in in relief. There were two guys on base and two out. I struck that guy out to end the inning. But when I went back out there with a clean slate next inning, I proceeded to walk two guys and ended up sending us home with our first loss. It was 5–5 when I came in, and we ended up losing 7–5. It makes you kind of think . . ."

Leach's voice trails off, and Fidge and I immediately jump in with all the standard wisdom.

"Don't do too much thinking."

"It's a long season."

"It's just one game."

"Turn the page."

Baseball has evolved an entire vocabulary to deal with the aftermath of a bad performance. It's no wonder. It really *is* a long season. Even in the short season rookie leagues. Before his season is over, Leach will have happy moments to reflect on, and his ERA will come back down.

And before the season is over, this cozy little Twins team in Elizabethton will be broken up. As many as half the guys on the roster may be gone, moved in various directions as the minor leagues continue to sort themselves out.

"That makes it tough," Leach reflects. "I'm set up now with a good roommate, a perfect setup. If one of us gets moved, it changes everything. You lose a friend, your arrangement changes. You have to look for someone else, or there could be financial problems. You want to progress, and you want your friends to progress, but you also want to avoid these hassles."

There's a very animated lecture on base stealing going on over at third base. The instructor, whose number doesn't appear on the Elizabethton coaching roster, has everyone's full attention. He's talking to them about footwork and body movement at a level most of them have probably never heard from their high school or college coaches. These guys are *learning* something! Here they are, many of them in their first week of professional ball, and, sure as hell, someone is teaching them something they don't know.

"They've got to unlearn so many bad habits." Larry Corrigan is talking to me with the same intensity he's just brought to his base-running lecture. He's the Twins' director of minor league instruction, which means he "roves." He's not on anybody's roster.

"A lot of these kids figured they'd just sign a pro contract, get out here, and their natural ability would carry them to the big leagues. It won't. They've got to be taught. And learning *that* is one of the first things they've got to learn.

"People don't realize how much it costs to scout and sign a player. I look around this team. There's guys here from Puerto Rico, Australia, Venezuela, the Dominican, Canada, all over the States, Ohio, Arizona, Virginia, Washington. And they've all come to Elizabethton to get on a bus to play a team in Bristol, Virginia. Somebody had to take all the time to find them and spend all the money to get them here. It's easy to underestimate that. For example, I know exactly how we got that shortstop." Corrigan gestures toward the infield, where a lanky kid named Ryan Lane is fielding grounders.

"I was the scouting director at the time, and I tried to see that kid in a game, six, seven, maybe eight times. We kept getting rained out, or they didn't play, or another game got in the way. He's from Bellefontaine, Ohio. We have a good scout out there, and he kept telling me, 'We've got a good kid out here. You better come out and see him.' Every one of these kids, I could tell you a story. There's a free agent signing out of New Jersey out in the bullpen. Another kid who played basketball, football, and baseball was All State in Indiana. He was going to play football in Indiana, but we got him here. It looks easy once they're here, but it took some doing to get them this far."

We're sitting on the sideline by first base. As long as we're talking about some prospect he saw in a cornfield in Iowa or the workings of the minor league system, Corrigan is full of enthusiasm. When the focus turns to him, the conversation grinds to a screeching halt. When I ask, "Who is Larry Corrigan?" I get, "Nothing there. Nothing to tell. I'm just another guy."

He keeps watching the action in front of him. "Keep your feet moving," he yells to the second baseman. "Play through it."

I finally get a confession. "I played in AAA in '75, '76, '77, and '78." After another silence, it emerges that he played for Albuquerque, with a final stint in Toledo. "That's back when the Mud Hens were still affiliated with the Twins."

After retiring from pro ball, Corrigan spent six years coaching at Iowa State. "The final four years I was head coach," he concedes. "After that I coached at Cal State Fullerton for two years. Then I scouted one year for Oakland, two years for the Twins, then I spent two years as scouting director. Now I'm field coordinator. And that's it."

And it would be, only I keep things going by wondering what it is he does.

"What programs we run out there, everything we do out there, that's my responsibility. I see everybody three or four times during the season. Travel all over. I stay here a few more days, then off to Chattanooga, then Nashville, then home for a few days, then off to Salt Lake City, then back to Nashville."

Like most people who spend a lot of their life on the road, Corrigan has developed a list of things he can't do without and those he doesn't care a lick about.

"You guarantee me a good shower and a remote control TV, and I'll stay there. I also have to have fresh toast. Not stuff that was prepared twenty minutes ago waiting for the next customer. Little things like that make traveling tolerable, or intolerable, for me."

A bit of Corrigan philosophy sneaks out: "There are only four acceptable answers in life. Yes, no, I don't know, and no excuse."

A moment later, outfielder Adrian Gordon blows a routine fielding play. Corrigan yells out to him, "Hey Adrian! How come you missed that ball there?"

Gordon immediately replies: I don't know.

"He's learning," says Corrigan.

Sometime later, I see Corrigan working out in right field with a first baseman named Jake Patterson. He's trying to teach him how to plant his feet to be

Larry Corrigan coaching Twins prospect Jake Patterson.

in position for a bunt. With admirable patience, Corrigan explains how the play should go. Then he throws a series of balls at Patterson's feet. He's a stocky kid, 6′1″ and 230 pounds, but he's surprisingly agile. Corrigan works with him, over and over.

During the fifth inning, I'm in the stands by myself, and Corrigan sits down next to me. I almost don't recognize him out of uniform. He points systematically to each of the Twins on the field, position by position. He recites the player's name, his hometown, what he hit in high school or college, and what his strengths and weaknesses are. This narrative is delivered with purpose and determination, as if to say, "*That's* what your book should be about." Somewhere around the sixth player profile, Corrigan stops for a moment, turns to me, and says, "Am I wearing you out?"

"No," I reply, genuinely interested. And so the narrative continues until the nine-man squad has been covered. We watch the game in silence for a few moments. Then, without turning his gaze from the diamond, he adds, "Don't put me in that book of yours. It's not worth it."

And with that, Larry Corrigan gets up and walks away.

One of the players Corrigan has spoken highly of is catcher Troy Fortin. Fortin was drafted in the eleventh round and contributes to the international character of the Elizabethton Twins. He is the Canadian representative on a

Team Canada's Troy Fortin.

team that hosts players from six countries and fifteen states. Although there have been exceptions, Canada is not a heartland of baseball. If nothing else, the climate mitigates against it.

"I got to play thirty games a season," laughs Fortin. "It doesn't give you much time to get anything done. There wasn't even a ball team in my hometown. I had to drive in to Winnipeg to play."

Actually, that's not particularly surprising since Lundar, Manitoba, has a population barely pushing eight hundred.

"My last season in Winnipeg I hit pretty well."

That's Canadian for the fact that Fortin hit .610.

"I wasn't really seen until I played for Team Canada. I made the All-Star team and had the most RBIs in the tournament. I have a big trophy back home."

No doubt, bragging is a capital offense back in Lundar, and these accomplishments are reported to me sotto voce. Fortin concludes, "Team Canada is where I got scouted."

I'm thinking that if superscout Corrigan could overhear this conversation, he'd shout "Not true!" and proceed to tell us stories about how he hid behind a snowbank watching Fortin hit home runs when he was still in high school. He'd probably explain that by the time Fortin joined Team Canada, the Twins already knew they wanted him. And it just might be true.

This is Troy Fortin's second season with the Twins. He spent last year playing in the Gulf Coast League. He can think of at least three other players from his Team Canada squad who were drafted by the pros. Obviously a banner year.

Would Fortin rather have been drafted by the Blue Jays?

"Oh, it didn't bother me at all. I just wanted a chance to play pro ball, and this is a good one."

How did Fortin avoid becoming a hockey player in a land where "He shoots! He scores!" is a national mantra.

"I did play hockey," Fortin concedes. "I just got tired of it. It was just no fun after awhile. It got very political, and I didn't enjoy that. Baseball was a lot more fun to play, and I seemed to be pretty good at it."

Actually, that seems to be an understatement. Larry Corrigan has already told me that Fortin has one of the sweetest swings he's seen. "The kid is going to do some hitting" was his simple assessment of Fortin's chances.

Troy Fortin is coming into pro ball with superb credentials. He can fall very far and still be exceptional. I ask him if he'd accept half of his Manitoba .610 batting average here.

"In a second," he replies without thinking.

Ray Smith, the Twins manager, is one of the friendliest-looking guys I've seen in professional baseball. He just seems to exude niceness without even trying. I can't even imagine him being angry. Obviously, you can't manage in the Appy League and not occasionally get pissed off at somebody: an umpire, a wayward player, a journalist . . . somebody. But in the time I spend around Smith, I never see anything to change my impression.

When I first approach him, Smith is talking several of his players into putting on a clinic the next morning for a local Cub Scouts camp.

"Just go over in uniform and show 'em how to hold a fastball. Just take you a half-hour, three-quarters of an hour, something like that. You know, just put

Ray Smith.

on a little show for the kids. A little clinic type of deal. Just get dressed about 11:30, then bop on down and big league it a little bit in front of the kids. They'll love it."

Smith talks kind of fast and jivey. His players are nodding, trying to follow his instructions. Arranging community things is part of the manager's job.

Fortunately, his players are still new enough to pro ball to enjoy this part of their work as much as the kids will tomorrow.

Ray Smith has been through it himself.

"I was signed by the Twins as a shortstop back in '77. I went to spring training, and they sent me out to Visalia to play in A ball. I was from San Diego so I liked being on the West Coast. I was swinging the bat pretty good, but I wasn't much of a shortstop. About halfway into the season we led the league in lawsuits. I had killed about half a dozen people sitting behind first base with my overthrows so they decided to change my position. Figured I could do less damage as a catcher.

"So they sent me back here, even though I had been hitting about .360, to work on a new position. I didn't find out until I got here that they were going to make me into a catcher. The next year I moved up to AA as a catcher. Then I was in AAA for a couple of years in Toledo with the Mud Hens. I got called up with the Twins in '81, but then I got sent back down in '82 and recalled for part of the season. Then I played all of '83 in the majors. I went back down in '84. I was one of those guys who bounces around a lot. I was like an insurance guy, a backup catcher. I never had a chance to play too consistently in the big leagues. I was usually a late inning defensive replacement.

"I got traded in '85 to San Diego, then traded again in '86 to Oakland. I started managing here in 1987. But my roots in this part of the country actually went all the way back to 1977, when I was a player. We'd visit our friends here every year when I was on my way south to spring training. And we'd come through here after spring training on the way back to Toledo, or Minnesota, or wherever I was playing. Often, we'd come back down here after the season too. We just grew to love the area.

"When I got done playing in '86, they offered me the job as manager here. I wasn't sure managing was what I wanted to do, but I tried it. I was burned out on traveling. I had done too much of it when I was a player, and by now I had a little girl and I wanted to see her grow up."

Smith discovered a unique compromise.

"I went to school in parks and recreation administration. A job opened up here in Elizabethton and I took it, running the city recreation center. It's a full-time position, and in the summer months they let me manage the Twins club. The Twins have been good to me also. They don't make any demands on my time during the rest of the year when I'm working here. So I work as both a field manager and also as a representative of the city administering the club. I'm sort of like my own boss, both the manager and GM. I'm the Twins rep back to the city and the city's rep back to the Twins.

"I can tell you, it makes for some long hours during the summertime! Just getting this field ready for the pro ball season is a lot of work! It gets used by all the local colleges and high schools. The soccer people use it in the fall, and so do all the local Babe Ruth leagues and Little Leagues. Just to get it into professional shape takes a lot of work in the last few weeks before the season. It's really a family business. My wife does all the painting on the outfield signs. She works real cheap, and we're on a shoestring budget. You just missed her today. She's out there every morning with a paintbrush in her hand."

All this small-town comfort sets an obvious limit on Ray Smith's career.

"I have no desire to be promoted at this point. I don't really want to go back to being in AA ball. I've been in the Southern League. I know all about those seventeen-hour bus trips from Orlando to Memphis. I'll take this league any day. We play most of our games against teams within an hour or two of Elizabethton. The lack of travel also helps professionally. This is a developmental league. We're on the buses less, and that leaves more time to work on player development."

Jim Lemon is not your average hitting instructor. It's not that he doesn't have the credentials. In fact, if anything, he has too many. Jim has been around for a while. He started his big league career with the 1950 Cleveland Indians.

"Yeah, I was called up in the middle of the season, then I went in the army for a couple of years. Then when I came back I had to start all over again. I played at Indianapolis for a portion of 1953, then I went to Washington in 1954. I was with the Senators until the club moved to Minnesota in 1961. I was there for three years, then I finished up with the Phillies in 1963. I played for the White Sox at the end of my career also, then I went back to the Twins as a coach in 1965. I stayed there for three more years, then I went back and managed the Washington club for one year.

"I got fired after that and I stayed out of the game for ten years. I found out there's a lot of life outside of baseball. Then the opportunity came to coach again, so I went back with the Twins in Minnesota back in '81 through '84. I started in the minor leagues in 1985. I've been in the minors for the last ten years.

"I've been here in Elizabethton for a while. It's just perfect for me. I work two and a half months a year. It's just enough to satisfy my appetite. I get a good workout in every day. I've been semiretired for about twelve years now. The rest of the time is my own. We live in South Carolina, play some golf . . ."

Would Jim Lemon prefer to be coaching in AA or AAA, to be closer to the major leagues? Echoing Ray Smith's sentiments, he replies, "No, this is ideal for me. I love working here. The travel is perfect in this league, no real long hauls. I don't ride any buses. I take my own car. I come and go as I please. I don't babysit these boys. That's for these younger managers and coaches to do. I have my job to teach and that's what I do."

Elizabethton coach Jim Lemon.

Jim Lemon is a bit uneasy about having this viewed as a "part-time" job.

"It's only part-time because of the number of months I'm working. But when I'm doing it, I'm doing it. Part-time has nothing to do with level of commitment. It's like that for players too. A player can't have other interests or commitments in his life at the same time as baseball. When you sign a contract, you have three or four years to learn everything you possibly can and display all the talent you have. If I were a player, I'd never want to wake up fifteen years later and say, 'If I had just worked a little bit harder, I would have made it.' I wouldn't ever want that hanging over my head. That's one of the things I try very hard to teach here. Your life in this game can be very short. You've got to be prepared to go all out. If you're not able to convince someone that you can play a little bit, you'd better be ready to start another vocation."

Lemon is dispensing wonderful advice, but I fear that, as often as not, the advice falls on deaf ears. To which Jim Lemon immediately replies, "Well, those people don't inherit the game."

Unlike most guys I've talked to, Jim Lemon occasionally turns the focus of the conversation on to me. When I mention that I saw him play for the Phillies when I was a senior in college, he wants to know where I went.

Columbia, I tell him.

Did I study journalism there, he wants to know.

No, psychology. Journalism evolved later on.

Is your book just about the minor leagues?

Yes, I tell him.

"Well, I hope you do a better job than the people who did that movie," he tells me.

"You mean *Bull Durham*?"

"Yeah," he says with a healthy measure of contempt. "Now I've never seen it," he explains, "but that's terrible. That's terrible," he repeats for emphasis. "The minor leagues are not like that. I don't know how they got that idea. They shouldn't be showing that. I've seen bits and pieces of it on TV."

I'm still not clear what it was that offended Lemon.

"Well for one thing, the guy was too old. He was on his way out. He'd never be playing at that level of ball."

I explain the premise, that Crash Davis was sent down to A ball just so he could babysit a young prospect.

"Oh, I didn't know that," he concedes. "Like I say, I haven't seen the movie." The conversation winds down without either of us mentioning the movie's rather explicit sexuality.

"I wish someone would write a book about the career minor league managers or coaches who really enjoy working with the young people. A lot of these coaches are more talented than just baseball. They could be successful outside of the game, but they love what they do and they dedicate themselves to teaching at this level. They love the challenge. They enjoy watching a guy progress and eventually make it all the way to the big leagues."

Lemon is being very careful to keep the conversation in the third person. We never once refer to him, the Twins, or his players. He is also plainly disappointed with how the minors are viewed from above.

"I would like to see more appreciation shown by the big league owners. There's some incredible disrespect for the minors. Very often you'll find there's as good and qualified a staff at this level as there is in the big leagues. I think the minor league staff could take over at the big league level and do an outstanding job."

We go on talking about cutbacks to minor league funding and how they've hurt the game. I mention the reduction in AA umpiring to two man crews.

"I didn't know that. Is that right? That's just typical. Instead of paying some star six million dollars, why don't they invest a bit of it down here where it will benefit the most?"

When our chat is just about over, I ask Jim Lemon if he can help me remember the starting lineup for the 1950 Cleveland Indians.

"No. There's no way," he says. "It's too long ago. I was only there for about a month and a half." And then it begins. "Well, Al Rosen played third," he recalls. “Boudreau played short . . .” And then Jim Lemon proceeds to name the remaining infielders, outfielders, catcher, and four starting pitchers of the 1950 Cleveland Indians. Lucky I didn’t ask for batting averages and uniform numbers.

I leave Joe O’Brien Field after about seven hours. The game is still in progress, but I’ve had a pretty full day. The parking lot is surprisingly full, and there’s a lot of noise coming from an adjoining diamond.

I walk over to see a women’s softball game in progress. A local church league, one of the spectators tells me. They’ve nearly got a full house here. Fans of all ages are seated along the sidelines on folding chairs they’ve brought from home. The aluminum furniture looks a lot more comfortable than the concrete bleachers I’ve just left at Joe O’Brien Field.

The players are women of varying sizes, ages, and colors. There seems to be as much racial integration in Tennessee church baseball as in the Appy League. The team uniforms are a little simpler on this diamond. The women are done up in pink T-shirts worn over jeans, shorts, or whatever was handy. All of them seem to be having a splendid time on this warm Tennessee night.

The spectators seem equally happy. The game has drawn about half as many viewers as the Twins next door. The level of play isn’t quite up to Appy League standards, but the admission price is surely right. Like the Appy League, most of the cheering is good-natured and on a first-name basis. Perhaps the biggest difference is that none of these ladies is likely to turn up on a highly priced rookie card.

Kingsport, Tennessee

"I've got a kid who just signed for a quarter of a million dollars and he's never faced a leftie. It's gonna be a long summer."
—Chuck Hiller, former Kingsport manager, about Darryl Strawberry

The journey to Kingsport leads me off the interstate and on to a road I traveled as a teenager in search of Tennessee music.

U.S. 11 still winds through mountainous country and is dotted with churches and automotive stores. Many roadside homes display religious signs, advertising their beliefs to passing motorists. At first, I think there must be a local election going on. Back home, it's common for people to display front yard signs touting their choice for city council for a week or two every few years. Down here, all the candidates seemed to be named Jesus or Lord. And the election is never over.

The car dealerships all sound appropriately rural: Stone Drive Motors, Hillbilly 'Vette. There are still independent motels here (Cleek's Motel — Truckers Welcome), but the chains have taken over the market. The price of gas has quadrupled in the thirty years since I've been down this road. The music has changed as well. Only baseball remains essentially the same.

About 40,000 people live in Kingsport. The area is rich in natural beauty and places to appreciate it. West of town there are nature preserves and even a planetarium. But, like most small towns, Kingsport has found its focus in the malls near the interstate. What's left of the downtown core is rapidly decomposing. Hillbilly Fried Chicken, tattoo parlors, and furniture shops are selling their wares, but for how long? There's still traffic on Center Street, but not much in the way of pedestrians. In twenty years, I'm betting most of the remaining storefronts will be vacant.

Interestingly, the Area Reference Map published by the Kingsport Convention and Visitors' Bureau makes no mention of professional baseball. You can find information on every

Arby's and Burger King, two local bowling alleys, Putt-Putt miniature golf, and the Carolina Pottery and Outlet Center. But if minor league baseball is played in Kingsport, it's apparently news to the Tourist Bureau.

Kingsport will be getting a new ballpark next season. It's not a moment too soon. J. Fred Johnson Stadium is the cheesiest facility I've seen in the Appalachian League. It is substandard by any reckoning. Maybe it looked good in 1956, when the Kingsport Appy League team played their first game here. But basically, this is a high school football field with a scoreboard to match. There is no warning track in the outfield and a scary looking chain-link fence bordering deepest right field. The scoreboard is useless for baseball; it doesn't even post the line score.

For now, Kingsport still draws surprisingly well. The park is decidedly family-oriented. The only beer you'll find here is contraband in the press box or clubhouse. It is neither sold nor permitted in the stands. Whether that helps or hurts the attendance in this small Tennessee town is anybody's guess. As the official program says, "We aim to provide you with a safe, clean and wholesale environment." Safe and clean seem to be working fine. It's not clear what a wholesale environment is, although the program only costs a dollar. That's a step in the right direction.

By the time you read this, Kingsport will have its new stadium, and all of this will be a memory. I'm not sure if my timing is lousy — just missing a look at the lovely new Kingsport Sports Complex — or extremely good — seeing a moment of history before it fades from view. In any case, quaint old Johnson Stadium will retire from minor league service, a role it never volunteered for in the first place.

You'd think after all the ball games I've seen lately, I'd become immune to the charms of the pregame rituals. Tonight I learn I'm not so jaded. In my travels thus far, I haven't heard a pregame prayer. The truth is, I'm not altogether comfortable with it. It reminds me more of a high school game than a professional contest. Yet there's something strangely affecting about this moment.

Right before the national anthem, a preacher walks out to the mound and picks up the microphone. A reflexive silence falls over the crowd.

"Lord, we thank You for these players. Protect them and bless them and let them play to the best of the abilities You have given them."

A few "amens" echo audibly from the parishioners in the stands. Immediately following the preacher's words, a local girl with no apparent pretensions of stardom sings a uniquely unaffected a cappella version of "The Star-

Fleer photographer Mark McIntyre gives outfielder David Sanderson a major league look.

Spangled Banner." When she is finished, I look down to see that I'm covered in goosebumps. Maybe the weather has something to do with it. It's quite misty out here.

For the second time, my journey has put me in the same town as the Fleer photographer. Today, he's going to have a tougher time than in Elizabethton. It's raining in Kingsport, Tennessee. It's not the kind of rain that sends everybody running for cover. That would almost be preferable. Instead, these baseball card photos are likely to feature steel gray skies, slightly soggy uniforms, and faces and gloves covered with beads of water that are plainly not sweat.

Mark McIntyre and I greet each other and shrug at the sky in a gesture of resignation. Let's get on with it, even though the weather threatens not only his work but tonight's game. Once again, I get to watch the making of a minor league card set with curiosity and admiration. Even on a sunny day, there aren't many photogenic corners in this park. Yet, Mark McIntyre is finding ways to make these barely professional players look like major league All-Stars.

Classic Cards photographer battles the elements to shoot Kingsport catcher John Turlais.

McIntyre has to share the field with a local photographer who has been hired by Classic Cards to shoot their version of the Kingsport Mets set. At this point, Fleer and Classic are in head-to-head competition to produce team sets in the low minors, although in 1995 there will be radical changes resulting in the lowest production of minor league cards since the boom started ten years ago.

For now, the Classic photographer is having his share of problems. The drizzle has become distracting enough for him to require a second player (Jesús Sánchez) to stand over him with an umbrella while he photographs one of the Kingsport catchers, bat on shoulder, attempting to look like a normal player going about his business on a sunny day.

Despite the rain, there is a police van on the field being filmed by the local TV station. Officer Joe Earles is being interviewed about the DARE program, designed to keep kids off drugs. He's got a bunch of the Kingsport Mets, along with their mascot, Foul Ball Freddie, in the show. I ask Earles if he visits high schools all over the area.

"High school?" he asks. "That's much too late. Most of the kids are beyond help by then."

Earles takes his antidrug message to the local fifth graders.

Janice Archer is in her fourth season as the Kingsport GM. Before this, Janice was the office manager for a local physician. "But my family and I were always big baseball fans. We kept a couple of players in our home and came out to a lot of games. When Kingsport was ready to lose its team, I wanted New York to know that not everybody wanted them to leave. There were some good people in town who wanted them to stay. So the Mets decided to give Kingsport another chance. But they still needed someone to do all the work. So they said, 'Why don't you do it?' I said, 'I won't know what I'm doing.' They said, 'You'll be all right. Just do it. We'll help out if you run into any problems.'

"There's not a lot of Mets fans in town. There's *Kingsport* Mets fans, but that's as far as it goes. New York City is a long way from here. People are more likely to be Braves fans or Cincinnati fans. They can drive there and see a major league game."

An interview with Janice Archer means following her through a maze of impromptu hallway meetings, in and out of souvenir stands, storage closets, phone calls, and minicrises. Our interview terminates in the snack bar, where Janice is chopping onions for tonight's chili. Amid the tears, Janice describes life as the Kingsport GM.

"I think I have it rougher than most of the men in this league. Even guys like Jim Holland in Princeton, who seems to do it all, have some advantages. They're employed twelve months a year. This is a ten-week job for me. The Mets only pay my salary between June and September. I'm a one-person staff. I depend on the Kingsport Baseball Association, which is really a booster club. Look around you. Everything you see happening here in preparation for tonight's game is done by volunteers."

With onions flying and tears running down her cheeks, I can't tell if Janice is enjoying herself.

"I'm happy. I'm stressed, but I'm happy. You've got to love baseball to do this. I'm plainly not getting rich. Nobody gets rich at this level, believe me. I'm here because I basically did not want the city of Kingsport to be without a professional baseball team. It's that simple. Nobody could even write a job description for this position. On top of everything else, I'm the mother hen. The players here have personal problems, they come to see me. I have to sort them out. They're my children for ten weeks.

"This job also gives me a chance to work with the kids in my own community. The team is always fun, but there's a lot of involvement with local kids as well. A lot of our promotions have impact on the town. For example, we started a program of high school scholarships based on sales from outfield signs. This is a chance to do something for the local youth, to put something back into the community."

GM Janice Archer sheds a few tears for the Kingsport Mets.

Janice and I are having our talk on the third night of the season.

"Yesterday was the worst day imaginable. Everything that could go wrong, did. Even my car broke down. We had thunder and lightning throughout the game. The circuit breakers kept kicking out. The Pepsi machine quit working in the middle of the ball game. We had cold food and no drinks. Even today, there's thunder and lightning again, and that means we have very little ice. But I know we're going to get through it."

Like most Appy League teams, there's a lot of Spanish spoken here.

"We have eight Hispanic kids. We encourage them to speak English as much as they can, but because there are so many of them it's easy for them to keep speaking Spanish a lot of the time. After the games, they come up here and I give them an English lesson and they give me a Spanish lesson. I'm doing pretty well. I know I'm learning how to swear in Spanish."

Thom Throp is the radio voice of the Kingsport Mets. He's a local boy who made good. In 1976 he graduated from high school and played football on the very same field the Mets call home nearly twenty years later.

"I do all the home games. I'd love to be out on the road with the team. I'm sure I'd enjoy all the antics on the road, except I have a wife and five kids. These days, I stay home."

Throp is a wealth of stories about Kingsport baseball. He can tell tales about former Mets like Darryl Strawberry, Dwight Gooden, Kevin Mitchell, Lloyd McClendon, Doug Sisk, and Jay Tibbs, who spent their formative years in Kingsport. He also remembers earlier Kingsport players from the Kansas City and Atlanta farm teams who went on to prosperous major league careers.

"Chuck Hiller was our manager back in 1980. I remember early that season Hiller was coaching at third, and a very young Darryl Strawberry comes up to bat. He's facing a big, tall 6′7″ left-handed pitcher. This guy whips a nasty-looking curveball in, and Strawberry bails out. His helmet goes flying, his bat goes flying, he hits the dirt. Strike one. Second pitch, exactly the same thing. Strawberry's in the dirt as this perfect curveball breaks in for strike two.

"Hiller calls time, and he and Strawberry meet halfway down the third baseline. They're standing there talking for a few minutes, and Hiller is starting to laugh. Then he's laughing even harder. It gets to where he can hardly stand up. Finally he motions Strawberry back to the batter's box. Darryl is just standing there looking sheepish, this eighteen-year-old kid straight out of high school. Third pitch, and exactly the same thing happens. Strawberry hits the deck as strike three is called. Darryl goes back to the dugout, and everybody in the stands is wondering what's going on.

"After the game, I go over to Hiller to find out what happened. He's still laughing, and he tells me Darryl looked him straight in the face and said, 'I've never seen a left-handed pitcher before.' He only played fourteen games as a senior in high school. He had never faced a leftie, yet he had signed for a $290,000 bonus. Hiller is thinking, Here I am in Kingsport, Tennessee. I've got a kid who just signed for over a quarter of a million dollars, and he's never faced a leftie. It's gonna be a long summer."

Another player Throp recalls is Jay Tibbs.

"Tibbs was one of the more arrogant guys we had come through here. He was a high round draft pick, and he'd just signed for a ninety-thousand-dollar bonus. The first thing he did was buy himself a brand new Cutlass with all the extras. First game of the season, he drove it up from Alabama and parked it right around the side of the stadium where everybody could see it. In the very first inning, a foul ball found its way right through Tibbs's windshield. You could hear it all over the park. Everybody knew it was his. From that day on, we never saw that Cutlass again. Tibbs either walked to the park or had the people he was living with drive him."

Throp makes no excuses for the Kingsport field.

"This is basically unchanged from when I graduated. It wasn't a very safe place to play baseball on back then, even at the high school level. It's basically a football field. The third base and shortstop area is in the end zone. Two years ago, a kid named Al Shirley made a great catch and went right through the outfield fence. The outfield is really dangerous. The standards for the lights and flagpole are actually inside the fence by about eight feet. We used to have pine trees growing there so nobody would crash into the poles. Sort of our own version of Wrigley Field, only with pine, not ivy. Then they cut the trees down, but they neglected to move the poles back or the fence in. To make matters worse, there's no warning track out there.

"Last season, one of those light poles caught fire. During our most popular games, like against Johnson City, there's usually a contingent of fans sitting out there. One night, they just decided to set the pole on fire. Maybe it was a boring game, maybe their side was losing. Anyway, the flames and smoke started to move up the pole. The inning went for two or three batters before it got to where everybody was watching the fire instead of the game. They had to halt play until they got it under control."

Throp has seen all kinds of personalities in his years with Kingsport.

"The wonderful thing about baseball, probably at any level, is how it brings such disparate people together. You'll have guys like Dickie Noles and Al Hrobosky playing side by side with real straight-laced types. Somehow they all mesh together into a team. Later they go their separate ways. Some are still jumping drunk into a pool somewhere while others are baptizing people in a pool. But while they're teammates, you never see their differences on the field.

"Minor league baseball gives you a wonderful chance to see kids grow up into men. Some of them do, anyway. The last week Darryl Strawberry was here, he almost drowned in my aunt's pool at a beer party. He was just a teenager, and he almost didn't make it out of Kingsport.

"There are all kinds of tragedies in baseball. It's a wonderful game, but it's also a cruel game. We have a kid on the Mets, a shortstop named Steve Lackey.

The Mets at play: Kingsport first baseman Jarrod Patterson takes a ride on the back of pitcher Justin Krablin.

This is his third season playing for Kingsport. That's a long time for this league. Sometimes, you can do that and still make it. Glen Hubbard played two years here and ended up being an All-Star with the Braves. But Lackey's not going to do that. He's yet to hit over .200. He's a solid defensive shortstop, but he's married with a family. He's got to start thinking of them. Instead he's still chasing this dream. How long do you chase it? It's one of those small tragedies. I can see it as someone in his midthirties who's found a life in this town. I can respect Lackey for trying. It's a dream I would have chased myself if I had been physically able. But you've got to know when to quit."

I'm watching the game with Dale Miracle, the bus driver for the visiting Bluefield Orioles. Dale is sharing some tales of life on the bus, which, like bullpen life, adds a dimension to one's understanding of minor league baseball.

Around the fifth inning, Dale points out a guy sitting in the stands about four rows in front of us. "Parent," he says. A single-word assessment born of hard experience.

"You sure?" I ask.

"Absolutely," he replies and goes back to watching the game. It's not even worth discussing.

During the half-inning, I move down several rows and sit down next to Lou Sauritch. Sure enough, his son Chris plays for Bluefield. But Sauritch has another story to tell.

"I'm a photographer for Fleer," he tells me. "I shoot mostly major league stuff. When my son got signed by Baltimore and assigned to Bluefield, I told them, 'I want to shoot the Bluefield set.' I was half-kidding because I know that normally they just use some local guy and do it on the cheap. But they said, 'Yeah, OK. And while you're at it, do the Princeton set as well.'"

After the game, Chris appears in the stands, still in uniform, cleats and all. I snap a couple of father and son photos to send off to the Sauritch family in California. The result captures what I saw: a combination of professional coolness and parental pride. It would have made a wonderful addition to the 1994 Bluefield team set, but, needless to say, it'll never end up in the package.

One hour after game time I take a walk down U.S. 11 looking for a late-night dinner. A block away I see a bunch of guys sitting at a Checkers hamburger outlet. Seven of the eight Hispanic members of the Kingsport Mets are enjoying an outdoor low-budget late-night meal. They're just finishing some burgers and fries and Cokes when one of them recognizes me. I'm still in my game clothes even if they aren't. He pantomimes taking a picture of me to confirm my identity.

The players are, as the GM explained, in various stages of learning English, and I am happy to stretch my high school Spanish to fit the occasion. So we converse as best we can, I in Spanish and they in English. It ain't pretty, but it gets the job done. I tell them they play well considering the quality of what they're eating. They point across the street to Applebees, a decidedly more upscale chain, where one of their teammates is eating indoors. Perhaps he alone signed a bonus contract. The food is better, we agree, but the meal is marginally beyond their means, as long as they're laboring in the Appalachian League.

But these young men all have plans to move beyond here, and the sooner the better. Most of them probably will. But few will make it through high A ball. And fewer still will make it to AA. And by the time one or two are laboring away in AAA, their fallen comrades will be back facing real life in Venezuela or the Dominican Republic.

Johnson City, Tennessee

"These are my boys. They're all so easy to please."
—"Mom" Joyce Schueller

Johnson City has been getting mixed reviews lately. On the one hand, they're receiving some unwanted attention as the backwater setting of Abraham Verghese's critically acclaimed book *My Own Country*, which documents how a small Bible Belt town comes to terms with AIDS and homosexuality. On the other hand, Johnson City continues to take pride in its baseball tradition, which includes membership in the Appalachian League since its inception back in 1921. One way or another, Johnson City has maintained its professional baseball heritage on a consistent basis few towns this small can match. Their present affiliation with St. Louis has run continuously since 1975.

The Johnson City Cardinals play in Howard Johnson Field. Like most outsiders, I wonder if the town and field were named for the same guy. They weren't. So I wonder if the facility is named after the restaurant and motel chain. It isn't. Then I figure maybe the erstwhile Mets' third baseman Howard Johnson spent his formative years in the Cardinals organization setting records in Johnson City. He didn't.

It turns out, you have to be a local to understand the park's name. It was selected to honor the founding member of Johnson City's Park and Recreation Board. Howard Johnson spent thirty-three years as its director before dying in 1979. Happily, the park was dedicated two years before his death.

Baseball is an important part of both recreation and civic pride in much of Appalachia. Johnson City's baseball roots go back well into the nineteenth century. By the time the city

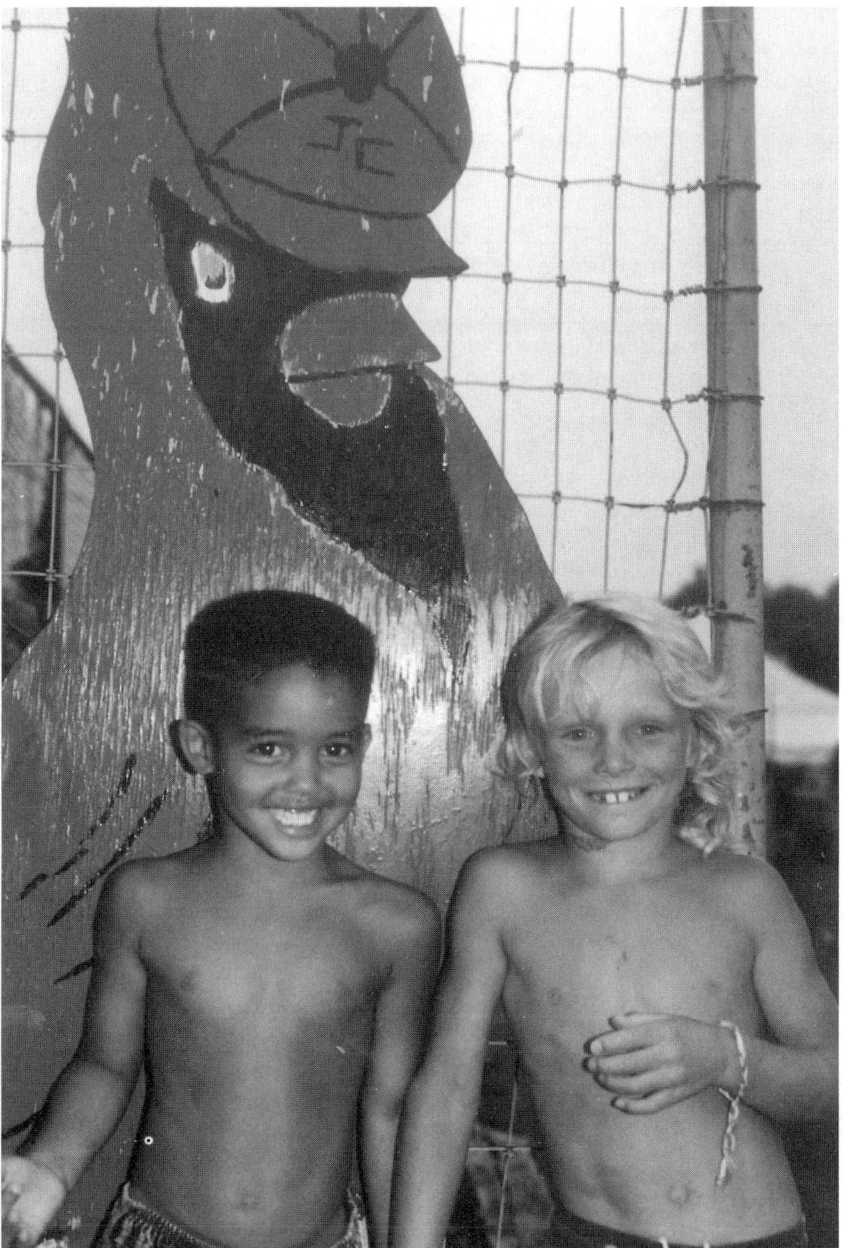

Young Johnson City Cardinal fans.

contributed a team (the Soldiers) to the fledgling Appalachian League in 1921, organized baseball in town was over fifty years old.

Like most small towns in America, Johnson City's affiliation with a major league club has been a mixed blessing. On the one hand, the majors have brought economic support to a venture that might otherwise have failed. It would take several hands to count the number of Appalachian League teams that have folded for lack of local money. Indeed, major league funding of salaries, uniforms, and travel expenses has been the sine qua non of survival for many teams.

However, the traditionalists will tell you that such funding has come at a cost. The minors are now there to serve the majors. Players were once local residents who lived and worked side by side with fans. Now they have become transients whose loyalty to Johnson City, or wherever, is as temporary as their local address. They are here for career development, and with any luck they'll be gone almost overnight. The good news is that Johnson City has a baseball team. The bad news is that it lacks the gritty civic pride that possessed the original Johnson City Soldiers.

The first guy I meet at the ballpark is Tim Redman. Redman is a coach for the Cardinals who looks young enough to be playing, if not in the Appy League, then somewhere in pro ball. But Redman's career is over.

"Yeah, I've gone as far as I was going to as a player," he concedes. "I got as far as AAA. That's not bad."

He's right. Redman was a catcher and spent a season with Louisville. He never got the callup to the Cardinals.

"That would have been nice, but I take some comfort in the fact that of all the guys I started out with when I played for Erie in '87, only one guy made it to the Show. I was the only one who made it as far as AAA. Maybe we weren't a very good team, but I was one of the survivors. You hold on to what you can."

Redman seems to be comfortable with what he's doing here, but the lifestyle is wearing him down.

"There's no way I'm going to be doing this in ten years," he tells me. "I'm just not cut out for this way of life. I'm not even married and all this traveling bothers me. I'll find something else. I'm not worried. I went to college so I'll have a fallback. I made a point of doing that. It means I'll never feel trapped here. When the time comes, I can move on."

I wonder how many of the guys I'm about to meet on the field can say the same thing.

Lonnie Lowe, the president and general manager of the Johnson City Cardinals, is giving me a tour of the park while we stand off behind third base. Like many Appalachian League parks, this one has undergone a recent upgrade. There are now shiny new aluminum benches for general admission and brightly painted seats down front for the more affluent fans. All this metal contrasts vividly with an unexpected brick wall that runs from the far edge of the visitors' dugout, all the way behind home plate, to the edge of the home team dugout. The brick interior of the dugouts offers a touch of class rare in the Appy League. Lowe admits that this brickwork was a conscious gesture of homage to Wrigley Field. All it needs is some ivy. Lowe also tells me, in more subdued tones, that the same convict laborers I met feeding ducks in Elizabethton provided the labor for Johnson City's brickwork.

While they were borrowing baseball images, the Johnson City architects didn't stop with Wrigley Field. They went on to recreate Fenway Park's famous "Green Monster" outfield wall, although here it's been moved to center field. Apparently, nothing in baseball design is sacred.

There is one feature of Johnson City's park that is a certified original. Everywhere I go, players talk about it. It's the one thing everyone seems to remember about playing in this league, although no one remembers it all that fondly. Most wonder if they've fixed it yet.

The object of all this attention is the right field hill. Unlike most outfields, which make an effort to be noticeably level, the Johnson City right field takes on a rather startling forty-five-degree incline about ten feet in front of the fence. "You get used to it" is the kindest thing I hear an outfielder say.

There was some fuss made about the situation awhile ago, so the grounds crew installed a warning track in front of the hill. Presumably other solutions were considered and rejected. Leveling the field would have been prohibitively expensive. Moving in the fence so that the hill lay outside would have made this park too inviting for left-handed power hitters.

League officials decided the warning track was sufficient. At the least, it met their safety concerns; nobody would stumble onto this incline without having been warned first. Prior to the new warning track, outfielders viewed the hillside itself as a warning that the fence was coming up. These days, Johnson City outfielders play in a park that warns them that they are about to be warned.

The question remains what to do with the hillside once you get there, since balls rolling up or down it are still in play. It can be daunting, to say the least. In the first inning of the game I see against Bristol, Johnson City's Miguel Rivera hits a ball up the hill in right. The Tigers' outfielder, who has apparently not prepared for this moment, finds himself chasing the ball up the hill. By the time he reaches the top, he is on all fours. He lunges for the ball but misses it and has to watch it roll back down the slope to level field. Predictably, the crowd roars with laughter as Rivera steams around the bases, ending up with an RBI triple. The season is just starting, and "their" field has fooled another outsider. It won't be the last time this season.

Jody Crump, who lives twenty miles north of Lexington, Kentucky, looks like someone from the original cast of *Tom Sawyer*. A hundred years ago, he might have been. In 1994, he's playing professional baseball, pitching for the Johnson City Cardinals.

"I was actually drafted by the Expos," he explains. "That was back in '91 when I was still in high school. I decided to turn them down and went to junior college in Florida. While I was down there, I was shagging flies my first year, and I broke my leg. It had just been raining, and the coach wanted to get some extra batting practice in. I went back on a fly ball and dislocated my ankle and broke my leg. My foot was like this, and my whole body was turned around this way."

Crump demonstrates what looks like an impossible combination to me. He shakes his head with the memory. "I remember thinking, What have I done?"

Crump had surgery on his broken leg, then sat around while it healed. He got a factory job and hated it. He was too young to see his dreams slip away so easily.

"I decided the best thing to do was go back to school. I started again last Christmas. I went to Volunteer State Junior College in Tennessee. I went for one semester and pitched for them. My record was 10–0, and I was the player of the year in our collegiate conference. The doctor certified that my leg had healed, and I got drafted by the Cardinals. Oakland had a lot of interest in me also, but my coach had some close contacts in the Cardinals organization, and they eventually signed me.

"I didn't hear anything for the first four days of the draft. On the fifth day I got a phone call at 8:30 in the morning. I was dead asleep when the phone rang. I was picked in the thirty-fifth round."

And suddenly, in a period of just weeks, Jody is standing in the Johnson City outfield talking to me. Actually, he is one of the least enthusiastic left-fielders I've ever seen, easing himself back into the shade and trying to carry on our conversation as inconspicuously as possible.

"I've learned it can be dangerous out here. This is not the way you want to end a career."

How have the first few weeks been?

Jody Crump.

"I'm having fun," he replies in a voice that sounds less than jubilant. "The money isn't too good, but it's more than I would have been making back in the factory. I worked third shift . . . it was unbelievable. It was like ninety or a hundred degrees in there sometimes."

I point out that that's pretty close to the temperature where we're standing right now. But at least we're outdoors.

"It's more than that," Jody adds. "At least you're not doing the same thing over and over again." Then he adds, "The only thing bad about playing baseball here is that I miss my family and my girlfriend."

I wonder how far he is from home.

"It's about a four-and-a-half, maybe five-hour drive. My folks drove me down here. We could have gone through the mountains and maybe got here quicker, but we decided to take the interstate. The main thing is it feels like a long drive. You can't just pick up and go home."

The image of casual outfield experience turning into an unexpected disaster will no doubt haunt Jody Crump for a while. Several moments after he tells me about his experience in Florida, a fly ball is hit directly toward us. Two guys are standing about thirty feet in front of us, talking while they shag flies. The ball is about six feet over their heads on its way to us. One of them throws his glove up toward the ball in the universal gesture of futility. Only this time, that one in a million happens. His glove hits the ball dead on, and it falls straight to the ground, as if felled by a hunter's bullet. The ball hits the second player squarely on the head, but by then its velocity is spent and no damage is done. Both Jody and I have witnessed it, and we look at each other in a moment of shared disbelief. We both know the unexpected can happen.

As usual, bullpen life is eventful. Pitching instructor Rick Mahler, who enjoyed a successful major league career with the Reds and Braves, is giving an impromptu juggling lesson. What juggling has to do with pitching mechanics is anybody's guess, but Mahler has eight or so future Cardinals enthralled. In the middle of all this, manager Steve Turco walks by. Aside from sporting a face that seems to wear every mile he's traveled in his thirteen years in the Cardinals organization, Turco has one of the slyest senses of humor I've run across.

Turco arrives to see his pitching coach with three baseballs suspended midair and most of his pitchers staring in rapt attention. As if he were witnessing a completely different scene, Turco nods proudly and says, "That's good, boys. Keep on working" and disappears into the clubhouse. If the scene needed an even further touch of the bizarre, Turco has just provided it.

The juggling demonstration over, normal life in the bullpen resumes. Mostly, that means stories, insults, and a crash course in obscenity that would have an anthropologist running for his notebook. Richie Lopez, a young outfielder from California, offers to help me with my book. He asks if it will be X-rated. I tell him I've got an open mind. "Good," he says. "Get your tape recorder."

Pitching coach Rick Mahler gives an impromptu juggling lesson.

And with that, Richie begins to spin tales of sex in the minor leagues. Soon, he's drawing as big a crowd as Mahler's juggling act. This is Richie's second season in pro ball. He spent last year in Johnson City as well as the Arizona Fall League, so he's got a head start on some of his teammates. An extra season of at bats and groupie encounters gives a man some status in Johnson City.

Richie's tales have two basic themes: sexual excess and vengeance. Interestingly, it is the women who seem most driven; the guys mostly seem to be in the right place at the right time. Anonymous multiple partners and acrobatics

Steve Turco.

seem to be the stuff of legends. Vengeance rears its head when one of Richie's former teammates, who apparently received a sizable signing bonus, had his sportscar trashed by an ex-girlfriend who disagreed with him about the permanence of their love affair. Somehow, there was a misunderstanding over whether this was recreational sex or a lifetime commitment to family values. This seems to be a frequent misunderstanding in the Appalachian League. However, the presence of a shiny new sports car allowed for a more creative expression of the conflict than usual.

If Lopez doesn't make it as an outfielder in the Cardinals system, he may have a career as a storyteller. When he is through, he turns to me expectantly and asks if I can use his stuff.

"Photographs, Richie," I tell him as earnestly as I can. "I need photos!"

He shakes his head in disbelief. "I don't have any pictures," he protests.

I put down my tape recorder and pretend to be losing interest. "Without pictures, there's no proof. There could be lawsuits," I tell him. "You need to be thinking ahead. You should have been right there under the table with that groupie, reeling off photos. Then, I'd be able to use this."

A couple of the guys are starting to laugh, and Lopez sees that I'm not serious. He waves his hand in exasperation and saunters away, assuming this whole episode will never make the book. Life is full of surprises.

Within minutes of Richie's X-rated tales, the scene in the bullpen shifts radically. Mama Joyce has appeared. Joyce Schueller is a local woman who has adopted the Johnson City Cardinals. She has taken over the role of team mom. She bakes for her adopted sons, she encourages them, she does what she can to turn this ragtag bunch of temporary orphans into a family.

Joyce literally wears it on her sleeve. She dresses in a Johnson City uniform. Above her number ("1") is the name "Mom." As soon as she appears, there is a palpable change in bullpen decorum. You might be hanging out in your bedroom with some buddies, listening to loud music and sharing one of Richie's sexual vignettes. Suddenly Mom comes in with some chocolate chip cookies, and everyone shifts from being a sex-crazed adolescent to a polite, cookie-craving young Republican. That age-old scene gets repeated in the Johnson City bullpen almost every day.

Joyce has been doing this for ten years. Since she usually appears laden with snacks, she is surrounded by hungry young men in a virtual feeding frenzy. There's lots of good-natured attention, and Joyce loves it. Today, she's getting a lot of kidding because all she's brought is a sack of candy bars and some sunflower seeds.

"Didn't you bake for us today, Mom?" they ask in mock disappointment. "Did you forget about us?" It's a wonderful ritual.

Joyce introduces me to all the guys in the pen. It's only the first week of the season, but there is already a lot of easy familiarity.

"These are all my boys," she tells me proudly. "They're all so easy to please."

"Yeah, Richie was just telling me about that," I reply. Joyce smiles, but a moment of sheer panic crosses Richie's face. "You wouldn't!" his eyes say to me. But then he realizes, of course I wouldn't. It was just too good an opportunity to miss.

Mama Joyce and some of her boys.

Today is Joyce's twenty-ninth wedding anniversary. Before she leaves, Joyce whispers to me, "These boys need a mama. They're all so far from home."

That's obviously not the side I get to see, but I can't imagine that Joyce is wrong. There haven't been many complaints in the decade Joyce has been on the job. Just before we finish talking, Joyce makes sure I've seen her sign. Out there in right field, Joyce has rented an outfield billboard. Among the ads for local restaurants and garages is a red and white sign announcing: MOM (Joyce) Says Good Luck Cardinals.

Mike Martin is not a typical Johnson City recruit. Unlike many of his teammates, Martin has not journeyed to Johnson City from hundreds or even thousands of miles away. Mike Martin is from Kingsport, Tennessee, literally minutes away from where he now pitches. Very few players in the Appalachian League share that advantage.

"This is great for me. I love playing here," Martin tells me. "I'm probably the only guy in the league who doesn't want to be promoted," he jokes. "No, actually, I do, but it'll never be like this again. Like I was just figuring it out. If I pitch every fifth day, I could end up starting a game in my hometown early next month."

Even if his calculations are off, Martin's family won't have far to travel to see him. Last night they made the hop to Johnson City to see his Appalachian League debut. Martin has his own cheering section: his parents, his grandparents, his brother (an aspiring catcher), and a whole bevy of friends from Kingsport. They weren't disappointed. Against the Huntington Cubs, Martin lasted seven innings, gave up just one earned run, and allowed only three hits.

Mike Martin and I are talking out in right field in front of the famous hillside, where the pregame temperature is in the midnineties and the humidity isn't far behind.

"Yeah, this feels about right to me," he jokes. "Last summer I pitched in the Arizona League. We used to play morning games in empty stadiums. It was even hotter than this, if you can believe it. The temperature was in the low hundreds, but there was no humidity. I'd much rather pitch here. I'm more effective with all this humidity. Perfect baseball weather."

I shake my northern head in disbelief, but Martin digs in deeper.

"I played some games up in Madison. Forty degrees at game time." He shivers. "I hated it. Now *this* is the way it's supposed to be."

My one look at the Johnson City Cardinals on the field is quite an eye-opener. I'm sitting in the left field bleachers in the fourth inning when designated hitter Steve Abbs come up and launches a moon shot out of the park. Two innings later, I'm trying out the fancy blue seats in the first row when Abbs again finds the Tennessee night air to his liking. Another moon shot. The man obviously doesn't care where I sit.

In the first four games of the season, Abbs is six for twelve with two home runs and five RBIs. After the game, he explains to the Johnson City sportswriter that he still isn't comfortable using a wood bat or hitting against the professional pitching in this league. He says the fans will have to give him some time to adjust before they see him at his best. It's a scary prospect.

Cedar Rapids, Iowa

"Wow, that's baseball!"
—Anonymous fan reaction to Veterans Memorial Stadium

It's incredibly hot as I leave some business behind in Nebraska and head for the lure of minor league baseball in Iowa. Every one of those little time and temperature signs in downtown Lincoln has been flashing a three-digit number. Even after 9 P.M., the temperature always seems to start with a 1.

I head east for what I hope will be the cool, swaying cornfields of Iowa. But nothing is very cool, and there isn't much swaying going on out there. There's no relief in sight. The whole Midwest is caught in the grip of what is becoming a record heat wave. Driving through Omaha, I hear radio warnings to stay at home. Conserve water. Try to conserve power. I can't imagine how these warnings help. If you're lucky enough to stay at home, you're probably showering or watering your lawn while the air conditioner runs full tilt.

Local radio stations have their news teams scurrying all over downtown Omaha to report on sidewalks that have come undone. Roadways are buckling in the heat, and motorists are being warned to stay away. I feel like a tourist on the interstate, zipping through a disaster area in my air-conditioned car.

There seems to be some consolation in knowing the problem goes beyond the immediate Iowa/Nebraska area. As I drive, there are tales of deaths in Chicago attributable to record heat. "It isn't just *us*," the disembodied voice assures local listeners. "It's *everywhere*." Such messages are usually followed by warnings to conserve power. The threats are getting more ominous. "If you don't cut down, there'll be blackouts." But with soaring humidity and temperatures near 110, who is likely to turn off their air conditioner? At a gas station just off the interstate, I hear vague grumbling. "Why should *I* be the one to conserve? How about the guy in the next apartment? Isn't *his* air conditioner still going?"

Heat waves have no difficulty crossing state lines. Council Bluffs, Iowa, directly across the border from Omaha, is an oven. Des Moines, lying almost directly in the center of the state, is also reporting road damage from high temperatures. I finally stop at a motel in Iowa City. The heat is so oppressive, I find myself planning even the briefest trip out of my air-conditioned room. It feels like there's a deluge out there. You don't want to be exposed to it any longer than you have to. Maybe in the good old days, the local kids would go swimming in a lake. But today swimming seems out of the question. I can't imagine lying around a motel pool on a day like this. Anyway, the water is barely refreshing when it's been heated above body temperature.

There's a pamphlet full of ads and consumer coupons in my room. It seems to have been printed very recently by someone who anticipated this heat. "Ice cold beer and pop delivered." That sounds just about right. Another proclaims: "Sidewalk Sizzle Sale on women's apparel." Maybe when it's thirty degrees cooler. Today, I can't see anybody browsing through Guccis with the sun beating down and the sidewalk buckling under their feet. Undoubtedly, the strangest ad comes from the local pet store, prophetically called Pet Degree. "Beat the heat with a *Cold Blooded* Pet," they encourage me. "25% off all reptiles in stock." I avoid the temptation to run out and buy a lizard and settle instead for a brief visit to a salad bar before settling in for the night.

It's a quick trip north to Cedar Rapids. That's the good news. The bad is that it's even hotter than yesterday when I arrive at Veterans Memorial Stadium, home of the Cedar Rapids Kernels. Like many teams in the Midwest League, the Kernels have recently changed their name and major league affiliation. Previously, they were tied to the Braves, Giants, Cardinals, and Cincinnati Reds. Their affiliation with the California Angels began in 1993, the year of *The Flood.* That was the season a vengeful Mother Nature did her best to sabotage baseball in the Midwest League. The Cedar Rapids franchise held its own against over sixty inches of rain and the following year won the league championship.

If bad weather has been a frequent guest at Veterans Stadium, so has victory. The Cedar Rapids team has won three league championships since 1988. They've also made a good living selling merchandise. The Kernels name resulted from a local contest. Their logo, featuring a baseball popping out of an ear of corn, is a merchandising dream. It appears on caps, bats, shirts, pants, pens, and paper. The franchise also sells T-shirts bearing a somewhat immodest (by Midwest standards) design featuring Titletown, USA — Cedar Rapids, Iowa. The old team logo of the Cedar Rapids Reds appears above the years '88 and '92, while the new Kernels logo is paired with the '94 championship year. Middle America or not, pride is pride.

Little of this success has translated into physical comfort. There's barely enough room in the general manager's office to carry on a conversation. Jack Roeder has held the position since 1991. He is easily the most formally dressed GM I have met. Despite the weather and the circumstances of his office, Roeder wears a suit and tie.

"I think it's part of our image. I'm real picky about how the team is presented. When people come out here, it's like they're going to a restaurant. They expect it to look clean. I think the staff should also look clean and well groomed. We want to convey a sense of professionalism. Looking tidy helps to say we know what we're doing and we take it seriously."

If that's the case, I want to tell Roeder that the suit is unnecessary in his case. Even in shorts and one of his Titletown, USA T-shirts, this GM would look professional. It's something he radiates. More than that, Jack Roeder seems like one of the most decent guys I've come across in baseball. He exudes *niceness.*

Roeder has been around the game for a while.

"I was coaching junior college baseball after I graduated from college. Then in 1979 I decided to go to graduate school. I wanted to get a master's degree so I could teach or coach at the college level. Right at that time, the sports administration field was starting to take off. So were the minor leagues. Up to that point, you really didn't need a degree to run one of these franchises.

"In order to graduate, I had to have an internship, and one of the positions that came up was with the Clinton Giants. Clinton is my hometown, so it really made the decision easy for me. After I graduated, the Giants hired me as their assistant GM. Then I went to Wassau, Wisconsin, as their general manager. I stayed with them until 1991, when the franchise was sold to Kane County. That's the year I came here."

Like all minor league GMs, Roeder works hard.

"This is a full-time job, to say the least. I average about ten hours a day and often end up working weekends as well. Even during the off-season. We really have two seasons here," Roeder explains. "The playing season and the nonplaying season. Most people don't realize the nonplaying season is far and away much more important. All the work that sets the table for the next season is done way before opening day. Once the actual season begins, it's just the day-to-day operations."

I ask Roeder to summarize the Midwest League for me.

"It's a mixture of older franchises like ours and some very new ones like Kane County and West Michigan. There are some beautiful facilities to see, and they're drawing incredible crowds. Kane County, for example, is drawing six or seven thousand people a night. That's exceptional for this league. So is the attendance at Grand Rapids [West Michigan]. They've been hitting about eight thousand a night. Both teams might end up in the top five in minor league attendance, which means they're outdrawing most AA and AAA teams in the country.

"We were just up to Grand Rapids for the league All-Star game last month. I was surprised to see there were guys out front scalping tickets. We didn't need any, but I asked how much they were. 'Thirty bucks,' he said. Thirty bucks! When you hit that for a single-A ticket, you know you've arrived. And you can bet he sold those tickets. The park was full."

I wonder if shiny new ballparks are the key to minor league success.

"No. Tradition is important too. This park is over forty years old. We still have fans who walk up that ramp, look at the field, and say, 'Wow, that's baseball!' Even so, a franchise like ours can't stand still. We draw pretty well. The metropolitan Cedar Rapids population is around 150,000. If you include Iowa City, which is just another half-hour south, there's another 60 to 70,000. Within a thirty- or forty-mile radius, we're nearly a quarter of a million people. Right now we're averaging about two thousand a game. Nevertheless, we have to think ahead and ask what we'll be doing in the year 2000. Teams are gone in this league that were there just a year or two ago. Towns like Wassau and Waterloo have lost their franchises. It can happen. Those teams go to bigger markets. You have to be concerned. We're trying to keep the charm and the tradition of this park but still add the amenities you need in order to stay competitive. That's the challenge."

Roeder is quick to add that a minor league franchise isn't an automatic ticket to riches.

"For every one of these minor league success stories, there are just as many struggling to make a go. And there are teams going under. There are no guarantees out there. This is still an iffy business. We're doing OK in Cedar Rapids, but we need to be careful. We have to work hard every year to come out in the black. Unlike the majors, the team itself is not the major factor. You want to win, obviously, and we've been fortunate to have some championship teams in the last few years. But that's just not enough at this level."

Even if he wanted to field a winning team, Roeder would be all but powerless. As usual, those strings are pulled by the head office. His team had just lost its best hitter yesterday. Outfielder Demond Smith was batting .343. Smith needed just a few more at bats to qualify as the league's leading hitter, not to mention setting a franchise record. But he won't get them this season. Bearing the curse of all minor leaguers, Smith has managed to do so well that he's lost his job. He's been promoted. Demond Smith is still in A ball, but now he plays for Lake Elsinore of the California League.

I wonder how the Kernels' new affiliation with the California Angels is working.

"It's too new to judge. So far things have gone well. We had a long relationship previously with the Reds. This was a Cincinnati team for thirteen years before 1993."

Why did such a long marriage end?

"The Reds felt they had two minor league teams at the same level. The Midwest League is considered mid- to low A ball. The Reds also had a team in the Sally League — Charleston, West Virginia. Their original thinking was to get one of those teams into a higher level A league. They were originally looking to the Carolina League, for example. They figured it would make more sense in terms of player development. I guess they were right. We were getting guys out of Charleston as the next step in their development. So the Reds were treating Cedar Rapids as their high-A team, but the rest of the league wasn't really up to that standard."

Lately, the Midwest League has been playing musical chairs with affiliations. Roeder prefers to describe it as "growing pains."

"Ultimately, I think all of this will strengthen the league. It's just that this has been a chaotic period."

Right now, Roeder has more immediate problems.

"We're hoping to get the attendance up to between twenty-two to twenty-three hundred a game. We're shooting for 150,000 for the season. We got off to a rocky start. April and May were unusually cold and wet here. Now we've got this heat wave. That's going to take its toll as well. I'm hoping it won't keep people away altogether. Maybe we'll just have a late-arriving crowd tonight. We were hoping for twenty-five hundred. With this temperature, I'd settle for fifteen hundred to be honest."

I leave the spartan air conditioning of Jack Roeder's office and walk out on to the ramp leading to the field. Before I can sigh "Wow! That's baseball!" I get hit with a wall of humidity that makes me want to run for cover. I'm amazed to see players taking BP and shagging flies as if it were forty degrees cooler. No one wants to look like a wimp, especially with the manager and coaches in sight. Despite all this macho madness, most guys are quick to confide that this is the worst heat they've ever experienced or played in.

I'm sitting in the Kernels dugout trying to keep cool. Pitcher Nick Skuse spots my Monterrey Bay Aquarium T-shirt and asks me if I'm from California. No, just a visitor to the aquarium, I tell him. We agree that it's a beautiful place, although he explains that he's from the Santa Cruz area: the mountains, not the seashore.

Pitcher Tony Shaver on a warm afternoon in Cedar Rapids.

Regardless, he admits that nothing in his California experience has prepared him for this weather. For what it's worth, the Cedar Rapids roster lists ten players who reside in California. The Angels seem to be scouting heavily in their own backyard. Ironically, one of the players who seems least dazzled by the heat is a pitcher named Jason Dickson. Dickson is out there shagging flies, fielding grounders, and relaying throws from the outfield. He seems to be operating in his own personal climate, impervious to the heat. Maybe it's the novelty. Dickson, it turns out, was born in Canada and still lives there. Half this temperature, literally, would be a normal day in London, Ontario, where Dickson grew up, or in New Brunswick, where he now lives.

"Oh, I just love it," he assures me. "It doesn't bother me at all."

The visiting Quad City River Bandits arrive at about four o'clock and launch into their own round of sweat-soaked workouts. I'm standing on the mound with several Quad City pitchers. Everyone is marveling at the heat when a reporter comes trudging across the infield with a large clocklike thermometer in his hand. The local paper wants to get a midafternoon reading on the pitcher's mound before tonight's game. This leads to a quick lottery, with everybody taking a guess at the temperature. Estimates range from the mid-90s (wishful thinking) to the unthinkable: 120. I weigh in at 115, which I'm hoping is high.

The thermometer has been in the reporter's car, and the air conditioner has kept it close to 70 degrees. It starts to climb in the afternoon heat, even as the final guesses are being logged in. We all gather round to watch. The verdict doesn't take long: you can see the hand move. First it glides through the 80s, then the 90s. Then 100 degrees goes by. The needle slows down as it hits 110, but it's still moving. It hits 115, and for a moment I think I'm going to be the winner. But the needle is still climbing. It finally comes to rest just beyond the 119 mark. The scale stops at 120. We look at each other in disbelief, and there is a moment of stunned silence.

I ask Tony Shaver, a pitcher from Orlando, Florida, to hold the thermometer while I take a couple of pictures. I figure without the photos, no one is going to believe this. Like fishing stories, tales of the heat wave of '95 will expand with retelling. Whether or not Tony Shaver maintains his 1.75 ERA and ends up winning a Cy Young Award, my photo guarantees that he will be able to show his friends and family that he stood on the mound in a pro ball uniform in Cedar Rapids, Iowa, when the temperature nudged 120 degrees.

I'm usually swarmed by players wanting to see my stat sheet when I walk on to the field. I notice that John Donati and Aaron Iatarola are keeping their distance. They take their turns in the Kernels batting cage but don't join in the rush to see how their seasons are going. Without looking, I assume both guys are having off-years and are in no hurry to see the statistical proof of what they already know.

Then I watch Donati in the cage. He is, to use the baseball expression of the midnineties, "going yard" with almost every swing. One of his teammates comments about the season Donati is having. So I look. A .304 batting average,

John Donati and Aaron Iatarola.

eleven HRs (second on the team), and fifty-three RBIs. For the hell of it, I scan down a few lines and check Iatarola. His average is a bit lower (.268), but he leads the team with fourteen HRs and fifty-nine RBIs. These two guys are having banner seasons.

So why won't John Donati look at his record?

"I don't like to look at stats," he tells me. "I figure they're pretty good right now, but it's a long season. Anything can happen."

I can't tell whether this is superstition or realism. But Donati doesn't like to tamper with fate. Our conversation drifts to Mitch Williams, whose legendary wildness has recently led the California Angels to send the Wild Thing back to his ranch in Texas.

"I'd hate to have hit against him. I don't care if he lost something off his fastball toward the end. It would still hurt. I wouldn't want to dig in against him. I'm sure that's how he got all those guys out for so many years. Everybody knew he threw hard and had lousy control. Who'd want to dig in against somebody like that?"

Donati plainly doesn't relish the idea of pain and injury.

"It's the same reason I'd rather hit against a pitcher in AA or AAA. Even though those guys have more experience than me and I'd be in over my head, at least they have command of their pitches. I feel like I'd be safe up there. I'd much rather face a guy like that than some guy from rookie ball who throws hard and has no idea where it's going."

About an hour later in the air-conditioned clubhouse, Donati is forced to confront some of his statistics. Only this time, it's his height, weight, and date of birth. GM Jack Roeder is carrying around proof sheets of the team baseball cards and wants to avoid the kind of errors that inevitably plague minor league sets. Neither Classic nor Procards, long the mainstays in minor league card production, will be printing team sets this year. That means that Roeder, like most minor league GMs, has been faced with printing his own set or having no product for his fans and players. He has chosen the former option and now finds himself in the quality control business.

Donati tries to look businesslike as he surveys the front and back of his card, but a smile is creeping across his face.

Tonight's crowd consists largely of employees and family members from one of the local hospitals. As part of their promotion, all visitors to the ballpark are getting a plastic squeeze bottle for cold drinks. It's not clear why anybody would want to drink from a container bearing the name of a hospital. Apparently, somebody believes that a logo of St. Luke's has all the allure of the Chicago Bulls. But forget the bottle. The giveaway that has everybody smiling is a small cardboard fan. Nobody seems to mind that this item sports the name of a hospital. What matters is that it moves air. This is something that air seems to have no ability to do on its own in Veterans Memorial Stadium.

It's hard to imagine a more appropriate giveaway on this night, with the temperature hovering near 100 degrees and not a breeze in sight. Minor league teams often have promotions late in the season called Fan Appreciation Night. Tonight's giveaway has brought a whole new meaning to that phrase.

I leave the ballpark at about 10 P.M. It's still hot as hell. The crowd that GM Roeder hoped for has never materialized. I drive back to the motel and walk a block or two to a Perkins restaurant for a late dinner. I'm sitting at my booth going over some game notes when it finally happens: the lights go out. And with them, the air conditioning and the ceiling fans. As if on cue, all conversation grinds to a complete halt. For a brief moment, fifty strangers are sitting together in a darkened, silent room. Some customers are still waiting for their dinners. Others are groping their way through an order of burger and fries. Silence slowly gives way to nervous laughter. The manager jokes that if the power stays off for any length of time, the restaurant will serve free ice cream rather than let it melt.

According to my waitress, I'm one of the lucky ones. My dinner appeared just minutes before the power company pulled the plug, as they've been threatening to do for days. The only light in the room is coming from a motel and restaurant across the way. The neighborhood seems to have been divided in a haphazard pattern that leaves my restaurant and, perhaps, my motel in the dark. I enjoy ice cream as much as the next guy, but I can't see waiting several hours for the chance of a free sundae served by flashlight.

It turns out that leaving is a little more complicated than usual. My meal costs about seven dollars. Using a charge card is out of the question since the processing equipment requires electricity. I'd use cash, except the register won't open because it, too, is electric. I've got a five and a twenty-dollar bill. The nice folks at Perkins accept the five as "close enough." Across the street, a Denny's restaurant is brightly lit. Presumably dinners are going for full price there.

Traffic is moving cautiously along 33rd Street, the motel and fast food strip. The road is unusually dark, and the traffic signals seem to be linked up to Perkins rather than Denny's. When I get back to my motel I find people milling about in the lobby and parking lot. Once again, I seem to be living on the wrong side of the street. Most guests have decided it's too hot to stay in their non-air-conditioned rooms. Without TV, air conditioning, and electric light, there is little to hold anyone in a Cedar Rapids motel room. There's a lot of joking and speculation about when power might be restored. Theories range from "any minute" to "it might be days." The truth lies somewhere in between. By two in the morning we're all happily ensconced in our air-conditioned nests again.

Brownouts in Iowa continue to appear ominously for the next several days, a grim reminder of how fragile our comfort and civilization are.

Burlington, Iowa

"You want me to jump?"
—Steve Wolfert, aka Wild Thing

Burlington, Iowa, is a small town. In fact, Burlington is the smallest city in America to host a full-season minor league team. Nestled in the corner of southeastern Iowa, Burlington seems more likely to sponsor an American Legion team or a tractor pull. Yet professional baseball has been part of Burlington's heritage since the 1880s.

"This is not a thriving business," Ryan Richeal says. He is in his first year as Burlington's GM and seems to be reeling from all the problems he's inherited.

"It's a good thing we're a community-owned nonprofit corporation. We're still in debt from two years ago when we had to go through renovations just to get up to league standards. We still haven't worked our way out of that. We've got a 372-foot fence in center field. We're under pressure from major league baseball to move it out to 400 feet. Who's going to pay for that? Last year we set a franchise record for attendance, and we still only made a few thousand dollars. For us to make any improvements here, to the field, the clubhouse, the money has to come out of our own pockets. We have to look for donations or city funding. Part of this job is learning how to beg.

"There are rumors that major league baseball is going to make things even tougher for the minors. They may start making the teams pay for their own bats and balls. What happens is that they look at that small percentage of teams that are making huge profits. Those teams can afford to take on additional expenses and still do just fine. But they're in the minority. Most minor league teams just can't do it. If they tighten the screws even a bit more some teams just won't survive.

"Up until recently, this has really been a mom-and-pop operation. People came out here to see a ball game, not to be entertained. The crowds were pretty decent, given our tiny fan base and the fact that there were almost no promotions. There were some lucky number giveaways, but nothing really happened beyond that. There was nothing for the customer who wasn't a diehard baseball fan. We've tried to change that recently. You can see from our promotion schedule that we're putting a lot of energy into providing entertainment and bringing families out to the park. This is a whole new audience."

On a strictly per capita basis, Burlington draws more fans than any team in the league and perhaps in all of A ball.

"If the weather is halfway decent here in July and August, we can draw 2,000 fans a night. When you consider the whole population is only 27,000, that's nothing to be ashamed of. We can take some credit for how we're marketing the game. The performance of the team hasn't been the reason people are coming to the ballpark. The truth is, this team hasn't been very good. We're in last place now. We started the year off with a 7–22 record. We've improved since then. Two of our best players are guys we got in the Salomon Torres trade. We got our shortstop, Wilson Delgado, and a pitcher, Shawn Estes. Delgado has played great for us. Unfortunately, we don't have Shawn any more. He was promoted to San Jose. On his first start for them, he threw five no-hit innings. Our other legitimate prospect is Jesse Ibarra. He's hitting .333 and leading the league in home runs and slugging percentage. Jesse really doesn't have a position on this team, so he's been DHing. As soon as the season is over, they're going to send him down to the Instructional League to convert him to a catcher."

About an hour later, I'm sitting in the Burlington dugout talking to two pitchers. Ibarra's name comes up, and they both speak of him with near religious devotion.

"Ibarra is just beyond belief," says one. "I've never seen anybody hit them so far. This is a little bandbox of a park, but Jesse doesn't hit any cheap shots here. He hits them over that scoreboard. Over the Marlboro Man. That kid could hit a ball out of any park. You see Cecil Fielder hit them on the roof in Tiger Stadium? Jesse Ibarra could hit them just as far."

I point out that pitchers at higher levels make a living by finding holes in someone's swing. Maybe Jesse Ibarra will never progress beyond the records he sets in A ball.

Both of his teammates disagree.

"Jesse was a completely different hitter last year when he played in the Northwest League. He hit a lot of home runs, but he had a lot of holes in his swing. He overswung a lot. This year, he's such a better hitter. He's more

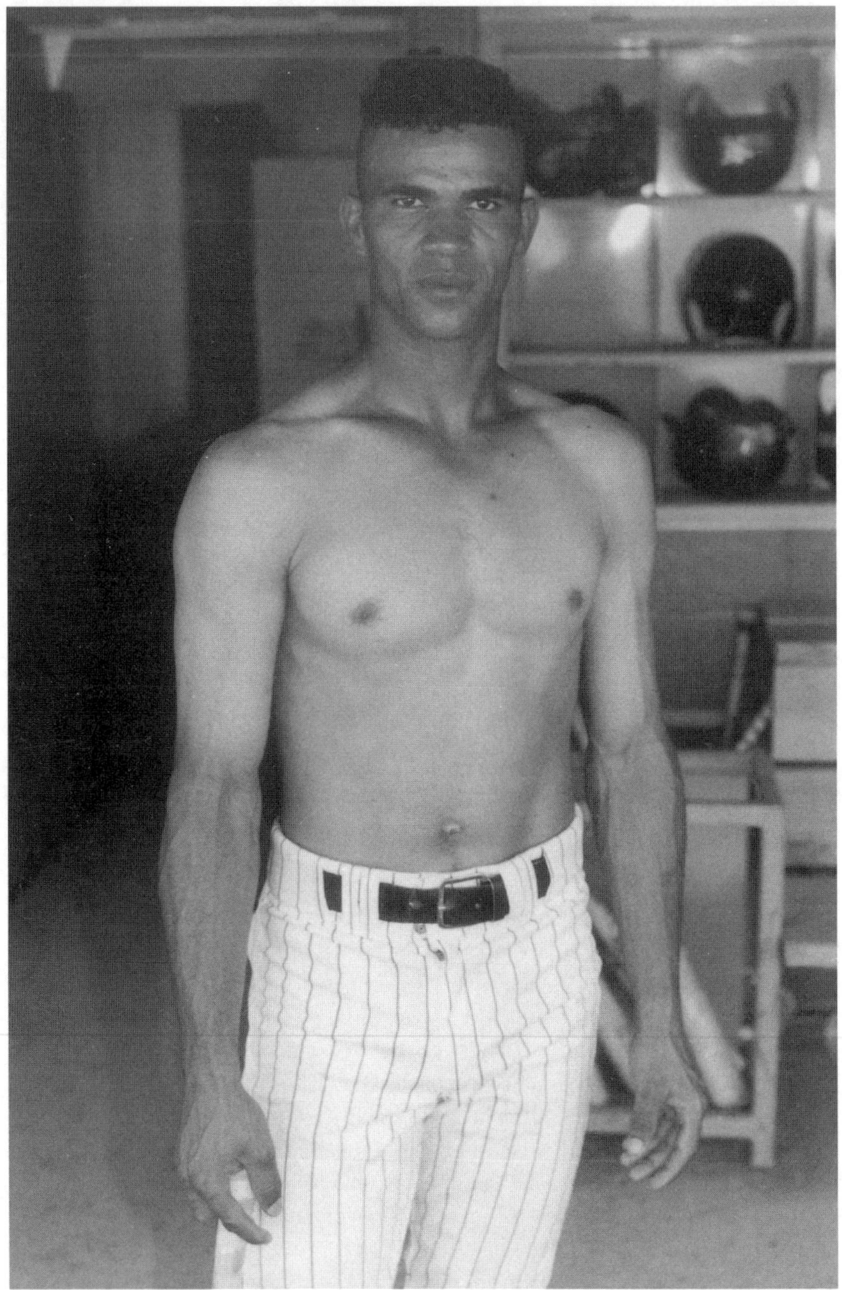

Wilson Delgado.

Jesse Ibarra.

disciplined. His swing is smoother. He hits the ball to the opposite field from both sides of the plate. I mean, sure, if he gets ahead in the count, he's going for it. That's why he was drafted. But now he shows patience. The fact that he's hitting .333 tells you something. If he hit .270, the organization probably would have been thrilled. The fact that he's hitting .333 with all that power, they must be having a heart attack."

Ryan Richeal is not the most ebullient GM I've met in my travels. Unless the topic is Paul Molitor. Then Richeal comes to life.

"He's my hero. No doubt about it. You know he played here in Burlington in 1977. He was almost singlehandedly the reason we won the Midwest League Championship that season. It turns out that was his only season in the minor leagues."

Richeal is right. After an outstanding A ball season for Burlington, Molitor was ticketed for a promotion all the way to AAA. A last-minute injury to shortstop Robin Yount caused the Brewers to speed Molitor's movement through the system even faster. He became their opening-day shortstop in 1978.

Richeal has followed Molitor's career to the present day. When Molitor was traded from the Brewers to Toronto, the Burlington GM was probably the only Blue Jays fan in town. An autographed picture of the two of them hangs over his desk.

In February 1995, Molitor returned to Burlington for his induction into the local Hall of Fame. He and Billy Williams, who also began his career playing for the Burlington team, were the first two inductees.

"So far, our membership is low, but our standards are very high. We've inducted a Hall of Famer in Williams and a future Hall of Famer in Molitor. A lot of good players have come through Burlington. We've had affiliations with the Rangers and Braves and Expos in recent years. Guys like Vida Blue, Chet Lemon, Doug Jones, Ruben Sierra, and Javy Lopez have played here. It's a safe bet our local Hall of Fame will grow."

Not surprisingly, the Burlington Bees' logo shows a pesky little insect, wings spread, bat cocked, wearing a cap with a *B* on it. The truth is, the original team name had nothing to do with stinging insects. When Burlington was a Kansas City farm team in the early sixties, someone decided it would be clever to name the team the "B's" since the big league club was the "A's." Years later, with the Kansas City affiliation a distant memory, someone had to come up with a sellable logo. And so the little stinging Burlington Bee was born.

I'm watching the game with Fernando Arango, a scout for the Yankees. One of the Bees gets on base, and I ask Fernando if he thinks the guy will try to steal in this situation.

"No way," he says. "The guy's a Hawaiian runner."

"A what?"

"A Hawaiian runner. Haven't you ever heard the term?" Fernando asks.

I shake my head, knowing my baseball vocabulary is about to be enriched.

"Remember the old TV show? Remember what it was called?"

"Hawaii 5–0," I reply, still not making the connection.

"Well, that's this guy's time down to first base. About 5.0. The average runner gets down there in about 4.3 seconds. Maybe 4.2 from the left side. This guy is slower. When someone takes at least five seconds to get down the line we call him a Hawaiian runner." Then he adds, "You see the stuff you learn hanging around with scouts?"

The temperature has come down to the low 100s by game time. The ballpark is oppressively hot. Nevertheless, Fernando is really excited about Quad City's starting pitcher tonight. His name is Scott Elarton.

"He's only nineteen years old, a high school kid from Colorado. He's 6′8″. Still growing." Fernando opens his briefcase and rummages through some stat sheets.

"Look at this. He pitched last year in the Gulf Coast League. He went forty-one innings and didn't give up a run. This kid is going to have a real chance."

Tonight he doesn't look exceptional. Fernando is clocking his fastball at about 90 mph. Fernando shakes his head.

"He can do better than that. It must be the heat."

Tonight's promotion is a traveling entertainer named Steve Wolfert. Professionally, he calls himself the Wild Thing. He deserves his name. This is Wolfert's second season on the minor league circuit. His reputation is deservedly spreading. The local kids will be talking about him for weeks. He'll drive the Baseball Purists crazy.

Wild Thing starts his antics by racing through the stands throwing popcorn at folks, working up the kids. He's just beginning.

In the bottom of the first inning, he climbs a light tower behind first base. He's wearing a wireless microphone so he can talk to the crowd while he climbs. Attention is deflected from the field as Wild Thing makes his way up the light tower. Technically, it may be an easy climb, but for most of us, it looks pretty scary up there.

By the middle of the second inning, all eyes are on the light tower.

"You want me to jump?" he asks the crowd.

"Yeahhhhhhhhhh!" comes the inevitable response.

"You people are sick!" he jokingly taunts. But a moment later he indulges them. Using mountaineering gear, Wild Thing rappels himself down the tower in several well-timed leaps. His screams while in free-fall are nearly obliterated by the crowd's response. Even the ball players have stopped to watch. This is no longer a ball game. It's become an aerial acrobatics show.

During the third inning, Wild Thing reappears riding a fake horse through the stands while "Chantilly Lace" plays over the PA system. An inning later, the horse and rider do a turn around the infield to the theme from *Bonanza*. The routine ends with Wild Thing's fake horse depositing a large but equally fake pile of manure over by the first base dugout. The crowd roars with laughter. The Bees' mascot, obviously part of the act, comes out and shovels up the imitation horse poop. The mascot later walks through the stands waving his shovel triumphantly.

It's interesting that I've seen two horses relieve themselves on a baseball field, both in towns named Burlington: North Carolina, and now Iowa. And in both cases, the landing site was just outside the first base coaching box. Burlington, Vermont, is close to Winooski, where the Expos currently have a team in the New York–Penn League. Maybe it's worth a trip there to keep this Burlington streak alive, just in case they have plans for an equestrian promotion.

The Bees have a promotion that I haven't seen before. Each night, a designated player is announced as "Tonight's Beer Batter." His performance affects the price of beer. Every time this batter comes up, the price of beer drops to fifty cents for the rest of the inning if he strikes out. Ideally, you want this guy to lead off an inning and whiff. You certainly don't want him flying out, hitting a single, etc. And if he has the decency to strike out, you certainly don't want him making the final out of the inning.

The first time our man comes up tonight, he works a 2–2 count, and fans start edging their way to the concession stands. He fouls a couple of pitches off, and you can almost hear the heartbeat of every alcoholic in the stands. On the next pitch, the beer batter lofts a fly ball to the center fielder. The crowd lets out an audible groan and returns to their seats.

The next time up, the man does it right. He leads off the inning and strikes out on four pitches. There is a predictable exodus from the grandstands as the vendors gear up for an onslaught.

Morgana, also known as the Kissing Bandit, is a busy act on the minor league circuit. Along with the Blues Brothers, she seems to turn up in every town hosting a minor league franchise. Although I've crossed paths with the Blues Brothers on numerous occasions, I've never managed to see Morgana perform. It's not clear what her act consists of. Historically, she is known for running on the field and kissing George Brett during a nationally televised game. But the real attraction goes beyond this historical footnote. Morgana is primarily known for her ample physical endowment. Simply put, the woman makes Dolly Parton look developmentally delayed.

For whatever it's worth, every GM I've talked to who has hired Morgana hastens to tell me, "She's an exceptionally nice person," or words to that effect. I can only assume it's true, coming, as it does, from so many different locales and employers. The life lesson seems to be: Even women with enormous breasts can be very nice.

Tonight, Wild Thing includes a Morgana impression as part of his act. This consists of stuffing two footballs into his tunic and running through the stands while blowing kisses to the fans. Since Wild Thing has already won the crowd over, the folks roar their approval to this touch of high comedic art. What they may not know is that in just fifteen days they can compare Wild Thing's antics to the real thing. Morgana herself will be coming to Burlington.

Jeff Keith is the Bees' closer. He's appeared in more games than any pitcher on the team. He leads the team in saves, strikes out more than one batter an inning, and has a stellar ERA around 2.00. Opponents are hitting .119 against him. In short, he has been having a hell of a season.

"I went to junior college in upstate New York, and I was expecting to get drafted. I even figured I'd go in a high round. I was a first team All-American."

All this is said with pride. Then Keith shakes his head.

"But it didn't happen. I was completely overlooked. So I went down to Florida. That's where all the scouts are, right? We played the University of South Florida one day. They were ranked number nineteen in the country. There must have been a dozen scouts there. I threw a one-hit shutout. I also beat the Miami Hurricanes last year when they were number two in the country. There were twenty-five scouts at that game. I figure, somebody must have seen me. But I still didn't get drafted."

Keith shakes his head slowly.

"I'm still a little bitter about that. It hurts when I think about it. I keep trying to figure out why I was passed over. First I thought it was because I was a senior. But I've seen seniors get drafted. Usually they go in a higher round,

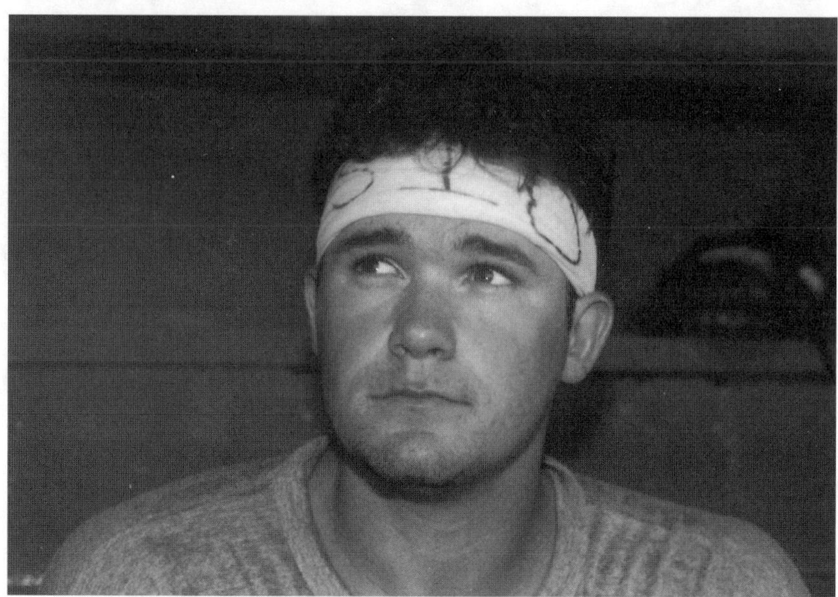

Jeff Keith.

but I would have been happy to get picked in the twentieth or even thirtieth round. But even that never happened."

Keith finally did sign.

"The day after the draft, I had four teams call me. All of a sudden I had my choice of organizations to play for. I asked the scouts, 'Why didn't I get drafted?' So they told me, 'I don't know. It's hard to tell. You were a senior. You probably just got overlooked.' They all told me they had put my name in. Only I never got the call.

"Come on. There's got to be a reason. I'm a left-handed sidearm pitcher throwing 88 miles an hour. The only thing I can figure is, it must be my personality. I'm kind of arrogant and hot-tempered. I've been told that scouts really don't like that. I'm a very intense person. Probably too intense. The funny thing is, when you get to the minor leagues, being intense and full of confidence is suddenly a good thing. Coaches like to see it. I keep hearing about guys with good stuff who get knocked around the park 'cause they lack confidence. You gotta pitch with a little fire in your ass. You gotta walk around that mound like you're the man. That's what I do. Only the trouble is, I've been doing it all along.

"I know I'm right for the bullpen. But I've been told I'm not going to be a closer when I move up the ladder. Even though I'm having a good season, Tony here is the closer of the future."

Keith gestures to Tony Mattos, standing next to us.

"Tony was our closer last year before he went on the DL. That's the only reason I've got the job now. As soon as he's healthy again, I'm gone. I'll go back to being his setup man. Or I'll be brought in to get lefties out."

I suggest to Keith that regardless of how he got here, he's now sitting in a dugout playing professional baseball. He's got a legitimate shot at the big leagues.

"You're right," he says quickly. "That's all that matters. I don't think the Giants look at me as a free agent anymore. I'm on their top prospect list. I've got their attention. But if I make it, I'll be the biggest bargain of the century. They didn't pay a dollar for me."

"But they will," I tell him. "Before it's over, they surely will."

Clinton, Iowa

"I wonder if I have to be a bitch to succeed at this."
—Leasa Brown, Lumber Kings GM

Unlike most of Iowa, Clinton rates close to a zero on the bucolic charm scale. Forget about idyllic visions of cornfields and century farms. All traces of agriculture along Highway 30 gradually disappear as you approach the Clinton city limits.

This is a tough, grimy, blue-collar town located on the easternmost point of Iowa. Many of its 30,000 residents are direct descendants of the hard-working, hard-drinking lumber workers who kept this place on the map through difficult times. Clinton features over six miles of riverfront along the Mississippi. Over the years, that's been a mixed blessing. Exposure to the river has kept commerce alive, but it has also maintained the threat of flooding. In 1976, Clinton decided to do something about it and built a twenty-million-dollar wall to keep the Mississippi at bay. Although the project was not without its detractors, all opposition was effectively silenced in 1993 when The Flood ravaged much of the Midwest. Clinton's wall held firm through it all.

Entertainment in Clinton typically means gambling and drinking. The town is well equipped for both. To its credit, Clinton also has professional baseball. The aptly named Lumber Kings (of the Midwest League) are the most recent in a string of teams that have represented this town. In the late 1930s, the Clinton Owls were a Brooklyn Dodgers affiliate playing in the Three-Eye League (Iowa, Indiana, and Illinois). When the Dodgers left town, their archrivals from New York took over, and the Clinton team was known as the Giants. After World War II, Clinton became a Cubs affiliate in the short-lived Central League, which lasted until 1948.

Professional baseball resumed in Clinton in 1954 with a Pirates affiliate in the Mississippi–Ohio Valley League. Two years later, the league underwent a name change to its present title, and Clinton has remained a charter member. The team's longest affiliation, with the San Francisco Giants, ended after fifteen years in 1994. During that final year, Clinton adopted its own name and colors when the Lumber Kings were born. In 1995, the newly minted Clinton Lumber Kings began their partnership with the San Diego Padres.

Riverview Stadium is aptly named. The mighty Mississippi flows just behind the outfield fence. There were some tense moments here in 1993 when the river rose higher than the level of the playing field. Needless to say, some games were canceled, although not as many as in nearby Davenport, where the Quad City team was farming out its home games to anyone within fifty miles who'd have them. The primary damage in Clinton was from seepage. The water actually came up through the ground rather than swamping it from above.

Looking from the stands, you can't actually see the Mississippi. However, you can pretty well assume there's a river out there since there are two riverboats bobbing behind left center field. I've looked at outfield fences and seen the Marlboro Man and billboards for Shoney's. I've looked beyond fences and seen trees — lots of them. But these are the first riverboats I've ever seen. And these are not your average riverboats; they're the kind Mark Twain would have been at home on. Both boats are part of Clinton's charm, such as it is. One is a restaurant and the other is a gambling boat.

Leasa Brown became general manager of the Clinton team in 1995. She knew she'd be working hard, but the job has been even more of a challenge than she expected.

"The truth is, I really don't know a lot about baseball, especially about the business side. I mean, I played Little League when I was a kid, and I played softball in high school. I've even done some umpiring. But I don't know anything about how players are signed or how they move up the ladder. I'm trying to learn more about that, as well as about batting averages, ERAs, stuff like that. I have to learn that at the same time I'm doing my job. Sometimes it feels like there just aren't enough hours in the day.

"When I interviewed for the job, I was honest about what my strengths and weaknesses were. They didn't seem to mind that I wasn't much of a professional baseball person. I had a good administrative background. I worked for the Clinton Tourist Board for three and a half years. That's what brought me here. I had to market what there was to see and do in this town. That obviously included baseball. People seemed to think that qualified me for the GM job. In some ways, it has. But in others, I feel like I've had no training. I was thrown into the fire.

"A lot of people told me I'd never get this job. I wasn't what they were looking for. I wasn't a man. During my interview, I told them, 'I can market your team. I can run it like a business. I can watch the cash flow. But if you want someone to sit around the locker room, scratch their balls, and talk baseball, I can't do that.' They knew what they were getting when they hired me.

"I know if I were a man, I'd be a lot more likely to know some basic stuff about baseball. But I still think that as a woman, I have some advantages. I have a better eye for certain things. For example, in trying to attract a crowd, I see things a man might overlook, like the appearance or cleanliness of the facility or the quality of the food.

"In some ways, it's been more than I bargained for. I've had some long thoughts about what kind of woman it takes to make it in a job like this. Am I tough enough? People who know me from the outside sometimes find it hard to believe I have this job. One guy I met said, 'How could she be the GM? She's so frail and fragile.' I laughed because that's very far from my perception. But I wonder if I have to be a bitch to succeed at this. It's a hard balance to find. I will admit that I have some vendors and staff upset 'cause I'm too picky. I had one of the people who wash the stadium quit on me. He thought I was too critical of his work.

"In a sense I'm kind of disappointed that there isn't more interaction with the players. I had expected that there'd be more day-to-day contact, or more involvement with their careers. That was probably a misconception on my part. We really have very little to do with them. They come by and say 'Hi' or 'Can I use the phone?' We do the rosters and find out who's coming and going. We take them to the airport. But that's it.

"I have to be very careful about my relationship with the players. Maybe if I were older, I could risk some more direct involvement. But I'm far from the motherly type. I'm twenty-four years old. The last thing I want is to get involved in some sort of relationship with one of them. Or even have people wondering about that sort of thing. When their parents come to town, I make a point of introducing myself. But otherwise, our paths don't really cross. That's their territory," Leasa says, gesturing to the field, "and this is mine here. Maybe next year when I'm a bit more comfortable with the position, I'll find it's OK to allow a little more closeness. But for now, I have to keep this distance."

The day I arrive, Leasa has just met with the Padres' director of minor league operations. Leasa has learned, and rather abruptly, that there were things she didn't understand about the operation of a professional baseball team.

"I was told there are things I should know and things I should be doing. That frustrates me. I had no idea. I thought I was doing my job well, and all of a sudden I find out I'm not. I've missed a whole side of things. It's not like I can't learn, but I like to think I understood what I was getting into here. And I obviously didn't. I could have done better if I had known what was expected of me."

Leasa now knows that she has to please not only the local investors but also the major league franchise located half a continent away. Worse yet, those priorities are often in conflict. Thankfully, both her employers agree on one thing: the virtue of packing the ballpark with enthusiastic fans. That'll make the ball players happy and also please the local investors, who love to see those turnstiles turning and that beer being swilled.

It's a rare moment when a minor league GM and the director of minor league operations have lunch together and you find two women at the table. Leasa's lunch partner is Priscilla Oppenheimer, who has worked for the Padres since 1983, where she began as a secretary for the scouting director. Today she is in charge of the day-to-day operations of the minor league system, which puts her in contact with GMs and players alike. Priscilla also handles contracts. "The guys in this league are looking at about $900 a month plus meal money. That's not much."

Speaking at a recent meeting of the Society for American Baseball Research, Oppenheimer reported that releasing players was the part of her job she liked least. In 1994, the Padres eliminated the Charleston, South Carolina, team from their organization. That meant that the Padres had to release about 30 of the 146 minor league players who had reported to spring training.

"Some of them sat for hours in my office. They just didn't want to go home. Some of them were afraid of facing their fathers. It's the same thing when a player is sent down to the minors from the major league roster. I tell them to take two days to feel sorry for yourself. Then make the major league team sorry they sent you down."

Although she's trying to be supportive, Oppenheimer is somewhat displeased with the situation she's found in Clinton.

"I know this is only the first year we've had an affiliation with them. And I know their GM is in her first year also. But there's some basic stuff that we'd like to see in place here, and it hasn't happened yet. It tells you something when your players feel more comfortable on the road than they do in their own park.

"I'll give you an example of the kind of thing that's missing. Baseball cards. This is the first year in a long time that none of the companies will be producing team sets for the lower minor league affiliates. Up till now, the minor league GM didn't have to do anything. The company photographer just came in, or a local guy was arranged for. And like magic, a set arrived about a month or two later. They could sell them or give them away as promotions. But most important, they had them for the players. You have no idea how important it is for some of these kids to see their face on a card. For a lot of them, it's the only card they'll ever be on. Most of these guys are never going to make it out of A ball. It's a big ego thing with them.

"When Classic and Fleer decided not to issue minor league team sets, a lot of other GMs arranged to produce their own. We would have liked our teams to be among them. That's the kind of thing I've had to explain to Leasa. I'm sure she would have done it if she had understood how important it was. Leasa is very concerned about expenses, and she's got a whole board of directors to answer to here. I told her, don't worry about the cost. We'll help out. I know a lot of parent clubs wouldn't get involved like that, but we do. It's a goodwill thing. I can see we're going to have to keep the communication channels open a bit wider."

Most of this is news to Leasa, who came into this job knowing or caring as much about baseball cards as she did jet engines. But now she's got to become a producer and a manufacturer almost overnight.

Despite the fact that tonight is Junior Baseball Night at Riverview Stadium, the attendance is way down. Kids in uniform are admitted free, but there are barely 500 people in the stands. The attendance is announced as 618, another exercise in creative bookkeeping. The Family Section is particularly deserted. This is the area of the stadium reserved for "family values," as GM Leasa Brown puts it. The rules are certainly well posted. "No Swearing. No Smoking. No Drinking." From what I've seen of Clinton's finest, that isn't going to be the most popular area of the park.

I'm sitting over on the third base side in the nonfamily section, and the beer is flowing in multiple twenty-ounce cups. The verbal abuse is running pretty well also. These $2.50 general admission tickets seem to buy a lot of license in Clinton. In the course of one half-inning, the third baseman blows a tough play and catches an earful from my neighbors. A few plays later, the umpire gets blasted with some memorable invective from these same folks. True, the call was marginal, and, worse yet, it went against Clinton. But the abuse seems all out of proportion. I've talked to enough minor league umpires and seen the conditions under which they work and travel. They deserve better than this.

Leasa Brown and Priscilla Oppenheimer aren't the only women involved in the operation of this club. Sitting in the stands, it takes me about four innings to realize I've been listening to a female PA announcer. Nowhere in my journey have I come upon the standard "Now batting for Clinton, number 42, Jason Tyrus" message delivered in a woman's voice.

"Oh, I'm sure I'm not the only one," Leslie Botkin tells me. "There's got to be more out there. But I'm glad I'm the first one you've met so you can mention me in your book."

What qualifies someone to be a PA announcer?

"I'm not sure. I'm a big baseball fan. As far as work experience, I don't know. I was a bill collector before this."

I'm talking with Jason Tyrus in the dugout before game time. Jason is from Milpitas, California, and attended the University of Washington.

"I didn't play college baseball. I was signed out of a tryout camp in Seattle. I was actually drafted in the twenty-first round. I worked out with different scouts in little parks in the area. It was a fairly unusual arrangement. If I hadn't gotten drafted, I would have started to play college baseball this year at the University of Washington. But when I went in a fairly high round, I decided it was time to begin my pro career.

"I haven't been playing as much as I'd like to but, you know, there's only so much playing time to go around. There's a constant turnover; we get draft picks in, guys are promoted. So I have to wait my turn."

Jason has appeared in about 70 percent of the Lumber Kings' games so far. But they're carrying six outfielders plus a full-time DH. Playing time is at a premium, to put it mildly. Jason is batting .226, striking out in nearly a third of his plate appearances. But the season is still young, and he's been slugging nearly a hundred points above his batting average. It's not time to pack it in yet.

"It's been frustrating," he concedes. "If I were near my home and I could do other things, it would make it easier. But I'm here in Clinton.

"I figure I'll give it another year or two. If I don't perform better than I have been so far or don't get more of an opportunity to play, then I'll go back to college. I was coaching basketball as an undergraduate assistant at the University of Washington. I'd like to get into that: coaching college basketball. I really love it. I'd enjoy doing that with my life.

"I loved Seattle. Even though it rained so much, it was a really great city."

Jason and I are talking about the old underground city of Seattle, and he

Jason Tyrus checks his batting average while Eduardo Cuervas contemplates the infield.

explains how that relates to the invention of the flush toilet. This is not your average dugout conversation. Eventually it returns to his own career.

"I was in a hotel just recently watching a TV movie about baseball. You ever see *The Ron LeFlore Story*? Part of it was about his minor league days after he got out of prison. There's this line in there where he says, 'This is the furthest I've ever been away from home.' So I guess it was when he was in the Midwest League. And I'm looking at the clubhouse and I say, Wait a minute. That's where *we* play."

Tyrus is right. Clinton was a Detroit farm team from 1971 until 1975. Ron LeFlore played his first minor league season here in 1973, batting .277. Jim Leyland was his manager.

Inevitably, the conversation turns to the weather.

"Have you ever seen a tornado?" Jason asks. "I've never seen one, but I heard the horns go off a couple of times. That's the one thing that scares me about living here. I'm not scared of earthquakes, coming from California. I've been in several. But tornadoes? Forget it. I don't want to see one."

Talk of the weather draws in more players. People in the Midwest spend a lot of time talking about the weather.

Gary Matthews, Jr.

"We've seen it all playing here," one guy chimes in. "We were freezing our asses off in April, and now look at it. Did you know the batboy here passed out from the heat two days ago?"

"Yeah," another adds. "It was over 110 degrees. Plus that humidity. The kid just fell over."

Jason has been thinking about inviting his parents to see him play ball, but he isn't sure he wants to subject them to Clinton.

"I think they'd be bored here. Maybe I'll wait until we're playing in Rockford. The Cubs have a team there. It'll be cheaper and easier to fly to Chicago, and there'll be more to do and see than there is here. If they come here, once they saw the riverboat, I'm not sure what else they'd do with their time."

I'm aiming my camera at number 36, a Clinton outfielder, when it occurs to me that this guy looks very familiar. Indeed, he should.

"You're Gary Matthews's son!" I report cleverly.

"That's right," he replies, showing commendable restraint.

"You really look like your father, minus the Afro."

"That's what everybody tells me," the younger Matthews reports. What I don't tell him is that I can still see some old TV images in my head of him running around at Veterans Stadium in Philadelphia during a fathers-and-sons game. The kid in my film clip is about four years old and doesn't look much like this 6′2″ twenty-one year old in front of me.

Matthews has one of his father's bats with him. It's a thirty-five-inch war club. The handle looks thicker than some bat heads I've seen.

"Do you *use* that?" I ask. Before Matthews can answer, a couple of his teammates contribute their thoughts.

"No way," says Jarman Leach, a left-handed pitcher. "He's gonna have to grow into that one." Then Leach adds, "Now *I* wouldn't have any trouble with it . . ." and makes his point by insisting on posing with the bat for his picture.

"You can see what a tough hitter I am," he says, taking several menacing swings.

"What is it with you pitchers?" I ask. "How come you care so much about your hitting?"

"Hey, I used to be an outfielder," he tells me proudly. "It's in the genes. My brother is an outfielder in the Yankees system. He plays for Columbus."

It's true. Jalal Leach is an outfielder for the Columbus Clippers. The curious thing is that his stats are virtually identical to Gary Matthews Jr.'s, right down to the number of at bats and .240 batting average. Their seasons are interchangeable.

A former Clinton GM is in the press box. Bill Kuehn, who now works for the *Clinton Herald*, is discussing the team's sagging attendance. In 1988, over 100,000 fans crowded into Clinton's Riverview Stadium to see their team. The following year attendance dropped by almost 50 percent and has pretty much stayed that way. Only 50,000 fans showed up in 1993, the year of The Flood.

"It doesn't mean that much," Kuehn insists. "They're not in danger of losing the franchise. It's a cyclic thing that tracks the economy. You think this is bad now? Look at some of the real bad years we had after the flood of '65."

In 1965, with the Mississippi lapping at their heels, the then–Clinton Sox drew just under 38,000 fans. The following year, when Pittsburgh moved in, attendance was down to 35,000. Kuehn is right. From that point of view, things are bound to get better.

Sometime in the sixth inning, a ball gets away from the catcher and rolls to the backstop.

"That used to be a regular play here," Kuehn tells me. "You see how the backstop is real close to the field? In 1983, the team was working on a play they were going to use in a game. The idea was, with a man on third, the pitcher would uncork what looked like a wild pitch. It was a set play. The runner would see it and break for home. But the ball would carom right off the backstop and bounce back to the catcher, who would tag out the runner. We figured we could use it a few times before the league got wise to us."

So what happened? I wonder. Did Clinton sucker a few teams into losing their runners on third?

"No. It backfired," Kuehn laughs. "The first time we ever used it in a game was the last. The ball hit a seam in the backstop and instead of bouncing back to the catcher, it caromed over toward first base, and the guy scored. We decided that was enough of trick plays."

As I leave the press box, Kuehn gives me his card, and I see how his last name is spelled. All night I've been assuming it's *Keen* or *Keane*. So I ask the question any baseball fan over forty would ask.

"Are you related to Harvey?"

"No," he laughs. "You're the first person in over three years to ask me that. I've missed that question."

After spending a summer apprenticing at Chicago superstation WGN, Pat Kinas began broadcasting the Clinton games in 1993. He stayed on for the '94 season as well, when the team went from being the Giants to the Lumber Kings. Pat has seen stars come through Clinton, guys who are destined for The Show. But, as often happens, one of the most memorable players he met won't be on anyone's major league roster. In reflecting on the '93 season, Kinas recalled, "Kevin Wong was a guy the Giants signed as a free agent to play at Clinton right before the 1993 season. He had a pretty good bat but, as with any organization, the bulk of playing time went to players originally drafted by the team, not veteran free agents. Although Kevin started as Clinton's opening day second baseman, his playing time quickly waned, and by early June, Kevin could be found sitting obediently on the bench. Injuries plagued him as well, costing him even more playing time.

"Kevin was one of my good friends on the team. He always had time to talk and joke. During a road trip to Burlington, Kevin was on the DL. He accompanied me to the press box in his street clothes. Actually, I think he wanted the free press box food; he ate up there like he hadn't eaten in days. When the Beegirl asked what he did, he told her he was my assistant.

"I wanted to have him on the air as a color analyst, but when I asked, Kevin laughed and said he wouldn't know what to say. He was pretty good help when it came to the Clinton batting order. He sat next to me and watched the manager in the coaching box for signs. He would mumble to me that the bunt sign was on and, with that knowledge in hand, I sounded like a genius. Of course, I cited Wong as my 'eye in the sky.' I guess he was my assistant.

"Kevin knew that his career was ending. He told me during that road trip that he was getting homesick for Hawaii, that he missed his girlfriend, and that he was ready to call it a career. We talked about it between innings quite a bit. It has to be one of the toughest decisions to make — admitting he was not going to make the majors — but I really admired his honesty. He felt it coming. Two days later, Kevin was released."

It's nearly midnight when I leave the ballpark, and I still haven't eaten. I'm pleased to see that a Country Kitchen restaurant lies en route to my motel. I've had good luck eating in this chain all through the Midwest. However, any joy I'm feeling turns to disbelief when I pull into the parking lot. This civilized, well-appointed chain usually serves good, affordable food in pleasant surroundings. Tonight all that seems to have changed.

The first hint is the parking lot. One guy is busy throwing up on his car. There aren't a lot of vacant spaces, and the parking spot I want has been taken over by a couple having a knock-down, drag-out fight. They see my car hovering nearby and move the brawl a few feet over so I can park and they can go about their business.

Inside, the restaurant is unrecognizable. The smoke is so thick it's hard to read the menu.

"Are you kidding?" asks a harried waitress. "The bars have just let out. Everybody smokes here. If you want no smoking, try the parking lot."

I would, except the parking lot is presently looking less than inviting. I order a meal, get through about half of it, and take the rest back to my room.

When I get to the motel, the scene isn't much different. The local Ramada is having its share of problems. The air conditioning plainly isn't up to the task, and the lone attendant at the front desk is about out of patience.

"Don't even tell me if your room is too hot" is his greeting. "There's nothing I can do for you. The air conditioners need to be replaced, OK? Everybody's already told me. And don't bother complaining about the noise. We're full, and there's nothing I can do."

With that warning, I head toward my room. When I get there, I understand what all the complaints are about. The air conditioners are old and noisy. They've managed to lower the temperature by about twenty degrees — no mean feat — but that still leaves it in the mid-80s. This, in turn, has forced people into the corridors, which seem marginally cooler. Guests are wandering around, laughing and drinking. Beer cans and cigarette butts litter the hallways. Saturday night in Clinton looks like a Fellini version of a biker film. *La Dolce Vita* meets *The Wild Bunch.*

In the morning, on my way out of town, I decide to try the Country Kitchen one last time for a late preroad breakfast. The place looks magically transformed. You can't even smell a cigarette. The after-church crowd has taken over. No one is fighting or puking in the parking lot. Even the waitresses seem to have been drawn from a different universe.

On the way out, I mention to the hostess that things seem quite calm this morning.

"Oh, you were here last night," she says, looking at me as if I had visited the netherworld and lived to tell the tale. "Yes, that *is* like a different establishment altogether." And then she adds matter of factly, "We do our best business during that shift."

The Postgame Show

Of Ballplayers and Goldfish

I've got a pond in my backyard. It's not very big — one of those vinyl-lined do-it-yourself jobs, about eight feet across. Soon after I got it, I decided it needed some fish. When I found out the cost of fully grown ornamental carp, I simplified the plan in a hurry. I made a trip to the mall and bought a dozen "feeders," pet store lingo for the cheapest kind of goldfish you can get. They even threw in a freebie, a total of thirteen fish for three dollars. Feeders are the runts of the litter, normally destined to be the dinner special for an Oscar or some equally large and showy specimen. Only my feeders got an unexpected lease on life. They got dumped into the backyard pond.

The first night eight of them disappeared, probably making a juicy midnight snack for some marauding raccoon. I figured the remaining five would be dessert by the next night, thus ending my fish experiment. But I was wrong. These guys had pond smarts. They were survivors. They lived, and they grew. Five years later, they're still alive. From undistinguished specimens barely an inch long, they've become beautiful, graceful, ornamental fish, nearly a foot in length. I never knew they had it in them. Maybe you can see the baseball analogy coming.

Along with their children and grandchildren, the original five fish spend the warmer months (there are six of them in southern Ontario) in their backyard paradise. During the remaining six months, when the Canadian climate asserts itself in no uncertain terms, the fish relocate into my house. Unlike the local fieldmice, who make the same move without my help, the fish require some assistance. Late in the fall when I drain the pond, I never know exactly how many fish I'll be bringing in. Here's where the baseball analogy forces its way to the surface.

There are hundreds, probably thousands of fish born in my pond every summer, but when it comes time to bring them in for the winter there are usually about thirty. The reason is simple: my backyard pond has become an ecosystem. I put in the water and the fish. The algae, frogs, snakes, and insects invite themselves. The place is perfectly in balance without my help. In *spite* of my help. It couldn't support hundreds or thousands of fish and so, no matter how many are born each year, only about thirty or so will survive. The rest are eaten by benign-looking frogs or by the equally benign-looking cousins, aunts, uncles, or grandparents of the fish themselves.

At the risk of insulting your intelligence, let me make the analogy clearer than my pond water. Baseball, too, is an ecosystem. It can only support so many players. The lucky twenty-five who make it to the major league roster are under constant pressure from the next generation. No one's job is really safe. The same pressure exists at every minor league level. The AA guys push the AAA players. The A guys are looking to be promoted to AA. Even within A-level ball, there is vertical movement. Rosters are limited and competition is fierce. Sometimes it comes from strangers. More often, your teammates, even your closest friends are your competitors. When Darwin talked about survival of the fittest, he wasn't talking about raccoons eating fish. He meant fish eating fish or working their fins a bit faster than the next guy to snag that juicy morsel on the surface. It really is a dog-eat-dog world out there, whether you're a fish or a ballplayer.

The Perils of Naming

My backyard pond has taught me one important coping strategy: never name the fish. I've never even named the original five. I know it's just a matter of time before they get careless and become snack food for some kind of hungry prowler. You're never safe out there. It's probably more fun than wintering in the house, but it's also more perilous.

Competition and selection pressure breed the strongest organisms. It works to the advantage of the species or the team, but it can be hell on individuals. That's what has occasionally made my baseball journey so difficult. I was smart in dealing with the fish. I avoided getting emotionally involved with individuals. There's no sense befriending somebody else's dinner. With minor league baseball players, I wasn't so smart. Maybe it's harder to stay detached with your own species. I made friendships. I grew to care about more than a few of the guys I met. In some cases that meant I got to watch a dream come true. Tim Crabtree spent the summer of 1995 pitching for the Toronto Blue Jays. José Lima graduated from his AAA no-hitter to the pitching staff of the Detroit Tigers. In some cases, the journey is still in progress. I'd bet almost anything that Bobby Estalella will end up catching for the Phillies and Richie Sexson will crack the Indians' powerhouse lineup.

But in too many other cases, I watched careers fizzle and die. After a promising start to the 1995 season, Jason Abramavicius hit a rough patch and was unceremoniously released by the Pittsburgh Pirates. Jason, you'll recall, was signed out of a tryout camp. There wasn't much invested in him, so when things got a bit rocky, the same system that chose not to draft him in the first place justified their wisdom by releasing him. Bryan Wiegandt, another tryout camp signee, suffered a similar fate by the Phillies.

A Rude Awakening

It goes without saying that the minor leagues represent a rude awakening for most players. Yes, these guys are good. Just months ago they were the stars of their high school or college teams. They were invincible. A .450 batting average, a 20–3 pitching record, an ERA under 1.50 can give you that feeling.

But what happens when suddenly *everybody* is that good, and some are even much better than you? Some players get messages like this and never adjust. For some, it's an inability to deal with a blow to the ego. For others, it's a limit to their physical talent.

But some do adjust. I always think of Richie Sexson here. Sexson underwent a transition from a rural Washington high school team to the rookie league Burlington Indians. He struggled mightily at first and barely survived. When I met him, he was in a near state of shock. But he pushed ego aside and didn't quit. And he finally reclaimed what the scouts had seen when they originally signed him. Once again, Sexson was better than the opposition — only this time the opposition was better than ever before.

Other than luck, there are two reasons why players succeed in pro ball: talent and motivation. These factors are independent. To be a major league player, or at least to stay a major league player, those two factors have to sum to some minimum level. Let's assume that talent and motivation are worth up to 100 points each. And let's assume, for argument's sake, that the major league minimum requirement equals 140. Some guys make it almost entirely on raw talent. Their work ethic is marginal; at least, it isn't the primary reason they're in the big leagues. Others make it with minimum talent and maximum hustle. Pete Rose is probably the most widely known example of this approach. Whether you like it or not, it takes both factors to reach that 140 minimum, although there's no requirement that the components have to be in balance.

In my experience, managers and coaches are most contemptuous of the great talent/minimum motivation category. Poor work habits are barely tolerated in minor league baseball, and then only in combination with massive physical gifts. When a high round draft pick washes out of pro ball, there is a lot of finger pointing. No one in the system wants to take the blame. The easiest way for the organization to look good is to concede that the guy had raw talent (thus, the scouts and the front office were right to sign him), but he also had the work ethic of a ferret — self-absorbed and headstrong. This takes the onus off the minor league manager and coaches ("Hey, we tried to teach the sumbitch something but the lazy bastard was uncoachable"). Now, everybody is off the hook, from the surveyors of raw talent to those entrusted with developing it. All that's left is a talented head case who is solely to blame for his failed attempt at professional baseball.

Owners, Raccoons, and Feelings

Let's face it. The front office of a major league baseball team cares about the feelings, fears, and dashed hopes of the minor league players it releases about as much as that raccoon cared about my eight goldfish on their first night in my backyard. The point is, they're not *supposed* to care. Natural selection, whether represented by the economics of baseball or the belly of a raccoon, is heartless. To do her job effectively, Mother Nature has got to be a bitch: "red in tooth and claw," as the expression goes.

It's one thing for a front office person like San Diego's Priscilla Oppenheimer to exercise some sensitivity when she gives this season's washouts their walking papers. But if the raccoon or, for that matter, the front office ever developed moral compunctions, it'd starve to death. In fact, the system would go under. You can't have three hundred fish living in a habitat designed for thirty. Nobody would thrive.

Likewise, you can't keep individual careers going because the player is a decent, likable guy. The first season I followed minor league ball, I got to know a catcher named Chris Calvert. We chatted with each other whenever Reading visited the AA London Tigers. Chris spoke matter-of-factly about the end of his career.

"If I don't get promoted at the end of this season, I'll just hang them up. There are plenty of other things I can do. I've had a good run, had plenty of adventures."

He talked of being part of a minor league trip to the Soviet Union.

"When would I have done that without baseball?" he asked rhetorically.

Sometime that season, or maybe it was after the Eastern League finished its schedule, Calvert was released. End of story.

Next spring, I chatted with Reading manager Don McCormack. When our conversation turned to Calvert, I mentioned that I was sorry to see him gone. McCormack turned on me with surprising energy.

"Why?" he demanded. "Because he was a good ball player helping this team and developing a career? Or because he was a nice guy?"

I wasn't prepared for the question, but the answer was clear.

"Nice guy," I mumbled.

"Right," said McCormack, releasing me from his gaze. He didn't have to add the next line, which would have been "That's not enough."

And, of course, he's right. If it were enough, professional teams would be awash in well-meaning mediocrity, the slightly upscale equivalent of a Sunday softball league. The quality of the game would suffer. Eventually the fans would turn away, the concessionaires would pack up, the owners would sell. Someone would build a parking lot over what was once a beautiful stadium. Professional baseball would shrivel and die. There'd be no one for kids to watch and emulate. Who knows how far it would go? Maybe after several generations even the sandlot games would be gone; no more fields of dreams in Iowa or stickball games on the streets of the Bronx. And all because we didn't have the heart to tell some nice guy to pack up his glove, go home, marry his sweetheart, and get a job at the filling station.

The Persistence of Players

If it's such a heartless, impersonal system, why is there an inexhaustible supply of talented young men willing to sell their souls to it? Minor league living conditions are far from luxurious. Seventeen dollars a day meal money can barely keep you alive, much less healthy. The travel is hard, and the glamour is decidedly low budget. The odds of success, however measured, are long.

Shannon Stewart of the Blue Jays and Ron Lockett, late of the Phillies, both talked openly about how tired they were. Others, like Richie Pratt, talked about how difficult it was to settle down after each night game and get sufficient rest to face the next day. I saw countless men playing in extreme weather conditions, from the freezing rain of London, Ontario, to the punishing heat of Cedar Rapids, Iowa. I can't recall anyone shrinking from either extreme. Guys *talked* about the heat or the cold, but they played hard in them. No one acts like a prima donna when his twenty-four teammates, not to mention his manager and coaches, are busting their asses under the same adverse conditions.

Why do these players persist? Maybe the question is no different from asking why there are so many musicians out there hoping to hit the big time. The odds of having a hit record are no better than making it to the major leagues. But that doesn't seem to stop anybody. Check out the number of local bands or self-produced cassettes being sold off the bandstand in every town in America.

But there's a big difference between aspiring musicians and aspiring baseball players. You don't have to quit your day job and put your life on hold to write a few songs and sell cassettes at a weekend gig. For guys taking a shot at professional baseball, real life is on hold for at least eight months a year. That kind of schedule wreaks havoc with higher education, normal jobs, and personal relationships. In virtually every case, minor league baseball represents some form of sacrifice in a young man's life.

Some, perhaps a lot, will tell you it's a love of the game that drives them. Sitting opposite me in a pancake house in Toledo, Ohio, Tim Crabtree put it as bluntly as I've heard it said.

"I've never been in it for the money. I signed within five days of being drafted. I just want to play baseball. That's what I'm here for. I'm not in it for drugs, money, or women. I want to play baseball."

But for a precious few, the money is reason enough: either the eventual prospect of a major league salary or the one-time signing bonus they can parlay from a great junior year. It may not be as romantic a motive, but why shouldn't money be part of it? In the last few years, books like Marvin Miller's *A Whole Different Game* or John Helyar's *Lords of the Realm* have laid bare the avarice of the owners. Even Ken Burns's epic documentary made it clear that player-owner conflicts are enshrined in the history of the game. As long as there have been owners, there have been accusations of greed and disputes over players' salaries. Unfair labor practices and worker exploitation hardly began in baseball's last decade. In truth, the relative passivity of the fifties and sixties that many of today's fans grew up seeing were an anomaly, a quiescent blip in the otherwise stormy economic history of the game.

For today's young men who have a chance to make an astounding amount of money quickly for something they do with effortless grace, it's worth taking a hard line. Their sense of self-worth has been bloated by praise from their coaches, the omnipresent scouts, the hovering agents, as well as their peers and families. Rookie cards sell today for more than yesterday's signing bonuses. The system has obviously gone nuts. Why not hold out for an extra quarter of a million before scrawling your name on a professional contract? Take all you can get.

But for every high round draft pick there are ten guys who'd kill just to get noticed at a tryout camp. Look at the backs of those minor league baseball cards. Every time you see the phrase *nondrafted free agent* you're looking at a story. Factor out the Hispanic names who were probably signed at wholesale sweeps of the Dominican Republic or Venezuela. Forget the Australian or Canadian kids who were lured into the fold during unregulated drafts. Think instead of those young players from Alabama or Ohio whose phones never rang despite the assurances of their coaches, teammates, and families. What went wrong? That question may haunt them for too much of their adult lives. Some, like Jeff Keith, will resent their nondrafted status even while pitching on a professional minor league team. It hurts just to sit in the dugout next to a guy who was drafted in the tenth round. It doesn't take much to tap into Keith's pain and anger. Everything about him says, "They're gonna pay before it's all over."

Others, like Bryan Wiegandt or Jason Abramavicius, clawed their way through tryout camps, beating astronomical odds to wear professional uniforms — only to be cut after a season or two of A-level ball. The organizations have taken the easy road. They'll tell you, "We were right in the first place not to draft them. There was a glimmer there, and just for a minute we thought they might have something. But when we turned up the light, it was just an illusion, just a shadow. Let 'em get on with their lives, 'cause they sure ain't gonna make it as pro ball players."

Organizational Egos

What those organization men won't tell you is that the same high intensity light used to condemn their low status signees might reveal similar flaws in a high round draft pick. But nobody wants to know that. You'd better be prepared to go to the wall and beyond with someone you've invested half a million dollars in. And if the money weren't enough of a reason, consider the personal and organizational egos at stake. Giving up on a first round draft pick is a public relations disaster. It tells the fans, "We were wrong. We don't know how to scout. We blew it. We pissed away a draft pick. We could have had Frank Thomas and instead we chose Jeff Jackson."

When the Phillies finally gave up on their 1989 first round pick at the end of the 1994 season, it was unclear whether they gained or lost face when Seattle immediately grabbed Jackson in the minor league Rule V draft. Yes, somebody else saw some worth in him and was willing to take a chance — at least at the AAA level. That was the good news. But when Seattle released Jackson just weeks into the following spring training, that seemed to confirm what everybody feared. It only took the Mariners several weeks to evaluate his potential. What were the Phillies thinking when they drafted him in the first place, or kept him around their minor league system for six seasons trying to justify their gamble?

Both Jeff Jackson and his Reading teammate Ron Lockett are gone — out of professional baseball. It doesn't matter that both men appeared as part of Upper Deck's inaugural set of minor league cards in 1992, proudly touted as major league stars of the future. Instead, I keep hearing Lloyd McClendon's words about the need for maturity and having other life options when a career is lost. I wouldn't want to be the documentary filmmaker searching for either Jackson or Lockett ten years from now on Chicago's mean streets. I want to believe that both these guys will finish school, embark on careers, and be surrounded by loving families.

That's what I wish for them, but it's a selfish wish. I've singled them out for concern because I knew both players. I spent hours leaning against outfield fences or sitting in the dugout talking with them. They're both good guys who shared their enthusiasm and frustration with me. But I know there are a lot of other minor league ball players who have been released to the unforgiving and unimpressed streets of their hometowns. On May 20, 1995, the day Jason Abramavicius was released by the Pirates off their Lynchburg roster, there were at least a dozen other minor league players cut — unceremoniously left to get on with real life.

People Die Every Day

You focus on the names you know. My mother used to read the obituary page of the *New York Times* every day. Like countless others who routinely scan that section of the newspaper, maybe she needed to reflect on her own mortality or find a focus for her grief. In any case, the *Times* never disappointed her. Every day there was a well-stocked obituary page. It's no news: people die every day.

In a sense, so do ball players. At least, their careers die every day, and maybe that is news. Major league fans might look at names like Chris Marchok, Jeff Jackson, Bryan Wiegandt, or Jason Abramavicius and say, So what? Those careers didn't die. They never even started.

That's where I beg to differ. I have sat in too many dugouts in too many small towns, talking to too many young men who have invested everything in the game being played in front of them. Those dreams, those identities as a *ball player* are not going to retreat without a fight.

In 1992 and 1993 I stood on the sidelines of Labatt Field in London, Ontario, watching travel-weary members of the Reading Phillies warm up. Casey Waller scooping balls out of the infield dust and firing them over to Sean Ryan at first base. Ed Rosado warming up Tyler Green, trying to catch his elusive knuckle-curveball. If any of those guys had a doubt about making it to The Show, they never discussed it while I was around.

Once, in a bout of enthusiasm, I wrote Sean Ryan a check for twenty bucks and told him he could cash it two years hence if he hadn't made it to The Show. He put it in his scrapbook, he later told me. He never cashed it, although, sadly, he earned the right. Within a couple of years, really not that long, Waller, Ryan, and Rosado had all been cut. Not one of them went gently into that good night. In 1994, Sean Ryan could be found playing for the Thunder Bay Whisky Jacks of the newly formed Northern League. In March 1995, when major league baseball was rattling its sabres, threatening to field replacement teams, guess who was listed as a first baseman on the Cubs' roster? Sean Ryan. Infielder for the Marlins? Casey Waller. And catching for the Pirates? Ed Rosado. Anything to prolong the descent into real life.

When the Dream Dies

And what do these failed athletes do when their minor league experience ends? The lucky ones get on with real life. The thing is, real life seems to come in a wide variety of sizes and flavors. Obviously, the descent is smoother when some higher education or a family business is part of the safety net. Poorly schooled kids, whether urban or rural, are at greatest risk. This was Lloyd McClendon's point as he sat on the outfield grass in Buffalo and told me how he counsels kids not to put their hopes in professional baseball. You've got to have some life skills in place, otherwise it's "a ticket to disaster," to use McClendon's phrase. "By the time the system chews them up and spits them out, they'll be too dazed or bruised to learn. That's when they're most vulnerable."

Consider Mike Lumley. When we last heard from him, Lumley was wondering if his next errant pitch was going to kill someone in the Eastern League. He was also stuck on the disabled list, nursing a mysterious sore shoulder and wondering about his future. Lumley had pitched in the Detroit minor league system for six seasons, but he wasn't considered a free agent yet.

"They got me on a technicality. That first year I spent with Fayetteville only counted as a half-season. I came over in the June draft so I lost a couple of months like that. I've got five and a half years of experience. You need six to be a free agent."

After last season, Lumley wasn't even sure if Detroit would want to re-sign him. But they did.

"Actually, it all went very well. I went in for arthroscopic surgery on my shoulder right after the season. It was a simple operation. They repaired what they call tears and frays. I started throwing a couple of weeks after the operation. I just had to get going again. That popping noise was gone, so I knew it was better. A month after the surgery I had my fastball up to 90 mph. The doctors tested my arm strength in December and were amazed. They wondered if I'd already begun throwing."

For a while, Lumley was riding a crest of good news. First, his wife gave birth to their son in September. Then Detroit came to him with a AAA contract. When I spoke to him, Lumley was packing for spring training.

"I'm really excited about this spring. Normally my arm is slow to come around. Living in Ontario, you don't get to throw much over the winter. This year, I've been throwing since last November. I'm ready. This season I'm going to be the man out of the gate. I've got velocity. My arm feels good. I'm hoping to start the season in Toledo [AAA], and then we'll see what happens."

Mike Lumley had his twenty-seventh birthday in January. He arrived in Florida for spring training barely a month later. Within days he was headed back to Ontario, his pro career over. It wasn't his performance that did him in. Lumley pitched four scoreless innings before the axe fell. The Tigers sent him out to the mound, confirmed that he was physically sound, and released him. The rules say you can't release a player when he's on the disabled list. So they fixed him, confirmed their handiwork, and cut him loose.

A dazed Mike Lumley arrived back in Ontario with the snow still on the ground, trying to make sense of his life and his career. The Tigers had other things on their minds, trying to put together a team that wasn't the laughingstock of the American League East. But Mike Lumley wasn't in their plans.

Lumley is one of the lucky ones. He's got a wife and family. He's known and respected in his hometown. Canadian TV viewers saw him several months later knocking down a barn with one of his fastballs in a nationally televised commercial for Molson beer. Even more important than his show business career, Lumley started up a baseball clinic for local youths in London, Ontario. He resumed his association with the London Majors, a team in the Southern Ontario Inter-County League. It wasn't the future he had in mind, but Mike Lumley survived.

So did Reading Phillies pitcher Chris Marchok. After seven seasons in the minors, Marchok decided to pack it in.

"I reached a crossroads in my life," he told me when we spoke in late February 1994.

"My wife and I decided it was time to call it quits. I became a free agent at the end of the season. I didn't pursue any teams and, the truth is, no one pursued me. If I were single and had a high school education, I might have tried to hang on. But it wasn't like that. My season ended great. I got consistent at the end. I was pitching for fun and pride with no thought to the future.

"I have no regrets. I gave it 100 percent. It was important for me to finish out well so I could be comfortable with my decision. I could have quit midseason. I could have walked away from it — a twenty-eight year old with an ERA over 7.00. But I didn't do that. I stayed on and fought back. It's not easy to get an ERA down. They go up real easily, but you have to battle to get them back down.

"I also feel good that I did what I could to help some of the younger guys on the team. That makes me feel good. I wanted to be a role model, and I think I did that. There are some young players on that team that have a real good chance to make it all the way. Ricky Botallico, Gene Schall, Phil Geisler — guys like that. I did what I could to convey a positive attitude.

"Right now I'm OK with my decision. I guess it'll hit me in a couple of weeks when spring training starts. This'll be the first season in I don't know how long that I won't be in Florida. It'll feel odd not being part of it. But this is what we've decided. My wife, Vicky, has been wonderful through all of this. I feel like I have real support here.

"The end was very emotional for me. I got into the last game of the season and pitched two scoreless innings. It was a perfect way to go out. After the game I just sat there in the dugout. After a while, I was alone. The other guys had gone into the clubhouse to pack up, but I just sat there, looking around, seeing it all for the last time.

"Yeah, I'll probably go to some games this season. I live real close to the new stadium in Trenton. I can get over there and watch Reading when they're in town. I'm sure some of the guys I played with will still be on the team. It'll be good to see them. But it'll be difficult. It's going to take awhile before I can do that. I'm not ready to become a fan yet."

There was one more curveball in Chris Marchok's future. He may have been through with baseball, but it wasn't quite done with him. The Florida Marlins came calling during major league baseball's flirtation with replacement players. For Marchok the decision to head for Florida was a no-brainer. It held a chance, albeit a long one, that he would march out of a dugout somewhere in a major league uniform.

"I got goosebumps thinking about that," he conceded.

The invitation also offered a major financial incentive. Marchok made more for traveling to Florida and briefly optioning his services to the Marlins than he did in most minor league seasons he played.

"That eighty dollar a day meal money wasn't too hard to take either," he observed.

When the specter of replacement baseball vanished, Chris Marchok returned to Pennsylvania and real life. Baseball finally gave him a bit of a payback. Last season he split his time between preparing to apply to medical school and playing for the Jenkintown Quakers of the semipro Penn-Delaware League. Like Mike Lumley, Chris Marchok only shows up on the days he's scheduled to pitch. Even on those terms, his manager is thrilled to have him.

Meanwhile, in the Midwest, another tale was emerging. Jason Abramavicius, our friend from Chicago who clawed his way into the Pirates' farm system through a tryout camp, had a good second season with Salem. It may not have ranked among the league's top ten, but it sure as hell told the Pittsburgh front office that this unheralded suspect might actually be a prospect. Jason's 3.12 ERA placed him fourth among a staff that numbered seventeen over the course of the season. That was good enough to get him an invitation to the Fall Instructional League held in Bradenton. The Pirates don't give out tickets to Florida like candy. They have to see something worth developing.

It was hard work, but Jason loved the experience.

"I learned a lot. It's really incredible. No one ever *taught* me like that before. I worked on pitch selection, holding runners on. Even the philosophy of pitching. I feel like I'm making up for lost time."

After the '94 season, Jason's coaches gave him the praise he deserved. They told him he had impressed a lot of people. They talked about him starting the next season in AA. Maybe even a promotion to AAA by end of the season.

Things were a bit rough at the start of spring training. Jason's first few outings were subpar, but he didn't worry.

"They were just intersquad games. By the time we started playing other teams, I could feel it coming together. I didn't allow any earned runs during my last fifteen innings. I felt ready to take on the world."

Apparently, that's not the way the Pirates' brain trust saw it. When camp broke, Jason was part of the Lynchburg roster, which meant another season in the A Carolina League. Worse yet, he had been demoted from the starting rotation to the bullpen.

"I couldn't believe it. I thought, What do you have to do to be promoted? I had shown them I knew how to pitch. I was getting all kinds of good messages from my coaches. The numbers were there. But when it came time to decide, they kept me right where I was. Worse yet, I didn't even have a starting job anymore. It felt like a demotion. I knew the guys who had moved up to AA. I honestly couldn't see that they had shown any more than I had. It really got to me."

Not surprisingly, Jason's attitude affected his game.

"I kept brooding about it. Until then I had this fire inside me. It drove me. It made me a fierce competitor. When I didn't move up, I could feel the fire just die. I had developed very high expectations, and when nothing materialized, I just lost my motivation. I lost that killer instinct that you need to pitch effectively. I couldn't believe how quickly it went away.

"Maybe I could have gotten it back, but I never got the chance. I pitched a total of eight innings for Lynchburg, and they were pretty poor. My ERA was up around 5.00. That was all they needed to see. I was released in May.

"Looking back, it really doesn't seem fair. If I wasn't good enough, I think I could live with this kind of ending. But it's not like that. I put up some good numbers the year before. Even my spring, once we got going, was fairly impressive. All it took was eight bad innings when I was in an admittedly bad state, and that was the end."

Jason went back to Chicago feeling demoralized.

"A couple of independent teams called me during the summer. I could have gotten right back into it, but I just didn't have the heart for it. Even the semipro team I had played with before I signed with the Pirates called. I turned them down too. I just couldn't bring myself to play ball. I figured it would pass, but I didn't know how long it would take.

"I decided it was time to get on with my life. I got a job in a bank, and I'm still working there. I'm hoping to become a loan officer.

"Last fall the owner of the semipro team called again and asked if I wanted to play. By then a few months had passed and I figured, why not? So I told him to go ahead and send me the papers to sign. There are some forms I have to submit certifying that I'm no longer a professional so I can play in that league. Somehow I never got around to filling them out. They're still sitting here. I don't know. Maybe with the winter meetings, I might get a call from someone. It's not like I *want* to go through all this again, but you never know what will happen. Baseball is like that. Once you get the hook in you, they have you for life.

"When I think about it, about having to prove myself all over again, about bouncing around the minors again, I say, 'No way!' I'm twenty-six now. It would have been great to make it to the majors, but life goes on. I have other goals.

"Then I think, what if somebody calls? Maybe it'll be different this time. And I feel my hopes starting to rise again. I've still got that hook in me."

Of Ballplayers and Musicians

I spent years interviewing musicians in order to write the liner notes for boxed sets of LPs and CDs. It was fascinating work, hunting these guys down, often years after their careers were over. Some had gone on to mundane jobs and family life. Their guitars, photos, and old records were gathering dust in the attics of mortgaged homes. Others were still making music in some small way: maybe working weekend gigs at the local Holiday Inn, playing uninspired versions of today's hits for bored and undiscriminating audiences. Sometimes they'd slip in one of their own tunes. Usually nobody noticed.

But most of these musicians, including those who had spent years on the road and recorded countless songs, differed from just about every ball player I ever met. I'd ask a musician about the details of his musical history and find that most could barely remember the songs they had written, much less who had played on what or where it had been recorded. It never failed to amaze me. White, black, country singer, blues singer, rock and roller — most of them were clueless about their own career.

Baseball players, for the most part, are a different breed. Events in a baseball player's life seem to be burned into his memory. I've heard players describe games from thirty years ago, nearly pitch by pitch.

"The guy threw me two sliders outside, trying to set me up. Then he came inside with a fastball, but I got just enough of it to line it over third for a two-run double."

You expect that kind of detail in a postgame interview. But it is just as likely to occur during the summary of a game from 1961. Why is there such a difference between musicians and ball players? The answer is more complex than assuming musicians are always drunk or high and ball players are always sober or straight. There are too many exceptions on both sides to relegate the difference to neurochemistry.

But neither can we conclude that ball players are exceptional men. These same guys will forget their wife's birthday or their own wedding anniversary, but it's a piece of cake to recall their ERA or batting average from years before they were married. Ask Greg Maddux or Ken Griffey, Jr., to tell you where they played before The Show, or what kind of season they had. You'll probably get an accurate transcript. Ask most of the musicians I interviewed to name the labels they've recorded for or who played the sax or guitar solo on one of their hits, and their eyes glaze over.

The simple fact is that most musicians just seem to be living the life. It's somebody else's job to take notes. Baseball players, on the other hand, are natural historians. They seem to have a tiny Camcorder implanted into their brains at the same time they're issued their first professional team caps and spikes. It doesn't take much looking to find the play button on those machines even years after the original recordings were made.

Nothing Is Sacred

Despite its low budget, down-home charm, minor league baseball is vulnerable to greed and short-sightedness from above. The 1994 season had barely dawned when major league baseball announced that it would be cutting the minors' four-million-dollar umpiring budget by $500,000.

Ideally, business decisions are driven by rational thought. In this case, there seemed to be little evidence that anyone had weighed cost against consequence. In an industry struggling to rationalize its obscene profits, the net savings to each major league team would be $20,000 per year. Petty cash. In return, minor league umpiring will be dealt a body blow.

The immediate impact included the reduction in AA crews from three persons to two, the reduction of minor league umpiring rosters from 210 to 173 persons, and a 40 percent enrollment cut in the umpire development evaluation course. This final cut affected the best students to come out of umpiring schools all over America. In addition, all Rookie Leagues, including the Appalachian League featured prominently in this book, were required to use amateur crews in at least one game per week. The amateur umpires we met in Bristol suggest there may not be much to worry about, but the ruthless cost cutting behind the move is cause for concern. Over 140 teams will be affected. The training and, potentially, the careers of about thirty-five hundred professional baseball players will be compromised each season. Inferior or insufficient umpiring will take its toll on player development. The effects may be subtle, but they will be there.

The owners of major league baseball seem to have lost sight of whose flesh they were trimming. It is not the Australian Soccer League they are wringing dry. It is minor league baseball, the same teams that are the lifeblood, indeed the very future of the major leagues. This parent has literally turned on its young. Infanticide is never pretty, but it is sometimes understandable in times of limited resources. That is hardly the case here. The total savings to the majors would not pay the salary of a single utility infielder hitting .220. What has a team with a forty-million-dollar payroll achieved by trimming $20,000 from its budget? Fiscal responsibility begins by questioning five-million-dollar salaries, not by watering down the mustard at the hot dog stand.

Subtle Mystique on the Altar

Baseball, both the major and minor league variety, has an undeniable and subtle mystique. It goes beyond hero worship and transcends locale. It is the stuff that keeps W. P. Kinsella on the best seller lists. It is the reason *Field of Dreams* touched so many moviegoers so deeply and continues to draw tourists to an obscure cornfield in Iowa. Ken Burns spent eighteen hours trying to capture that magic and learned, like poets, novelists, and cinematographers before him, just how elusive it is.

Arguably, the best way to capture the magic of baseball is to stand back and let the game unfold. The smells, sights, sounds, and rhythms of baseball will emerge spontaneously. All they need is a sympathetic venue.

Such venues are surprisingly hard to find in the minor leagues. To its credit, major league baseball is often more sensitive to this process than the minors. Certainly, the minors are not wholly sacrilegious; nor are the majors uniformly wise in their respect for baseball's subtle magic. But for every place like Bluefield or St. Catharines, where general managers seemed satisfied to let the game unfold, I visited a dozen towns where silence was viewed as a challenge: a black hole that needed to be filled with anything from a few rounds of Baseball Bingo to a performance by Captain Dynamite.

Purists of any persuasion, and baseball is but one of them, rarely make good accountants. Professional baseball has ceased to be a "sport" in any real sense of the word. Even calling it a "business" no longer does justice to what it has become. Baseball is now commercial entertainment. In the majors, ownership of teams by family groups is no longer viable. After nearly four years of negotiations, Walt Disney now owns the California Angels. Time/Warner is presently attempting to acquire Turner Broadcasting and, with it, the Atlanta Braves.

Even in the minor leagues, baseball is entertainment. Fans equal revenue. If you can triple attendance and concession sales by booking the Blues Brothers, why not do it? A. J. Maloney, the Buffalo Bisons mascot who considers himself something of a baseball purist, told me he found Fenway Park eerily quiet. It's no wonder. Anything would seem peaceful compared to the nightly doings at Pilot Field, where fans turn out in record numbers and rave about the value of their entertainment dollar.

As long as minor league general managers are entrusted with turning a profit, they will do everything they can to *entertain*. Baseball is just one way to entice spectators. Why not combine the game with a few contests, giveaways, and sideshow acts? The tough answer is that those business-oriented GMs are sacrificing the subtle rhythms and mystique of the game on the altar of a three-ring circus. An emerging no-hitter might be interrupted at any moment by the aerial shenanigans of Wild Thing or the bountiful charms of Morgana, the Kissing Bandit. The GMs know it. They'll tell you there just aren't enough Kinsella-type purists out there to keep the franchise afloat.

Maybe this is true, although most GMs I met were simply unwilling to test this germ of economic folklore. And so the stakes escalate and the sideshow grows. In fairness, part of the minors' quirky charm probably involves the crass commercialism and aggressively lowbrow taste that combines a three-hit shutout with aerial acrobatics and fifty-cent beer.

A Portal to Yesteryear?

Much of what is written or broadcast portrays minor league baseball as being lost in a time warp, a doorway into the offbeat zaniness of small-town life. Come on through and experience the pleasures of simpler times. Vendors still sell cotton candy aisle to aisle, and scorecards still cost a buck. Step up and meet P. T. Barnum and a cast of hawkers and gawkers. See life on the midway: the clowns and the freaks. Folks in their shirtsleeves enjoying a concert in the park on a hot July night. The melodies are familiar, but the arrangements are a bit ragged. A return to traditional values. Norman Rockwell, alive and well in the nineties.

You've got to wonder how long this can go on. Can anyone stop the loss of innocence? Those sweet-faced kids in uniform stand tall and obligingly sign autographs. Their faces and feats appear in the local paper. But will these small-town heroes become tomorrow's aloof, self-indulgent superstars? Should you keep that Boomer Whipple autograph as a precious memento or sell it to a dealer on the day Boomer makes it to The Show and no longer greets his old friends?

Most of what you read about minor league baseball is true. It *is* all those hokey things that ooze Americana. And despite all the media attention, the PBS documentaries, the segment on *60 Minutes*, the coverage in the *New York Times*, minor league baseball will probably retain its quirky charm for the foreseeable future. Too much of what makes the minors special is rooted in human nature. Greed, pride, innocence, hero worship. Those things, as we all know, are slow to change. Nor will the essential character of small-town life change.

Bluefield, West Virginia, and Elizabethton, Tennessee, to name but two, are not likely to lose their essential culture just because you can see softcore porn or the New York Yankees on cable TV. Small-town culture has withstood bigger challenges and survived relatively unscathed. And so the Orioles and Twins affiliates playing in those towns will continue to perform in a different universe than their counterparts in Baltimore or Minneapolis. Somewhere along the line, the team ownership may change. And when that happens, someone with dollar signs in his eyes will want to change the name of the local team from the Orioles or Twins to something flashier. Maybe Warthogs or River Bandits, or have those already been taken? A new logo will be created, and merchandising specialists will be called in. There will be licensing fees paid and earned. But the essential character of the players and the folks who attend the games will be as unchanged as the Appalachian night.

What's in a Name?

Ten years ago, most self-respecting minor league teams were named after their major league overseers. You went to see the Greenville Braves, the Reading Phillies, or the Pawtucket Red Sox. While lacking in ingenuity, these names made it clear that your small-town franchise had a direct link to the big time. True, there have always been exceptions. Minor league teams like the Durham Bulls, the Albuquerque Dukes, or the Rochester Red Wings maintained their independent titles, even in an era when major league identity was worn proudly.

All that has changed. In 1996, the majority of minor league teams are uniquely named in ways that belie their ties to the majors. Instead of Yankees, Mets, and Cardinals we have Sea Dogs, SeaWolves, and Jammers. As has always been the case, animal names predominate. Some, like Cobras, Lynx, and Hawks, are fairly conventional specimens. Other franchises have opted for the more exotic. The Beloit Snappers seem to be named after the turtle, not the red fish. The Brevard County Manatees have honored one of nature's least understood and mildest mannered creatures. In the case of Greensboro, it remains unclear whether the Bats in question are flying mammals or baseball equipment. To its credit, the logo does nothing to resolve the issue.

Some leagues are plainly more indulgent than others. Probably none is more permissive than the South Atlantic League, which includes Polecats, Tourists, Greenjackets, Riverdogs, Alley Cats, Bombers, Boll Weevils, Redstixx, Generals, the aforementioned Bats, Suns, and Crawdads. Only the Macon Braves and Savannah Cardinals remain true to their major league affiliates, and how long can such loyalty last?

In the Midwest League, the new franchise in Battle Creek, Michigan, created an instant legend when they named their team the Golden Kazoos. Undoubtedly, the front office will provide a press release explaining what kazoos have to do with baseball. In other cases, the team name is shrouded in mystery. Consider the Wilmington Blue Rocks of the Carolina League. The Wilmington franchise was wildly successful during its inaugural 1993 season. Wilmington drew 332,000 fans in a park that seats just over 5,000. Quite a few AAA teams would have been proud of that attendance figure.

Journalist Matt Wall joined me in addressing a simple question: just what are Blue Rocks, and why has this franchise taken their name? According to the official press release, blue rocks refers to the "distinctive granite for which Delaware is known." Nonsense, says Matthew Wall. Delaware simply isn't known for granite. In his words, "Delaware ain't exactly New Hampshire; the few rocky outcroppings in this sea-level state are hardly distinctive."

So why the fabrication? Wall believes that the team didn't want to get tangled in a complex web of imagery. And just what might that web look like? It's here that Wall did some checking and learned that the Blue Rocks were the name of Wilmington's original minor league team that closed shop in the 1950s. The name is even older than that. Teams called the Blue Rocks played in several industrial leagues, including a shipbuilders' league that has become famous for one of its participants — a certain George Herman Ruth.

So what did the name Blue Rocks mean eighty years ago? Wall checked the newspaper archives and found two accounts. In the first, blue rocks were the name for coal, mined in Pennsylvania and shipped through the port of Wilmington. The name referred not only to the coal they handled but to the handlers themselves. Not a bad name for a rough-hewn industrial league team. But perhaps a bit too rough for a team offering clean-cut family entertainment?

Actually, it's a Sunday picnic compared to the alternative theory. Blue rocks, in Wall's words, referred to "a certain medical condition caused among males working on the ships who were without female companionship for an extended period of time." A wonderful story, indeed, even if it isn't true. Given the apple pie image of most successful franchises, it is not surprising that tales of sexual deprivation weren't part of the official press release. But what a terrible waste of potential for the team logo!

Durham Revisited

Perhaps some places are more resistant to change than others. For all its economic and cultural progress, Durham, North Carolina, remains surrounded by a haze of zaniness as persistent as the ozone layer.

At the end of the '93 season, the biggest story was the demise of the fabled old Durham Athletic Park. The teary final game was held on September 4, 1993. A sellout crowd of forty-five hundred fans stayed as long as they could, but an afternoon squall ultimately washed away their tears along with the final game.

Game or no game, Durham went ahead with its funeral and its wake. The *Herald-Sun* published a special section in its August 31 edition to celebrate the death of an institution. It contained photographs, banner headlines, some history, and a section of quotes about "What the DAP means to me." Everyone from the Braves' Ron Gant to the real Crash Davis, on whose career the movie *Bull Durham* was based, had something reverent to say.

Then reality set in. It turned out that reports of the DAP's death were premature. As red-faced city planners and team officials met, it became obvious that the eleven-million-dollar new park wouldn't even be close to completion in time for the start of the '94 season. Maybe, just maybe, the Bulls could move there by mid- or late season, but even that wasn't guaranteed. Rather than risking further embarrassment, the Durham Bulls simply apologized for the miscalculation and announced they would be playing their 1994 games at the DAP. Local residents may have recalled an old hillbilly tune called "How Can I Miss You If You Won't Go Away."

I visited Durham in November 1994. There still wasn't much to see in the way of a new ballpark. Some attractive masonry seemed to loom out of a sea of red Carolina mud. It was going to be a long haul to opening day in 1995. But, as usual, the Bulls made it work. The park wasn't quite ready for prime time when they opened the gates, but the beer was flowing and the sod was down. That was enough for the umpires to shout, "Play ball!"

If anyone expected the new ballpark to puncture the looniness that hangs over Durham, they were mistaken. As the Bulls' management predicted, there was little resistance to the new DAP. Crowds came out in record numbers. As usual, the gods of lunacy continued to smile on Durham. Even attempts at social responsibility and political correctness backfired in near-mythic proportions.

On May 22, 1995, the Durham Bulls put on their pious face and sponsored Strike Out Domestic Violence Night at the ballpark. The players responded with one of the most spectacular brawls in the history of minor league baseball. The game almost made it through three innings before visiting pitcher Jason Kummerfeldt hit John Knott, the Bulls batter, on the arm with a pitch. That in itself might not have caused a melee were it not for the fact that this was not Kummerfeldt's first victim of the evening. Worse yet, Kummerfeldt had just given up back-to-back home runs to Durham batters and was plainly feeling a bit peevish.

Actually, the Bulls were hardly blameless. In the top of the same inning, Durham pitcher Jamie Arnold nailed Aaron Boone of the Winston-Salem team with a pitch. And so tempers were running appropriately high on Strike Out Domestic Violence Night. When Knott decided to charge the mound, his teammates followed him. This, of course, led Kummerfeldt's colleagues from the Warthogs to join the party. When the dust cleared thirty-two minutes later, there were bloodied bodies and ambulance crews in attendance. Warthog pitcher Glen Cullop, who wasn't even involved in the game, took the biggest beating. He was knocked unconscious and had to undergo surgery to repair a broken jawbone. Cullop also faces some serious dental bills to replace the five teeth that Durham player Earl Nelson kicked out during the brawl. But Nelson's loss may ultimately be greater than Cullop's. Almost immediately, the Atlanta Braves released him from their minor league system. Teeth, you can replace. A career in professional baseball is another matter.

Matt West, the Bulls' manager, broke the news to Nelson, who "took the decision like a man and a professional." Along with the expected "the Bulls do not condone this kind of behavior," West made one observation worthy of our attention.

"When Earl went on to that field, he did not intend to go out and kick somebody in the face."

Probably no one doubts that, including the Atlanta front office, who summarily released Nelson. They understood that kind of violence, whether in the home or on the field, lies within all of us. Certainly, it lay within Atlanta's major league manager, Bobby Cox, whose arrest for wife battery was well publicized. Under normal conditions, however, the social contract requires us to keep violent impulses in check. In wartime, they may be encouraged. In some sports, such as hockey and football, they lie closer to the surface or, at least, are better tolerated by management and the media. In baseball, however, violence is unseemly.

Nelson's fate was probably sealed by two things. One was a video tape record of him repeatedly kicking Cullop in the head while he lay on the ground. Even so, violence alone might not have cost Nelson his job. Indeed, there were forty-eight player suspensions and over $6,000 in fines (serious money in the Carolina League). Yet, no one else lost his career except Nelson. He was in a class by himself. Nelson was more than violent. He fought dirty. He kicked a fellow when he was down. That you don't do, whether in minor league ball or American folklore. That will get you banished.

The other factor that might have weighed in the decision to release Nelson was his record. He was 0–1 with an ERA hovering around 5.00. The man was not having a good season, which is plainly not the time to go kicking people in the face.

Don't Be Deceived

Although many fans and towns take pride in their minor league teams, you'd have to be pretty naive to think that such homespun loyalty is a two-way street. The major league owners don't mind if you watch their players develop. They're happy to let them train in low budget venues like your hometown. But the bottom line *is* player development. And that means, when it's time for a promotion (or, occasionally, a demotion), kiss your slugger or star pitcher or hometown hero good-bye. Off he goes to another spot in the food chain, one that makes sense to someone in the organization whose face you'll never see and whose logic remains inscrutable. The local chamber of commerce will not be consulted. The feelings of that starry-eyed eleven year old whose baseball was signed last week will not be factored into the equation. The local prom queen whose heart he's going to break will, likewise, not sway the course of player development. Not even the team manager who works for the same organization will be consulted when the time comes. If anything, the manager is supposed to understand! It was his nightly reports in the first place that contributed to this promotion. The fact that this poor manager has been piloting a winning team for the past month — something that not only felt good but might even look good on his record when a major league coaching job opened up — counts for naught. Nothing matters. The fans, the local team owners, the general manager, the field manager, the teammates who are staying behind — everyone is a bystander. Natural selection is at work. Stand back! Nature takes no prisoners.

How does the player himself feel on such occasions? Some of them told me, "Are you kidding? A promotion? I'm outta here. Yeah, it'd be tough leaving friends, but this is about my career. My chances! Anything to get closer to The Show, I'm for it."

That doesn't sound like a role Jimmy Stewart or Kevin Costner might play, but it's hard to blame a guy for saying those things. Should my five goldfish have felt badly for having been the ones to survive? Would it bring back the other eight? Would it please Darwin or, for that matter, Abner Doubleday?

But I also heard the other kind of reaction, the one closer to Hollywood's idea of traditional American values.

"I'd hate to leave this team, especially if we were doing well. Winning is important. You don't break up a winning team. It's taken us half the season to develop this chemistry. We're playing well together. Everyone knows his role. We've got pitching, timely hitting, defense. We pull together and we're winning. Nothing can replace this experience. Even if some of us make it to The Show, this might be the only time we get to play on a winning club. I'd do anything to preserve this, and I'd certainly turn down a promotion if that's what it took."

Maybe nobody said *exactly* those words to me. But those feelings were there, and I heard most of those phrases even if they weren't spoken that clearly or strung together in that order. The truth is, those sentiments were usually expressed by guys whose teams *were* playing well. I don't recall hearing anything about turning down promotions from someone whose team was playing .400 ball.

The interesting thing is that the "winning team" argument goes beyond sentimentality. It goes to the heart of "intangibles," a sports phrase that has fallen from favor in the eyes of statheads and in the face of Sabremetrics. The era of *range factors* and *major league equivalence* has replaced airy-fairy notions such as "team chemistry." If intangibles are truly irrelevant to predicting or analyzing baseball performance, then who cares if a guy has experience playing on a championship team before he makes it to The Show?

But if playing on a winning team counts for something, then unless the stakes are very high, it makes no sense to promote a player and disrupt a team on the brink of victory. There are too many stories of valuable contributors who were pulled from the rosters of contending minor league teams late in the season only to sit idly in the dugout of a major league team going nowhere. Is it better to experience that September callup to The Show and serve as an occasional pinch runner or to lead your minor league teammates to victory? Even if that victory is only a divisional title in some A league, winning is winning. I've never heard anyone say, as the beer was flowing and the music was blaring, "Hey, what are we so excited about? This is only the Appalachian League!"

Afterword

SPECIAL TO THE BISON BOOKS EDITION

It's been ten years since I first packed up my car and headed off in search of the stories and pictures that led to this book. A lot has changed since then and not everything ended up exactly as I would have predicted. The bases are still 90 feet apart and most ballgames still last nine innings, but when you look beyond the basics there are quite a few differences today from the world I wrote about.

Ten years may not seem like a long time, but in the world of baseball—especially minor league baseball—ten years can be a lifetime. Certainly ten years is long enough to see whether the promise spotted in an athlete by some roving scout or high school coach has been fulfilled. It's long enough for lives and careers, especially those of young men, to change direction. It's long enough for stadiums to wear out or slip below league standards. It's long enough for players and personnel to retire and for new ones to take their places. Sometimes the process is sad to watch, but it is also the strength of the game and the key to its survival.

At the time this book was first published I tried to produce something like an afterword in the final chapter, but there wasn't enough distance between the stories and the book's publication date to make it as useful as I had hoped. A decade comes closer to the timing you need to provide a "Where Are They Now?" section. Obviously there is never enough time to get it right. These are real lives and the men who live them continue to evolve and reinvent themselves, which is as it should be. But since *Small-Town Heroes* is essentially a baseball book, I can afford to be selective. Suffice it to say, what you are about to read is only a glimpse of what happened to some of the people and places you encountered in the preceding pages.

Time Marches On

Nearly two-thirds of the teams I visited have changed. Some are gone altogether and others go by different names. Some have changed their major league affiliations or play in new stadiums. For some even if the city, the team name, the affiliation, or the park is the same, the personnel are different. You expect the players to change—that's what the minors are all about. But most of the people I met in the front offices—everyone from GMs and their assistants to the ticket takers—have moved on to other pursuits. That's a lot of change in a short time and it tells you something fundamental about minor league baseball: though there is a lot of enthusiasm and youth associated with it, it is rare for people to grow old in the field.

Some of the changes that have occurred were predictable. Durham Athletic Park was in the process of shutting down even as the original edition of *Small-Town Heroes* went to press. The old park was photogenic as hell and drew tourists and romantics by the hundreds, but it was a crumbling, obsolete facility. Durham still has a franchise, of course, but it has upgraded itself from single-A to triple-A, and it plays its games in a spiffy new ballpark. Toledo, Ohio, still has its AAA team, but as of the 2002 season it has been playing in a new ballpark: venerable old Ned Skeldon Stadium is now part of the Mud Hens' long history. In Erie, Pennsylvania, the problem was just the opposite: the park was too good. The SeaWolves were playing in a short-season A league with a AA facility. Not any more: they are now proud members of the AA Eastern League.

Southern Ontario, the starting point for my journey, has fared the worst. Of the four teams I visited in the mid-nineties none still exist. The Hamilton Redbirds were the first to go, departing their pathetic Bernie Arbour Stadium and leaving it in the hands of local softball teams. Welland was the next, allowing the Pittsburgh Pirates to find a more favorable location for their New York–Penn League affiliate. The saddest departure was already in the works when I was wrapping up the manuscript: the Detroit Tigers gave up their AA franchise in London, Ontario, and headed southeast to New Jersey, more than quadrupling the distance from Detroit in the process. Most recently the Toronto Blue Jays pulled the plug on their St. Catharines franchise, choosing to cross the border into upstate New York. St. Catharines was anything but picturesque but it must have set some kind of record for proximity to its major league affiliate; you could almost see the Toronto skyline from St. Catharines.

Other teams like Greensboro, Hickory, and Martinsville have stayed put but changed their major league affiliations. Since 1996 the Burlington Bees have managed to change team affiliations four times. To their credit they have competed in the playoffs (2002) and won the league championship (1999) during that same period. They have also marshalled every available resource in tiny Burlington, Iowa, and completed some much-needed renovations to their ballpark.

Where Are They Now?

As expected, the team rosters have changed too. You don't expect many guys who played minor league ball in the early nineties to be toiling away in the same trenches in the twenty-first century. Still, there are some exceptions on that score. When we met Johnny Carvajal in Princeton, West Virginia, in 1993, no one would have guessed he'd still be in the minors ten years later. Last year (2002) he played for Shreveport in the AA Texas League and he seems destined for more of the same this season. Since we met him Carvajal has been traded twice, signed as a free agent three times, and bounced around between A and AAA like a yo-yo. In November 2002 he signed with Arizona. The 2003 season will be his eleventh year in the minors.

Some of the players we previously met have moved up. Most of them have moved out, creating space for an endless supply of hopefuls to fill their ranks. Some of the success stories were to be expected. Derek Jeter is, as almost everyone predicted when I met him in Greensboro in 1993, a star. He is the Yankees' shortstop for now and for the foreseeable future. Despite some early struggles Carlos Delgado has become the offensive machine for the Toronto Blue Jays that nearly everyone predicted he would be. Richie Sexson went from being the tall gangly kid we met in Burlington, North Carolina, to a legitimate major league slugger. But predicting stars, or even success, is a tricky business. Even those who made it to the majors had no guarantee their success would last. You often hear that it's easier to "get there" than it is to "stay there," and you'll get no argument from the likes of Tyler Green.

Green, a former number one draft pick, not only made it to the major leagues but pitched well enough during the first half of his rookie season (1995) to make the All-Star Team. Just as quickly, however, Green lost his touch. The second half of 1995 was pretty dire, as injuries took their toll. A sore shoulder cost him all of 1996. He pitched sporadically in '97 and '98, amassing a combined 10-16 record with an ERA of 5.00. Some further stints in AAA and a season of winter ball in Venezuela didn't turn his situation around. Tyler Green never pitched an inning of major league ball after 1998. He now works as a broker, selling group insurance for a large banking company.

Fortunately there is a whole other dimension to Green's life. "I've been involved in music for a long time. Even when I was in the minor leagues I was carrying a keyboard around with me, jamming whenever I could. I've got a studio in my home now and I write lyrics and music. In fact, we lived in Nashville for three and a half years, trying to take advantage of the [music industry] opportunities there. I'll keep trying; you never know how things are going to work out. It's all a process. One thing I know: I got out of baseball when I should have. I could have hung on, hoping to pitch my way back out of the minors, but I knew it was over. It was time."

Jose Lima also made it big, winning twenty-one games for Houston in 1999 and appearing in the All-Star Game. His 2002 salary with Detroit was a staggering $7.25 million, for which he turned in a 4-6 record and an ERA near 8.00. He was released by the Tigers in September 2002 and is presently a free agent. Lima may have to sign a minor league contract to make it back to the majors, although it's a cinch he won't end up pitching in London, Ontario—which is where we first met him.

We crossed paths with Jason Dickson while he was pitching for Cedar Rapids, Iowa, in the A-level Midwest League. He, too, played in the major league All-Star Game only two years after we met him in 1995. Since then he has been plagued by injuries. He spent the 2002 season pitching for AAA-Durham and is presently under contract to Tampa Bay. It is anybody's guess whether he'll regain the form that led to his meteoric rise to the majors.

We also met some "can't miss" prospects who washed out before they really even got started. Ryan Karp's career went from the spectacular heights we observed in Greensboro in 1993 to an injury-plagued, unexceptional career and eventual release. Over parts of two seasons (1995 and 1997) Karp pitched a total of fifteen major league innings, amassing an overall ERA of 5.29. All and all it wasn't much to show for his much-ballyhooed minor league career. Terrell Wade continued to impress minor league observers, as he did when we met him in Durham in 1993. But Wade's brief stint in the majors never matched those expectations; he pitched well for the Braves in 1996 (5-0, 2.97 ERA) but never returned to form. Wade joined Tampa Bay's expansion team in 1998 and pitched a total of ten innings with an ERA over 5.00. The name Terrell Wade has not graced a major league roster since.

Others, like Wayne Gomes—whom we met pitching for Batavia in 1993—never quite put it together and went from college phenom to prospect to suspect. At this writing Gomes is hoping to catch on as bullpen help with Tampa Bay. He pitched a total of twenty-one major league innings in 2002 with an ERA near 5.00. Gomes's erstwhile teammate, Bobby Estalella—first observed with Martinsville in 1993—made the most of his early major league career with some dramatic multi–home run games. He then settled into a frustrating injury-plagued career of unfulfilled promise, going from the Phillies to the Giants to the Yankees to the Rockies in less than two years. At present Estalella is under contract to Colorado. He works out daily, hoping this season will be the one when he can finally put it together.

Just as intriguing are the minor league players who became serviceable major leaguers, despite a near-total lack of enthusiasm about their prospects when we met them. In the mid-1990s pitcher Mike Williams was wearing out the northeast extension of the Pennsylvania Turnpike, commuting between unsuccessful stints with the Phillies and frustrating interludes with the AAA Scranton–Wilkes-Barre Red Barons. Williams is now an established and much-coveted closer for the Pittsburgh Pirates.

Reliever Tim Crabtree made it to the major leagues with Toronto in 1995 soon after we met him pitching for Syracuse. Crabtree showed he had the goods and quickly established himself as a solid middle-reliever. In 1998 he was traded to Texas, and the Rangers announced that Crabtree would be their closer for the 2001 season. Then injuries began to take their toll. "First I hurt my back, and then my shoulder went out in July. It shows how you can be on top of the world one minute and then have it vanish the next," he observes. In July 2001 Crabtree had surgery to repair a 70 percent tear in his rotator cuff. Eager to get back into the game, Crabtree signed with the Dodgers three days before spring training for the 2002 season. He stayed in

Florida with the Vero Beach team but by June he knew it was a mistake. "My shoulder wasn't healed and I wasn't doing it any good by rushing it. I had been through too much to hang around in A ball with no hope of making it back to the majors." Crabtree secured his release from the Dodgers and went back home to Texas. "I've been here for nearly eighteen months now. I keep going back and forth about whether to retire. I have a good career waiting for me in criminal justice if I want it. I just passed my FBI exam. My wife and I have two daughters and I love being with my family. Still, I'm only thirty-three. My shoulder has been feeling pretty good lately. I've been throwing every day without pain. Maybe I could sign a minor league deal with the Tigers and see what I could show them during spring training. I've had six and a half years in the majors but I know I have to reestablish myself. I don't mind doing that. I grew up in Jackson, Michigan. It would be great to pitch for the team I watched growing up. I could probably fill a whole section of the park with friends and family every night. It would be a nice way to finish my career. I guess one way or another I'll know if I still have a career after this year."

Troy Fortin, whom we met in Elizabethton in 1994, did not make it with the Twins. By 1999 he was playing for Winnipeg (close to his home) in the independent Northern League. In 201 at-bats he hit a respectable .323, perhaps making Minnesota wonder if they had lost a good thing. The following year Fortin returned to Winnipeg and the results were not so stellar. After 176 at-bats his average had dropped to .250. A sore shoulder had taken its toll and by June 19 Troy Fortin had gone home. He is now married with a young son and has a job with the local cable company.

Troy's brother Blaine also tried his hand at pro ball, signing a contract with the Toronto Blue Jays. After several seasons in the low minors a knee injury ended Blaine's chances. "I'm glad my boys are home," reports Judy Fortin. "I supported them totally as long as they were out there trying, but I was one happy mom when they left professional baseball. It wasn't worth it for all the injuries. I watch my sons play in the local seniors league and enjoy every minute of it, but I won't even watch pro baseball on television anymore. I've just lost all respect for it."

Jeff Keith never did make the San Francisco Giants pay for overlooking him in the amateur draft. The 1999 season found him pitching for Atlantic City in the independent Atlantic League. He got through five innings, giving up nine walks and surrendering a .294

average to opponents. At that point his career in professional baseball was over.

Jesse Ibarra surprised a lot of people by going nowhere. In December 1997 the Tigers signed him as a free agent, hoping they could harness his raw power and talent. As late as 1999 he was still playing AA ball for Tulsa. With 325 plate appearances his average had dropped to .222 but, more alarming, those mammoth home runs were getting fewer and farther between. He hit only 11 of them for Tulsa. Ibarra could no longer interest a major league team in signing him, so he switched to the independent Northern League and spent the 2000 season with St. Paul, where his batting average climbed into the respectable range again. But his home run total—Ibarra's meal ticket—remained stuck at an unspectacular 13. He began the 2001 season with St. Paul but after 100 at-bats the writing was on the wall. A .245 average with only one home run sent him packing to another Northern League team in late June. Ibarra finished out the season playing for Adirondack. His .229 average and 10 home runs closed the door. Jesse Ibarra has not played professional ball since then.

Chris Marchok, whose life was updated in *The Post-Game Show*, still misses baseball nearly ten years after his official retirement. Marchok's life is anything but empty; in fact it is admirably full: he has a good marriage, two lovely daughters, and a career as a financial advisor. Yet, as he ruefully admits, every spring it's as if there is some sort of biological imperative calling him to spring training. He is presently volunteering his time as a baseball coach at his old high school.

In 1993 we met Harry Muir and Shannon Stewart playing for St. Catharines. When we crossed paths with them the following year in Hickory, North Carolina, both players had been promoted to Hagerstown. Both also were having shoulder problems; Muir was pitching through the pain and Stewart was on the DL. It turns out that 1994 was the final season for Muir before being released, whereas Stewart—a first round draft pick—remained in the Blue Jays' minor league system. Stewart got brief call-ups in 1995, 1996, and 1997 before becoming an everyday major league player in 1998. Harry Muir went on to pitch in the Premier League in France in 1995 and, after returning to Canada the following year, played on and off in the Ontario Inter-County League for four more years. He is now married with a ten-month-old son. Muir considered becoming an airline pilot and almost completed his commercial flying license before opting for a job in construction as an architectural design technician.

Darren Fidge, who hails all the way from Adelaide, Australia, never made it to the big leagues although he spent six years in the Twins organization. I caught up with him in 1999 when he was pitching for the league champion London (Ontario) Werewolves in the independent Frontier League. Fidge remembered our conversation and little picture-taking session back in Elizabethton when he was a Twins prospect: "You bet I remember it!" he told me. "It cost me twenty bucks. I got fined for talking to you when I should have been running laps." Fidge went on to pitch for Catskill in the Northern League in 2000 and then returned to Australia. In 2001 he was part of the Australian National Senior World Championship team. He was last seen in November 2002 pitching—quite effectively—for the Goodwood Indians in the Championship Playoffs of the Senior Australian Baseball League. One footnote to Fidge's story concerns the Werewolves, the team he pitched for in 1999. London, Ontario, has again lost its franchise. In 2002 the Werewolves moved out of Canada to Canton, Ohio. They now play in Thurmon Munson Stadium, former home of the AA Canton Indians who in turn have moved to a new stadium in Akron.

Although pitcher Ryan Duffy had a bat in his hand when I met him in Erie, Pennsylvania, in 1995, our conversation did not result in a fine. Neither, however, did it result in a big league career for Duffy: he was traded to Arizona after the 1995 season, although the Diamondbacks did not yet exist as a major league team. He spent 1996 pitching for Lethbridge and Visalia, posting respectable numbers for both teams. In 1997 he was claimed by the Mets in the Rule 5 Draft and went to spring training expecting a speedy journey through the ranks. Unfortunately his shoulder had other plans. "I just couldn't pitch through the pain and I finally told them about it." An MRI revealed a torn labrum and surgery was scheduled almost immediately. Duffy spent the rest of the '97 season rehabbing in Florida.

By the start of spring training 1998 the pain was no better and Duffy was released. While not a success story by major league standards, Ryan Duffy has ended up well. He married Sandy (whom we met in the chapter on Erie, Pennsylvania), has two young daughters, and works at a job with the local roads department that leaves him time for farming with his father and brother. It also leaves him time to play for the Wilkesport (Ontario) Channel Cats of the Senior Mens League. Duffy has become a powerhitting outfielder and leaves the pitching to others. "My shoulder is still pretty sore, even after all this time." The verdict? "I have no regrets. I met some great people and got to travel to places I [otherwise] never would have seen. About the only thing I wish I had done differently is say something when my shoulder first started hurting. But it's that old hockey mentality—you just want to play through the pain."

Chad Brown, aka "Psycho," made it out of St. Catharines all the way to AAA ball in the Blue Jays' system. Then he was traded to Pittsburgh, where he found himself pitching for the AA Carolina Mudcats. His shoulder, a recurrent source of problems, was scoped and cleaned on two separate occasions. Sometime during the 1999 season Chad got tired of all the pain and rehabbing and called it quits. He went back home and resisted the inevitable calls from various independent league teams. Brown is presently living in his hometown in North Carolina, working as a paint salesman. In one sense he is still pitching for Pittsburgh, only this time he's pitching paint to customers of the Pittsburgh Paint Company. It's not surprising that he has won the Salesman of the Year Award each of the past two years. As his former GM Ellen Harrigan once told him, "You may not make it in the major leagues, but you'll always be a success at public relations."

"They don't call me 'Psycho' anymore," he confided. "I've got some new nicknames now." But one thing hasn't changed: Chad is still a devoted consumer of Sun Drop soft drink. As we spoke he retrieved a can of it from a well-stocked refrigerator. "There are nine cases waiting to replace those," he assured me. I also learned that Sun Drop now comes in caffeine-free and diet versions. "I keep some [of those] around," he admitted, "but they're for guests only." As our conversation drew to a close Chad asked, "Do you think we could say that I'm looking for a wife? I really am." Then he reasoned, "When somebody buys the book, they could read about me and look at my picture on page 70. If they're interested, they could contact me. We could give out my email address." I suggested that a lot of things—including Chad's e-mail address—might change in the time between our conversation and publication of the book. "I suppose," he conceded, "but just in case." And so we offer the following: One former professional pitcher, left-handed. Present age, 31. Owns his own home. Gainfully employed outside of baseball. Extremely outgoing. Well-stocked with

Sun Drop, diet, caffeine-free, and regular. Seeks bride. Apply to the author in care of the publisher. All submissions will be forwarded to the man formerly known as "Psycho."

In case you were wondering, Cathy Sokal, formerly known as the "Belle of the Bull," has changed vocations. She now runs a garden design business on an island off the coast of North Carolina. And while we're on the subject of nonplayers, a few others have broken the mold and stayed put since we met them a decade ago: Jim Holland, the tireless GM of the Princeton team in the Appy League is still putting in twenty-six-hour days. True to form, Holland won the 2002 Appalachian League Promotional Award for publicizing his team best. Maybe it's something in that Southern air, but Ray Smith is also still the manager of the Elizabethton Twins. And if Holland and Smith show no signs of letting up, neither does Boyce Cox. This devoted servant of baseball just completed his twentieth year as president and GM of the Bristol, Virginia, club in the same Appy league. Since our visit in 1994 the club itself has changed affiliations from the Detroit Tigers to the Chicago White Sox, but Cox labors on. Last August he celebrated his seventy-seventh birthday while doubling as the club's public address announcer—a job he's had since 1981. Fortunately the good people of Bristol, Virginia, recognize the gem they have in their midst. Two years ago the mayor officially changed the name of their ballpark to Boyce Cox Stadium.

Finally, a word about Boomer Whipple—the player whose picture is on page 111 and had graced the cover of the original edition of *Small-Town Heroes*. Over the years more than a few readers have commented that "the guy on the cover looks like a young Mickey Mantle." "Well, I can tell you one person the book impressed," reports Boomer, a big smile crossing his face. "My wife. Only she wasn't my wife at the time. We were on our second date and things weren't going all that well. When she sort of unexpectedly saw me on the cover, I think it made her stop and think. She was even more impressed with the fact that I hadn't mentioned it to her or try to show off with it. I can't say she married me *because* of the book, but it sure didn't hurt my chances."

Boomer's baseball career ended after the 1997 season. He spent 1996 with Augusta, making the Sally League All-Star Team. "I had become a utility guy; I played every infield position and DH'd. I enjoyed the variety, but I don't think it was doing my shoulder any good. It really started to hurt at the end of the '96 season. [With] the first ball I threw preparing for spring training in '97 I knew I was in trouble. I had an MRI and it showed a torn rotator cuff. I had surgery in March and rehabbed 'til the end of May in Florida. I went back to Augusta but I wasn't playing much. The rest of the '97 season was a write-off. For the first time ever it felt like a job.

"I knew I was going to get released. A registered letter came from the Pirates in January 1998. It was so impersonal, my parents and I were laughing at it. It was like 'Dear Player,' and then there were several different boxes they could select. The one they checked off said, 'You have been given your unconditional release.' It probably would have happened even without the injury. I can't say it was a horrible shock or a major disappointment. I have absolutely no regrets. Remember, I wasn't originally drafted. I'm one of those guys who signed as a free agent for a plane ticket and some spikes. There were low expectations all around. I loved it, and when it was over, it was over." Today Boomer Whipple is vice president of an insurance company, working as an employee benefits consultant. Does he miss playing ball? "I love to watch it, I'm still a big fan, but I have no real desire to play. For three summers—1998, 1999, and 2000—I played in a coed softball league. It was very noncompetitive. That took care of all my baseball needs." Coaching? "Maybe down the road when my wife and I have some kids."

Then there are stories like Lloyd McClendon's. When we met him in 1995 McClendon already had a major league career behind him. There he sat in Buffalo, New York, plagued by minor injuries but hoping to keep it together for a few more years in baseball. McClendon has succeeded better than most. As of this writing he is the manager of the Pittsburgh Pirates.

So, as in all things, there are both happy endings and not-so-happy endings. Some were predictable and some came as relative surprises. Who can predict physical mishaps or the sudden erosion of skills? For some of these men baseball was but one phase of their lives, a youthful digression on a path to bigger and "more mature" pursuits. For others, probably for the majority of others, their time playing professional baseball was a defining moment. Everything else will be second best and nothing will feel as fulfilling. If you retire or are pushed aside at age twenty-five from what you value most, how do you fill in the rest of your life? A half a century can be a long period to mark time.

A number of young men I met turned to coaching when their playing days were over. Some did it professionally. Others worked in their spare time at the community level, sharing their knowledge and enthusiasm for the game with local kids. Men like Dan Held, whom I met in Martinsville in 1993 and again in Reading in 1997, never got the game out of his blood. I last saw him in August 2002 working as a hitting instructor for single-A Batavia. When his buddy Scott Rolen was traded to the Cardinals in 2002 Held also signed a contract to spend the 2003 season with St. Louis. The press release indicated Held would pitch batting practice for the club. The bottom line is he will be wearing a major league uniform and drawing a major league paycheck. It might not have as many zeroes on it as his buddy Scott Rolen's, but no matter. Held will be keeping the real world at bay. And that, as for most of the guys in this book, is what minor league baseball is really all about.

Stories Untold

I knew I'd regret it when the original edition of *Small-Town Heroes* went to press. No sooner had I turned in the manuscript than new characters and new stories began to assault me from all sides. I wanted to tell Tim Hewes's story because it is proof of Yogi Berra's old maxim that "Half the game is 90 percent mental." Tim is a former minor league catcher who finally quit because he took his daily failures so seriously he could no longer enjoy playing. Baseball was his first love, and it had become a cruel mistress—a source of worry and shame. Wisely, Hewes quit and eventually became a counseling psychologist. But the game still had its hooks in him. When I met him in 2000, Tim was pitching batting practice for the Syracuse Sky Chiefs and working as a roving counselor for the Toronto Blue Jays, helping others maximize their talent and avoid the pitfalls that had cut short his own career.

In 1997 I revisited St. Catharines and met a young right-handed pitcher named Woody Heath. Heath was the Blue Jays' fourth round draft pick and was enjoying a fine season with the Stompers. In fact, he finished the season with a 7-4 record and led his team with a 2.42 ERA. Opponents were batting only .213 against him. Heath was voted Pitcher of the Year by his coaches but he still wasn't satisfied. When I met him in August, Woody Heath was working on another tool for his arsenal: he was learning how to pitch with his left arm. While his teammates were lounging around the clubhouse or changing slowly into their game uniforms, there he was, about an hour before game time, throwing in the bullpen with a glove on his right hand. For an hour that evening Heath was a southpaw. Could Heath pull it off? The scenarios were fascinating. Would the rules of baseball allow him to switch pitching arms freely within an inning as he worked through the batting order? He could neutralize every managerial move they threw at him. A whole new era of strategy might begin. If Heath faced a switch hitter the game might be delayed for hours as the two opponents flip-flopped endlessly within a single at-bat.

Fortunately for baseball the adventure never played itself out. It appears that it isn't enough to throw with both arms; you also have to stay healthy and pitch effectively with at least one of them. In 1998 Woody Heath was no longer Pitcher of the Year. He was struggling in A ball with Dunedin, trying to pitch around a sore shoulder. He missed half the season. When he returned in '99 his shoulder continued to plague him, which led to elbow problems. His record was 6-4, but his ERA was 5.00 and opponents were hitting .268 against him. "They kept offering surgery and I kept turning them down. They started to question my commitment. They also saw me as injury-prone. I had broken my collar bone when I was in high school and now I had all these shoulder problems." By the spring of 2000 Heath was starting to feel pretty good. And then disaster struck. "Some buddies and I were playing football on the beach and I broke some bones in my foot, kicking the ball. I think that was probably the last straw for the Blue Jays."

With twenty innings under his belt at Dunedin, Heath had an 0-2 record with a 6.30 ERA and had already given up 16 walks. By the end of May 2000 Woody Heath was no longer on the roster. What had happened to his experiment in switch-pitching? "That never really got very far. You probably saw me at my peak. My pitching coach at St. Catharines [Bill Monbouquette] didn't take it too seriously. He actually thought it was a pretty bad idea. 'You're here to learn,' he told me. 'Why not master one thing before you move on to another?'" But the final blow to Heath's career as a part-time southpaw came in the winter of 1998. "I was camping and I fell off a log and broke my left arm. Maybe I really am accident prone." Today Woody Heath runs a gym in Seattle and works as a personal trainer. Has he had enough of baseball? "Last season I pitched in a local adult league. For a while I felt pretty good and I wondered if maybe I could play in one of the independent leagues. I contacted some teams but they told me their rosters were pretty well set."

And Finally . . .

This afterword is about wrapping up stories, not starting them. Still, it would be unfair to give you the impression that anything about minor league baseball is cut and dried. And so I'll leave you with one teaser—a story in progress that you can monitor over the next several years.

The Rule 5 Draft is part of what makes baseball so endlessly fascinating. It essentially says to every major league team, "If you don't value the players in your own minor league system, someone else will." One team's ballast is another team's treasure. Case in point: in 2000 the Phillies signed third baseman Travis Chapman. Chapman is the kind of player who gets selected in the late rounds of the amateur draft and is signed for a small, even token, bonus. You don't expect much from him; he's essentially there to fill up a spot on a minor league roster. He'll stick as long as there's a need for him and he doesn't embarrass himself. Only Chapman didn't play by the rules. He surprised a lot of people. He brought an admirable work ethic with him and then he bulked up, adding some eye-opening power to his game. By 2002 Chapman turned into the AA Eastern League's All-Star third baseman, hitting .301 with 15 home runs. Still, the Phillies didn't protect him on their forty-man roster, which meant he was ripe for the picking by another team. In the Rule 5 Draft for the 2003 season Cleveland snatched Chapman the first chance they got. For a while it looked like revenge might have been part of their motivation. Barely a month earlier the Indians had lost their best player—Jim Thome—to the Phillies. But it turned out their motives were even less pure. Within a week the Indians turned around and sold Chapman's contract to the Detroit Tigers (presumably for more than the fifty-thousand-dollar price they paid for him in the draft). Will Chapman continue to develop and become an everyday third baseman for the Tigers? (According to the rules of the draft he has to remain on the Tigers' major league roster for the full season or be offered back to the Phillies for half of what Cleveland paid for him.) Or will Chapman drift back into the obscurity originally predicted for him?

Through tenacity and hard work one player has transformed himself from suspect to prospect. By the time this edition of *Small-Town Heroes* appears some early returns will be in on the Travis Chapman story. Like other stories in this book, time will unravel its mysteries. Most of the players profiled in *Small-Town Heroes* had careers that were only beginning. As with many things in life, the view is a lot different ten years down the road.

Index